As It Was in the Beginning

As It Was in the Beginning

An Intertextual Analysis of New Creation
in Galatians, 2 Corinthians, and Ephesians

BY
Mark D. Owens

☙PICKWICK *Publications* · Eugene, Oregon

AS IT WAS IN THE BEGINNING
An Intertextual Analysis of New Creation in Galatians,
2 Corinthians, and Ephesians

Copyright © 2015 Mark D. Owens. All rights reserved. Except for brief quotations in critical publications or reviews, no part of this book may be reproduced in any manner without prior written permission from the publisher. Write: Permissions. Wipf and Stock Publishers, 199 W. 8th Ave., Suite 3, Eugene, OR 97401.

Pickwick Publications
An Imprint of Wipf and Stock Publishers
199 W. 8th Ave., Suite 3
Eugene, OR 97401

www.wipfandstock.com

ISBN 13: 978-1-4982-0240-4

Cataloguing-in-Publication Data

Owens, Mark D.

    As It Was in the Beginning: An Intertextual Analysis of New Creation in Galatians, 2 Corinthians, and Ephesians / Mark D. Owens.

    xviii + 242 p. ; 23 cm. Includes bibliographical references.

    ISBN 13: 978-1-4982-0240-4

    1. Bible. Galatians—Criticism, interpretation, etc. 2. Bible. Corinthians, 2nd—Criticism, interpretation, etc. 3. Bible. Ephesians—Criticism, interpretation, etc. 4. Creation—Biblical teaching. I. Title.

BS2650.52 O91 2015

Manufactured in the U.S.A.   10/15/2015

Gratefully dedicated to my mother (Darlene Owens-Elliott), my step-father (Lee Elliott), and my father-in-law and mother-in-law (Rev. Dr. Gerald and Kay Bontrager).

Without their love and support, this project would not have been possible.

Contents

Preface | ix
Acknowledgments | xi
Abbreviations | xiii

1 Introduction and Method | 1
2 New Creation in the Prophecy of Isaiah | 14
3 New Creation and Restoration in the Old Testament and Second Temple Judaism | 43
4 New Creation in Galatians and 2 Corinthians | 68
5 New Creation in Ephesians 1–2 | 121
6 Conclusion | 171

Appendix One: The Use of ANE Temple-building Traditions outside of Isaiah's Prophecy | 181

Appendix Two: Isaiah's New Exodus in the Writings of Second Temple Judaism | 187

Bibliography | 193
Index of Authors | 211
Scripture Index | 217
Ancient Document Index | 235

Preface

THIS MONOGRAPH PRINCIPALLY INVESTIGATES the relationship between the portraits of new creation in the Hauptbriefe (specifically, in 2 Corinthians and Galatians) and Ephesians. Part of the underlying impetus behind this book is to provide a detailed response to those scholars who argue for a limited understanding (whether cosmological, anthropological, or ecclesiological) of the phrase καινὴ κτίσις in 2 Cor 5:17 and Gal 6:15. This book also partly responds to the lack of attention devoted to the new creation theme in Ephesians by investigating the depiction of new creation in Eph 1-2.

Chapters 2 and 3 of this book investigate the background of new creation in the Pauline tradition through an analysis of various texts in Isaiah, Jeremiah, Ezekiel, 1 Enoch, and Jubilees. These chapters demonstrate that new creation and restoration within these Jewish texts were frequently associated with anthropological and cosmological renewal, the salvation of the Gentiles, and an *Urzeit-Endzeit* typology. The strong correlation between Isaiah's new exodus and ANE temple-building traditions is a particularly significant contribution of the inquiry of Isaiah.

Chapters 4 and 5 of this work primarily analyze the depictions of new creation in Gal 6:11-16; 2 Cor 5:11-21; and Eph 1-2. A salient point of this analysis is the suggestion that Eph 1:20—2:22 may be understood as an extended discussion of new creation modeled after Isaiah's portrait of the new exodus as an act of temple-building. This examination demonstrates that the descriptions of new creation in all three of these texts are strongly linked with anthropological, eschatological, and ecclesiological notions, as well as an *Urzeit-Endzeit* typology. This book also points to a number of other correspondences between the portraits of new creation in the Hauptbriefe and that of Ephesians.

Acknowledgments

THIS MONOGRAPH IS A revised version of my PhD thesis, "'Behold, I Make All Things New': An Intertextual Analysis of New Creation in Galatians, 2 Corinthians, and Ephesians," submitted to the University of Aberdeen. This book therefore represents the culmination of several years of hard work and occasional anxiety. While I undoubtedly will miss some of the people who have assisted me in the completion of this project, the following are worthy of special gratitude.

I am particularly thankful to my *Doktorvater*, Dr. Andrew Clarke, for his careful supervision of my PhD thesis. His sharp eye and attention to detail were immensely valuable throughout that journey. Without his encouragement, support, and sage guidance, I would have never been able to complete that project. My PhD thesis examiners, Prof. N. T. Wright and Dr. Tomas Bokedal, are also deserving of recognition. Their careful scrutiny of my thesis allowed me to produce a finished product that was undoubtedly superior to the version I originally submitted. Despite the work of these three scholars in guiding and evaluating that project, any shortcomings of this volume are undoubtedly my own.

Mere words cannot express how indebted I am to my dear wife, Rachel. She endured the demands of graduate work for some ten years right alongside me and sacrificed much during that time. She is a remarkable woman and I am blessed to call her my wife!

The care and assistance of my mother (Darlene Owens-Elliott) and in-laws (Rev. Dr. Gerald Bontrager and Kay Bontrager) must be noted. My mother has always exhibited a keen interest in my education and has sacrificed much over the years so that I might pursue my academic goals. Without her financial assistance, my life as a graduate student would have been significantly more complicated! I am truly thankful for her love. I am also blessed to have incredible in-laws and their role in the completion of this larger project has been notable. Their willingness to endure my presence in their home for eighteen months is a testament to their abounding patience and Christian virtue! At the same time, opening their home to my wife and me is only one of numerous ways in which they have supported us over the past twelve years.

I am also grateful to the administration, faculty, and staff at Luther Rice College & Seminary. I owe a special debt of gratitude to our President, Dr. James Flanagan, and Dr. Brad Arnett, for taking a chance on me. Luther Rice is an incredible place to serve the kingdom and it is largely so because of their leadership and vision. I genuinely appreciate the time, space, and encouragement they have given me to pursue my research interests.

The following individuals also helped me throughout the course of this journey in various ways: Rev. Travis Williams; Rev. Dr. Josh Malone; Dr. Chris Green; Dr. David Morgan; Richard & Vicki Huffman; Alan & Elaine Cordiner; Rev. Estriberto Britton; Dawn Jones; Brian Kinney; Rev. Dr. Abi Ngunga; Dr. Christopher Spinks; Robert Rose; Daryl & Linda Sharp; Sherri Humphrey; Kristin Cook; Don & Jane Smith; Dr. Jeff Aernie; John Dixon; Rev. Gary and Janice Laroy; Rev. Dr. Joshua Stewart; Rev. Jack Lewis; Ivan Annison; Rev. Daniel Wilson; Robert and Pat Fields; Rev. Tom and Olive Hudson; Brad Isbell; Rev. Steve Leigh.

Finally, I am deeply grateful to God for the strength and grace needed to complete this project. His goodness to me over the years has been amazing! I am particularly grateful that our lives post-graduate work looks very different, not only in terms of employment, but also in terms of our family structure. God has blessed us with the opportunity to adopt a precious two-year-old girl and we are thankful the long journey of becoming parents is over!

Abbreviations

AnBib	Analecta Biblica
AB	Anchor Bible
ATD	Das Alte Testament Deutlich
BCOTWP	Baker Commentary on the Old Testament Wisdom and Psalms
BDAG	Danker, F. W., ed. *A Greek-English Lexicon of the New Testament and Other Early Christian Literature*. Chicago: Chicago University Press, 2000.
BDF	Funk, R.W., ed. *A Greek Grammar of the new Testament and Other Early Christian Literature*. Chicago: Chicago University Press, 1961.
BECNT	Baker Exegetical Commentary on the New Testament
BETL	Bibliotheca Ephemeridum Theologicarum Lovaniensium
BHT	Beiträge zur Historischen Theologie
Bib	*Biblica*
BibTS	Biblisch-theologische Studien
BIS	Biblical Interpretation Series
BKAT	Biblischer Kommentar Altes Testament
BNTC	Black's New Testament Commentaries
BTB	*Biblical Theology Bulletin*
BTS	Biblischer-Theologische Studien
BZAW	Beihefte zur Zeitschrift für die alttestamentliche Wissenschaft

BZNW	Beiheft zur Zeitschrift für die neutestamentliche Wissenschaft und die Kunde der älteren Kirche
CBET	Contributions to Biblical Exegesis and Theology
CBQ	*Catholic Biblical Quarterly*
CBQMS	Catholic Biblical Quarterly Monograph Series
CEJL	Commentaries on Early Jewish Literature
ConBNT	Coniectanea Biblica: New Testament Series
ConBOT	Coniectanea Biblica: Old Testament Series
Conc	*Concilium*
CRINT	Compendia Rerum Iudaicarum ad Novum Testamentum
CTJ	*Calvin Theological Journal*
EKKNT	Evangelisch-Katholischer Kommentar zum Neuen Testament
EvT	*Evangelische Theologie*
ExpTim	*Expository Times*
FAT	Forschungen zum Alten Testament
FB	Forschung zur Bibel
FN	*Filologia Neotestamentaria*
FOTL	Forms of Old Testament Literature
FRLANT	Forschungen zur Religion und Literatur des Alten und Neuen Testaments
HAR	*Hebrew Annual Review*
HCOT	Historical Commentary on the Old Testament
HNT	Handbuch zum Neuen Testament
HNTC	Harper's New Testament Commentary
HSM	Harvard Semitic Monographs
HTKAT	Herder's Theologischer Kommentar zum Alten Testament
HTKNT	Herders Theologischer Kommentar zum Neuen Testament
HTR	*Harvard Theological Review*
IBS	*Irish Biblical Studies*
ICC	International Critical Commentary
Int	*Interpretation*
JBL	*Journal of Biblical Literature*

JETS	*Journal of the Evangelical Theological Society*
JNES	*Journal of Near Eastern Studies*
JNSL	*Journal of Northwest Semitic Languages*
JSHRZ	Jüdische Schriften aus hellenistisch-römischer Zeit
JSJSup	Supplements to the Journal for the Study of Judaism
JSNT	*Journal for the Study of the New Testament*
JSNTSup	Journal for the Study of the New Testament Supplement Series
JSOT	Journal for the Study of the Old Testament
JSOTSup	Journal for the Study of the Old Testament Supplement Series
JSP	*Journal for the Study of the Pseudepigrapha*
JSPSup	Journal for the Study of the Pseudepigrapha Supplement Series
JSSMS	Journal of Semitic Studies Monograph Series
JTS	*Journal of Theological Studies*
KEK	Kritisch-exegetischer Kommentar über Das Neue Testament
KJV	King James Version
LHBOTS	Library of Hebrew Bible/Old Testament Studies
LNTS	Library of New Testament Studies
LSJ	Liddell, H. G., R. Scott, H. S. Jones, and R. McKenzie, *A Greek-English Lexicon*. 9th ed. Oxford: Clarendon, 1996.
LSTS	Library of Second Temple Studies
MBPS	Mellen Biblical Press Series
MNTC	Moffat New Testament Commentary
NCB	New Cambridge Bible Commentary
NCBC	New Century Bible Commentary
NIBC	New International Biblical Commentary
NICNT	New International Commentary on the New Testament
NICOT	New International Commentary on the Old Testament
NIGTC	New International Greek Testament Commentary
NovT	*Novum Testamentum*
NovTSup	Supplements to Novum Testamentum
NSBT	New Studies in Biblical Theology

NTL	New Testament Library
NTOA	Novum Testamentum et Orbis Antiquus
NTS	*New Testament Studies*
OBO	Orbis Biblicus et orientalis
OTK	Ökumenischer Taschenbuchkommentar zum Neuen Testament
OTL	Old Testament Library
OTNT	Ökumenischer Taschenbuchkommentar zum Neuen Testament
PCNT	Paideia Commentaries on the New Testament
PNTC	Pillar New Testament Commentary
PS	Pauline Studies
RevExp	*Review & Expositor*
RevQ	*Revue de Qumran*
RST	Regensburger Studien zur Theologie
RSV	Revised Standard Version
SBEC	Studies in the Bible and Early Christianity
SBLSCS	Society of Biblical Literature Septuagint and Cognate Studies
SBLDS	Society of Biblical Literature Dissertation Series
SBLMS	Society of Biblical Literature Monograph Series
SBS	Stuttgarter Bibelstudien
SemeiaST	Semeia Studies
SNT	Studien zum Neuen Testament
SNTSMS	Society for New Testament Studies Monograph Series
SNTW	Studies of the New Testament and its World
SP	Sacra Pagina
ST	*Studia Theologica*
STDJ	Studies on the Texts of the Desert of Judah
StPB	Studia Post-Biblica
SupJSJ	Supplements for the Journal for the Study of Judaism
SVTP	Studia in Veteris Testamenti Pseudepigrapha
TB	*Tyndale Bulletin*

TDNT	*Theological Dictionary of the New Testament*
THKNT	Theologischer Handkommentar zum Neuen Testament
TJ	*Trinity Journal*
TTZ	*Trierer theologische Zeitschrift*
VT	*Vetus Testamentum*
VTSup	Supplements to Vetus Testamentum
WBC	Word Biblical Commentary
WMANT	Wissenschaftliche Monographien zum Alten und Neuen Testament
WUNT	Wissenschaftliche Untersuchungen zum Neuen Testament
ZAW	*Zeitschrift für die Alttestamentliche Wissenschaft*
ZBK	Zürcher Bibelkommentare
ZECNT	Zondervan Exegetical Commentary on the New Testament
ZNW	*Zeitschrift für die Neutestamentliche Wissenschaft und die Kunde der älteren Kirche*

1

Introduction and Method

An Overview of the New Creation Debate in the Hauptbriefe

PRIOR TO 1935, THE phrase καινὴ κτίσις in 2 Cor 5:17 and Gal 6:15 was interpreted within a purely anthropological framework, which is reflected in the English translation "new creature" (e.g., KJV).[1] However, with the arrival of R. Strachan's commentary on 2 Corinthians, what was once an inactive crater suddenly became a bubbling volcano.[2] Rather than understanding this Pauline expression in anthropological terms, Strachan proposed to interpret it through the lens of Jewish apocalyptic literature and opted for the translation "new creation."[3]

Since the publishing of Strachan's commentary, a number of works have been written that attempt to elucidate the meaning of καινὴ κτίσις in 2 Cor 5:17 and Gal 6:15.[4] These studies generally seek to probe what may

---

1. Cf. Hubbard, *New Creation*, 2; pace Jackson, *New Creation*, 7–9. Jackson helpfully notes that there were several voices in the early church that interpreted the phrase καινὴ κτίσις along anthropological *and* cosmological lines. Nonetheless, one can reasonably conclude that this phrase has been primarily interpreted anthropologically over the past few centuries.

2. Strachan, *Corinthians*, 113–14.

3. Beginning with the RSV, major English translations of the New Testament [NT] since the publication of Strachan's commentary have translated the phrase καινὴ κτίσις in 2 Cor 5:17 and Gal 6:15 with the phrase "new creation." Throughout this study, the phrase "new creation" will be used not only as a translation for the expression καινὴ κτίσις in 2 Cor 5:17 and Gal 6:15, but also as a shorthand way of capturing the various ideas associated with this theological concept.

4. Aside from discussions in commentaries, more specialized studies include: Stuhlmacher, "Erwägungen," 1–35; Hoover, *New Creation*; Mell, *Neue Schöpfung*; Hubbard, *New Creation*; Adams, *Constructing the World*; Aymer, *Paul's Understanding of 'KAINE KTISIS'*; Kraus, *Das Volk Gottes*; Schneider, *KAINH KTISIS*; Schneider,

be described as the essential theological nature of Paul's idiom. Over the years, scholars have predominantly understood the expression in three main ways: anthropologically, cosmologically, and ecclesiologically.[5] Most scholars have combined these three interpretations in various ways. Others, however, demonstrate a marked tendency to prioritize one interpretation over the others. Thus, there exists a strong measure of debate concerning how this important phrase should be understood. This lack of consensus may partly reflect the absence of a sustained discussion of new creation in 2 Cor 5 and Gal 6.

Jesusüberlieferung und Christologie, 357–71; Schneider, "Die Idee der Neuschöpfung," 257–70; Gloer, *New Creation*; Jackson, *New Creation*. Romans 8:18–25 is another pertinent text in this debate. See Jackson (*New Creation*, 150–69) for an especially helpful discussion of new creation in Rom 8:18–25. Colossians 1:15–20 is another significant text related to new creation in the Pauline corpus, though it has received scant attention within this larger debate. Space limitations prevent a detailed analysis of these two texts.

5. The anthropological reading of new creation primarily focuses on conversion and the inward/ethical transformation of individual Christ-followers. According to Schnelle (*Anthropologie*, 1), "Die neutestamentliche Anthropologie fragt nach dem Grund, der Ermöglichung, der Struktur und dem Vollzug menschlicher Existenz." This definition provides a suitable basis for considering potential anthropological notions that might be associated with the portrait of new creation in the Pauline corpus. Generally speaking, I will approach this reading of new creation more from the perspective of systematic theology than the social scientific discipline of anthropology.

The cosmological reading of new creation primarily interprets the phrase καινὴ κτίσις as the partial fulfillment of Isaiah's promised "new heavens and new earth." According to Adams ("Graeco-Roman and Ancient Jewish Cosmology," 5), cosmology refers to the attempt "to explain the origin, structure, and destiny of the physical universe." This definition provides a suitable framework for this research project as it orients the discussion and interpretation of the phrase καινὴ κτίσις around the future of the created order.

In terms of the ecclesiological reading of new creation, a close analysis of the literature on this subject suggests the need for greater precision in this area. A significant question that has been featured in this debate concerns whether new creation in Paul encompasses individual Christ-followers or the entire community of believers. While this is an important question, the answer to this question may not sufficiently account for the complexity of Paul's understanding of new creation, particularly in Gal 6:15. Kraus and Jackson rightly note that the corporate element within Paul's understanding of new creation particularly focuses on the identity of the church as composed of Jewish and Gentile Christ-followers (e.g., Kraus, *Das Volk Gottes*, 251–52; Jackson, *New Creation*, 111–13). The distinction between an anthropological and an ecclesiological understanding of new creation thus reaches beyond an individualized versus corporate reading of καινὴ κτίσις. I should point out that Jackson does muddy the water a bit by framing the anthropological reading of new creation within an individualized and corporate framework (e.g., Jackson, *New Creation*, 4). Adams (*Constructing the World*, 227–28, 235) may also fall into the same trap.

Review of Research on New Creation in the Hauptbriefe

This project will interact primarily with major works devoted to investigating the meaning of new creation in the Pauline corpus. Special attention will be devoted to: 1) scholarly studies that argue for a limited conception of new creation; and 2) scholarly studies that have made claims regarding the relationship between the portraits of new creation in the Hauptbriefe and that of Ephesians. I will now briefly discuss the contributions of the major figures within this debate.

The contribution of U. Mell to this debate is representative of a firmly cosmological reading of καινὴ κτίσις in the Hauptbriefe. Mell's understanding of new creation in 2 Cor 5:17 and Gal 6:15 is weighted heavily by his cosmological reading of the noun κόσμος in Gal 6:14. Yet Mell also places great stress on a history-of-traditions analysis and argues that the Pauline understanding of new creation is derived from apocalyptic Judaism. Mell's *traditionsgeschichtliche* analysis of new creation is problematic on two fronts. First, he engages in a highly selective analysis of Second Temple Jewish texts that overlooks the anthropologically oriented portrait of new creation in such texts as *Joseph and Aseneth*. Second, his attempt to explain the development of the new creation concept (beginning with Isaiah, proceeding through apocalyptic Judaism, and culminating in the Hauptbriefe) not only downplays the complexity (and significance) of new creation in Isaiah and Second Temple Judaism but also the Pauline corpus itself.

Hubbard's contribution to this debate warrants special attention because of his strictly anthropological reading of new creation. While Mell may be rightly chided for a prejudicial selection of texts, Hubbard falls into the identical trap. According to Hubbard, the key to understanding the nature of new creation in the Hauptbriefe lies in the anthropocentric new covenant promises of Jeremiah and Ezekiel, as well as the import of the death-life metaphor for understanding the new creation motif in the Hauptbriefe.[6] While Hubbard judiciously stresses the anthropological nature of new creation in the Hauptbriefe, like Mell he firmly divorces theological categories that Paul in all probability would have never severed.

An exclusively ecclesiological reading of καινὴ κτίσις is associated particularly with Kraus's *Das Volk Gottes: Zur Grundlegung der Ekklesiologie bei Paulus*. Kraus's central concern in this work is presenting an alternative to the traditional supersessionist approach regarding the place of Jewish identity within the Christian community. According to Kraus, καινὴ κτίσις in both 2 Cor 5:17 and Gal 6:15 is best understood as a "Gemeindewirklichkeit"

---

6. Cf. Hubbard, *New Creation*, esp. 91–122.

inaugurated by the death and resurrection of Jesus Christ.⁷ Kraus is to be commended for not only appreciating the ecclesiological nature of new creation in the Hauptbriefe, but also the manner in which this concept implicitly draws upon the eschatological expectations related to the conversion of the nations in such texts as Isa 66:18–24. Nonetheless, Kraus fails to grapple with how Paul's portrait of new creation (and the Isaianic texts that inform his understanding of this theological concept) is related to Scriptures' basic story of redemption and how this question of who constitutes the people of God is related to an *Urzeit-Endzeit* typology.⁸ That is, Kraus fails to consider how the union of Jew and Gentile in Christ is related fundamentally to God's plan to put right the crisis depicted in Gen 3.

While the meaning of the phrase καινὴ κτίσις in the Hauptbriefe plays a minor role in his analysis, Adams's *Constructing the World: A Study in Paul's Cosmological Language*, nonetheless, represents a major peak in this debate. The importance of Adams' contribution is seen primarily in the complex understanding of new creation for which he contends in this monograph. For Adams, new creation in the Hauptbriefe encompasses both anthropology and cosmology, and also looks beyond individual Christ-followers to

---

7. Kraus, *Das Volk Gottes*, 251.

8. Wright (*People of God*, 38–44, 77–80, 215–19, 262–68) provides a helpful explanation of the place of "story" within biblical interpretation, as well as important insights into the fundamental stories of Israel, early Judaism, and early Christianity. For now, one should note that: 1) the creation and fall narratives in Gen 1–2 and Gen 3 respectively, constitute significant points in the biblical plot-line; and 2) the Abrahamic covenant is to be understood as God's remedy for the crisis depicted in Gen 3. The translation of the verb נרד in Gen 12:3 MT aside (note the use of the passive participle ἐνευλογηθήσονται in the LXX, however), it is reasonable to conclude that Gentiles somehow benefit through a positive relationship with Abraham (cf. Gen 17:4; 18:18; Gal 3:8; 1 *En.* 10:3, 21). Cf. ibid., 262–63. There is thus a sense in which the identity of God's people plays an important role in Scripture's grand narrative of salvation.

The nomenclature "*Urzeit-Endzeit*" will be used throughout this project to refer to the well-known pattern within Jewish eschatology that suggests the new age will be somehow related to the primordial age of Gen 1–3. Cf. Isa 11:6–9; 51:3; 65:17–25; Ezek 47:1–12; 4 Ezra 6:13–28; *Sib. Or.* 3:785–95; 2 *Bar.* 73:1–7; 1 *En.* 24:1—25:7; L. A. B. 3:10; Rev 21:1—22:7. This typological pattern was first extensively examined by Gunkel (*Creation*, esp. 231–33). For the sake of clarity, the various ways in which this correlation between the beginning and the end may be construed should be considered. The ways in which the new age might be related to the primordial age include: 1) a complete and precise return to the primordial age; 2) a return to the primordial age that involves a high degree of continuity between the end and the beginning, such that the new age may be understood as something of a reenactment of the primordial age; and 3) a return to the beginning that involves some degree of continuity with the primordial age, yet at the same time making it clear that the end is superior to the beginning. Goppelt (*Typos*, 32–38, 228–29) rightly notes that portraits of the end in Second Temple Judaism and the NT generally follow the third option. Cf. Hanson, *Dawn*, 407.

the entire community of believers. Significantly, Adams does not seem to address the ecclesiological nature of this community.

Jackson's recent monograph, *New Creation in Paul's Letters: A Study of the Historical and Social Setting of a Pauline Concept*, warrants attention because of the complex portrait of new creation advocated in this study. His central thesis is that new creation explicates Paul's "eschatologically infused soteriology which involves the individual, the community and the cosmos and which is inaugurated in the death and resurrection of Christ."[9] Jackson is to be especially commended for appreciating the interrelationship between anthropology and cosmology not only within Paul's thought but also within his Jewish background. His study is also significant because of his contention that Isaiah constitutes the primary background for Paul's understanding of new creation. Despite these strengths, Jackson's analysis does not account sufficiently for the relationship between Paul's understanding of καινὴ κτίσις and an *Urzeit-Endzeit* typology. Jackson's treatment of new creation also does not account for the implications of the temple imagery in 2 Cor 6:16.

The Letter to the Ephesians and the New Creation Debate

While the nature of new creation in the Hauptbriefe has sparked a great deal of interest among scholars, this topic has received relatively little attention in the letter to the Ephesians. Several studies have explored individual passages that comprise the new creation theme in Ephesians.[10] Scholars also have pointed to a variety of similarities between the new creation theme in Ephesians and the Hauptbriefe.[11] Both Hubbard and Jackson have also appealed to the discussion of new creation in Ephesians in support of their divergent readings of new creation in the Hauptbriefe.[12] Nonetheless, to date a full analysis of the precise points of continuity and discontinuity between

---

9. Jackson, *New Creation*, 6.

10. Turner ("Mission," 138–66) is an important exception. Though brief, Turner's essay closely connects new creation with the letter's larger theme of cosmic reconciliation. While his methodology is questionable, McHugh ("Reconsideration," 302–9) extensively discusses Irenaeus' recapitulatory understanding of Eph 1:10. Finally, Miletic (*"One Flesh"*) explores the significance of new creation theology for understanding subordination within the husband-wife relationship.

11. For example, Beale ("Reconciliation," 578–79) notes the presence of allusions to Isaiah's new exodus in 2 Cor 5:17 and Eph 2:13, 17, as well as the close connection between new creation and reconciliation in both texts. Cf. Webb, *Returning Home*, 117–20.

12. Cf. Hubbard, *New Creation*, 7; Jackson, *New Creation*, 184.

the portraits of new creation in the undisputed Pauline epistles and the letter to the Ephesians has yet to be undertaken. Thus, the primary aim of this study is to explore how strongly aligned the portraits of new creation in the Hauptbriefe and Eph 1–2 are with one another via an intertextual analysis of the relevant texts.

In contrast with 2 Cor 5 and Gal 6, there is a more extensive discussion of new creation in the letter to the Ephesians. For now, it is sufficient to note the entire context of Eph 2:1-22 is set within a new creation framework.[13] Interestingly, new creation theology in Eph 2:11-21 is grounded in the context of Isaiah's proclamation of a new exodus (cf. Isa 52:7; 57:19; Eph 2:13, 17). These allusions to Isaianic tradition in Eph 2:13, 17 establish a significant parallel with new creation in the Hauptbriefe as it is generally agreed that Isaiah's new exodus forms the backdrop for new creation in 2 Cor 5:17. These preliminary observations regarding new creation in Eph 2 raise the question of this theme's relationship to new creation theology in the Hauptbriefe.

The extent to which new creation theology in the Pauline tradition is linked with Isaiah's prophecy indicates that an examination of relevant Isaianic traditions could bring greater clarity to this debate. Paul's allusion to Isaianic tradition in 2 Cor 5:17 (τὰ ἀρχαῖα παρῆλθεν ἰδοὺ γέγονεν καινά) has certainly played a role in this discussion.[14] However, the significance of new creation in the Pauline tradition has yet to be investigated by means of a full-scale intertextual analysis.[15] Such an investigation would extensively

---

13. It is helpful to comment briefly at this point on several features of Eph 1–2 that will be explored more fully below. First, there is strong evidence to suggest that new creation in this letter carries anthropological connotations (cf. Eph 2:1-6, 10, 15; 4:24). Second, the emphasis on inaugurated eschatology in Ephesians suggests that new creation in that text may also carry cosmological overtones (cf. Eph 1:10, 20-23; 2:5-6, 10). Third, the use of temple imagery in Eph 2:19-22 to describe the union of Jewish and Gentile believers indicates that new creation in Ephesians may also convey the ecclesiological orientation emphasized by some scholars. Further ecclesiological overtones pervade Eph 2:11-19 with its discussion of the uniting of Jew and Gentile through the death of Christ. New creation in this segment of the Pauline tradition thus does seem to resist the tidy divisions proposed by some scholars.

14. The Isaianic texts that scholars generally attempt to link with 2 Cor 5:17b include: Isa 42:9 (τὰ ἀπ' ἀρχῆς ἰδοὺ ἥκασιν καὶ καινὰ ἃ ἐγὼ ἀναγγελῶ); 43:18-19 (μὴ μνημονεύετε τὰ πρῶτα καὶ τὰ ἀρχαῖα μὴ συλλογίζεσθε ἰδοὺ ποιῶ καινά); 48:3, 6 (τὰ πρότερα ἔτι ἀνήγγειλα . . . ἀκουστά σοι ἐποίσα τὰ καινά); 65:16-17 (τὴν πρώτην . . . ὁ οὐρανὸς καὶ ἡ γῆ καινή . . . τῶν προτέρων). Cf. Stuhlmacher, "Erwägungen," 6; Mell, *Neue Schöpfung*, 38-39, 47; Webb, *Returning Home*, 121-28; Jackson, *New Creation*, 119-23; Beale, "Reconciliation," 552-59; Hubbard, *New Creation*, 182; Gignilliat, *Paul*, 97; Hoover, *New Creation*, 169; Schneider, "Die Idee der Neuschöpfung," 265; Wilk, *Jesajabuches*, 276-80; Kim, *Origin*, 18.

15. See below, pp. 8–13, for a discussion of intertextuality.

explore the Isaianic texts evoked in 2 Cor 5:17; Eph 2:13, 17 and assess the extent to which Isaiah's prophecy informs the understanding of new creation in the Pauline tradition.[16] Investigating these texts intertextually could be especially advantageous since the relationship between new creation in the Hauptbriefe and Isaianic tradition is, in fact, a major issue within this larger debate.[17]

At this stage, it is also necessary to discuss a helpful methodological tool for evaluating the relationship between new creation in the Hauptbriefe and Ephesians. In his work exploring the correlation between the Qumran *Songs of the Sabbath Sacrifice* and *The Celestial Hierarchy* of Dionysius the Areopagite, P. Alexander employs what he has termed a heuristic analysis to address the complexities of the relationship between these two texts.[18] For Alexander, such an analysis involves a comparison and contrast of notions revolving around a theme and generally circumvents issues such as differences in the dating, authorship and provenance of separate literary works. The intent of using this methodological approach within this present analysis is to deal with the deutero-Pauline status of Ephesians in a critical manner.[19] The application of a heuristic analysis to this wider issue will first require that the theological content of new creation in each of these letters be investigated on their own terms, and then the degree of continuity and discontinuity between the texts will be assessed.

Summary of This Investigation

This analysis of new creation will proceed in four major steps. First, I will analyze major texts that form part of Isaiah's new exodus theme with a view toward assessing its precise theological content and determining how this motif might inform the understanding of new creation in the Pauline

16. Jackson (*New Creation*, 17–30) provides one of the more extensive examinations of the relevance of Isaiah for this question, yet his analysis does not engage closely with the Isaianic texts alluded to in Eph 2:13, 17.

17. Of the scholars who have closely investigated new creation in the Hauptbriefe, Jackson most strongly emphasizes the importance of Isaiah. Others stress the new covenant promises of Jeremiah and Ezekiel (particularly Hubbard and Schneider) or the apocalyptic traditions of early Judaism (Mell).

18. Cf. Alexander, *Qumran Songs*.

19. While I personally do not find the arguments against the Pauline authorship of Ephesians strong enough to deny its authenticity, the nature of this project will nonetheless require I take these concerns seriously. I will therefore not refer to Paul as the author of Ephesians and will occasionally use E. Best's designation "AE" (i.e., "author of Ephesians"). See Van Roon (*Ephesians*) and Hoehner (*Ephesians*, 2–61) for helpful defenses of the Pauline authorship of Ephesians.

tradition. A prominent feature of this analysis will be considering the relationship between Isaiah's new exodus and ANE temple-building traditions.[20] Second, I will examine significant traditions related to new creation and restoration in Ezekiel, Jeremiah, *1 Enoch*, and *Jubilees*. Special attention will be given in this chapter to considering the extent to which restoration in Ezekiel and Jeremiah is presented in purely anthropological terms and how Isaiah's "new heavens and new earth" is developed in the Second Temple period. Third, I will consider the descriptions of new creation in Gal 6:11–16 and 2 Cor 5:11–21. The goal of this analysis is to determine how narrowly or broadly Paul conceives new creation in these two passages and the extent to which they are related to an *Urzeit-Endzeit* typology. Finally, I will offer a detailed treatment of Eph 1:9–10 and Eph 1:20—2:22. Once again, the aim of this chapter will be to evaluate the theological scope of new creation in these passages and more closely consider how the portraits of new creation in these two texts are informed by Isaianic traditions.

Intertextuality and the Pauline Tradition

The relationship between the Old Testament [OT] and the documents in the Pauline corpus has been a subject of much scholarly debate. Throughout this discussion, an assortment of issues has come to the forefront.[21] This enquiry found new direction through the influential work of R. Hays. In his monograph, *Echoes of Scripture in the Letters of Paul*, Hays investigates the use of Israel's Scriptures in the Pauline corpus by means of the literary phenomenon of intertextuality.[22] According to Hays, intertextuality refers to

---

20. By ANE temple-building traditions I am referring to texts from the ANE (e.g., *Enuma Elish* 1:37–40, 73–76; 6:1–70) that correlate the creation of the universe with the defeat of a god's enemies and the consequent construction of a temple in that god's honor. Two points of clarification regarding the nature of a temple within the ANE worldview are particularly germane to this discussion. First, a temple was understood as the earthly locus of the divine presence (e.g., Exod 25:8; 29:44–45; 1 Kgs 8:10–13; Ps 25:8 LXX). Second, temples were viewed as a microcosm of heaven and earth (cf. *Enuma Elish* 6:112; Ps 77:69 LXX; 131:8–9, 13–14 LXX; Josephus, *Ant.* 3:123, 179–87; Philo, *Plant.* 1:47–50; Wis 9:8). Cf. Lundquist, "Temple," 205–19. Finally, the designation "LXX" is used throughout this study to refer to the critical text of the Septuagint.

21. See Hays (*Echoes*, 37–52) for further discussion. Watson (*Paul*, 2–5) has also recently demonstrated the fundamentally textual nature of Paul's theology, which is firmly grounded in a careful reading of the OT. Watson (ibid., 2–5) has also advocated the use of a three-way model that intertextually explores Paul's reading of the OT by bringing together the OT, texts from Second Temple Judaism, and the Pauline text itself into a single inquiry.

22. Hays's approach is similar to and in some ways builds on M. Fishbane's work on inner-biblical exegesis in the Old Testament (see Fishbane, *Biblical Interpretation*).

"the imbedding of fragments of an earlier tradition within a later one."[23] An important feature of Hays's approach is his suggestion that the relationship between the Pauline corpus and the OT may be associated profitably with the literary phenomenon known as metalepsis.[24] For the purposes of this study, Hays's approach to intertextuality provides a theoretical framework for recognizing that the presence of an intertextual reference in the Pauline corpus *may* require the reader to examine the precursor text for possible implicit connections between the Pauline text and the OT text. Hays's proposal raises the question of just how closely the portraits of new creation in 2 Corinthians and Ephesians are related to Isaianic tradition.

While Hays's work is indeed a valuable contribution to Pauline studies, it does raise two questions that are particularly relevant to this project. First, what is the role of the reader in the interpretative process? Second, what are suitable criteria for validating proposed allusions to the OT? These issues will be treated in the following analysis.

An issue in Hays's work that has attracted a great deal of subsequent interest is his reader-oriented hermeneutic. This is an important concern given the strong emphasis among some intertextual theorists on freeing a text from the constraints of authorial intention.[25] Admittedly, Hays does not attempt an explicitly post-structural reading of the Pauline epistles. Hays, in fact, notes five possible loci of meaning—the author, original readers, the text, contemporary readers, an interpretative community—and seeks "to hold them all together in creative tension."[26] It is hard to escape the conclusion, however, that Hays places great stress on the interpreter's role in the exegetical process.[27]

It would no doubt be naïve not to recognize the danger of subjectivism that is inherent in reading any text intertextually. At the same time, however, it is also necessary to account for the cognitive distance between Paul and modern exegetes. More specifically, we must not overlook the fact

---

Regarding his specific approach to intertextuality, Hays depends strongly on the work of J. Hollander (cf. Hollander, *Echo*). See Clayton and Rothstein ("Figures," 3–36) for a helpful description of intertextuality.

23. Hays, *Echoes*, 14.

24. Cf. Hays, *Echoes*, 20, 87–88, 155. Hays (ibid., 20) suggests that an instance of metalepsis "functions to suggest to the reader that text B [the later text] should be understood in light of a broad interplay with text A [the text that is alluded to], encompassing aspects of A beyond those explicitly echoed."

25. Cf. Clayton and Rothstein, "Figures," 12, 14–16, 21–26. Others argue that the author's intended meaning does not exhaust a text's full semantic potential. See Vanhoozer (*Meaning*) for a balanced discussion of this issue.

26. Hays, *Echoes*, 26–27.

27. Cf. ibid., 31–33.

that Paul's worldview is drastically different from that of the typical twenty-first-century interpreter. Our ability to interact with the Pauline tradition in an objective manner can be hampered not only by doctrinal biases but also by broader worldview commitments such as scientific rationalism.[28] Even a casual reading of Paul's writings indicates that he was quite willing to engage with the OT in creative and imaginative ways (e.g., 1 Cor 10:3-4). Thus, there is a strong sense in which interpreters must keep their "feet" in both the past and the present. More specifically, while it is necessary to adjudicate any potential intertextual reading according to valid and scientific criteria, one must also be willing to simply "let Paul be Paul."

This now brings us to the matter of suitable criteria for validating potential quotations and allusions to the OT. To engage in an intertextual analysis is admittedly to pursue a somewhat subjective enterprise where plausibility can sometimes be in the eye of the beholder. Hence, there is a need to establish principles that will aid the exegete in assessing the probability that a tradition is being alluded to in a later text.

One of the lasting contributions of Hays's monograph, *Echoes of Scripture in the Letters of Paul*, is the seven criteria he proposed to assess the feasibility of a proposed allusion. These seven "tests" (as he refers to them) have frequently been utilized in intertextual investigations of the Pauline corpus. The tests Hays developed are:

1. availability—this test primarily addresses the accessibility of the precursor text;
2. volume—this test assesses the degree of formal correspondence between the precursor text and the later text;
3. recurrence—this test considers the frequency with which the same author evokes the precursor text in other texts;
4. thematic coherence—this test evaluates the degree of conceptual correspondence between the precursor text and the later text;
5. historical plausibility—this test weighs the likelihood that the author would have intended to evoke the precursor text and the likelihood that the original readers would have detected the intertextual reference;
6. history of interpretation—this test attempts to validate a proposed intertextual reference by determining whether other interpreters have previously detected the suggested quotation or allusion;

---

28. Cf. Wagner, *Heralds*, 11-12.

7. satisfaction—according to Hays, this test seeks to determine if "the proposed reading offers a good account of the experience of a contemporary community of competent readers."[29]

While none of these tests are free of difficulties, they have generally been well received within the scholarly community.[30] Nonetheless, a number of them require additional comment and clarification. Hays's seventh test, satisfaction, is especially problematic. Hays himself notes it is challenging to describe this measure without committing the affective fallacy, the misleading notion that a text's meaning is related to its emotional impact on the interpreter.[31] Much of Hays's description of this test seems to overlap with the explanation of his fourth criterion, thematic coherence. That is, both tests seem to assess the "quality" of the reading produced by the proposed allusion.[32] In light of these two factors, this test will not be employed in this analysis.

Hays's historical plausibility test also warrants careful consideration at two points. First, one must recognize that this is not an entirely objective criterion since it requires the interpreter to construct an image of Paul as a writer/theologian.[33] This is not an insurmountable objection, however, since there is a fair amount of primary data present in the Pauline corpus to construct such an image. Second, as noted above, this test also considers the original reader's ability to detect proposed allusions. Hays does allow for the possibility that Paul may have penned statements that were not readily intelligible to his original audience.[34] C. Stanley, however, has extensively argued that many of Paul's allusions, echoes, and implicit quotations would have been overlooked by Paul's original readers.[35] Stanley's work on the literary competence of first-century readers does establish the importance of considering how accessible a potential allusion was to Paul's original readers. However, to adopt his reader-centered approach to this matter unduly limits Paul's creativity as an interpreter of the OT. While a cautious, conservative analysis of the primary data is laudable, in order to understand Paul's use of the OT, one again should seek to "let Paul be Paul" (though this

---

29. Hays, *Echoes*, 31–32.

30. See Berkeley (*Broken Covenant*, 65) and Wagner (*Heralds*, 11–13) for helpful assessments of Hays's criteria for adjudicating allusions.

31. Hays, *Echoes*, 31.

32. Cf. Wagner, *Heralds*, 13.

33. Cf. Berkeley, *Broken Covenant*, 65.

34. Hays, *Echoes*, 30.

35. Cf. Stanley, *Arguing with Scripture*, 48.

undoubtedly can be difficult).[36] Finally, as Wagner notes, one has to account for the probability that less competent readers/interpreters of Paul might have received sufficient instruction from other Christ-followers concerning how to understand Paul's use of the OT.[37]

Finally, Hays's suggestion that a text's prominence within Paul's intertextual framework (the recurrence test) can serve as a means of validating proposed allusions also requires a closer look. In particular, one should consider the frequency a given OT text is referenced outside the Pauline corpus. For example, the Watchers tradition (Gen 6:1-4) holds a prominent place within a variety of Second Temple Jewish texts (e.g., *1 En.* 6-16; Philo, *Gig.* 6, 16, 19, 58; 1QS 3-4; *Jub.* 5:1-11). A proposed allusion to Gen 6:1-4 in the Pauline corpus could gain some measure of viability simply on the basis of its importance in early Jewish literature. A text's place within the NT documents outside the Pauline corpus would hold even greater relevance. Hays himself identifies the relevance of C. H. Dodd's analysis of the early church's Bible to this larger discussion.[38] If the early church did assign a great deal of weight to certain texts within the OT, a proposed allusion by Paul to one of these texts would thus gain a strong degree of probability.

In summary, intertextuality provides a useful hermeneutical tool for investigating the new creation motif in the Pauline tradition. Nonetheless, careful use of this interpretative method is necessary because of the subjective nature of this approach to analyzing texts. Where relevant, the following examination of new creation in the Pauline corpus will focus on two forms of intertextual references—quotations and intentional allusions— and will implicitly use six of Hays's tests (availability, volume, recurrence, thematic coherence, historical plausibility, history of interpretation) to assess the viability of allusions to the OT.

Conclusion

Despite a long history of association with anthropological renewal, recent interpreters have argued for a much broader understanding of the phrase καινὴ κτίσις in 2 Cor 5:17 and Gal 6:15. More specifically, a number of

---

36. Stanley (ibid., 34) himself notes, "The cost of this measure of security [afforded by a reader-centered approach] is the exclusion of a number of passages whose closeness to a particular biblical passage reveals a clear intent to reproduce the wording of that passage within the later Pauline context (e.g., Rom 2:6; 1 Cor 5:13; 15:32; 2 Cor 13:1)."

37. Wagner, *Heralds*, 36-39.

38. Hays, *Echoes*, 201. Cf. Dodd, *According to the Scriptures*, 61-110.

scholars have contended that the traditional reading of new creation in 2 Cor 5:11–21 and Gal 6:11–16 neglects significant cosmological and/or ecclesiological associations within these two texts. At the same time, the traditional account of new creation in these two texts has recently been championed by Hubbard. The nature of new creation in 2 Cor 5:11–21 and Gal 6:11–16 thus remains a matter of serious debate.

The portrait of new creation in Eph 1–2, however, has not received as much scholarly interest as the same material in the Hauptbriefe. Commentators frequently note that Eph 2:1–22 is replete with new creation imagery and concepts. Nonetheless, only a few minor studies have specifically examined the discussion of new creation in this text. A few scholars have also noted a variety of similarities between the conception of new creation in Eph 1–2 and that of the Hauptbriefe. Interestingly, both Hubbard and Jackson appeal to Ephesians in support of their opposing understandings of new creation in the Hauptbriefe. The combination of these factors raises the question of the conceptual relationship between the significance of new creation in these three texts.

In contrast with most investigations of new creation in the Pauline corpus, this inquiry will attempt to give due weight to the allusion to Isaianic tradition in 2 Cor 5:17. While it is often observed that this allusion links new creation in 2 Cor 5:17 with Isaiah's new exodus, a number of interpreters give greater weight to the new covenant traditions of Jeremiah and Ezekiel or Jewish apocalyptic traditions. The intertextual method will be employed throughout this study to determine just how closely new creation in the Pauline tradition is aligned with Isaiah's vision of divine deliverance. The fact that Isaiah's new exodus is also evoked in Eph 2:13, 17 reinforces the viability of the intertextual method for this particular project. In summary, this inquiry will explore the degree of continuity and discontinuity between the depictions of new creation in the Hauptbriefe and the letter to the Ephesians by means of an intertextual analysis.

2

New Creation in the Prophecy of Isaiah

Introduction

A CENTRAL POINT OF contention within the new creation debate in the Pauline corpus pertains to how this concept is related to Isaianic traditions. While scholars agree Isaiah is alluded to in 2 Cor 5:17b and Eph 2:13, 17, much less accord exists regarding several other significant questions.[1] The relationship between new creation in Paul and Isaiah's "new heavens and new earth" is a particularly important issue. The precise nature of Isaiah's new exodus is yet another subject of debate. The relationship between Isaiah's new exodus and the "new heavens and new earth" of Isa 65–66 is also an issue in need of further study.

It is my belief that one of the principal causes for the existence of this ongoing debate is the relative lack of attention devoted to Isaiah by those who have attempted to understand new creation in the Pauline tradition.[2] The absence of serious engagement with the book of Isaiah in this debate is, of course, a methodological issue.[3] Generally speaking, those who have extensively analyzed the background of new creation in Paul have employed

---

1. Throughout this analysis of new creation in Isaiah, emphasis will be placed on understanding how Isaiah is being interpreted in the Pauline tradition. A number of critical questions such as the authorship and redaction of Isaiah will therefore be bypassed. As Jackson (*New Creation*, 18) notes, focusing on the unity of Isaiah may help in clarifying the nature of new creation in Paul's letters.

2. The recent work by Jackson is an important exception. Further effort, nonetheless, is needed to determine how Isaiah is related to new creation in the Pauline corpus.

3. One may attribute this state of affairs either to a passé approach to the use of the Old Testament in the NT or to a tendency to overemphasize the use of the phrase καινὴ κτίσις in Second Temple Jewish texts over against the allusion to Isaianic tradition in 2 Cor 5:17b.

the *traditionsgeschichtliche* method.[4] I have already noted the scholarly trend to interpret quotations of and allusions to the OT within the Pauline corpus through the lens of intertextuality (see above, p. 8–9). Viewing 2 Cor 5:17b and Eph 2:13, 17 as literary tropes opens up the possibility that closer engagement with Isaianic texts may shed light on the nature of new creation in the Pauline tradition.

One may even suggest that the evocation of Isaiah in 2 Cor 5:17b is particularly suited to an intertextual investigation. While there is a strong consensus that this phrase picks up on Isa 43:18–19, less certainty exists regarding which other texts Paul may be alluding to in Isaiah.[5] The allusive nature of the intertextual reference in 2 Cor 5:17b raises the question, "What is the function of such a veiled allusion to Isaiah?" The use of imagery capable of being linked with a variety of Isaianic texts intimates that Paul is associating καινὴ κτίσις in 2 Cor 5:17a with Isaiah's new exodus motif *in toto* rather than connecting new creation with *specific* texts in Isaiah.[6] A close examination of texts associated with this Isaianic theme may thus shed important light on new creation theology in the Pauline tradition.

Prior to my actual analysis, a few comments are in order regarding my selection of texts. First, in keeping with the intertextual method, particular emphasis will be placed on carefully considering the texts most strongly evoked in 2 Cor 5:17b and Eph 2:13, 17. Special attention therefore will be devoted to Isa 43:16–21; 52:7–12; 57:14–21.[7] Second, Isa 40:1–11 will also be examined in an effort to determine how this programmatic new exodus text might inform the portrait of the new exodus in Isaiah.[8] Third, I will also closely study the descriptions of the "new heavens and new earth" in Isa 65:17–25 and Isa 66:18–24. Throughout this analysis, I will pay careful attention to determining the extent to which Isaiah's new exodus encompasses anthropological, cosmological, and ecclesiological concerns.

---

4. This is especially true of the contributions to this debate of Mell and Hubbard.

5. See above, p. 6.

6. Cf. Gignilliat, *Paul*, 97. This is obviously not an entirely new suggestion. One is forced to conclude, however, that the implications of this hypothesis have yet to be fully worked out.

7. Space constraints preclude a detailed examination of other texts that may be evoked in 2 Cor 5:17b beyond Isa 43:16–21. At any rate, the new exodus imagery in Isa 43:16–21 is much stronger in comparison with Isa 42:9–16 and Isa 48:1–11.

8. Cf. Lund, *Way*, 72, 101; Elliger, *Deuterojesaja*, 34. Pace Jackson, (*New Creation*, 20) who argues that Isa 43:18–19 "may well be the key passage of Isaiah's new exodus theology."

New Creation in Isa 40:1–11

I have already noted the lack of lexical correspondence among 2 Cor 5:17b; Eph 2:13, 17; and Isa 40:1–11. Nonetheless, an analysis of Isa 40:1–11 is relevant to this discussion on the basis of the following points of evidence: 1) the status of Isa 40:1–11 as the introductory new exodus text in Isaiah; and 2) the predominance of allusions to Isa 40:1–11 in Isa 52:7–12 and Isa 57:14–21 (see below, esp. p. 26–32).[9]

Exegesis of Isa 40:1–11

The prologue of Isa 40–55 begins in vv. 1–2 by introducing a subject that will play a significant role in the remainder of the book. Isaiah 40:1–2 consists of a general proclamation of salvation for God's people (v. 1) and is followed by a more explicit elaboration of that declaration (v. 2). The development of the oracle of salvation in v. 2 begins by concretely identifying those intended to receive this message of consolation. "Jerusalem" is personified in v. 2 and in doing so the author highlights the close relationship between the people of Israel and their religio-political capital.[10] Understood within the overall message of Isaiah, v. 2 announces the end of God's judgment and the restoration of Jerusalem. Within the context of Isa 40:1–11, it becomes clear that this message of consolation is to be understood largely in the form of restoration from exile (vv. 2, 10–11). However, when understood within the larger framework of Isaiah's final form, this message of comfort not only looks back to the thanksgiving song of Isa 12:1–6, but also introduces the theme of the restored Jerusalem/Zion to be developed more extensively in Isa 56–66 (cf. Isa 33:20–24; 60–62; 65:17–25; 66:18–24).[11]

---

9. As already noted, τὰ ἀρχαῖα παρῆλθεν ἰδοὺ γέγονεν καινά in 2 Cor 5:17b is best understood as an allusion to Isaiah's new exodus theme rather than specific texts within Isaiah (see above, p. 15). If this is the case, it is natural to consider this foundational new exodus text in Isaiah to determine how it contributes to the portrait of Isaiah's new exodus.

10. Jackson (*New Creation*, 24) notes, "The city and its holy mountain are used in Isaiah as symbols of hope for the continuing covenant relationship between YHWH and his people (cf. Isa 37:31–2)."

11. According to Rendtorff ("Jesaja," 318), "Das Thema 'Zion' wiederum hat in jedem der drei Teile seine deutliche Funktion und bildet in gewisser Weise das stärkste Bindeglied zwischen ihnen." Cf. Dumbrell, "Purpose," 111–28; Barstad, *Way*, 10; Jackson, *New Creation*, 24–27.

There are three major portraits of the restored Zion/Jerusalem in Isaiah's prophecy: Isa 60–62, Isa 65:17–25, and Isa 66:18–24 (see esp. Isa 59:20; 60:10–22; 61:4–7; 62:1–4, 10–12; 65:18–19, 25; 66:7–14). Several observations regarding the description of the restored Zion/Jerusalem in Isa 60–62 are worth briefly noting. First, there is a strong

The announcement of salvation in Isa 40:1-2 raises the question of the nature of the restoration envisioned in this passage. Despite a change in speaker, it is evident that vv. 3-5 does address this concern. According to Westermann, vv. 3-5 describes how "comfort" will come to the Israelites and indicates that this is strictly by means of divine agency.[12] Scholars generally agree that the imagery of a "way in the wilderness" in v. 3 forms part of Isaiah's new exodus theme.[13] Less agreement, however, exists regarding how this imagery and theme are to be interpreted.[14]

For a number of scholars, v. 3 is best understood to refer to a way home for the exiles from Babylon to the promised land.[15] Recent interpreters, however, have questioned this reading and argued on the basis of several factors that the "wilderness" and "way" of Isa 40:3 are best understood metaphorically. Historical and geographical concerns make a strictly literal reading of v. 3 largely untenable.[16] The literary relationship between Isa 35:1-10 and Isa 40:3-5 also creates problems for the attempt to interpret this new exodus solely as a return from Babylon. There are a number of lexical points of contact between Isa 35:1-10 and Isa 40:3-5, and the prior

emphasis in Isa 60-62 on the salvation of the nations (e.g., Isa 60:3-7, 10-16). Second, the concluding imagery in Isa 62:10-11 (note especially the "way" imagery in v. 10 and the modified quotation of Isa 40:10 in v. 11) suggests that the description of the restored Zion/Jerusalem in Isa 60-62 is to be understood as the fulfillment of Isaiah's prophecy of a new exodus (cf. Isa 40:3, 10; 43:19; 49:11; 52:7; 57:14; *T. Dan* 5:8-13; *Sib. Or.* 3:767-95; 1QM 12:9-18). This observation allows for the conclusion that while there are no explicit references to the building of a temple in new exodus texts such as Isa 40:1-5, 9-11; 43:16-2, the concept is nonetheless present since the goal of Isaiah's new exodus is the restored Zion/Jerusalem. The phrase "worshiping community" will thus be used when discussing the presence of temple-building traditions in Isaiah's new exodus as a means of capturing the essentially cultic nature of its eventual outcome. Third, the allusion to Isa 62:8-9 in Isa 65:22-23 suggests that the picture of a "new heavens and a new earth" in Isa 65:17-25 is closely related to the eschatological vision of a restored Zion/Jerusalem in Isa 60-62 (cf. *Jub.* 1:28-29; 4:26; *2 Bar.* 32:1-6; 44:5-15; see below, p. 35-37). See below, p. 187-191, for further analysis of the relationship between Isaiah's new exodus, the restored Zion/Jerusalem, and the "new heavens and new earth" in Second Temple Judaism.

12. Westermann, *Jesaja*, 30, 33.

13. Cf. Childs, *Isaiah*, 299; Watts, *Isaiah 34-66*, 80-81; Stuhlmueller, *Creative Redemption*, 74, 82.

14. See Lund (*Way*, 3-21) for an extensive survey of literature on this topic.

15. Cf. Stuhlmueller, *Creative Redemption*, 82; Goldingay, *Message*, 18; Westermann, *Jesaja*, 30, 35; Elliger, *Deuterojesaja*, 17-18.

16. Oswalt (*Isaiah 40-66*, 51-52) notes, "The way back from Babylon did not come through the desert but went around it." Blenkinsopp (*Isaiah 40-55*, 182) further observes that those texts in the Old Testament that describe a journey from Babylon to the promised land depict a voyage through the Fertile Crescent (cf. Neh 2:7-11). Cf. Lund, *Way*, 19.

text clearly addresses the Assyrian threat.[17] At the same time, since v. 11 probably describes the divine warrior of vv. 9-10 bringing the exiles home (see below, p. 19-20), it remains difficult to separate the Babylonian exile completely from the historical situation of v. 3. In summary, when the entire context of vv. 1-11 is accounted for, it is likely that the new exodus of Isa 40:1-11 encompasses the historical return of the exiles from Babylon, yet also looks beyond that to a greater act of divine deliverance.[18]

Further evidence for this reading of Isa 40:3 is found in the author's reference to preparing "the way of the Lord" (τὴν ὁδὸν κυρίου). Regarding this phrase, Lund notes that advocates of a literal interpretation of Isa 40:3 fail to give sufficient stress to the author's statement that this "way" is directly connected with YHWH and not the Israelites.[19] The meaning of this phrase is helpfully elucidated by considering its relationship to theophany traditions in the OT. Several scholars observe that the account of the constructing of a "way" in v. 3, the altering of the terrain in v. 4, and the unveiling of God's glory in v. 5 are all common features of theophanic texts (cf. Hab 3:1-13; Nah 1:2-8; Ps 67:1-11 LXX).[20] Understood in this light, vv. 3-5 portrays God coming to save and deliver his people during their time of need. Significantly, the description of geographic transformation in Isa 40:4 adds an element of cosmological renewal to this new exodus text.[21] The presence of the phrase τὸ σωτήριον in Isa 40:5 LXX strengthens the possibility that the "way" of v. 3 carries connotations of deliverance.[22] Within the context of Isa 40:1-11, the call to "prepare the way of the Lord" therefore refers to the means by which God himself will rescue his people.

Given the possibility that new creation in the Pauline tradition encompasses ecclesiological concerns, it is especially important to consider the significance of the clause ὄψεται πᾶσα σὰρξ τὸ σωτήριον τοῦ θεοῦ in v. 5.[23] The

17. Cf. Blenkinsopp, *Isaiah 40-55*, 181-82.

18. See Gignilliat (*Paul*, 63-68) for the suggestion that the lack of historical specificity within Isa 40-66 requires a "theological" reading, which closely relates the message of Isa 40-55 with that of Isa 56-66.

19. Lund, *Way*, 89. Cf. Watts, *Isaiah 34-66*, 80; Baltzer, *Deutero-Isaiah*, 85; Whybray, *Isaiah 40-66*, 50; Goldingay and Payne, *Isaiah 40-55*, 75; Koole, *Isaiah III*, 59.

20. Goldingay and Payne, *Isaiah 40-55*, 77; Seitz, "Divine Council," 335-37; Lund, *Way*, 86.

21. Cf. *Sib. Or.* 3:777-79.

22. Cf. Lund, *Way*, 88. Lund (ibid., 87) also notes that even though the MT does not overtly express a connection between this theophanic manifestation of God and the salvation of his people, this relationship finds more thorough elaboration in Isa 40:9-11. Thus, it is likely that Isa 40:9-11 LXX continues this reading of vv. 3-5.

23. Within the context of Isa 40:3-5, v. 5 expresses the divine attendant's description of the consequences of God's march through the wilderness—his glory will be revealed

emphasis on the restoration of Jerusalem in the immediate context of Isa 40:5 makes it difficult to conclude that the salvation of Gentiles is being conveyed in this passage. Nevertheless, if the "new heavens and new earth" of Isa 65–66 represents the ultimate fulfillment of Isa 40:1–11, it then becomes plausible to presume that the salvation of Gentiles is ultimately in view.[24]

A close examination of Isa 66:18-24 reveals that this is a distinct possibility. The phrase πᾶσα σάρξ is used in Isa 66:23 to describe Jews and Gentiles worshiping YHWH in the "new heavens and new earth." A careful reading of Isa 66:18-23 indicates that those pictured worshiping in v. 23 are also those from among the nations who behold (ὄψονται) God's glory (δόξαν) in vv. 18–19.[25] The presence of the noun δόξα and the verb ὁράω in this context creates strong lexical ties to Isa 40:5.[26] While it is difficult to discern whether the nations experience God's salvation in Isa 40:5, this possibility certainly becomes more plausible in Isa 66:18-19.[27]

Given the climactic role of Isa 40:9-11, it is important to consider how these statements elaborate on vv. 1–5.[28] This section of Isa 40:1-11 continues the message of hope presented in vv. 1–5 by personifying Zion and Jerusalem as heralds of deliverance (v. 9). The clause εἰπὸν ταῖς πόλεσιν Ιουδα in v. 9 offers a particularly helpful interpretative clue. By building upon the theophany imagery of vv. 3–5, the proclamation "here is your God" in v. 9 probably implies Zion and Jerusalem have already experienced the

---

to πᾶσα σάρξ (v. 5).

24. Goldingay (*Message*, 22) notes that later uses of the phrase "all flesh" in Isaiah clarify its meaning in Isa 40:5. The emphasis on universalism in Isaiah (e.g., Isa 2:1–4; 19:18–25; 56:1–7; 60:1–4; 66:18–24) also makes it natural to consider whether Gentiles might experience the salvation described in v. 5. See Kaminsky ("Election," 135–44) and van Winkle ("Relationship," 446–58) for helpful discussions of the difficult question of the place of universalism within Isa 40–55.

25. Isaiah 66:18-22 primarily describes the process by which God establishes the multi-ethnic worshiping community pictured in v. 23. See below, p. 38–40, for further discussion of universalism in Isa 66:18–24 and its relationship to Isa 40:5. Jackson (*New Creation*, 153–54) also observes the presence of the phrase "all flesh" in Isa 40:5 and Isa 66:23 and concludes that these two texts might have relevance for understanding the nature of new creation in Paul.

26. Cf. Childs, *Isaiah*, 543. Childs observes a number of other correspondences between Isa 40:1–11 and Isa 65–66.

27. The message of Isa 66:18 seems closely related to Isa 60:1–4, which describes the restored Zion/Jerusalem as a place where "all nations" (גּוֹיִם) assemble to behold YHWH's glory (cf. Isa 2:1–4; Mic 4:1–8; Zech 8:20–23).

28. See Goldingay (*Message*, 27) and Blenkinsopp (*Isaiah 40-55*, 185) for helpful discussions of how vv. 9–11 are linked with the preceding eight verses (pace Watts, *Isaiah 34-66*, 78).

deliverance described in vv. 1–5.²⁹ When Isa 40:9 is read within the context of vv. 1–8, it suggests that the promised redemption of Zion/Jerusalem in vv. 1–5 is an accomplished reality and this redemption will ultimately extend throughout the land.

One may conclude on the basis of Isa 40:9 that Zion/Jerusalem is the goal of the new exodus of vv. 3–5. If Isa 40:9–11 represents an elaboration of vv. 3–5 and v. 9 implies that Zion/Jerusalem has already been delivered, it is reasonable to conclude that the "way" upon which God traverses in v. 3 to bring his people comfort leads to Zion. Once again, Isa 40:1–11 forms part of a larger thematic movement within Isaiah that depicts the restoration of Zion/Jerusalem and ultimately beyond to the "new heavens and new earth" of Isa 65–66.³⁰

The presence of divine warrior imagery in v. 10 is also worth noting. Isaiah 40:10 primarily elaborates on v. 9 by describing the manner in which YHWH returns to deliver his people. It is clear from v. 10 that YHWH is coming as a victorious warrior-King (v. 10a).³¹ According to some scholars, the use of arm imagery in v. 10 constitutes an allusion to the exodus tradition of the Pentateuch (cf. Exod 6:1, 6; 15:16; 32:11; Deut 4:34; 5:15; 6:21; 7:8, 19; 9:26, 29; 26:8).³² Despite the faint volume of this proposed allusion, the degree to which the imagery of YHWH's arm forms a part of the exodus

---

29. Childs, *Isaiah*, 301; Baltzer, *Deutero-Isaiah*, 63; Westermann, *Jesaja*, 39. The phrase "here is your God" in v. 9 also implies that YHWH is returning to Zion now that the era of judgment of the covenant people has reached its completion. YHWH's return to Zion is an important feature of several Isaianic new exodus texts and represents an adaptation of the ANE temple-building narrative pattern (cf. Isa 40:9–10; 49:9–10; 52:8, 12; 57:18). One may then suggest that the Isaianic new exodus application of ANE temple-building traditions (generally speaking) adheres to the following outline: divine conflict . . . conquest . . . YHWH's return to Zion . . . temple-building.

30. Isaiah 40:1–11 is certainly not the only new exodus text in Isaiah that focuses on the restoration of Zion/Jerusalem. Isaiah 51:9–11, a text that alludes to the first exodus in vv. 9–10, does explicitly mention Zion, and this text too concludes with a description of the exiles as a worshiping community (v. 11). Much the same can be said regarding Isa 49:1–21. The lexical links between Isa 49:11–13 and Isa 40:1–4 (ὁδόν, πᾶν ὄρος, παρεκάλεσεν) are particularly interesting to note. For our purposes, it is worth observing that this oracle of salvation describes the end of Israel's captivity by means of a way through mountains in vv. 11–13 (cf. Isa 40:3–4) and then proceeds to address the reversal of Zion's state of desolation in vv. 14–21. Implicit behind this progression of thought is that the exiles are journeying from Babylon to Zion. See below, pp. 112–16, for further discussion of Isa 49:11–13.

31. Cf. Blenkinsopp, *Isaiah 40–55*, 186. Importantly, a number of texts in Isaiah depict YHWH as a divine warrior and occasionally these texts are linked with new creation imagery and/or the restored Zion/Jerusalem (cf. Isa 11:1–27; 27:1–2, 12–13; 30:27–33; 31:4–9; 34:5–7; 51:9–11; 52:7–12; 59:16–21; 63:1–6; 66:14–24).

32. Blenkinsopp, *Isaiah 40–55*, 186; Goldingay and Payne, *Isaiah 40–55*, 89.

tradition makes this a plausible reading of v. 10.³³ The use of divine warrior imagery continues in v. 10b, yet with a slight modification; whereas divine warrior traditions typically describe slaves accompanying the conquering warrior, vv. 10b-11 portrays the warrior being attended by his own people.³⁴ The suggestion that YHWH is leading his people back to the land once again raises the question of whether Isa 40:1-11 should be interpreted historically or theologically. Despite the strength of a theological reading of Isa 40:3-5, it must be admitted that since Isa 40:11 seems to clarify v. 10, it is difficult to avoid the conclusion that v. 10 describes YHWH being accompanied by his people. This reading of v. 10 more effectively accounts for the use of the verb παρακαλέω in v. 11, which closely binds the reassuring statements in that context to the preceding ten verses.³⁵ Thus, there seems to be a distinct interplay between history and theology within Isa 40:1-11 that correlates the return from Babylon with a greater act of redemption.

Summary

While Isa 40:1-11 is not evoked in 2 Cor 5:17 or Eph 2:13, 17, this passage's status as the prologue to Isa 40-55 and Isaiah's introductory new exodus text makes it relevant to this study. An analysis of this text indicates Isa 40:1-11 sets the stage for other new exodus texts that are more commonly related to new creation theology in the *corpus Paulinum*. Importantly, Isa 40:1-11 closely associates the new exodus with: 1) the end of YHWH's judgment upon Israel's sin (vv. 1-2); 2) the alteration of the created order in v. 4; and 3) the salvation of the Gentiles (v. 5). Isaiah 40:1-11 thus links the new exodus with anthropological, cosmological, and ecclesiological notions. It now remains to consider the degree to which other Isaianic new exodus texts more commonly associated with new creation in the Pauline corpus develop this multifaceted portrait of YHWH's redemption of his people.

33. In this regard, the pervasive use of divine warrior imagery in the "Song of the Sea" (Exod 15:1-19) is also relevant to this issue. The presence of exodus imagery in Isa 40:3 should also be considered. Finally, Isa 51:9 establishes even stronger connections between arm imagery and the exodus tradition (cf. Isa 63:11-13). The combination of these factors strengthens the viability of an allusion to the exodus tradition in Isa 40:10.

34. Cf. Baltzer, *Deutero-Isaiah*, 62-63; Goldingay and Payne, *Isaiah 40-55*, 90.

35. The presence of intertextual links between Isa 35:3-4; Isa 40:9-11; and Isa 62:8-12 also confirms this reading of vv. 10-11. See Blenkinsopp (*Isaiah 40-55*, 181-82) and Childs (*Isaiah*, 301, 513) for helpful discussions of the relationship between Isa 40:9-11 and these other two texts. It must be admitted, however, that the LXX does not convey quite as strongly as the MT the links between Isa 40:9-11 and Isa 62:8-12. Nonetheless, it does seem plausible to read these texts as a critical part of the larger message of Zion's restoration in the book of Isaiah.

New Creation in Isa 43:16–21

As already noted, one of the few points of consensus among scholars who have analyzed new creation in the Pauline tradition is that 2 Cor 5:17b constitutes an allusion to Isa 43:18–19. There is no need to challenge this assertion. What is needed, however, is a closer analysis of this passage to determine how this text might inform the conception of new creation in the Pauline corpus.

Exegesis of Isa 43:16–21

Isaiah 43:16–17 continues the discussion of God's ability to redeem from the preceding context (cf. Isa 43:8–15) by alluding to the exodus tradition. Despite the impreciseness of the imagery in v. 16, a definite allusion to the exodus tradition is confirmed when one examines v. 17.[36] Within v. 17, the reader finds explicit references to the chariots, horses, and Egyptian army that play such a vital role in the exodus tradition. Furthermore, Ps 76:20 LXX also employs the imagery of a "way through the sea" and a path through powerful waters; within that context, the metaphor also is meant to recall the events surrounding God's deliverance of the Israelites from Egypt (cf. v. 16, 21).[37] On the basis of these two points of evidence, there is thus a strong degree of probability that the imagery in v. 16 is meant to recall the exodus tradition.

Despite the strength of this allusion to the exodus tradition, one must still determine if this passage should be read strictly within the confines of the Babylonian exile. A close examination of Isa 43:16–21 indicates that this is not the case.[38] Perhaps the most compelling evidence for a metaphorical reading of this passage is the description of wild animals praising God in v. 20.[39] Yet even within vv. 16–17, one finds that while the author alludes to the

---

36. The presence of the nouns ὁδόν and τρίβον in v. 16 may constitute an intertextual link with Isa 40:3 (cf. Isa 43:19).

37. Goldingay, *Message*, 208. It should be noted that like Isa 43:1–15, Ps 76 LXX also revolves around a problematic situation (vv. 1–2), emphasizes God's acts of salvation in the past (vv. 3–6, 11–12, 14), and contains explicit allusions to the exodus tradition (vv. 15–20).

38. It is perhaps best to suggest that while this passage envisions the return from Babylon, it nonetheless also points to an even greater act of deliverance. Cf. Lund, *Way*, 191; Blenkinsopp, *Isaiah 40–55*, 228.

39. Cf. Lund, *Way*, 182; Kiesow, *Exodustexte*, 77–78; Koole, *Isaiah III*, 336. Isaiah 43:19–20 is almost certainly one of the most difficult new exodus texts in Isaiah to connect with a literal exodus from Babylon. Goldingay (*Message*, 211) concedes on the basis of this passage that the referent of this theme cannot be strictly limited to the return from Babylon.

exodus tradition, his modification of the tradition signifies an entirely literal reading is probably not intended. Specifically, while accounts of the exodus describe God leading the Israelites from Egypt (cf. Exod 7:4–5; 13:14–16; 14:11; Ps 104:37 LXX; Bar 1:19–20; 2:11), Isa 43:17 portrays God leading "chariot and horse, army and warrior" to their demise.[40] Finally, if Isa 43:19–20 represents an intertextual allusion to Isa 40:3–4 as some scholars propose, the conclusions drawn there regarding the nature of the new exodus should probably affect how one interprets this passage.[41] The emphasis in v. 17 on YHWH's defeat of his enemies raises the possibility that the author is appealing to another aspect of the exodus tradition. In particular, rather than focusing on the tradition's narration of the Israelites' deliverance from Egypt, the author of Isaiah may be drawing from the tradition's depiction of YHWH's defeat of the Egyptians as a cosmic event. This interpretation of the deliverance from Egypt is perhaps clearest in what is commonly described as the "Song of the Sea" (Exod 15:1–19), a text which is also something of a poetic retelling of this climactic event in Israel's history.

At this point, it is helpful to consider how Exod 15 and Isa 43:16–21 begin and conclude. Specifically, both texts commence by portraying YHWH as a divine warrior (cf. Exod 15:1–3; Isa 43:16–17) and conclude by describing the formation of a worshiping community (cf. Exod 15:13, 17; Isa 43:20–21). Within Exod 15, YHWH is not only portrayed as a victorious warrior in v. 3, but there is also a decided emphasis on YHWH's victory over the Egyptian army (the only concrete reference to the delivered Israelites in the "Song of the Sea" is found in vv. 13, 17, and 19).[42] The presence of this structural arrangement suggests that Exod 15:1–19 and Isa 43:16–21 are both modeled after ANE temple-building traditions.[43] Exod 15 is thus a

40. Cf. Lund, *Way*, 186. The emphasis, at least in Isa 43:16–17, is therefore on God's sovereignty and his victory over his enemies (cf. vv. 11–13), as opposed to a description of God guiding his people from a place of oppression to one of freedom.

41. Isaiah 43:19–20 evokes Isa 40:3–4 through the phrase καὶ ποιήσω ἐν τῇ ἐρήμῳ ὁδόν and the description of ecological transformation (ὅτι ἔδωκα ἐν τῇ ἐρήμῳ ὕδωρ καὶ ποταμοὺς ἐν τῇ ἀνύδρῳ). Cf. Patrick, "Epiphanic Imagery," 133; Goldingay, *Message*, 212–13.

42. In Exod 15:3, the LXX reads κύριος συντρίβων πολέμους ("the Lord crushes wars"), which is a curious rendering of the MT's יהוה איש מלחמה ("the LORD is a warrior"). According to Wevers (*Exodus*, 228), Exod 15:3 LXX depicts YHWH as "one who is victorious in warfare." The meaning of Exod 15:3 LXX and Exod 15:3 MT is thus essentially the same.

43. Cf. Propp, *Exodus 1–18*, 558; Cross, *Canaanite Myth*, 137; Batto, *Mythmaking*, 113; Goldingay, *Message*, 213; Clifford, "Cosmogonic Language," 3–4. See Batto (*Mythmaking*, 114) for the suggestion that the sanctuary in view is Mt. Zion (a suggestion which would further strengthen the eschatological character of this text). The reverberations of ANE temple-building traditions are established in Exod 15:17–18 by

poetic reiteration of the original exodus that aims to compare the creation of Israel with the creation of the cosmos.[44] Viewed through the lens of Exod 15, the portrait of a new exodus in Isa 43:16–21 thus comes to signify an act of temple-building comparable to the exodus from Egypt.[45] The allusions to the exodus narrative do not seem to describe a literal journey of the Israelites from Babylon back to the promised land. Instead, the events of the first exodus have been incorporated into an eschatological framework in order to depict God's future redemption of his people.[46]

The significance of Isa 43:18–19 for understanding Isaiah's new things/former things theme is especially relevant to understanding new creation in the Pauline tradition.[47] Within Isa 43:18–19, this theme is expressed by means of two parallel colons in v. 18 (μὴ μνημονεύετε/μὴ συλλογίζεσθε) and the phrase ἰδοὺ ποιῶ καινά (v. 19a). Recent interpreters building upon arguments for the unity and coherence of the book of Isaiah have suggested that the "former things" in all likelihood refer to the prophetic message of judgment presented in Isa 1–39, while the "new thing" refers to the message of promise developed in Isa 40–66.[48]

---

means of the explicit mention of the sanctuary and the concluding statement the "Lord will reign forever and forever." Regarding Isa 43:16–21, the appositional phrase in v. 21 implicitly expresses YHWH's purpose in electing Israel as the creation of a nation who would worship him. With this statement in v. 21, the text establishes further links to the "Song of the Sea" and the portrait of the "new thing" in v. 19 as a divine act of temple-building is concluded (cf. Exod 4:23; 7:16; 8:1, 20; 15:13, 16–17; Ps 77:52–55 LXX).

44. The poetic nature of Exod 15:1–18 should not cause one to lose sight of the fact that the exodus from Egypt eventually led to the construction of the tabernacle, a structure that may be sufficiently understood as a temple (cf. Exod 25–40).

45. Cf. Haag, "Der Weg," 21, 23, 42; Zenger, "Der Gott," 17; Simian-Yofre, "Deuteroisaias," 544; Lund, *Way*, 186, 197.

46. Isaiah 51:9–12 MT establishes even more explicit connections between the first exodus, God's coming deliverance, and the defeat of chaos. In this text, a personified Zion calls upon God to act on its behalf by reminding him of his prior victories over the forces of chaos (vv. 9–10). God himself then seems to become the speaker in vv. 11–12 and expresses the natural conclusion from the statements in vv. 9–10: the same God who defeated chaos in the past will do so again and will thus bring his people back to Zion.

47. The allusion to Isaianic tradition in 2 Cor 5:17b places Paul's new creation theology firmly within Isaiah's new things/former things motif. It is therefore important to consider how Isa 43:18–19 might inform Paul's perception of new creation. Finally, the new things/former things motif of Isaiah 40–66 is chiefly developed in Isa 41:22; 42:9; 43:9; 46:9; 48:3; 61:4; 65:7, 16–17.

48. Cf. Childs, *Introduction*, 325–38; Clements, "Prophecies," 421–36; Clements, "Unity," 117–29. This is in contrast with those scholars utilizing historical criticism who argue "the former things" refer to God's saving acts that preceded 587 BC and "the new things" are best understood as God's new plan of salvation involving Cyrus. Cf. North, "Deutero-Isaiah," 111–26; Barstad, *Way*, 94–95; Hoover, *New Creation*, 13.

While this is a helpful account of the book of Isaiah as a whole, one must consider that this motif carries a more concrete meaning within Isa 40–55. More specifically, within Isa 40–55, the "new thing" generally refers to God's new act of deliverance (depicted as a new exodus), while the "former things" (again generally) point to his prior acts of deliverance.[49] The pervasiveness of exodus imagery in Isa 43:16–17 provides a strong measure of support for this interpretation. When these allusions to the exodus tradition are considered, it becomes likely that Isa 43:18 refers to the exodus from Egypt and other divine acts of deliverance in the distant past.[50] Isa 43:19a (ἰδοὺ ποιῶ καινά) then clarifies v. 18 by explaining why the reader should not dwell on the past redemptive acts of God. According to v. 19a, the reader is to forget the past because God is doing something new (cf. Isa 42:9).[51] Within the context of this passage, this "new thing" is best understood as a new act of redemption that will surpass the magnitude of the exodus from Egypt. When the entire message of Isaiah is taken into account, this new act of redemption probably encompasses the "new heavens and new earth" of Isa 65–66.[52]

Summary

Isaiah 43:16–21 is an oracle of salvation that depicts YHWH's deliverance of his people as a new exodus. This passage mirrors Exod 15:1–19 by framing the new exodus as a divine act of temple-building. YHWH is depicted as a divine warrior (vv. 16–17) and his people as a worshiping community (vv. 20b–21). Highly metaphoric language is also employed in v. 20a that

49. Cf. Isa 41:22; 42:9; 43:9, 18–19; 46:9; 48:3, 6; 51:9–11. Cf. Lund, *Way*, 187–89; Stuhlmueller, *Creative Redemption*, 137–68; Koole, *Isaiah III*, 329–31.

50. Cf. Oswalt, *Isaiah 40–66*, 154–55; Blenkinsopp, *Isaiah 40–55*, 227–28; pace Goldingay and Payne, *Isaiah 40–55*, 298.

51. Despite the strong parallelism between Isa 42:9 and Isa 43:18–19 (note the presence of the root αρχ-, the interjection ἰδού, the adjective καινά, and the verb ἀνατέλλω), there is no hint within the immediate context of Isa 42:9 of an allusion to the exodus tradition. The "song" of Isa 42:10–17, however, does contain allusions to divine warrior traditions (vv. 13–16) and v. 16 does describe God leading "the blind" along a "road" (ὁδῷ).

52. It is helpful at this point to recall the suggestion that the goal of Isaiah's new exodus is the restored Zion/Jerusalem. While there is no concrete reference to Zion or Jerusalem in Isa 43:16–21, the description in vv. 20–21 of YHWH's formation of a worshiping community suggests the "new thing" YHWH is doing and the terminus of the "way in the wilderness" (v. 19) is ultimately a place of worship. Cf. Clifford, "Cosmogonic Language," 4. Given the frequent cultic connotations associated with Zion/Jerusalem in Isaiah, it is reasonable to conclude the "way" (and the "new thing" associated with it) leads to this place of hope (cf. Isa 4:3–5; 35:10; 51:3).

indicates this grand new exodus directly impacts the created order.[53] Close analysis of Isa 43:16–21 once again reveals that Isaiah's new exodus looks ahead to the "new heavens and new earth" of Isa 65–66. Perhaps most importantly, Isa 43:19 describes the new exodus as a "new thing," thus also placing the new exodus within Isaiah's new things/former things theme (cf. Isa 65:16–17). Finally, if Isa 43:16–21 should be understood through the lens of ANE temple-building traditions, despite the absence of an explicit reference to the restored Zion/Jerusalem, it is likely that this is the reality (and thus Isaiah's "new heavens and new earth") ultimately in view. Thus, Isaiah's account of the new exodus in Isa 43:16–21 is replete with cosmological undertones, which calls into question any attempt to exclude such notions from the depiction of new creation in the Pauline corpus. The extent to which Isa 43:16–21 utilizes ANE temple-building traditions to describe this new exodus also suggests that it may be related to the portrait of new creation in Eph 1–2.[54]

New Creation in Isa 52:7–12

There is general agreement that Eph 2:17 constitutes a conflated allusion to Isa 52:7 and Isa 57:19. Within Eph 2:17, it is evident that only the clause εὐηγγελίσατο εἰρήνην strongly evokes Isa 52:7. The brevity of the allusion to Isa 52:7 in Eph 2:17 naturally raises the question of the relevance of Isa 52:7–12 to this discussion. The following analysis of Isa 52:7–12 will explore the possibility of reading this passage as part of Isaiah's new exodus motif and assess its relevance for understanding new creation in the Pauline tradition.

Exegesis of Isa 52:7–12

The general content of this passage and its overall place within Isa 40–55 provide a suitable starting point for this discussion. Isaiah 52:7–12 may be understood as a hymnic celebration of Zion's deliverance. The imagery that is used here is of a city under siege, waiting to hear the outcome of a decisive battle (cf. Nah 1:15; Rom 10:15).[55] It is clear from the content of v. 7 that Zion's enemies have been defeated and the victory has been won

---

53. Cf. Isa 32:12–20; 35:4–10; 41:17–20; 44:3–4.

54. See below, pp. 135–37, on the relationship between ANE temple-building traditions and Eph 1–2.

55. Cf. Oswalt, *Isaiah 40–66*, 367.

by none other than God himself. The remainder of Isa 57:7-12 describes the significance of this conquest for Zion and YHWH's people. Concerning the import of Isa 52:7-12 within Isa 40-55, the volume of allusions to Isa 40:1-11 may provide a helpful clue for addressing this issue. More specifically, the extent to which Isa 40:1-11 is evoked within Isa 52:7-12 suggests that the latter text represents a portrait of the fulfillment of this critical passage within Isa 40-55.[56]

The links between Isa 52:7-12 and divine warrior traditions are particularly significant for this discussion. These traditions are primarily evoked through: 1) the emphasis in the wider context on YHWH's defeat of his enemies (cf. Isa 51:22—52:6); 2) the cry of victory in v. 7, "your God reigns"; and 3) the clause ἀποκαλύψει κύριος τὸν βραχίονα αὐτοῦ τὸν ἅγιον in v. 10 (cf. Ps 97:1-3 LXX; Ezek 20:33-44).[57] On the basis of this echoing of ANE traditions, YHWH's victory over the enemies of his people is again being compared with his conquering of chaos at creation, and the restoration of Zion pictured in this passage again becomes portrayed as an act of temple-building (cf. Isa 40:9-11; 43:16-21).[58]

Other features of this passage indicate that the restoration of Zion is depicted here as an act of temple-building. The statement "for in plain sight they will see the return of the LORD to Zion" in v. 8 expresses the reason for the joyful (εὐφρανθήσονται) reaction of the city's watchmen. The clause ὀφθαλμοὶ πρὸς ὀφθαλμοὺς ὄψονται is anthropomorphic in tone and suggests that the watchmen will witness God in theophanic form approaching Jerusalem.[59] Despite the presence of minor differences between the MT

---

56. According to Oswalt (ibid., 367), "everything from [Isa] 40:1 to [Isa] 52:12 is about the anticipated return of God to his people ... [n]ow it is about to be realized." Childs (*Isaiah*, 406) further suggests, "In a very real sense, vv. 7-10 form a suitable conclusion to the eschatological drama first announced in chapter 40 and then unfolded in chapters 40-55." Links between these two texts are especially pronounced in Isa 52:7 (cf. Isa 40:9). Cf. Baltzer, *Deutero-Isaiah*, 382; Goldingay and Payne, *Isaiah 40-55*, 262, 264. The use of the verb ἐλεέω in Isa 52:8-9, however, represents something of a departure from the predominant image of salvation (παρακαλέω) in Isa 40-55 (cf. Isa 40:1-2, 11; 49:10, 13; 51:3; 57:18). Nonetheless, there is a close connection between these two verbs within Isa 49:10, 13, which suggests that they are used synonymously in Isaiah LXX.

57. Cf. Blenkinsopp, *Isaiah 40-55*, 342-43; Goldingay, *Message*, 453-54; Westermann, *Jesaja*, 203. The presence of the exclamation, "Marduk is King" in *Enuma Elish*, 4:28 is especially significant on this point.

58. Cf. Goldingay, *Message*, 453-54; Baltzer, *Deutero-Isaiah*, 381-82.

59. The imagery in v. 8 is frequently thought to recall the language of Isa 40:3-5, 9-11. E.g., Westermann, *Jesaja*, 202-3. The presence of the verb ὄψονται in v. 8 constitutes a particularly strong link with Isa 40:5 where the singular form (ὄψεται) is used to describe the revelation of God's glory and witnessing God's salvation of his people.

and LXX, the allusion to temple-building traditions in Isa 52:7 intimates this theophany may be understood as a description of YHWH returning to dwell in his temple.[60]

Second, the description of the return of the exiles in Isa 52:11 also correlates the restoration of Zion with ANE temple-building traditions. While the Babylonian exile provides the immediate setting for the plea to "depart" (cf. Isa 48:20), it is questionable to limit the intent of that command solely to that particular historical setting.[61] Instead, as with other texts in Isa 40–55, a much greater restoration is likely in view. The remark directed to those bearing "the vessels of the Lord" in v. 11 may provide an important clue regarding the significance of these verses. As Goldingay notes, "Their returning presupposes an expectation that the temple will be rebuilt."[62] Thus, these verses look backward to such texts as Isa 40:1-11, but as with other passages in Isa 40–55 they also look forward to the "new heavens and new earth" of Isa 65–66.

Finally, Isa 52:10 again raises the question of the relationship between universalism and Isaiah's new exodus. Specifically, the final clause in v. 10 (καὶ ὄψονται πάντα τὰ ἄκρα τῆς γῆς τὴν σωτηρίαν τὴν παρὰ τοῦ θεοῦ) invites the reader to consider the extent to which this passage might depict the salvation of the nations. The use of divine warrior imagery in v. 10a admittedly envisions the judgment of the nations. Furthermore, the immediate context of Isa 51:12—52:10 focuses on the judgment of the nations for their oppression of the exiles. It is thus difficult to conclude Isa 52:7-12 foresees the redemption of the nations. Nonetheless, if the phrase καὶ ὄψονται πάντα τὰ ἄκρα τῆς τὴν σωτηρίαν τὴν παρὰ τοῦ θεοῦ in Isa 52:10 represents an intertextual allusion to Isa 40:5 (καὶ ὄψεται πᾶσα σὰρξ τὸ σωτήριον τοῦ θεοῦ), this would at the very least indicate that Isaiah's new exodus is intimately concerned with the fate of the nations. Furthermore, if Isaiah's new exodus ultimately looks forward to the "new heavens and new earth" of Isa 65–66,

---

That this verb is used in Isa 52:8 to describe the watchmen beholding the Lord's return to Zion further strengthens the plausibility of this link.

The use of the verb ἐλεέω in v. 8 as a translation for the MT's בשׁו certainly diminishes the connections between this passage and Isa 40:1-11. The use of the verb ἐλεέω in this context may represent an attempt to soften the anthropomorphic connotations of Isa 52:8. See Goldingay and Payne (*Isaiah 40–55*, 267-68) for a helpful discussion of the correction of the MT's anthropomorphism in the history of tradition. Finally, the reading of Isa 52:8 found in 1QIsaa testifies to the antiquity of the MT reading.

60. Cf. Baltzer, *Deutero-Isaiah*, 382-83. *Tg. Isa.* 52:8 makes this point explicit through the following rendering, "for with their eyes they will see the prodigies which the Lord will do when he will return his Shekhinah to Zion."

61. Oswalt, *Isaiah 40–66*, 371-72; Childs, *Isaiah*, 406-7; Westermann, *Jesaja*, 204.

62. Goldingay, *Message*, 459.

the strong emphasis on the salvation of the nations in Isa 66:18-21, 23 suggests that the question surrounding the destiny of the nations in such texts as Isa 40:5 and Isa 52:10 receives a positive answer in Isa 66:18-24 (cf. Isa 2:2-4; 43:6; 49:6-12; 56:1-8; Zeph 3:8-10).[63]

Summary

Scholars widely recognize that Isa 52:7-12 employs imagery and concepts from Isa 40:1-11 and therefore represents an elaboration of the prologue of Isa 40-55. The links with ANE temple-building traditions in vv. 7-8, 10-11 suggest that Zion's renewal is to be understood as a cosmic event and has as its goal the formation of a worshiping community. Isaiah 52:10 importantly also raises the issue of the fate of the nations. This passage thus paints Isaiah's new exodus in fairly broad brushstrokes and suggests that it is a complex reality that cannot be subsumed under any single theological category (whether anthropology, cosmology, or ecclesiology).

For some scholars, Eph 2:17 primarily draws upon Isa 52:7 in order to elucidate the significance of Christ's ministry.[64] The foregoing discussion has shown that there may be stronger connections between Eph 2:17 and Isa 52:7-12 than previously recognized. Specifically, a close examination of Isa 52:10 again raises the question of the degree to which Isaiah's new exodus ushers in the salvation of the Gentiles (cf. Eph 2:11-22). The presence of allusions to ANE temple-building traditions in Isa 52:7-12 also opens up the possibility that these traditions formed part of the background for AE's discussion of new creation in Eph 2:1-22 (cf. Eph 1:20-23; 2:19-22).[65]

New Creation in Isa 57:14-21

As already noted, Isa 57:19 is one of two Isaianic texts alluded to in Eph 2:17. The presence of this allusion to Isaianic tradition once again raises the question of the degree to which AE intends the phrase εἰρήνην ὑμῖν τοῖς μακρὰν καὶ εἰρήνην τοῖς ἐγγύς in Eph 2:17 to function as a literary trope which is meant to guide the reader to probe the wider context of Isa 57:19 for further connections between these two texts. A close reading of Isa 57:14-19 reveals links between these two texts are indeed present. Equally as important,

63. Cf. Goldingay, *Message*, 457; Oswalt, *Isaiah 40-66*, 371.
64. Schnackenburg, *Epheser*, 118; Moritz, *Profound Mystery*, 51.
65. I will argue in my discussion of new creation in Ephesians that ANE temple-building traditions provide a viable means of appreciating the unity of Eph 1:20—2:22 (see below, esp. pp. 132-37, 140-42).

careful examination of Isa 57:14–19 uncovers a number of intertextual allusions to Isa 40:1–11 and in the case of Isa 57:14–19 LXX these links seem to provide something of a commentary on that earlier programmatic text.

Exegesis of Isa 57:14–21

It is helpful to begin our analysis of this passage by considering its significance within the immediate context of Isa 57:3–13 and the wider context of the entire book. Given the stress on restoration in Isa 57:14–21, one may understand this text as an elaboration on the promise of salvation in Isa 57:13c. The volume of allusions to Isa 40:1–11, however, suggests that Isa 57:14–21 sets that rescue within the confines of Isaiah's new exodus.

Isaiah 57:14 LXX begins with what may be understood as yet another command from the divine council (cf. Isa 40:3) calling for the preparation of a "way" (ὁδούς/ὁδοῦ). This act of preparation is described in v. 14 by means of the imperatives καθαρίσατε and ἄρατε and also strongly evokes Isa 40:3.[66] The use of the noun σκῶλον in the remainder of the LXX suggests that v. 14 may be related to the idol polemic of Isa 57:3–13.[67] If this is the case, the clause ἄρατε σκῶλα ἀπὸ τῆς ὁδοῦ τοῦ λαοῦ μου in Isa 57:14 LXX then could be read as YHWH's response to the wayward tendencies of his people. Further analysis of Isa 57:14–21 LXX reveals the presence of additional links with Isa 40:1–11 LXX and a tendency to extend the scope of Isaiah's new exodus beyond the Babylonian exile.

The intertextual significance of the phrase ἀπὸ προσώπου αὐτοῦ ὁδούς in Isa 57:14 LXX should not be overlooked.[68] The use of the noun πρόσωπον in conjunction with the noun ὁδός probably conveys the thought of a divine theophany and may be intended to strengthen the connection between this passage and Isa 40:1–11 (cf. vv. 3–5, 9–11).[69] If Isa 57:14 is read in the light of the wider context of Isa 56:9—57:13, the presence of the promise in v. 13c suggests that: 1) the "way" in v. 14 is a path to Zion; and 2) this "way" is

---

66. Since the prepositional phrase ἀπὸ προσώπου αὐτοῦ probably depicts a theophanic manifestation of God, the use of the verb καθαρίζω in this context could imply this "way" should be "cleansed" in preparation for God's holy presence.

67. The noun σκῶλον is used four other times in the LXX (cf. Exod 10:7; Deut 7:16; Judg 8:27; 2 Chr 28:23). Of these four, Exod 10:7 is the only text that does not relate this noun to idolatrous practices.

68. See Childs (*Isaiah*, 441–42) for a helpful discussion of the intertextual relationship between Isa 40–55 and Isa 56–66.

69. *Tg. Isa.* renders Isa 57:14b, "remove the obstruction of the wicked from the way of the congregation of my people." This translation places v. 14 outside of the Babylonian exile and may also refer to idolatrous practices.

God's response to the sinful condition of his people that features so prominently in Isa 56:9—57:13.[70]

Isaiah 57:17 exhibits further connections to Isa 40:1-11. In Isa 57:17, the author presents the grounds for the divine anger described in v. 16—Israel's sin. The LXX's use of the phrase ἁμαρτία βραχύ in v. 17 as a translation of the MT's בְּעֲוֹן בִּצְעוֹ ("wicked covetousness") could represent an attempt to generalize further the already historically indeterminate language of v. 17. The use of the noun ἁμαρτία in v. 17, however, also establishes stronger ties with Isa 40:1-11 (cf. Isa 40:2). The statements in Isa 57:17 LXX may thus be an additional attempt on the part of the LXX translator/s to provide an interpretative commentary on Isa 40:1-11. On this reading, Isa 57:17 LXX confirms the plight (and thus the corresponding solution) envisioned in the book of Isaiah as a whole extends beyond the temporal confines of the Babylonian exile.

One encounters further links to Isa 40:1-11 in Isa 57:18. This text primarily continues the thought of v. 17 by again noting Israel's obstinate rebellion (τὰς ὁδοὺς αὐτοῦ ἑώρακα). Isaiah 57:18, however, also presents a divine promise of restoration. Significantly, this pledge of restitution is couched in language highly evocative of Isa 40:1-11 and also utilizes imagery (specifically that of healing) which is frequently used in Isaiah to describe salvation (cf. Isa 6:10; 19:22; 30:26; 53:5; 61:1). The use of the verb παρακαλέω in Isa 57:18 LXX further links these two new exodus texts together.

When read within the context of Isa 57:14-18, v. 19 is best understood as a climactic summary of the salvation of God's people. The concept of peace (εἰρήνην) is also frequently used in Isaiah to describe God's act of delivering his people (cf. Isa 9:7; 32:17-18; 52:7; 53:5). The precise identity of the two groups mentioned in v. 19 (τοῖς μακρὰν καὶ τοῖς ἐγγύς) and the nature of the antagonism in vv. 14-18 aid in clarifying the nature of the peace described in v. 19. The degree to which Eph 2:13, 17 evokes Isa 57:19 also makes the identity of the "far" and "near" an especially significant issue. The adverbs μακράν and ἐγγύς in v. 19 may indeed refer to Jews in the diaspora and Jews still within the land respectively (cf. Isa 33:13).[71] At the same time, the likelihood that the Babylonian exile serves as a typological medium within the book of Isaiah to describe a greater act of restoration

---

70. The concluding promise in Isa 57:13 (those who trust in YHWH "shall possess the land and inherit my holy mountain") is worth noting. Since the phrase "holy mountain" frequently denotes Zion/Jerusalem in the Old Testament (cf. Ps 2:6 LXX; 47:2-3 LXX; Joel 2:1; 4:17; Zech 8:3; Isa 27:13; 63:18; 66:20; Dan 9:16, 19-20), this text may envision the eschatological salvation of God's people. Once again, Isa 57:14-21 may therefore be read as a direct continuation of the preceding passage.

71. Cf. Lincoln, "Use," 27.

points to the need to look beyond this concrete *Sitz im Leben*. If the use of the noun σκῶλον in Isa 57:14 LXX represents an attempt to shift the new exodus of Isa 40–55 outside the realm of the return from Babylon as I have suggested, it would be difficult to associate the "far" and "near" of v. 19 with this historical event. The wider concern for the fate of Gentiles in the book of Isaiah (see above, esp. p. 18–19, 28–29) also allows for the possibility that the "far" and "near" of v. 19 may refer to those distanced from salvation (Gentiles) and those in closer proximity (Jews).[72] Given the volume of allusions to Isa 40:5, there also may be a sense in which Isa 57:19 continues the ambiguity of Isa 40:5 regarding the potential salvation of Gentiles by means of God's "new thing." In summary, a close analysis of Isa 57:14–21 indicates it is difficult to interpret the adverbs μακράν and ἐγγύς exclusively within the historical setting of the Babylonian exile.

The nature of the "peace" referred to in v. 19 is best clarified by considering the preceding statements. Much of Isa 57:16–18 concerns the sinful condition of God's people. Furthermore, the verb ἰάομαι is used in Isa 57:18 to describe God's response (τὰς ὁδοὺς αὐτοῦ ἑώρακα καὶ ἰασάμην αὐτόν) to the waywardness of his people. When these two factors are taken into account, it is evident that the "peace" referred to in v. 19 describes the new state of affairs (involving the absence of hostility) which occurs as a result of God's decisive work in addressing the sin of his people.

Without engaging in a detailed treatment of Eph 2:13, 17 at this point, it is helpful to consider briefly how AE is interpreting Isa 57:19. While there is some degree of uncertainty regarding how the "far" and "near" of Isa 57:19 are best interpreted within their original context, it is nonetheless evident that AE understands the former to refer to Gentile Christians and the latter to Jewish Christians. The presence of the verb κτίσῃ and the phrase καινὸν ἄνθρωπον in Eph 2:15 set the author's overall discussion of the union of Jew and Gentile in Christ within the context of new creation theology. Furthermore, when the wider context of Isa 57:19 is examined, it again becomes clear that as is the case with the undisputed Pauline epistles, new creation in Eph 2:13–17 is associated with Isaiah's new exodus (cf. Isa 57:14).

Additional connections between Isa 57:14–21 and the context of Eph 2:11–22 are evident when one considers the stress placed in the Isaianic text on God's deliverance of his people from their sinful condition (cf. Eph 2:12–13, 16–22). That the new exodus of Isa 57:14–21 addresses Israel's sinfulness is apparent from: 1) the use of the healing imagery in v. 18; and

---

72. This is how AE interprets Isa 57:19 in Eph 2:13, 17 (see below, p. 150–51, for further discussion).

2) the declaration of "peace ... to the far and the near" in v. 19.[73] One may, therefore, conclude that both Isa 57:14–21 and Eph 2:11–22 are concerned with describing God's response to humanity's iniquity.

Summary

The text of Isa 57:14–21 exhibits a number of links with Isa 40:1–11. Both passages employ new exodus imagery, focus on covenant disobedience, and explore the fate of the Gentiles. Importantly, the LXX rendering of Isa 57:14–21 also seems to betray a tendency to make the connections between these two oracles in Isaiah more unequivocal at a number of points (cf. vv. 14, 17–18).

These observations have important implications for understanding the LXX text of Isa 57:14–21. Admittedly, there are no explicit references to Zion/Jerusalem and its restoration within this text. Nonetheless, if Isa 57:14–21 fundamentally develops the promise expressed in Isa 57:13, then there is a sense in which this passage indeed looks forward to the restored Zion/Jerusalem and ultimately to the "new heavens and new earth" of Isa 65–66.[74]

This analysis of Isa 57:14–21 also has ramifications for understanding the relationship between Isaiah's new exodus and new creation in Ephesians. More specifically, the preceding investigation of Isa 57:14–21 has demonstrated that anthropological, ecclesiological, and cosmological concerns are present within this text. Thus, this analysis of Isa 57:14–21 again demonstrates that Isaiah's new exodus may be understood as an act of divine deliverance which encompasses a number of theological realities. This observation may have implications for understanding the portrait of new creation in Eph 2:1–22.

---

73. I will address the place of vertical reconciliation within Eph 2:11–22 in greater detail in my analysis of new creation in Eph 2:11–22.

74. The presence of an intertextual allusion to Isa 57:14 in Isa 62:10 further strengthens the possibility that Isa 57:14–21 points to the restored Zion/Jerusalem since Isa 60–62 constitutes an extended description of this eschatological reality. On the literary relationship between Isa 62:10–11 and Isa 40:3, 10–11; 57:14, see Childs (*Isaiah*, 513). Finally, the presence of the clause ἐξάρατε σύσσημον εἰς τὰ ἔθνη in Isa 62:10 again relates Isaiah's restored Zion/Jerusalem with the salvation of the nations (cf. Isa 11:10; 49:22; 66:18–23).

New Creation in Isa 65:17–25

One of the central questions relating to the development of new creation theology in the Pauline tradition is its relationship to Isaiah's "new heavens and new earth." For a number of scholars, the phrase τὰ ἀρχαῖα παρῆλθεν ἰδοὺ γέγονεν καινά in 2 Cor 5:17b constitutes a concrete allusion to Isa 65:16–17.[75] However, the lack of firm correspondence between these two texts is problematic. Despite this word of caution, one need not conclude that Isaiah's "new heavens and new earth" is completely irrelevant to this issue. I previously argued that the phrase τὰ ἀρχαῖα παρῆλθεν ἰδοὺ γέγονεν καινά in 2 Cor 5:17b is best perceived as a broad allusion to Isaiah's new exodus theme (see above, p. 15). Isaiah 65:16–25 forms an integral part of this theme and is, therefore, pertinent to this overall discussion.[76]

Exegesis of Isa 65:17–25

A close look at Isa 65:17b suggests that it forms part of Isaiah's new things/former things theme.[77] I have already argued that Isaiah's new exodus represents an integral feature of this motif. In attempting to understand how Isa 65:17b relates to Isaiah's new things/former things theme, we should begin by noting this motif is expressed slightly differently within the major sections of Isaiah. Strictly speaking, there is no direct statement regarding a "new thing" in Isa 1–39 and 56–66. Nonetheless, as Webb posits, the contrast between the adjective προτέρων and the creation of a "new heavens and a new earth" in Isa 65:17 is not unlike imagery used in relation to the new exodus in Isa 40–55 (cf. Isa 42:9; 43:19; 48:7).[78] I have also previously maintained that the "former things" of Isa 40–55 generally refers to YHWH's prior acts of salvation. The treatment of the "former things" in Isa 1–39 and Isa 56–66, however, carries much more negative connotations than its corresponding usage in Isa 40–55. Within Isa 1–39 and Isa 56–66, three principal texts speak of "former things": Isa 9:1 (8:23); 61:4; 65:16–17. In each of these three texts, the roots προτ- and πρωτ- are used in connection with Israel's judgment, as it is exemplified in the Babylonian exile.[79] When

---

75. Cf. Schneider, "Die Idee der Neuschöpfung," 265; Schneider, *KAINH KTISIS*, 78; Webb, *Returning Home*, 121–25; Kraus, *Das Volk Gottes*, 258; Stuhlmacher, "Erwägungen," 6; Beale, "Reconciliation," 553, 555, 557; pace Hubbard, *New Creation* 182.

76. Cf. Hoover, *New Creation*, 19; Webb, *Returning Home*, 124–25.

77. Childs, *Isaiah*, 537.

78. Cf. Webb, *Returning Home*, 124.

79. Jackson, *New Creation*, 21.

understood within the broader framework of Isaiah, the "former things," therefore refers to the suffering and hardship experienced by God's people.

The preceding observations raise the question of the relationship between the "new heavens and new earth" of Isa 65–66 and the new exodus of Isa 40–55. It is, admittedly, difficult to deny that while both these literary features of Isaiah describe YHWH's deliverance of his people, the "new heavens and new earth" presents a much grander picture of salvation. For those scholars who reject the essential unity of Isaiah, the differences between these two portraits may be explained by appealing to separate authors.[80] That is, the literary genesis of the "new heavens and new earth" of Isa 65–66 may be understood as the work of an individual (or community) who has deliberately emulated language in Isa 40–55 associated with the new exodus yet expanded its scope beyond the Babylonian exile to encompass the renewal of the entire cosmos. The preceding analysis of Isa 40–55, however, has demonstrated that it is difficult to read the new exodus strictly as a prophetic account of the return from Babylon. Furthermore, if the goal of the new exodus is the restored Zion/Jerusalem, it becomes possible to read the "new heavens and new earth" of Isa 65–66 as an explicit description of what is implicit in Isa 40–55.

More can be said regarding the precise character of the "new heavens and new earth" of Isa 65:17–25. It is helpful to begin by considering the significance of Zion traditions within this passage. Zion traditions are primarily found in Isa 65:17–25 through the association of the "new heavens and new earth" with Jerusalem (vv. 18–19) and God's "holy mountain" (v. 25). For our purposes, it is significant to note that the repetition of the nouns ἀγαλλίαμα and εὐφροσύνη in vv. 18b–19a establishes an implicit identification of Jerusalem and God's people with the "new heavens and new earth" in v. 17.[81] The correspondence between the "new heavens and new earth" and Jerusalem in all likelihood is meant to recall the numerous texts in

---

80. Cf. Mell, *Neue Schöpfung*, 61; Westermann, *Jesaja*, 324; Hanson, *Dawn*, 156–61. While Hubbard (*New Creation*, 16) affirms the unity of Isaiah, he, nonetheless, sharply distinguishes between the portraits of salvation in Isa 40–55 and that of Isa 56–66. Several scholars note the differences between the portraits of deliverance in Isa 40–55 and that of Isa 56–66, yet also helpfully observe the presence of paradisiacal imagery in such new exodus texts as Isa 43:20 and Isa 51:3 (cf. Isa 11:6–8). Cf. Webb, *Returning Home*, 124–25; Jackson, *New Creation*, 20; Hoover, *New Creation*, 16–17, 19, 22, 23. Jackson (*New Creation*, 18–19) also suggests, "The force of the imagery of [Isa] 65–66 is impossible to understand without the framework which has been developed in the earlier parts of the book."

81. Finally, the parallelism between these three concepts is perhaps even stronger in the MT, which reiterates the verb בוֹרֵא in v. 18.

Isaiah which describe the restoration of Zion/Jerusalem.[82] The phrase "holy mountain" in v. 25 is frequently connected with Zion/Jerusalem throughout the OT.[83] Perhaps even more importantly, the phrase "holy mountain" in the OT is often associated with cultic concepts and imagery.[84] The degree to which the phrase "holy mountain" is associated with the Israelite cultus suggests that the "new heavens and new earth" of Isa 65:17-25 likewise acquires similar connotations (cf. Isa 66:18-24).[85]

In summary, the association of the "new heavens and new earth" in Isa 65:17-25 with "Jerusalem," God's people, and God's "holy mountain" strongly colors this account in a cultic direction. The cultic overtones in Isa 65:17-25 have two significant implications for this project. First, in light of the repeated allusions to temple-building traditions in Isa 40–55 (e.g., Isa 40:9-10; 43:16-21; 52:7-11), they establish stronger connections between Isaiah's new exodus and the "new heavens and new earth." Second, the cultic images in Isa 65:17-25 suggest that this eschatological portrait exhibits the influence of an *Urzeit-Endzeit* typology.[86]

The intertextual links between Isa 65:17-25 and the creation narrative of Gen 1–3 confirm the presence of this typological pattern. First, the use of the phrase τοῦ ξύλου τῆς ζωῆς in Isa 65:22 LXX strongly evokes Gen 2–3 (cf. Gen 2:9; 3:17, 22, 24).[87] Second, lexical links with Gen 1–3 are created through the reference to the "offspring" in v. 23 (cf. Gen 3:15; 9:9; 12:7)

---

82. Cf. Isa 1:21-27; 2:1-4; 4:1-6; 11:1—12:6; 18:5-7; 24:19-23; 27:6-13; 30:18-19; 31:1-5; 33:20-22; 35:8-10; 37:31-32; 40:1-2, 9; 41:25-27; 44:23-28; 46:8-13; 49:13-21; 51:1—52:10; 59:16-21; 60:10-22; 61:1-6; 62:1-12.

83. Cf. Ps 2:6 LXX; 47:2-3 LXX; Joel 2:1; 4:17; Zec 8:3; Isa 24:22; 25:6-10; 27:13; 63:18; Dan 9:16, 19-20. In an analysis of the role of the temple in Isa 56–66, Middlemas cautions against making a strict identification of the concepts "holy mountain," "Zion," and "Jerusalem" with the Jerusalem temple. Cf. Middlemas, "Divine Reversal," 165-69. Middlemas' analysis does provide a helpful corrective to those scholars (e.g., Hanson) who attempt to place Isaiah's discussion of the temple in chapters 56–66 within the context of a specific historical situation that centers upon disputes over the Jerusalem cult. In contrast, Middlemas (ibid., 169-71) argues the discussion of the temple in Isa 60:1—63:6 sets its restoration within the context of an even grander act of deliverance.

84. Cf. Ps 14:1 LXX; 23:3 LXX; 42:3 LXX; 98:9 LXX; Isa 56:7; 63:18; 65:11; Ezek 20:40; 48:10.

85. Cf. Watts, *Isaiah 34-66*, 355. The presence of such strongly cultic language in Isa 66:18-24 confirms this suggestion.

86. It would be unwarranted to conclude, however, that a new (physical) temple exhausts the meaning of Isaiah's "new heavens and new earth." Nonetheless, one may describe the "new heavens and new earth" as a temple-like reality (much like the "garden of Eden") that signifies the completion of God's plan to restore the cosmos.

87. Cf. Stordalen, *Echoes of Eden*, 440; Beale, *Temple*, 136.

and the "serpent" in v. 25 (cf. Gen 3:1, 2, 4, 13, 14–15).[88] Third, according to T. Stordalen, conceptual links between these two texts are present "in the motives of extended human life span and animal peace in vv. 20, 25."[89] Fourth, given how frequently the verb ποιέω is used in Gen 1–2 to describe God's creative activity, the use of this verb in Isa 65:18 is possibly meant to evoke the creation narrative (cf. Gen 1:1, 7, 16, 21, 25, 26, 27, 31; 2:2–4, 18).[90] There is thus an underlying *Urzeit-Endzeit* typology in Isa 65:17–25 that broadly views eschatology through the lens of protology.[91]

Summary

When read within its wider context, Isa 65:17–25 may be understood as an expansion of the declaration in Isa 65:16b, "the former troubles are forgotten." Of particular importance for understanding new creation in the Pauline tradition is the relationship between this passage and Isaiah's new things/former things theme (cf. 2 Cor 5:17b). While the "new heavens and new earth" is not described explicitly as a "new thing," there are similar statements in Isa 40–55 associated with a new exodus (cf. Isa 42:9; 43:19; 48:7). Thus, one may conclude that the "new heavens and new earth" of Isa 65:17–25 constitutes an integral component of Isaiah's new things/former things theme and is directly related to the new exodus of Isa 40–55.

This raises the question of the relationship between Isa 65:17–25 and Zion/Jerusalem traditions within Isaiah. The parallelism between Isa 65:18 and Isa 65:19 suggests that the "new heavens and new earth" is closely related to the restored Zion/Jerusalem that plays such an important role in much of Isaiah. Further links with Zion traditions may also be discerned in the use of the phrase τῷ ὄρει τῷ ἁγίῳ in Isa 65:25. The presence of these Zion traditions not only implies that the "new heavens and new earth" should be understood in temple-like terms but also confirms that the portraits of the new exodus as an act of temple-building in Isa 40–55 ultimately point ahead to Isa 65:17–25 (and Isa 66:18–24). The allusions to Gen 1–3 within

---

88. Cf. Watts, *Isaiah 34–66*, 355; Van Ruiten, "Intertextual Relationship," 40.

89. Stordalen, *Echoes of Eden*, 440. Cf. Stuhlmueller, *Creative Redemption*, 69–70.

90. The verb ποιέω is undoubtedly an extremely common lexeme in the LXX. However, given the strength of the other echoes of Gen 1–3 in this passage, this suggestion is not outside the realm of possibility. Steck ("Beobachtungen, 357–58) likewise argues the use of the verb ברא in Isa 65:17 is best explained as an allusion to Gen 1:1.

91. Mauser, "Isaiah 65:17–25," 181–86; Watts, *Isaiah 34–66*, 357; Blenkinsopp, *Isaiah 56–66*, 287–88, 290; Oswalt, *Isaiah 40–66*, 656–66; pace Childs, *Isaiah*, 537–38; Westermann, *Jesaja*, 324. Cf. *1 En.* 72:1; 91:15–17; *4 Ezra* 6:13–28; *2 Bar.* 32:6; 44:7–15; 2 Pet 3:5–13; Rev 21:1—22:7.

Isa 65:17–25 are also relevant to this project (cf. vv. 18, 20, 22, 25). Based on these reverberations of the creation account, one may conclude that the "new heavens and new earth" is aligned with an *Urzeit-Endzeit* typology.

New Creation in Isa 66:18–24

The absence of an allusion to Isa 66:18–24 within the Pauline tradition naturally raises the question of the relevance of this text for our current investigation.[92] While this is a significant concern, it is not an insurmountable objection, especially if one considers my suggestion that 2 Cor 5:17b does not so much allude to specific texts within Isaiah but instead to Isaiah's new exodus motif as a whole. Isaiah 66:18–24 also constitutes the climax of an important theme in Isaiah—universalism—which is directly related to new creation in the Pauline corpus (cf. Gal 6:12–16; 2 Cor 5:14–17; Eph 2:11–22). Finally, there are also scholarly precedents for investigating the relationship between Isa 66:18–24 and new creation in the Pauline tradition.[93]

Exegesis of Isa 66:18–24

It is helpful to begin our analysis of Isa 66:18–24 by noting that the hope expressed in this passage centers around the restored Zion/Jerusalem. Much of this text pertains to the means by which Jerusalem is repopulated. According to vv. 19–20, Jerusalem will be reinhabited by a two-fold process: 1) Israelites are sent by God to proclaim his glory among pagan nations; and 2) as a result of this missionary endeavor, Gentiles will bring Israelites back to Jerusalem as an "offering to the Lord."[94] The presence of the phrase τὴν ἁγίαν πόλιν Ιερουσαλημ in v. 20 is particularly significant. While the MT doubtless represents the original text (הר), the use of this phrase once again connects the "new heavens and new earth" with Isaiah's restored Zion/Jerusalem motif (cf. Isa 52:1; 60:14).[95] By connecting this account of the "new heavens and new earth" with these traditions, the author thus closely relates this passage to Isa 65:17–25. Furthermore, given the importance of

---

92. Several scholars have attempted to link Paul's universal gospel with Isa 66:19 by means of his statements in Rom 15:24, 28. E.g., Aus, "Paul's Travel Plans," 232–62; Scott, *Paul*, 44–47. Das ("Paul," 60–73) has recently offered a trenchant critique of this hypothesis.

93. Cf. Kraus, *Das Volk Gottes*, 23–25; Hoover, *New Creation*, 22.

94. Cf. Blenkinsopp, *Isaiah 56–66*, 315; Westermann, *Jesaja*, 339.

95. The lack of external support for the LXX reading suggests that it is an interpretative rendering. Cf. Oswalt, *Isaiah 40–66*, 682.

the restored Zion/Jerusalem in Isaiah's new exodus theme, the author also suggests that this text is connected to the message of Isa 40–55.

The suggestion that Isa 66:18–24 is related to the theology of Isa 40–55 is confirmed when one considers the presence of allusions to Isa 40:1–11 within this text. In my analysis of Isa 40:5, I noted that Isa 66:18, 23–24 primarily evokes this earlier text by means of the phrases καὶ ὄψονται τὴν δόξαν μου and πᾶσα σάρξ. Along with these lexical connections, the presence of theophanic imagery in Isa 66:15–17 also establishes further links between these two texts, especially given that both texts employ divine warrior imagery to describe divine judgment and salvation (cf. Isa 40:3–5, 9–11).[96] Since Isa 66:18–24 depicts the "new heavens and new earth" as a restored Zion/Jerusalem, the presence of these allusions to Isa 40:3–5 confirms our earlier suggestion that the goal of Isaiah's new exodus is the restored Zion. What is more, Isa 66:18–24 (as with Isa 57:14–21) may be understood as an elaboration of the programmatic new exodus promises in Isa 40:1–11. In particular, the discussion of the "new heavens and new earth" of Isa 66 makes clear not only that the identity of those referred to in Isa 40:5 as "all flesh" encompasses Jews and Gentiles but that Gentiles will also experience the salvation promised in that earlier text.

The emphasis on the salvation of Gentiles in Isa 66:18–21 raises important questions for understanding the nature of new creation in the Pauline tradition.[97] As already noted, several scholars have argued that new creation in the Pauline corpus is closely connected with ecclesiological concerns (cf. Gal 6:15–16; Eph 2:15).[98] It must be forthrightly acknowledged that no new creation text in the Pauline tradition quotes or alludes to Isa 66:18–24. Nonetheless, if the allusion in 2 Cor 5:17b is meant to evoke Isaiah's new exodus theme more generally (rather than specific texts in Isaiah), it becomes reasonable to conclude that Isa 66:18–24 played an important role in formulating the conception of new creation one encounters in the *corpus Paulinum*. The restored Zion/Jerusalem functions as a significant metaphor within the new exodus theme of Isaiah and a number of texts indicate that this restored Zion will be populated not only by Israelites but also Gentiles (cf. Isa 2:2–4; 42:1–16; 56:1–8; 60:1–16).[99] If Isa 66:18–24 is understood as the culmination of those promises, it is possible the final portrait of the

---

96. Cf. Westermann, *Jesaja*, 334; Watts, *Isaiah 34–66*, 364.

97. According to Westermann, *Jesaja*, 337, Isa 66:18–21 "ist zum erstenmal ganz eindeutig von Mission in unserem Sinn die Rede."

98. Cf. Kraus, *Das Volk Gottes*, 250–51, 258–61; Adams, *Constructing the World*, 235; Jackson, *New Creation*, 111–13, 144.

99. Cf. Mic 4:1–2.

"new heavens and new earth" in Isa 66:18-24 exercised a formative role in the development of new creation in the Pauline corpus.

The overall interest in cultic concerns within Isa 66:18-24 requires further comment. According to v. 23, the "new heavens and new earth" may be understood as a place of continual worship by all of humanity (cf. Zech 14:16-21). If Isa 66:18-24 is integrally related to the initial portrait of the "new heavens and new earth" in Isa 65:17-25, the presence of allusions to Gen 1-3 in the latter text should probably influence our understanding of Isa 66:18-24.[100] As already discussed, the "garden of Eden" may be understood as a divine sanctuary (see below, p. 181-83). Given the eschatological and cultic flavor of Isa 65:17-25, the allusions to Gen 1-3 in this text suggest that it may be read within the framework of an *Urzeit-Endzeit* typology.[101] The universalistic concern and cultic imagery that pervade Isa 66:18-24 indicates that one may then describe this text as an elaboration of Isa 65:17-25 that heightens the cultic dimension of the "new heavens and new earth," as well as its association with an *Urzeit-Endzeit* typology.

Summary

Isaiah 66:18-24 is chiefly a description of the restored Zion/Jerusalem and focuses on the process of its repopulation (vv. 18-21). Significantly, Isa 66:18, 23-24 indicates that the new Zion/Jerusalem will be reinhabited by Jew and Gentile (cf. Isa 40:5; 52:10). If one reads the allusions to Isaianic tradition in 2 Cor 5:17b and Eph 2:13,17 as more than mere proof-texts, this opens up the possibility of reading Gal 6:15 and Eph 2:15 at least partially in ecclesiological terms.

The cultic nature of the "new heavens and new earth" of Isa 66:18-24 is also worth considering (cf. vv. 20-21, 23). The emphasis on worship in this text is likely an elaboration of similar notions that underlie the initial account of the "new heavens and new earth" in Isa 65:17-25 (cf. v. 25).[102] These observations are particularly important for this present discussion because they strengthen the likelihood that Isaiah's "new heavens and new earth" should be understood within the framework of an *Urzeit-Endzeit*

---

100. The addition of the phrase ἐν Ιερουσαλημ in Isa 66:23 suggests the LXX translator/s are here connecting the portrait of the "new heavens and new earth" in Isa 66:18-24 with its initial representation in Isa 65:17-25.

101. Cf. Oswalt, *Isaiah 40-66*, 692, 695.

102. The allusions to Gen 1-3 within Isa 65:20-25 are also relevant at this point, given my prior suggestion that the primordial garden may be interpreted as a divine sanctuary (see above, pp. 36-37).

scheme. Finally, the manner in which the discussion of new creation in Eph 2 concludes by describing the church (composed of Jew and Gentile) as an expanding temple (vv. 19–22) again raises the question of Isaianic influence upon the conception of new creation in the Pauline tradition and will be discussed in my analysis of Eph 1:20—2:22.

Conclusion

The preceding analysis of new creation in Isaiah has raised a number of fruitful findings for understanding the nature of new creation in the *corpus Paulinum*. Perhaps most importantly, this study has revealed that the prophecy of Isaiah depicts new creation as a complex notion that resists a reductionistic reading. More specifically, a variety of texts which comprise the Isaianic new exodus motif indicates that YHWH's new act of salvation encompasses anthropological, cosmological, and ecclesiological concerns.[103] This observation raises questions regarding prior attempts to limit new creation in the Pauline tradition to one or two of these theological categories.

I have also demonstrated that there is a close relationship between Isaiah's new exodus and the restoration of Zion/Jerusalem. Several new exodus texts within Isaiah exhibit links with ANE temple-building traditions in that these passages describe YHWH as a divine warrior and depict the restoration of Zion/Jerusalem as a consequence of his victory over the enemies of his people.[104] These new exodus passages frequently depict YHWH returning to Zion, accompanied by his covenant people (e.g., Isa 40:9–10; 49:9–10; 52:7–10). Given the cultic significance frequently attributed to Zion/Jerusalem within Isaiah's prophecy, one may then describe the restored Zion/Jerusalem as the goal of Isaiah's new exodus and the formation of a worshiping community as its intended outcome.[105]

This reading of Isaiah's new exodus has important implications for understanding new creation in the Pauline corpus. As noted in my survey

---

103. Cf. Isa 40:1–5; 43:16–21; 51:3–5, 9–11; 52:7–10; 57:14–19; 62:10–12; 65:17–25; 66:18–24.

104. Cf. Isa 40:3–5, 9–11; 43:16–21; 51:9–11; 52:7–10.

105. Cf. Isa 2:1–4; 4:2–6; 35:1–10; 51:3–5, 9–11; 56:1–8; 64:10–11; 66:18–23. One of the distinguishing features of this analysis of new creation in Isaiah is the incorporation of recent research on Isaiah's new exodus that observes several problems with historically linking these prophetic texts with the return from Babylon. While I do not completely deny the relevance of this historical event for understanding the new exodus of Isa 40–55, I do question critical attempts to establish a sharp distinction between the message of Isa 40–55 and that of Isa 56–66 and do conclude that Isaiah's new exodus looks ahead to the "new heavens and new earth" of Isa 65–66.

of secondary literature on new creation in Paul, a number of scholars have interpreted new creation along cosmological and ecclesiological lines. The ambiguity of 2 Cor 5:17b, however, makes it difficult to link concretely the phrase καινὴ κτίσις in 2 Cor 5:17a with Isaiah's "new heavens and new earth." Nonetheless, if Isaiah's new exodus points to the "new heavens and new earth" of Isa 65–66 as I have suggested, it becomes problematic to exclude these cosmological and ecclesiological understandings of new creation in Paul.[106] Furthermore, the dual portrait of new creation in Eph 2:1-22 concludes with a description of the church as a temple (vv. 19–22). The degree to which ANE temple-building traditions are associated with Isaiah's new exodus raises the question of the extent to which new creation in Ephesians is likewise related to these ANE traditions.[107] Finally, the frequency with which the salvation of the Gentiles is linked with Isaiah's new exodus also raises the possibility that new creation in the Pauline corpus is somehow related to ecclesiological concerns.

---

106. It is helpful at this point to recall my earlier suggestion that the evocation of Isaianic tradition in 2 Cor 5:17b does not so much direct the reader to specific texts within Isaiah but to Isaiah's larger new exodus motif. If Isa 65:16-17 is closely related to Isaiah's new exodus as I have argued above, further difficulties arise for attempts to separate Isa 65:17-25 and Isa 66:18-24 from the conception of new creation in the Pauline corpus.

107. This issue will be addressed more fully in my analysis of Eph 1:20—2:22 (see below, esp. pp. 135-42).

3

New Creation and Restoration in the Old Testament and Second Temple Judaism

Introduction

The intent of this chapter is not to provide an exhaustive discussion of every relevant primary text related to the concepts of new creation and restoration within the OT and Second Temple Judaism.[1] Instead, I will examine several of the more significant texts from these two corpora to determine how new creation and restoration were conceived by a variety of ancient Jewish thinkers.[2] The chief aim of this chapter is to respond to those scholars who advocate a fairly minimalistic conception of new creation in the Pauline corpus (i.e., strictly anthropological, strictly cosmological, etc.) by demonstrating the complexity with which new creation and restoration are depicted in these works. Since one of the major proposals of this study is that new creation in the Pauline tradition is firmly rooted in Isaianic soil, this chapter will also seek to demonstrate how Isaiah's "new heavens and new earth" was interpreted within two important Jewish texts from the Second Temple period and explore the relationship between Isaiah's new exodus and the prophecies of Ezekiel and Jeremiah.

1. See Mell (*Neue Schöpfung*, 47–257) for a fairly exhaustive survey of important Jewish texts related to new creation.

2. It is necessary to make a careful distinction between new creation and restoration throughout this discussion, especially as one considers the relevant material in Jeremiah. More specifically, while expectations related to new creation generally exhibit some degree of discontinuity with the old order, those associated with restoration are often best understood in close relation to Israel's historical deliverance from exile. This distinction allows one to appreciate the significance of compositions such as Jeremiah and Ezekiel within their original historical settings.

New Creation and Restoration in Ezekiel

The Relevance of Ezekiel

Despite my thesis that Isaiah provides the primary background for understanding new creation in the Pauline corpus, I nonetheless must affirm that the book of Ezekiel also probably played an important role in formulating the understanding of new creation in the Pauline corpus. Hubbard's analysis of new creation gives great weight to Paul's death-life antithesis and helpfully proposes Ezekiel's discussion of the Spirit provides a critical background for this aspect of new creation in Paul's letters.[3] R. Suh has also recently suggested that Ezek 37 provides the fundamental background for Eph 2:1–22, a passage replete with new creation overtones.[4] While the absence of any direct evocation of Ezekiel in Eph 2:1–22 presents a serious challenge to Suh's proposal, there do seem to be a number of plausible parallels between Ezek 37 and Eph 2:1–22.[5] Further analysis of new creation and restoration in Ezekiel is therefore in order.

Examination of Relevant Texts in Ezekiel

The book of Ezekiel is generally regarded as an exilic work, set within the historical context of the early sixth century BCE.[6] The events described in Ezekiel's prophecies center around the initial stages of the Babylonian exile (cf. Ezek 1:2; 29:17). The city of Jerusalem and its temple have yet to fall and Jeremiah's prophecy of a seventy year exile (Jer 25:11–12) has yet to run its full course. Given the emphasis in Ezekiel on the judgment of those Israelites still in Jerusalem (e.g., Ezek 5–9), it can be read as something of a continuation of Jeremiah's message of judgment.

To understand the significance of new creation and restoration in the book of Ezekiel, one must first appreciate Ezekiel's emphasis on God's presence. The book begins with a vision of God's heavenly throne-room, which forms the setting for Ezekiel's commissioning as a prophet to unfaithful Israel (Ezek 1:1, 26–28; 2:3–4; 3:4–5). Significantly, God's presence is mysteriously described in Ezek 1:28 as, "the appearance of the likeness of the glory of the Lord" (ἡ ὅρασις ὁμοιώματος δόξης κυρίου). Within this visionary

---

3. Hubbard, *New Creation*, 91–122.
4. Suh, "Ephesians 2," 715–33.
5. The presence of allusions to Isa 52:7 and 57:19 in Eph 2:13, 17 suggests that the material in Isaiah provides a more viable background for Eph 2:1–22.
6. Joyce, *Ezekiel*, 3–4; Greenberg, *Ezekiel 1–20*, 12–17.

account, there is a description of a cherubim chariot that is meant to be understood as a replacement for the cherubim throne within the Jerusalem temple (cf. 1 Sam 4:4; 6:2; Ps 98:1 LXX).[7] According to Renz, "The emphasis on the cherubim forming a chariot rather than a throne . . . puts emphasis on the mobility of Yahweh, a crucial presupposition in later chapters."[8] The book of Ezekiel therefore begins with a visionary account that presupposes the spatial freedom of the divine presence and sets the stage for YHWH's eventual abandonment of the temple.

YHWH's desertion of the Jerusalem temple is largely depicted in Ezek 9–11.[9] Within Ezek 9–11, God's departure from the temple is described as a multi-staged event in which his glory gradually proceeds from the temple to the Mount of Olives (cf. Ezek 9:3; 10:3–4, 18–19; 11:22–23). Significantly, Ezek 11:16 suggests that the divine presence has now taken up residence among the exiles (καὶ ἔσομαι αὐτοῖς εἰς ἁγίασμα μικρὸν ἐν ταῖς χώραις οὗ ἂν εἰσέλθωσιν ἐκεῖ).[10] This theme concludes in Ezekiel with a visionary account of the return of God's glory to a restored temple in Ezek 40–48 (cf. Ezek 43:2–5; 44:4).

The question as to what gives rise to Ezekiel's restored temple can be helpfully understood within a plight-solution framework.[11] The central issue for Ezekiel is not that God has abandoned the temple. Rather, God's departure from his sanctuary is merely the consequence of a much larger problem—Israel's sinful condition. Much of Ezek 4–7 consists of a series of symbolic acts that picture Israel's coming judgment and exile from the land. It is clear throughout this section that the punishment is in response to Israel's sin (cf. Ezek 5:6–7, 9, 11; 6:1–7, 9, 11; 7:4, 8–9, 20). In this regard, the sin of idolatry is particularly emphasized and leads to the defilement of the temple in Ezek 7:21–22 (cf. Ezek 6:1–7; 7:20). The abandonment of the Jerusalem temple therefore is expressed as a consequence of Israel's

---

7. Renz, *Rhetorical Function*, 63.

8. Ibid., 63–64.

9. The destruction of Jerusalem had already been symbolically portrayed in Ezek 4:1—5:4 and the basis for this divine judgment is Israel's covenantal disobedience (cf. Ezek 6:1–7; 7:4, 8–9, 20; 8:5–18).

10. See Greenberg (*Ezekiel 1–20*, 190) and Zimmerli (*Ezechiel*, 250) for helpful discussions of the sense of Ezek 11:16. It is also important to note the ensuing verses in this context use language strongly evocative of Ezek 36–37 to describe the restoration of the exiles (cf. Ezek 11:17–20; 36:25–28; 37:23). That Ezek 37 concludes with a divine promise of the restoration of the Jerusalem temple in vv. 37–38 explicitly links the new covenant texts of Ezek 36–37 with the theme of God's abandonment of the temple.

11. Hubbard (*New Creation*, 19–20, 23, 52–53) adopts a similar approach in his analysis of Ezekiel and other Jewish texts.

disobedience. Since this is the definitive plight in Ezekiel, it is natural to assume that the apposite solution would be a reversal of Israel's wayward condition.[12]

The shift from plight to solution in the book of Ezekiel occurs in Ezek 33–48.[13] Within this section, Ezek 36:22—37:28 plays a particularly significant role in describing God's plans for the restoration of his people, the land, and the temple. The cultic connotations associated with this renewal are particularly worth observing. Within this passage, the *plight* of the exiles is described in terms of ritual defilement, and the *solution* is depicted as a divine act of cultic purification (cf. vv. 25, 38).[14] The parallelism between the clause καὶ καθαρισθήσεσθε ἀπὸ πασῶν τῶν ἀκαθαρσιῶν ὑμῶν and the clause καὶ ἀπὸ πάντων τῶν εἰδώλων ὑμῶν καὶ καθαριῶ ὑμᾶς in v. 25 indicates that false worship is also a central feature of the dilemma God is addressing. As much is implicit in God's promise to give the exiles a καρδίαν καινήν in v. 26. Frequently within the book of Ezekiel, the exiles are described as having idolatrous hearts (cf. Ezek 6:9; 11:18–19, 21; 14:3–7; 20:16).[15] It is likely within this context that the promises in the second half of v. 26 should be understood; that is, for God to remove their "heart of stone" and give them a "heart of flesh" is to perform an act of new creation which addresses a problem that lies at the core of this book.[16] Cultic concerns thus play a strong role in this section of Ezekiel's portrait of God's restoration of the exiles.

Interestingly, the restoration of the land in v. 28 is closely related to the new creation of the exiles. The return to the land in Ezek 36:28 is directly connected (note the use of the preposition καί) to the two purpose clauses of v. 27. Furthermore, God's removal of the exiles' impurity (ἀκαθαρσιῶν) in v. 29a is directly related to his promise to return the land to a state of blessing in vv. 29b–30. The repopulation of the land in v. 33 is similarly conditioned on God's act of cleansing (καθαριῶ) the exiles of their sin. There thus seems to be a consistent emphasis in Ezek 36:25–33 on the new creation of the exiles as an act of purification, which is in turn linked with the return *to* and

---

12. Ibid., 21–23.

13. See Renz (*Rhetorical Function*, 102) and Joyce (*Ezekiel*, 42) for the suggestion that Ezek 33 serves as the book's fulcrum.

14. Cf. *Tg. Ezek.* 36:38.

15. Cf. *4 Ezra* 3:20–22, 26.

16. The ensuing statements in v. 27 (note the linking of v. 26 and v. 27 through the use of the verb δίδωμι) indicate that God is promising to do more in this passage than address Israel's idolatrous tendencies. Nonetheless, there is sufficient warrant to conclude that idolatry remains a significant problem within Ezekiel's rhetoric. Cf. Ezek 6:9; 11:18–19, 21; 14:3–7; 20:16.

restoration *of* the land. This complex of ideas may also pave the way for the description of the new temple in Ezek 40–48.[17]

Ezek 37:1–28 also sheds light on the relationship between new creation and restoration in the book of Ezekiel. This passage consists of two distinct, yet related, literary units: vv. 1–14 and vv. 15–28. The first section describes the renewal of the exiles and their return to the land. The second section clarifies how the unification of Judah and Israel (which is assumed in Ezek 36:22—37:14) is achieved.[18] It is important to note that Ezek 37:1–28 continues yet also develops some of the major themes from Ezek 36:22–28. The statements in Ezek 37:11 play an integral role in the passage in that they: 1) identify the dry bones in the vision with the "whole house of Israel" (v. 11a; cf. Ezek 36:17, 21–22); and 2) indicate that the entire vision serves as a metaphoric description of the exiles' hopeless condition (v. 11b).

Ezek 37:1–28 also expands upon the portrait of restoration presented in Ezek 36:22–38. The divine πνεῦμα operative in Ezek 36:25–27 is also clearly active in Ezek 37:5–6, 9, 14. The imagery in Ezek 36:26 suggestive of an anthropological transformation also becomes more explicit in Ezek 37:1–14 as the prophet describes the metaphoric renewal of the exiles.[19] The revitalization described in Ezek 37:1–14 clearly focuses on ethical concerns. The parallelism between Ezek 37:14 and Ezek 36:27 implies the life spoken of in the former text "denotes a moral (and national) renewal which would allow God's people to keep his statutes."[20] Both these passages therefore present the Spirit as an agent of renewal and focus the restoration in terms of human obedience to the divine will.

Despite its obvious shift in content, Ezek 37:15–28 also contributes to our understanding of the restoration envisioned in Ezekiel. According to Joyce, the two sections of Ezek 37 "constitute largely self-contained sections, even though they share the theme of restoration."[21] More can be said regarding the connections between vv. 1–14 and vv. 15–28. First, the reference to the "whole house of Israel" in v. 11 seems to foreshadow the unification

---

17. The reestablishment of a new temple, after all, would require the cleansing of the exiles and their return to the land. The renewal of the land in Ezek 36:29–35 is conceivably related to the portrayal of the temple in Ezek 40–48 as the restored Eden-temple. Cf. Beale, *Temple*, 340.

18. Allen, "Structure," 140.

19. The replacement of the exiles' "heart of stone" (τὴν καρδίαν τὴν λιθίνην) with a καρδίαν σαρκίνην in v. 26 particularly intimates that their problem is of an anthropological nature.

20. Hubbard, *New Creation*, 118. The promises in Ezek 37:12–14 regarding the return to the land could also assume knowledge of the related statements in Ezek 36:28–38.

21. Joyce, *Ezekiel*, 208.

of Judah and Israel that is described in vv. 15–28. Second, both sections of Ezek 37 describe God addressing the very problem that gave rise to the exile—the sinfulness of his people (vv. 5–6, 9–10, 14, 23–24). Third, the return to the land also plays an important role in these two literary units (vv. 12–14, 21–22, 25–28). Ezekiel 37:15–28 is consequently directly related to Ezek 36:22—37:14 and continues the text's stress on Israel's restoration.

Importantly, Ezek 37:15–28 helps clarify this text's larger ecclesiological concern. By means of the sign act in vv. 16–17 and its interpretation in vv. 18–28, this passage makes explicit what is merely implicit in the previous two restoration passages—the restoration envisioned in Ezekiel must be understood as *both* an individual and corporate reality. The text has already indicated that the previous two restoration passages are addressed to the "house of Israel" (cf. Ezek 36:22, 32, 37; 37:11). The presence of the covenant formula in Ezek 36:28 also indicates the author is describing more than the renewal of individual Israelites in this context (cf. Ezek 37:23, 27).[22] One need not deny that Ezek 36:22—37:28 describes the inward/spiritual restoration of individual Israelites. Yet, at the same time, the reader must also consider these three passages are recounting God's plan to address a problem that directly impinges upon his entire covenant people.

The promises of the return of the divine presence in Ezek 37:26–28 are also relevant to this discussion.[23] While the thought of a new physical temple is not absent from Ezek 37:26–28, a close examination of this passage suggests there is more of an emphasis on the return of God's presence. The phrase τὰ ἅγιά in v. 26 and v. 28 admittedly does envision a new physical structure.[24] Nonetheless, the connotation of God's presence seems to be conveyed by: 1) the clause ἔσται μετ' αὐτῶν in v. 26; and 2) the use of the covenant formula in v. 27a. When these contextual features (along with Ezekiel's wider narrative concerning the departure of God's presence from the temple) are kept in mind, there does seem to be greater stress in this passage on God's presence with his people. Ezekiel's account of the restoration

---

22. Ibid., 205. The presence of the construction λαόν μου in Ezek 37:13 has a similar rhetorical effect.

23. As already noted, Ezek 8–11 describes the gradual departure of God's presence from the Jerusalem temple. Ezekiel 37:26–28 therefore may be understood as a promise of its return.

24. This is especially true in light of the use of the noun κατασκήνωσις in v. 27 (cf. 1 Chr 28:2; Tob 1:4; Wis 9:8). Furthermore, the phrase τὰ ἅγιά is used in a variety of texts to describe the Jerusalem temple (cf. Exod 36:1; Lev 20:3; 1 Macc 2:12; 3:51; *J. W.* 4:201, 323).

of the exiles therefore climactically ends with a series of promises which all envision the return of God's presence to dwell among his people.[25]

No discussion of restoration in the book of Ezekiel would be complete without an analysis of Ezek 40–48.[26] According to Renz, Ezek 40–48 may be understood as "a vision of New Israel, a transformed society."[27] The precise nature of this new society, however, is a subject of much debate.

For the sake of simplicity, it is perhaps best to begin this discussion by considering whether this vision should be understood literally or symbolically. Taken at face value, Ezek 40–48 describes what seem to be detailed plans for an actual physical temple (this is especially true of Ezek 40–42). This has led a number of scholars to interpret this vision in a strictly materialistic fashion.[28] Generally speaking, this reading of Ezek 40–48 is driven by the assumption that Scripture should always be interpreted literally unless the context clearly demands a symbolic reading.

Despite the presence of such patent architectural features, several points of evidence within Ezek 40–48 suggest this vision is best understood metaphorically. First, Ezek 40:2 describes the prophet being taken to "the land of Israel" and being placed on "a very high mountain." Since the elevation of Jerusalem is only 2500 ft above sea level, it is argued that the introduction to this vision situates it in something of an otherworldly setting.[29] Second, scholars also argue the description of the water flowing from the temple in Ezek 47:1–12 creates problems for a strictly literal reading of Ezek 40–48.[30] Third, S. Tuell argues for a literary connection between Ezek 1:1–3; 8:1–3 and 40:1–2 on the basis of the presence of the following threefold combination in each passage: 1) a date formula; 2) the expression "the hand of the Lord was upon me"; and 3) the expression "in visions of God." In light of this

25. Cf. Beale, *Temple*, 337–39.

26. Scholars generally recognize that Ezek 37:26–28 foreshadows Ezek 40–48. Cf. Renz, *Rhetorical Function*, 121; Greenberg, *Ezekiel 21–37*, 760. The emphasis in Ezek 37:26–28 on the divine presence may have important implications for understanding Ezek 40–48. If Ezek 37:26–28 is directly related to Ezek 40–48, then the stress placed on the divine presence in the former text may aid in interpreting the notoriously difficult final section of Ezekiel and provide further evidence that an actual literal temple is not in view. Finally, it is helpful at this point to note Niditch's proposal ("Ezekiel 40–48," 220–23) regarding the links between Ezek 38–48 and ANE temple-building traditions.

27. Renz, *Rhetorical Function*, 122.

28. Literal interpretations of Ezek 40–48 are especially associated with Dispensational readings of this text (e.g., Feinberg, *Ezekiel*, 233–39).

29. Cf. Beale, *Temple*, 336; Blenkinsopp, *Ezekiel*, 197–98; Block, *Ezekiel: Chapters 25–48*, 501.

30. Block, *Ezekiel: Chapters 25–48*, 501, 694; Blenkinsopp, *Ezekiel*, 230–32; Tuell, "Rivers of Paradise," 176–80.

relationship, Tuell argues that the emphasis in the first two passages on the divine presence (principally expressed through the concept of God's glory) should be imported into one's reading of Ezek 40–48.[31] Finally, the absence of vertical dimensions in Ezek 40–48 implies that this passage can hardly be understood as a blueprint for the construction of a physical temple.[32]

The description of the river flowing from the temple in Ezek 47:1–12 is especially important for understanding the nature of restoration in the book of Ezekiel (cf. Ps 45:5 LXX; Joel 3:18; Zech 14:8).[33] Despite the absence of concrete lexical links between Ezek 47:1–12 and Gen 1–3 within the LXX, the description of the life-giving river and the bountiful trees in the former text is almost certainly meant to evoke the description of the "garden of Eden."[34] The presence of these conceptual ties with the creation narrative intimates that the temple of Ezek 40–48 is being portrayed as a restored Eden-temple.

Also notable is the place of Gentiles within the restoration program of Ezek 40–48. This subject is first broached in Ezek 44:5–9 and forms part of the vision's discussion of who may and may not enter the temple (vv. 5–16). In vv. 6–9, the prophet is instructed to inform the Israelites that they are no longer to permit foreigners "uncircumcised in heart and flesh" to enter the temple (cf. Deut 23:2–6).[35] Ezek 47:21–23, however, mandates the allotment of an "inheritance" within the land to proselytes (cf. Lev 19:33–34).[36] As

---

31. Cf. Tuell, "Rivers of Paradise," 180; Beale, *Temple*, 337–38; Block, *Ezekiel: Chapters 25–48*, 496, 505.

32. Beale, *Temple*, 342; Block, *Ezekiel: Chapters 25–48*, 510–11; Greenberg, "Design," 193.

33. Ezekiel 47 begins by observing the presence of water within the temple (vv. 1–2). In vv. 3–5, the angelic guide takes the prophet outside the temple to demonstrate the massive proportions of this river. Regarding this description of the river, Allen (*Ezekiel 20–48*, 279), helpfully notes, "Normally one would envisage tributaries and drainage as the cause of such phenomenon." On this basis, he concludes that this requires a supernatural explanation. Cf. Beale, *Temple*, 343; Block, *Ezekiel: Chapters 25–48*, 692. The account concludes in vv. 6–12 by describing the restorative nature of the river. Finally, see Blenkinsopp (*Ezekiel*, 230) for the suggestion that "the water flowing from inside the temple is the direct consequence of the return of the *kabod* to the inner sanctuary" in Ezek 43:1–5.

34. Importantly, Ezek 36:35 MT has already compared the restored land with Eden (cf. Isa 51:3). Cf. Morales, *Restoration of Israel*, 33. Furthermore, commentators on the MT frequently connect these two texts. Cf. Levenson, *Theology*, 27; Tuell, "Rivers of Paradise," 171–89; Allen, *Ezekiel 20–48*, 280. According to Block (*Ezekiel: Chapters 25–48*, 694–95), the phrase כל־נפש חיה אשר־ישרץ in the MT of Ezek 47:9 establishes a explicit link with Gen 1:20–21.

35. See Block (*Ezekiel: Chapters 25–48*, 622–23) on the identity of these foreigners.

36. It should be noted that the LXX explicitly identifies these Gentiles as proselytes through the use of the noun προσήλυτος in v. 22. That these individuals reside

Joyce notes, these two texts should not be viewed as inconsistent since they both address different concerns and individuals of different standing within the Israelite community.[37] The representation of new creation and restoration in Ezek 40-48 therefore encompasses a measure of hope for Gentiles who convert to the Israelite religion.

Summary of New Creation and Restoration in Ezekiel

As with any well constructed literary work, to understand the book of Ezekiel one must play close attention to its introduction (ch. 1) and conclusion (ch. 40-48). Ezekiel begins with a theophanic vision that places great stress on the divine presence (Ezek 1:1, 4, 26-28). Within this vision, a great deal of attention is given to describing a cherubim chariot and its mobility (vv. 5-24). The cherubim chariot of Ezek 1 is generally understood as a symbolic replacement for the cherubim throne in the Jerusalem temple, and its mobility is meant to imply the consequent mobility of the divine presence. This introductory account sets the stage for the progressive departure of the divine presence from the Jerusalem temple in Ezek 9-11 (cf. Ezek 9:3; 10:3-4, 18-19; 11:22-23). Finally, within the extensive description of the restored temple in Ezek 40-48, the author notes that the divine presence returns to inhabit the temple in Ezek 43:2-5 and 44:4.

This thematic interest in the divine presence is important for understanding the nature of new creation and restoration in Ezekiel for a number of reasons. Sandwiched between Ezek 1 and Ezek 9-11 is an extensive description of Israel's impending judgment and exile. Throughout this section, it is clear that YHWH is executing this punishment because of his people's covenant unfaithfulness, which is frequently linked with idolatry (cf. Ezek 5:6-7, 9, 11; 6:1-7, 9, 11; 7:4, 8-9, 20; 8:3-18). YHWH's departure from the Jerusalem temple may therefore be understood as his response to Judah's sin, especially as it manifests itself in terms of idolatry and defilement of the temple (cf. Ezek 8:6). The solution to the people's plight is mainly depicted in Ezek 36-37. Importantly, within this passage salvation from sin is portrayed as an act of cultic purification (Ezek 36:25-26, 29, 33, 38). Furthermore, this section of Ezekiel concludes with a promise of a restored temple

---

permanently in the land and procreate also strengthens this conclusion.

37. Joyce, *Ezekiel*, 238. Cf. Block, *Ezekiel: Chapters 25-48*, 718. The LXX makes it especially clear that different groups of individuals are described in these passages through its use of the adjective ἀλλογενής to describe the foreigners barred from entering the sanctuary in Ezek 44:7, 9, while the noun προσήλυτος is employed in Ezek 47:22-23.

and the return of the divine presence (Ezek 37:27–28). There is thus a strong sense in which the description of restoration in Ezek 36–37 prepares for the restored temple of Ezek 40–48.

A number of other factors within Ezek 36–37 add to the complexity of Ezekiel's portrait of new creation and restoration. Both these subjects are treated in a decidedly comprehensive manner in this passage. A prominent feature is the promise of a "new heart" and a "new spirit" in Ezek 36:26. This statement has frequently been used in discussions of the background of καινὴ κτίσις in the Pauline tradition to support an individualized, anthropological reading of that concept. While this promise undoubtedly concerns individuals, one must not overlook the presence of corporate overtones within the passage's larger context (cf. Ezek 36:22, 28, 32, 37; 37:11, 15–28). The promises in Ezek 36:26 are also closely linked to the return of the exiles to the land (Ezek 36:24, 28, 33).[38] Furthermore, the cultic purification of the exiles in Ezek 36:26 is also directly connected to the restoration of the land to a state of fruitfulness (vv. 29–30, 34–35). Finally, the restoration promises in this passage culminate with the climactic promise of a reestablished temple in Ezek 37:26–28, which itself sets the stage for the discussion of the new temple in Ezek 40–48.

Two features of the program of restoration elucidated in Ezek 40–48 are particularly worth noting. First, the presence of allusions to Gen 1–3 in Ezek 47:1–12 at the very least suggests that the restored temple of Ezek 40–48 is being portrayed as a restored Eden-temple (cf. Ezek 36:35; Isa 51:3). Second, the question of the status of Gentiles within the restoration program of Ezek 40–48 is also raised in Ezek 47:21–23. Admittedly, Ezek 44:5–9 does deny Gentiles "uncircumcised in heart and flesh" entry into the sanctuary. A picture of Gentile hope is, however, found in Ezek 47:21–23, which grants an inheritance to proselytes of the Israelite religion and thus may implicitly describe the salvation of the Gentiles.

New Creation and Restoration in Jeremiah

The Relevance of Jeremiah

Jeremiah has longed played a role in deciphering the background of new creation in the Pauline tradition.[39] Schneider goes so far as to suggest Jeremiah's new covenant promises provide *the* conceptual framework for new

---

38. Cf. Ezek 37:9–14, 21, 25.

39. Cf. Hubbard, *New Creation*, 17–20; Schneider, "Die Idee der Neuschöpfung," 258–59.

creation in the Pauline tradition.⁴⁰ In contrast to Schneider, Mell hardly deals with Jeremiah in his investigation of new creation.⁴¹

Two factors warrant a consideration of the text of Jeremiah in this project. First, new covenant traditions from Jeremiah (and Ezekiel) likely played an important role in developing Paul's argument in the wider context of 2 Cor 2:14—5:10 (e.g., 2 Cor 3:3, 6; 4:16; 5:5).⁴² Second, an examination of Jeremiah is warranted on the basis of the likelihood that new exodus traditions in Isaiah seem to draw upon traditions from within Jeremiah (cf. Jer 31:21–22).⁴³

Examination of Relevant Texts in Jeremiah

The book of Jeremiah is generally regarded as an exilic document, though there is evidence that its final form developed over a relatively long period of time.⁴⁴ With regard to its historical setting, the book focuses on the period between Josiah's reforms and Jehoiachin's release from prison (cf. 2 Chr 34:3–7; 2 Kgs 22–23; Jer 51:31–34). The contents of this book focus strongly on Judah's sinfulness and God's response of judgment (Jer 2:1—25:14). Furthermore, the fact that the fall of Jerusalem is narrated twice in Jeremiah (cf. Jer 39:1–10; 52:1–30) allows one to conclude that this historical event plays an important role in this book's final form. The book of Jeremiah, nonetheless, closes with an implication of hope by recounting King Jehoiachin's release from prison (Jer 52:31–34; cf. Jer 33:15–26), which may imply the restoration of the Davidic dynasty (cf. 2 Kgs 25:27–30).

---

40. According to Schneider (*Jesusüberlieferung und Christologie*, 361), "der Ursprung des Neuschöpfungsgedankens in der Bundestheologie des Propheten Jeremia liegt."

41. Mell's work on new creation in Paul does not contain any significant analysis of Jeremiah. Mell (*Neue Schöpfung*, 39), however, does propose that the new covenant promises of Jeremiah have "mögliche Anknüpfungspunkte" with the new creation concept in Paul; however, he concludes that these promises are more relevant for understanding the "Gesetzeskritik" of 2 Cor 3:3, 6.

42. Cf. Webb, *Returning Home*, 72–111.

43. According to Thompson (*Jeremiah*, 566), "it may be that the theme of the New Exodus was already current in Judah long before it was taken up by Second Isaiah." Sommer (*Isaiah 40–66*, 46–50) goes further and suggests, "Jeremiah 30–31 and 33 provide the richest mine for Deutero-Isaiah as he restates positive prophecies from Jeremiah." Whatever the literary relationship between Isaiah and Jeremiah may have been, the new exodus traditions in Isaiah are clearly more developed than that of Jeremiah and take on a decidedly more eschatological form.

44. Carroll, *Jeremiah*, 51.

Much of the scholarly discussion regarding the relationship between new creation in the Pauline tradition and the book of Jeremiah has centered on Jer 31[38]:31-34. This justly famous passage describes the promise of a new covenantal relationship (διαθήκην καινήν) between YHWH and his people.[45] A central feature of this new covenant is the internalization of the law on the hearts of God's people.[46] Jeremiah has already firmly located the sinful inclinations of the Israelites within their hearts (Jer 4:6; 5:20-25; 17:1, 9; 18:2).[47] The covenant of Jer 31[38]:31-34 may therefore be understood as God's answer to the primary malady which plagues his people.[48]

According to H. Wolff, Jeremiah may be charged with establishing a shift in Israelite religion away from the community and towards the individual.[49] This is primarily the result of the emphasis on interiority within the new covenant. Accordingly, the new covenant of Jeremiah is frequently described in such terms as the individual creation of a new person.[50] On the basis of this reading of Jer 31[38]:31-34, some interpreters of new creation in the Hauptbriefe have argued for a strictly anthropological reading of καινὴ κτίσις.[51] One must note, however, that Jeremiah's new covenant is instituted with the "the house of Israel and the house of Judah" (v. 31; cf. v. 33).[52] A rigorous anthropological reading of the new covenant thus does not

---

45. For some scholars, the new covenant described in Jeremiah is best understood in close continuity with the Mosaic covenant, and Jer 31:31-34 thus describes the restoration of that prior covenant. Cf. Rendtorff, *Kanon und Theologie*, 185-87; Levin, *Die Verheißung*, 138-41. Other scholars suggest the covenant described in Jer 31:31-34 is an entirely new covenant. Cf. Potter, "New Covenant," 349-50; Lalleman-de Winkel, *Jeremiah*, 196-201; Von Rad, *Theologie*, 225. While there may be some elements of continuity between these two covenants, the full force of v. 32 should be considered when addressing this question. It is therefore best to conclude that though there is some degree of continuity with the Mosaic covenant, the covenant of Jer 31:31-34 is nonetheless a largely distinct covenant in its own right. Cf. Lundbom, *Jeremiah 21-36*, 466; Dumbrell, *Covenant and Creation*, 177-81.

46. While there is some debate among scholars regarding what precisely is new about the covenant of Jeremiah 31, there is little doubt this promise constitutes a central feature of its innovation. Cf. McKane, *Jeremiah 2*, 818; Thompson, *Jeremiah*, 581; Weinfeld, "Jeremiah," 28.

47. Cf. Deut 6:6; 11:18; 30:5, 6, 14.

48. Hubbard, *New Creation*, 19-20; Jackson, *New Creation*, 30.

49. Wolff, *Anthropologie*, 319-20.

50. According to Von Rad (*Theologie*, 226), "Es sind hier die Umrisse des Bildes von einem neuen Menschen gezeichnet, von einem Menschen, den Gott durch ein Wunder zu einem vollkommenen Gehorsam behähight." Cf. Weippert, "Neuen Bund," 347.

51. Cf. Stockhausen, *Moses' Veil*, 175; Hubbard, *New Creation*, 185, 236; Schneider, *Jesusüberlieferung und Christologie*, 357-71.

52. Further corporate overtones are also found: 1) in v. 32, which compares the new covenant with the covenant instituted with the "ancestors" of Jeremiah's audience; and

fully apprehend the scope of the renewal envisioned in Jer 31[38]:31-34.[53] Rather than merely describing the restoration of individual Israelites, this passage is also depicting the restoration of YHWH's covenant community.[54]

It is also important to recognize that Jeremiah's vision of restoration extends beyond the establishment of a new covenant between YHWH and his people. Jeremiah 31[38]:31-34 occurs within a key section of Jeremiah, the so-called Book of Consolation, which makes a strong shift from oracles of judgment to oracles of salvation (Jer 30-33[37-40]). The controlling idea of the Book of Consolation is God's promise to "restore the fortunes" (ἀποστρέψω τὴν ἀποικίαν) of his people (Jer 30[37]:3).[55] This motif generally involves the return from the exile (Jer 30[37]:8, 10; 31[38]:7-10, 15-17, 27-28), the reestablishment of the Davidic kingdom (Jer 30[37]:9, 21), and the restoration of Zion (Jer 30[37]:17-22; 31[38]:4-7, 12).[56] The new covenant of Jer 31[38]:31-34 therefore forms part of a larger program of renewal which involves more than the anthropological renewal of the exiles.[57]

The expansive nature of restoration within the Book of Consolation is particularly evident in Jer 30[37]:18-22. Despite the presence of a number of textual difficulties, it is at least clear from this passage that Jeremiah foresees the rebuilding of Jerusalem (v. 18d) and the reinstatement of the Davidic kingship (v. 21).[58] The prospect of a restored temple is less certain. The use of the noun ναός in Jer 37:18 LXX as a translation of the noun אַרְמוֹן (Jer 30:18 MT) does shift the promise in the MT away from the rebuilding of palaces in the land to an explicit promise of the restoration of the Jerusalem cult (cf. *Tg.* Jer 30:18). The presence of cultic associations in v.

---

2) in the use of plural pronouns throughout vv. 32-34.

53. Jackson (*New Creation*, 30) also notes, the renewal "of the earth's productivity and the geocentricity of Zion so important in the wider Jewish tradition" also plays a role in Jeremiah's conception of restoration (cf. Jer 31:12-14, 23-24).

54. Cf. Carroll, *Jeremiah*, 611-12.

55. Ibid., 568, 571.

56. One of the valuable features of Webb's analysis (*Returning Home*, 87-88) of the background of 2 Cor 3:1-6 is his observation that new covenant and new exodus are closely linked in Jeremiah and Ezekiel (cf. Jer 31[38]:31-33; Ezek 11:19; 36:26-27a). On this basis, Webb (ibid., 88) concludes, "It is important to keep in mind the joining of these two features (exilic return promises and new covenant promises) when the function of exilic return promises within the context of Paul's inaugurated new covenant theology is examined—the two are inextricably linked."

57. The prominence of the return from exile in Jer 32[39]:36-44 should not be ignored. Within this passage, vv. 39-40 is strikingly similar to the new covenant promises of Jer 31[38]:31-34. The similarity between these two sets of promises suggests anthropological transformation and the return to the land are closely related concepts within Jeremiah. Cf. Ezek 36:25-28, 33, 37-38.

58. Cf. Jer 23:5; 30[37]:9; Ezek 34:24; 37:24-25.

19 may have served as the basis for this rendering.[59] The phrase וְעֲדָתוֹ לְפָנַי תִּכּוֹן in Jer 30:20b MT also envisions a restored temple, yet the use of the noun μαρτύριον in the LXX complicates the situation.[60] While it is difficult to account for the LXX rendering of this statement, the external evidence does allow one to presume that Paul and AE would have been familiar with the reading of the MT. In summary, a restored temple forms an integral element of God's plans to "restore the fortunes of the tents of Jacob" in Jer 30[37]:18–22.

Another important text within the Book of Consolation which gives form to Jeremiah's portrait of restoration is Jer 31[38]:38–40. This passage follows an oracle that describes God's enduring faithfulness to his covenant people (vv. 35–37) and focuses on the rebuilding of Jerusalem.[61] The geographical locations mentioned in vv. 38–40 indicate the reconstruction project described in this passage will extend Jerusalem's boundaries beyond its historical limits (cf. Rev 21:15–17; 4Q554 1–2).[62] Several features of this text, however, imply that more is going on in this passage than a mere construction undertaking. First, the southward expansion of the city's borders suggests that the land will be purified.[63] Second, the cleansing of the land in vv. 38–40ab allows the city to serve as a ἁγίασμα τῷ κυρίῳ (v. 40).[64] Third, the promise of Jerusalem's inviolability in v. 40 suggests that the primary problem that led to its destruction—the sinfulness of its people—has been addressed (cf. Jer 31[38]:31–34).[65] In summary, Jer 31[38]:38–40 is con-

---

59. Cf. Keown, Scalise, and Smothers, *Jeremiah 26–52*, 104; McKane, *Jeremiah 2*, 772–73; Holladay, *Jeremiah 2*, 177.

60. See Becking ("Jeremiah's Book of Consolation," 156) and Fischer (*Jeremia 26–52*, 120) for further discussion of the LXX reading.

61. According to Lundbom (*Jeremiah 21–36*, 490), Jer 31[38]:38–40 may be understood as "a walking tour of the city's boundaries before its destruction, beginning in the northeast quadrant and proceeding in a counterclockwise fashion until it ends up near where it began."

62. Despite uncertainty regarding the exact location of some of the places mentioned in vv. 39–40, the suggestion in v. 40 that the measurements for this restored Jerusalem will extend as far as the Kidron Valley indicates this text describes a Jerusalem larger than the historical city. Cf. Keown, Scalise, and Smothers, *Jeremiah 26–52*, 137; pace Lundbom, *Jeremiah 21–36*, 490.

63. According to v. 40, Jerusalem's walls will extend to "all the fields as far as the Wadi Kidron." For our purposes, it is enough to note that vv. 38–40 describes the enlargement of the city's fortifications to include land used for idolatry, burial, and waste. Cf. 2 Kgs 23:4, 6, 10, 12; Jer 2:23; 19:4–5, 13; 32[39]:35.

64. The noun ἁγίασμα is used to refer to a cultic sanctuary in a number of texts (e.g., Exod 15:17; 25:8; Jer 17:12; Ezek 48:21; 1 Esd 8:75; Jud 5:19; 1 Macc 1:21, 36; 5:1; Sir 36:12).

65. Cf. Keown, Scalise, and Smothers, *Jeremiah 26–52*, 139.

cerned with more than the rebuilding of Jerusalem; it also depicts the restoration of the land, the transformation of God's covenant people, and the construction of a temple.

Summary of New Creation and Restoration in Jeremiah

Throughout the quest to comprehend the background of new creation in the Pauline tradition, the book of Jeremiah has generally played no small part in the debate. This is a natural development given the importance of Jeremiah's new covenant and its promise of the internalization of the divine law (Jer 31[38]:31-34). These notions are appealed to by scholars (primarily Hubbard and Schneider) who argue that Paul's conception of new creation is to be firmly associated with the anthropological renewal of humanity.

A closer look at the wider context of the Book of Consolation, however, reveals that the presentation of new creation and restoration in Jeremiah is much more grandiose. First, one must note the new covenant of Jer 31[38]:31-34 is directly addressed to "the house of Israel and the house of Judah" (v. 31). While this new covenant no doubt concerns individual Israelites, v. 31 thus indicates it also involves the entire covenant community. Second, the broader framework of the Book of Consolation is dominated by God's promise to "restore the fortunes" of his people (Jer 30[37]:3).[66] This theme in turn covers a wide range of ideas such as the return of the exiles, the restoration of the Davidic kingship, and the renewal of Zion.[67] Finally, there are a number of passages in the Book of Consolation that foresee the establishment of a new temple (cf. Jer 30:20 MT; 37:18 LXX; 38:40 LXX).

The conception of restoration in Jer 31[38]:38-40 is not only far-reaching but also starkly similar to that of Ezek 36:24-38. This passage from the Book of Consolation is a description of the rebuilding *and* expansion of Jerusalem. According to vv. 39-40, the rebuilding of Jerusalem will extend to the "Wadi Kidron" and give rise to a permanently secure city. The underlying implication behind vv. 39-40 is that: 1) defiled land used for burial, idolatry, and waste will be cleansed; and 2) God has addressed the problem which gave rise to the destruction of Jerusalem—the sinfulness of the Israelites. These ideas find fuller development in Ezek 36:24-38, which also combines the cleansing of the Israelites (vv. 25-27, 29, 33, 37-38) with their return from exile (vv. 24, 28, 33) and the rejuvenation of the land (vv. 29b-30, 34-35). Since the restoration envisioned in Ezek 36:24-38 probably culminates with the new temple in Ezek 40-48, the suggestion in Jer

---

66. Cf. Jer 29[36]:14; 30[37]:18; 31[38]:23; 32[39]:44; 33[40]:7, 11, 26.
67. Cf. Jer 30[37]:8-10, 17-22; 31[38]:4-10, 12, 15-17, 27-28.

38:40 LXX that the cleansed land will become a divine sanctuary (ἁγίασμα) establishes further parallels with the portrait of restoration in Ezekiel.

New Creation and Restoration in 1 Enoch

The Book of 1 Enoch

In the words of one prominent scholar, *1 Enoch* is "arguably the most important Jewish text of the Greco-Roman period."[68] The presence of the phrase καινὴ κτίσις in *1 En.* 72:1 makes this ancient Jewish composition particularly relevant to this project.[69] The book of *1 Enoch* is a pseudonymous work that relates a series of divine revelations given to the patriarch Enoch (cf. Gen 5:21–24). *1 Enoch* is best described as a collection of related traditions concerning Enoch and consists of five major sections, followed by two shorter appendices. These traditions are generally dated between the fourth and first century BCE. (though the Parables are likely much older).[70] While it is difficult to understand *1 Enoch* as a unified composition, one can, nonetheless, note that its focus is generally on "the coming judgment in which God will adjudicate the injustices that characterize life as the authors and their readers experience it."[71]

New Creation and Restoration in The Book of Watchers

The first passage in the Book of Watchers that is helpful for understanding new creation is *1 En.* 10:1—11:2.[72] As with other texts surveyed in this chapter, *1 En.* 10:1—11:2 presents a multi-faceted portrait of new creation. It is clear from this text that the judgment of the Watchers and their offspring has a direct effect on the earth. The archangel Raphael is commissioned in

---

68. Nickelsburg, *1 Enoch 1*, xxiii.

69. Given the parenthetical reference to new creation in *1 En.* 72:1, the foregoing analysis will focus on passages within *1 Enoch* with more extensive discussions of this concept. For now, it is sufficient to observe the strong cosmological overtones (particularly, the parallelism between "world" and "new creation" in this text) associated with new creation in *1 En.* 72:1.

70. Nickelsburg, *1 Enoch 1*, 1; Collins, *Apocalyptic Imagination*, 33–34; Vanderkam, "1 Enoch," 33–34.

71. Nickelsburg, *1 Enoch 1*, 7. Regarding the difficulty in reading the contents of *1 Enoch* as a unified whole, Black (*1 Enoch*, 12) suggests that "there is no Ariadne's thread to lead him [the reader] through the Enochian labyrinth."

72. The Book of Watchers is generally dated to the third century BCE. Cf. Wright, *Evil Spirits*, 23–28.

1 En. 10:7 to "restore the earth" and "announce" its renewal. Michael is likewise instructed to "cleanse the earth" (*1 En.* 10:20; cf. *1 En.* 10:22).[73] These divine commands suggest the sin of the Watchers has had an immediate impact on the earth.[74] Finally, an effect of the divine judgment is a dramatic improvement in agricultural productivity (*1 En.* 10:18–19, 11:1; cf. *2 Bar.* 74:1–2). This linking of divine judgment with an increase in farming efficiency symbolizes the return of the divine blessing upon the land and draws upon deuteronomic traditions.[75]

New creation in *1 En.* 10:1—11:2 is also somewhat anthropological in scope. A significant effect of the divine judgment in this passage is extended human longevity (*1 En.* 10:16–17; cf. *1 En.* 10:3; 24:6). This linking of divine judgment with an increase in human life span evokes Isa 65:15–20.[76] The cleansing of the earth also leads to a righteous humanity (v. 21).[77] While this statement receives little elaboration in the immediate context, the eschatological setting of *1 En.* 10:16—11:2 allows for the possibility that humanity has somehow been transformed.

Finally, the salvation of the Gentiles also plays an important role within *1 En.* 10:1—11:2. In this text, a "plant of righteousness and truth" appears which "will become a blessing" (cf. *1 En.* 10:3). According to Nickelsburg, the plant spoken of here is none other than Abraham and the promise of blessing alludes to Gen 12:2–3.[78] This allusion to Abraham and God's covenant with him then prepares for the statement in v. 21, "all the peoples will worship me."

1 En. 24:2—25:7 is another passage within the Book of Watchers that illustrates the development of new creation in Second Temple Judaism. The presence of Eden traditions in *1 En.* 24:2—25:7 is especially significant.[79] Beginning in *1 En.* 25:3, the archangel Michael provides an angelic

---

73. While these statements could feasibly refer to the flood, their presence within such a utopian context suggests they should be understood eschatologically.

74. The presence of the statement, "And the world was changed" in an important manuscript of *1 En.* 8:2 explicitly expresses this idea (Knibb, *Enoch*, 81).

75. Cf. Deut 28:16, 22, 24, 38–40, 42; 30:1–5, 9, 16.

76. Cf. Nickelsburg, *1 Enoch 1*, 226. Nickelsburg (ibid., 227) further suggests that the description of the righteous enjoying the fruits of their labour in *1 En.* 10:18–19 also alludes to Isa 65:21–22.

77. It should be noted that the statement "righteousness and truth will they plant in joy for ever" in *1 En.* 10:16c already envisions the ethical transformation of humanity.

78. Nickelsburg, *1 Enoch 1*, 226.

79. This passage is primarily an eschatological description of seven mountains that closely parallel the seven mountains of *1 En.* 18:6–9. Special attention is given in this account to the seventh mountain (which is said to surpass the other six in height) and one of the many fragrant trees which surround this mountain (vv. 3–5).

interpretation of Enoch's vision, first focusing on the seventh mountain (v. 3) and then explaining the nature of the tree of *1 En.* 25:4–5 (vv. 4–6).[80] Regarding the tree of *1 En.* 24:3–5, the archangel Michael begins his explanation by implicitly identifying it as the "tree of life" of Gen 2–3 and suggesting that it will not be made accessible to humanity until the inauguration of the eschatological age (vv. 4–5a). Once the tree is available to the righteous, it will give rise to an amazing growth in human life span (v. 6d; cf. *1 En.* 10:17). Also notable in this regard is the statement in v. 6 regarding the termination of human anguish and suffering. The combination of these traditions once again points to the importance of the *Urzeit-Endzeit* typology within Second Temple Judaism.

Despite its ambiguity, the account of the relocation of the tree of life in v. 5bc also helps clarify the portrait of new creation in this passage. According to Nickelsburg, this passage suggests that the tree of life will be taken from the seventh mountain and placed in the New Jerusalem.[81] Furthermore, *1 En.* 25:5–6 closely links the tree of life with the divine sanctuary in the New Jerusalem. According to v. 5b, the tree of life will be transferred to "a holy place, by the house of Lord." In v. 6a, the chosen are then described worshiping God. Given the presence of sanctuary symbolism in the creation account of Gen 1–3, *1 En.* 25:5–6 may then be read as the restoration of the Eden-temple.

New Creation and Restoration in The Animal Apocalypse

1 En. 90:28–38 is the passage most relevant for understanding the depiction of new creation in the Animal Apocalypse.[82] This account begins with the destruction of the old temple and its replacement with "a new house, larger and higher" than its predecessor (vv. 28–29). There is some debate regarding the nature of this "new house." According to Vanderkam, the "new house" of *1 En.* 90:28–29 symbolizes a restored Jerusalem devoid of a temple.[83] The allegorical nature of this passage warrants a degree of caution on this matter. Since the noun "tower" is always used in the Animal Apocalypse to refer

---

80. According to the archangel Michael, the seventh mountain, with its throne-like apex, will be the place upon which God will sit when he comes to execute the final judgment (v. 3; cf. *1 En.* 18:8; 22:4, 11, 13).

81. Nickelsburg (*1 Enoch 1*, 315) bases this conclusion on both the connections between *1 En.* 25:5bc and *1 En.* 10:21 and their common echoing of Isa 65.

82. The postdiluvian world is also depicted as a new creation in *1 En.* 89:8–9. Cf. Tiller, *Animal Apocalypse*, 266–67. The text of *1 En.* 89:8–9, however, presents a much less developed portrait of new creation.

83. Vanderkam, *Apocalyptic Tradition*, 168. Cf. Rev 21:22.

to the temple, it is perhaps best to conclude that *1 En.* 90:28–29 does not describe the reestablishment of the Jerusalem temple.[84] At the same time, Nickelsburg suggests, "If the house is thought of as city and temple, it will be a temple in which God dwells (v. 34) and where no traditional cult is necessary both because of God's presence and because the human race has been fully and permanently purified of sin."[85]

Another important element within this passage is the transformation of the "sheep," "wild beasts," and "birds of heaven." *1 En.* 90:32 states that after their deliverance from exile, the "sheep" are "white" and their wool is said to be "thick and pure." This symbolic description of the Israelites could well refer to their bountiful righteousness.[86] The narrative further asserts in v. 35 that the "sheep" have also regained their sight. Throughout the Animal Apocalypse, the imagery of blindness is used to convey Israel's sinful tendencies and rebellion against the divine will (e.g., *1 En.* 89:32–33, 41, 54, 74; 90:7, 26).[87] For the "sheep" to have eyes able to see in the eschatological age suggests that their sinful condition has been addressed. Finally, the scope of restoration clearly widens after the birth of a "white bull" in v. 37, since all the species of animals in the narrative are said to be "changed" and become "white cattle" (v. 38). The transformation described in this portion of the narrative must include the "wild beasts" and "birds of heaven"; it is natural then to read this account as an allegorical description of the salvation of the Gentiles.[88]

The identity of the "white bull" in *1 En.* 90:37–38 is also important to consider. This "white bull" has traditionally been interpreted as a symbol for a messianic figure.[89] Despite the validity of this suggestion, Milik's observation that Adam was also symbolized within the allegory of the Animal Apocalypse as a "white bull" deserves attention (cf. *1 En.* 85:3).[90] There is ultimately no need to establish an unwarranted bifurcation between these two readings of this "white bull" since the "white bull" is said to reign over

---

84. Ibid., 168. *1 En.* 89:50 is especially helpful in this regard in that it distinguishes between a "house" and a "tower." That the "tower" of v. 50 symbolizes the Solomonic temple is probable from the description of "the Lord of the sheep" standing on the "tower" and the spreading of a "full table," which likely is a metaphor for sacrifices. Cf. *1 En.* 89:73.

85. Nickelsburg, *1 Enoch 1*, 405. Cf. Black, *1 Enoch*, 278; Tiller, *Animal Apocalypse*, 376.

86. Charles, *1 Enoch*, 257; pace Tiller, *Animal Apocalypse*, 380.

87. Cf. Deut 29:4; Isa 6:10; Ezek 12:2.

88. Bryan, *Cosmos*, 62; Black, "New Creation," 19.

89. Cf. Black, *1 Enoch*, 279–80; Black, "New Creation," 19–20.

90. Milik, "Problèmes," 359. Cf. Vanderkam, *Apocalyptic Tradition*, 168; Lindars, "1 Enoch XC. 38," 483–86.

all the cattle (v. 38).⁹¹ If the "white bull" is a symbol of a second Adam, the implication in *1 En.* 90:28–38 is that after the judgment of cosmic and human evil, humanity (both Jew and Gentile) will be restored to a state of perfect righteousness and brought under the headship of a new Adam.⁹²

New Creation in The Apocalypse of Weeks

The primary description of new creation within the Apocalypse of Weeks occurs in *1 En.* 91:12–17. As with other portions of *1 Enoch*, the Apocalypse of Weeks correlates the new creation with an *Urzeit-Endzeit* typology. This typological structure is especially prominent in the tenth week, which combines the destruction of "the first heaven" with its replacement by "a new heaven" and a state of eternal righteousness (*1 En.* 91:16–17).⁹³ The text conveys a similar point through the description of the rebuilding of the *eternal* temple in *1 En.* 91:13 (cf. Gen 2:1–4).⁹⁴ Further connections with the primordial state are also apparent in the text's portrait of the new creation as a state of sinless perfection (vv. 16–17). The depiction of new creation in the Apocalypse of Weeks also has important ramifications for humanity. At the very least, the events described in the ninth week ("all men will look to the path of uprightness") likely gives rise to the conversion of the Gentiles (*1 En.* 91:14d).⁹⁵

Summary of New Creation and Restoration in 1 Enoch

The text of *1 Enoch* is particularly relevant for appreciating the background of new creation in the Pauline tradition due to the presence of the phrase καινὴ κτίσις in *1 En.* 72:1. The work also exhibits a strong interest in the eschatological era and the restoration of God's people. The scope of new creation in *1 Enoch* encompasses not only cosmological renewal (e.g., *1 En.*

---

91. Cf. Nickelsburg, *1 Enoch 1*, 406–7.

92. Cf. Tiller, *Animal Apocalypse*, 15–18, 388; Bryan, *Cosmos*, 101.

93. The account of the destruction of the "first heaven" and emergence of a "new heaven" in v. 16 probably draws upon Isa 65–66 (cf. *2 Bar.* 32:1–6; *Jub.* 1:29). Cf. Van Ruiten, "Influence," 161–66; Stuckenbruck, *1 Enoch*, 149; Dexinger, *Henochs Zehnwochenapokalypse*, 142.

94. This portion of the Apocalypse of Weeks also draws upon expectations of an eschatological temple. Cf. Dexinger, *Henochs Zehnwochenapokalypse*, 140; Stuckenbruck, *1 Enoch*, 138.

95. Cf. Stuckenbruck, *1 Enoch*, 144–45; Dexinger, *Henochs Zehnwochenapokalypse*, 141; pace Black, *1 Enoch*, 294.

10:18-19; 11:1; 91:16), but also anthropological transformation (e.g., *1 En.* 10:3, 18-19, 21; 25:6; 90:32-33, 37-38) and ecclesiological restoration (e.g., *1 En.* 10:16, 21; 90:37; 91:14). The restoration of the temple also plays an important role within several accounts of new creation in *1 Enoch* (e.g., *1 En.* 25:3-6; 90:28-29; 91:13). Further evidence for the presence of an *Urzeit-Endzeit* typology within *1 Enoch* may also be present in *1 En.* 90:37-38.

New Creation and Restoration in Jubilees

The Book of Jubilees

The book of *Jubilees* is best categorized as an example of the ancient Jewish genre "rewritten Bible."[96] This composition presents itself as an interpretative account of the scriptural narrative from creation to the time of Moses. Scholars generally date this work to around the time of the Maccabean conflict.[97] If *Jubilees* was composed within this period, its explicit retelling of the biblical material may be understood as an interpretation of contemporary events that aims to ward off Hellenistic influences among its Jewish audience.[98]

As with *1 Enoch*, the book of *Jubilees* is regarded as one of the most important extant Jewish works from the Second Temple period.[99] *Jubilees* provides the modern reader with an insightful look into how the OT was reinterpreted by Jews living around the time of the development of early Christianity. Furthermore, the use of the phrase καινὴ κτίσις in *Jubilees* establishes a direct link between this text and the Pauline tradition (cf. *Jub.* 1:29; 4:26).

---

96. Cf. Endres, *Jubilees*, 15-16; Vanderkam, *Book of Jubilees*, 11, 135-36; Van Ruiten, *Primaeval History Interpreted*, 3-4. While *Jubilees* primarily belongs within the genre "rewritten Bible," there are features within this text that give it an apocalyptic flavor. It is, after all, an account of an angelic revelation given to Moses (cf. *Jub.* 1:27-28) and exhibits some interest in the eschatological age (cf. *Jub.* 1:7-29; 4:26; 23:11-31). Collins' (*Apocalyptic Imagination*, 63-67) suggestion that *Jubilees* has a "borderline case for the apocalyptic genre" may therefore be appropriate.

97. Vanderkam, *Textual and Historical Studies*, 214-85; Wintermute, "Jubilees," 43-44.

98. Berger, *Jubiläen*, 298-300; Vanderkam, *Book of Jubilees*, 139-41.

99. Cf. Wintermute, "Jubilees," 46.

Examination of Relevant Texts in Jubilees[100]

The primary topic of *Jub.* 1:7–29 is a dialogue between God and Moses concerning the history and fate of the Jewish people. This passage begins by extensively recounting the sinful waywardness of the Israelites, which culminates in exile from the land (vv. 7–14). Exile is, however, followed by restoration (vv. 15–18). The promise of return to the land is followed by a plea from Moses that God would definitively deal with the sin of his people by forming "a pure heart and a holy spirit for them" (vv. 19–21). This is then followed by a lengthy divine speech that discusses God's plans for the renewal of his people and the land (vv. 22–29).[101]

An important feature of the program of renewal in *Jub.* 1:7–29 is its emphasis on the establishment of an eternal sanctuary (vv. 17, 27–29).[102] Scholars frequently note that the use of the phrase καινὴ κτίσις in *Jub.* 1:29 is likely an allusion to Isa 65–66.[103] One may also discern further connections to the "new heavens and new earth" of Isa 65–66 in the text's promise of a new sanctuary. This is especially plausible in v. 28bc and v. 29f, which both connect this divine abode with Mt. Zion and Jerusalem.[104] The establishment of a sanctuary in the new creation account of *Jub.* 1:7–29 may thus provide further evidence that this text represents a development of the traditions found in Isa 65–66.

The description of new creation in *Jub.* 4:26 further links cosmic renewal with the appearance of a restored temple. As Hubbard notes, the

---

100. My analysis of *Jubilees* builds upon Hubbard's analysis of new creation in *Jubilees* by discussing a few aspects of these texts he fails to address. Hubbard's discussion of *Jubilees* is to be especially commended for: 1) pointing out the relevance of *Jub.* 23:11–32 (despite the absence of the phrase καινὴ κτίσις) for understanding this important theme within *Jubilees*; 2) showing that in contrast to other works from the Second Temple period with apocalyptic features, *Jubilees* places great emphasis on anthropological renewal (cf. *Jub.* 1:7, 22–23, 29; 5:12); and 3) proposing that new creation in *Jubilees* is presented as the solution to the three-fold plight of sin, Satan, and the Gentiles (cf. *Jub.* 1:26–30). Cf. Ibid., 36–46.

101. Given the prominence of the sanctuary in vv. 27–29, *Jub.* 1:22–29 may be understood as something of an elaboration on *Jub.* 1:15–18.

102. According to vv. 17–18, the presence of this sanctuary indicates that God has restored his relationship with his covenant people (cf. v. 13).

103. Cf. Mell, *Neue Schöpfung*, 156; Stuhlmacher, "Erwägungen," 12–13; Schneider, "Die Idee der Neuschöpfung," 260.

104. In this regard, one should note: 1) the "new heavens and new earth" of Isa 65–66 is described as a "new Jerusalem" in Isa 65:17–18; 2) Jerusalem and Zion traditions are closely linked throughout Isaiah (cf. Isa 33:20; 40:9; 52:1–2, 7–9; 64:10); and 3) cultic concepts and terminology are particularly evident in Isa 66:20–24. See above, esp. pp. 16–17, 35–37, 40, for further discussion of these points.

concept of new creation receives little development in this text.[105] Two features of this account, however, warrant closer consideration. First, this new sanctuary is again linked with Zion traditions.[106] Second, the purification of this temple on Mt. Zion gives rise to the cleansing of the whole earth from the defilement of sin. The discussion of new creation in *Jub.* 4:26 therefore builds upon similar ideas found in *Jub.* 1:7, 27–29.

The parallelism between *Jub.* 1:7–29 and *Jub.* 23:22–31 suggests that the latter passage is also pertinent to this discussion.[107] According to *Jub.* 23:22–31, new creation is preceded by an increase in the sinfulness of God's covenant people and exile from the land (cf. *Jub.* 1:7–14).[108] However, whereas *Jub.* 1:7–29 places great stress on the ethical transformation of the Israelites, the account of new creation in *Jub.* 23:22–31 focuses on their bodily renewal (cf. *Jub.* 23:27–29).[109] This physical rejuvenation is primarily described in *Jub.* 23:27–29 as an increase in life span.[110] The shift from physical decline to restoration pictured in *Jub.* 23:27–29 likely evokes Isa 65:20–23.[111]

The suggestion in *Jub.* 23:27 that the Israelite's life span will eventually approach one thousand years is also worth additional comment. Several scholars propose this statement builds upon *Jub.* 4:29–30, which notes that Adam "lacked seventy years from one thousand years" and alludes to Ps 90:4 MT, which equates one thousand earthly years with a single heavenly "day."[112] The implication in *Jub.* 4:30 is that because Adam ate the fruit of "the tree of knowledge" his life was cut short of the ideal human life span. Returning to *Jub.* 23:27, the gradual rise in human longevity to one thousand years thus represents not only the undoing of the desperate situation described in v. 25 but also should be understood as Israel's return to Adam's glory. The picture

---

105. Hubbard, *New Creation*, 36. Nonetheless, since this statement does place a new sanctuary within the new creation, it testifies to the dominance of this idea within Second Temple Judaism.

106. According to *Jub.* 4:26, Mt. Zion is one of four sacred sites on the earth that will be consecrated in the new creation.

107. Davenport, *Jubilees*, 1–2, 45; Hubbard, *New Creation*, 37–38.

108. It is probable that this link between sin, exile, and restoration is deuteronomic in nature (that is, drawing upon the well-known sin-exile-restoration pattern described in Deut 28–34). Cf. Scott, *Restoration*, 114–17.

109. Hubbard, *New Creation*, 46.

110. *Jub.* 23:27–29 may be understood as a description of the reversal of the decline in human longevity pictured in *Jub.* 23:25.

111. Charles, *Jubilees*, 150; Scott, *Restoration*, 121–25.

112. E.g., Scott, *Restoration*, 117. The allusion to Ps 90:4 MT in *Jub.* 4:30 is found in the phrase "for a thousand years are like one day in the testimony of heaven."

of new creation presented in *Jub.* 23:22–31 thus also includes a subtle indication that the end is presented within an *Urzeit-Endzeit* framework.[113]

Summary of New Creation and Restoration in the Book of Jubilees

An analysis of *Jubilees* sheds significant light on the traditions that underlie new creation in the Pauline literature. First, *Jub.* 1:17, 27–29 and *Jub.* 4:26a point to the presence of a restored temple in Jerusalem within the eschatological age. This temple is connected with Zion traditions within both texts (cf. *Jub.* 1:28bc, 29; 4:26). The presence of this "sanctuary" is directly connected to the phrase καινὴ κτίσις and the renewing of heaven and earth in 1:29. The combination of these textual features thus creates strong links with the "new heavens and new earth" of Isa 65–66. These three texts also depict the inauguration of the eschaton as a multi-faceted program of restoration. Once again, new creation is associated with cosmological renewal (cf. *Jub.* 4:26) and anthropological transformation (cf. *Jub.* 1:17–29; 4:26; 23:27–29).[114] Finally, the suggestion in *Jub.* 23:27 that the Jews will live to one thousand years ultimately aligns the portrait of new creation in *Jubilees* with an *Urzeit-Endzeit* typology (cf. *Jub.* 4:29–30).

Conclusion

Perhaps most importantly, this chapter has demonstrated that new creation is conceived quite broadly within a number of important ancient Jewish texts (both in the OT and from the Second Temple period). When one gives careful attention to the wider context of these passages, it is clear that the restoration associated with new creation is depicted with rather expansive brushstrokes. Generally speaking, the portrait of new creation one attains from these passages is of a reality that is anthropological, cosmological, and

---

113. Cf. Halpern-Amaru, "Jubilees," 142. The importance of Eden within *Jubilees* is also worth noting (see esp. Brooke, "Miqdash Adam," 294). Though this is not made explicit, it is probable that the eschatological sanctuary of *Jub.* 1:28–29; 4:26 is meant to be understood as a restored Eden-temple. This would establish further links between *Jubilees* and an *Urzeit-Endzeit* eschatology.

114. The absence of ecclesiological restoration in Jubilees, however, warrants further comment. This, indeed, is in contrast to expectations found in Isaiah, Ezekiel and *1 Enoch*, and may reflect the pro-Maccabean leanings of the community that produced the book of *Jubilees*.

ecclesiological in scope.¹¹⁵ This evidence calls into question previous attempts to argue that new creation in the Pauline corpus is strictly anthropological, or strictly cosmological, or strictly ecclesiological.¹¹⁶ All four of the texts surveyed in this chapter also link new creation with the establishment of a restored temple (Ezek 37:27-28; 40-48; Jer 38:40 LXX; *1 En.* 25:3-6; 90:28-29; 91:13; *Jub.* 1:28-29; 4:26).¹¹⁷

As already discussed in the analysis of new creation in Isaiah, there are a number of intertextual links between Isa 65:18-25 and Gen 1-3. The presence of these links allows the "new heavens and new earth" of Isa 65-66 to be read within an *Urzeit-Endzeit* typological scheme. This typological pattern is also a prominent feature of a number of the texts discussed in this chapter (cf. Ezek 47:1-12; *1 En.* 25:3-6; 90:37-38; *Jub.* 1:29; 23:22-32). Of these passages, Ezek 47:1-12 and *1 En.* 25:3-6 are especially interesting in that they connect this *Urzeit-Endzeit* typology with a restored temple. These two texts thus seem to foresee a restored Eden-temple in much the same way as Isa 65-66.

Finally, I would like to make a few comments regarding the relevance of *1 Enoch* and *Jubilees* to this project. One of the primary aims of this overall analysis is to understand the meaning of the phrase καινὴ κτίσις in the Hauptbriefe. On one level, the presence of this phrase in *1 En.* 72:1 and *Jub.* 4:29 establishes a strong parallel with 2 Cor 5:17 and Gal 6:15. At the same time, one can readily conclude that there are important differences between these two Second Temple texts and the Pauline corpus.¹¹⁸ Despite these major differences, one should not overlook the fact that, like Paul, the authors of *1 Enoch* and *Jubilees* are fundamentally interpreters of the OT. Thus, their literary creations, as in the case of Paul, bear witness to the OT's semantic potential. Viewing the authors of *1 Enoch* and *Jubilees* as interpreters of the OT gives these two texts a legitimate place at the table in that they provide a measure of validation for the particular reading of new creation in the Pauline tradition offered in this analysis.

---

115. Cf. Ezek 36:26, 29-30, 34-35; 37:26-28; 40-48; Jer 30:20 MT; 31[38]:31-34; 37:18 LXX; 38:40 LXX; *1 En.* 10:3, 18-19, 21; 11:1; 25:3-6; 90:28-29, 32-33; 91:13, 16; *Jub.* 1:17-29; 4:26; 23:27-29.

116. I am here thinking of the work of Hubbard, Mell, and Kraus respectively.

117. Niditch's linking of Ezek 38-48 with ANE temple-building traditions (see above, p. 49) establishes additional parallels between new creation in Ezekiel and Isaiah and further confirms Ezekiel's relevance to this analysis.

118. For example, while *1 Enoch* may be readily described as an apocalypse, the writings of Paul generally do not exhibit any of the *literary* qualities associated with this genre. One could also conclude that Paul has a much more favorable perspective on the fate of Gentiles when compared to the author of *Jubilees*.

4

New Creation in Galatians and 2 Corinthians

Introduction

UP TO THIS POINT, this study has primarily addressed the nature of new creation in the OT and Second Temple Judaism. Taking a panoramic look at these texts reveals several significant commonalities. Perhaps most importantly, we have seen that these disparate traditions all depict new creation in such a way that this concept is closely aligned with cosmological, anthropological, and ecclesiological notions. We have also seen that there is a strong tendency to associate depictions of new creation with primordial conditions, the salvation of the Gentiles, and temple-building.

The primary concern of this chapter is to understand the nature of new creation in Gal 6:11–16 and 2 Cor 5:14–17. As already noted, scholarly efforts to investigate new creation in the Pauline tradition have chiefly focused on these two texts.[1] I have also observed the propensity among some interpreters to limit the scope of new creation in these passages to either cosmology, anthropology, or ecclesiology.[2] A significant matter for consideration within this analysis will be determining the degree to which such narrow conceptions of new creation in 2 Corinthians and Galatians represent legitimate appraisals of the meaning of this theological concept.

---

1. These are indeed the two central segments of 2 Corinthians and Galatians where Paul most explicitly expresses his understanding of new creation. The extent to which new creation is associated with temple imagery in the OT, Second Temple Judaism, and the letter to the Ephesians, however, also raises the question of how Paul's description of the church as the "temple of the living God" in 2 Cor 6:16 might be related to the scope of new creation in 2 Cor 5:14–17. This is an area of inquiry that has been overlooked in prior studies of this subject and will comprise an important aspect of my contribution to this ongoing debate.

2. This is especially true of the works of Mell, Hubbard, and Kraus on this subject.

New Creation in Galatians 6:14–16

From the outset of this letter, Paul makes the seriousness of the threat to the Galatian churches patently clear. While Paul begins this letter with his customary greeting (Gal 1:1–5), he nonetheless departs from his standard practice by omitting a statement of thanksgiving. Instead, Paul immediately scolds the Galatian believers for their willingness to entertain a "different gospel" (v. 6). The very nature of the nature of Jesus Christ is thus a central concern within this letter.

Paul's chief discussion of new creation in his letter to the Galatians occurs within Gal 6:14–16. These statements constitute part of this letter's postscript and as such provide a concise summary of the entire letter.[3] The points of contact between Gal 6:11–18 and the remainder of this letter have already been extensively discussed in a number of helpful works.[4] The following analysis of Gal 6:11–18 will therefore focus on providing a detailed exegesis of this passage that aims to understand the central meaning of καινὴ κτίσις in v. 15.

The Immediate Context of Galatians 6:11–13

Galatians 6:11–13 begins with a statement that directly highlights the significance of this section within the overall letter (v. 11). The clause ἴδετε πηλίκοις ὑμῖν γράμμασιν ἔγραψα in v. 11 has a distinct rhetorical function in that it draws attention to the subsequent statements and may be helpfully described as the ancient equivalent of bold or italics print.[5] The remainder of v. 11 (τῇ ἐμῇ χειρί) indicates Paul has ceased using an amanuensis and has taken up the pen himself (cf. Rom 16:22; 1 Cor 16:21; Col 4:18; 2 Thess 3:17; Phlm 19).

Paul then immediately returns to the central problem he is attempting to address in his correspondence with the Galatian churches—the place of Torah in the new age (vv. 12–13). The focus in Gal 6:12–13 is on clarifying the fundamental motivations of the Galatian agitators.[6] Galatians 6:12

---

3. Cf. Betz, *Galaterbrief*, 529–32; Weima, "Hermeneutical Key," 90–93. Lührmann (*Galater*, 100) observes that the extended length of this subscription (when compared to Paul's other letters) testifies to the seriousness with which Paul viewed the theological crisis confronting the Galatian church.

4. E.g., Weima, "Hermeneutical Key," 93–106.

5. Cf. Longenecker, *Galatians*, 290; Matera, *Galatians*, 224, 229–30; Martyn, *Galatians*, 560. For the comparison with modern fonts, see Dunn (*Galatians*, 335) and Betz (*Galaterbrief*, 532–33).

6. While the identity of the agitators remains a fairly contested issue, it seems safe

begins with the rather gnomic statement ὅσοι θέλουσιν εὐπροσωπῆσαι ἐν σαρκί. According to some scholars, the phrase ἐν σαρκί in v. 12 refers to the rite of circumcision.[7] Hubbard persuasively argues on the basis of several factors, however, that the construction ἐν σαρκί here draws upon the Spirit-flesh opposition so important within Paul's theology and his "biography of reversal" in Gal 1–2 (cf. Gal 1:10, 13–14; 3:3; 5:16; Phil 3:1–6).[8] While it may be nothing more than mere coincidence, Hubbard's observation that Paul's treatments of new creation in Gal 6:11–18 and 2 Cor 5:11–21 are both "introduced by means of an internal-external antithesis" is at least worth observing (cf. 2 Cor 5:12).[9]

The remainder of Gal 6:12 shifts from describing the general bent of Paul's opponents to specifying their precise aim in relation to the Gentile Christ-followers in Galatia (v. 12bc). The clause οὗτοι ἀναγκάζουσιν ὑμᾶς περιτέμνεσθαι focuses Paul's polemic against these agitators on their attempt to convince the Galatian believers of the need to undergo the rite of circumcision (cf. Gal 2:3–5; 5:2–3; 6:13; Josephus, *Ant.* 13:257–58; *Vita* 112–13).[10] The clause μόνον ἵνα τῷ σταυρῷ τοῦ Χριστοῦ μὴ διώκωνται then expresses another motivation underlying the actions of the agitators—the desire to avoid persecution. The historicity of this revealing statement has not gone unchallenged.[11] Scholars also debate the identity of the potential persecutors of these Jewish Christians and the basis of their animosity. Jewett represents

---

to conclude that there is still a strong consensus among interpreters that they were Jewish Christians from Jerusalem. See Sumney ("Studying Paul's Opponents," 17–24) for a recent summary of research on this issue.

7. Cf. Dunn, *Galatians*, 336; Martyn, *Galatians*, 561; Bruce, *Galatians*, 268.

8. Hubbard, *New Creation*, 210–11. Hubbard appeals to: 1) the "maxim-like character" of Gal 6:12a; 2) the presence of the article in Gal 6:13c (in contrast to the anarthrous phrase ἐν σαρκί in v 12a); and 3) the use of the pronoun ὑμετέρᾳ in v. 13c. Cf. Jervis, *Galatians*, 157; Mussner, *Galaterbrief*, 411.

9. Hubbard, *New Creation*, 211.

10. It is generally conceded that the place of circumcision within Judaism derives from its status as a central symbol of God's covenant with Abraham and his physical descendants (cf. Gen 17:1–14; 1 Macc 2:46). On the importance of circumcision within early Judaism, see Cohen (*Jewishness*, 39–47).

11. A number of scholars argue that the polemical nature of Gal 6:11–18 makes it is difficult to determine how much of Paul's statements in vv. 12–13 actually conform to reality. Cf. Sumney, "Servants," 136; Mussner, *Galaterbrief*, 412; de Boer, "New Preachers," 47–48. No doubt, the adverb μόνον in v. 12 is at least somewhat rhetorical (so for example Dunn, *Galatians*, 336). Nonetheless, Paul's reminder of his own personal familiarity with suffering (διώκομαι) due to his law-free gospel in Gal 5:11 supports the historical value of Gal 6:12c (cf. Gal 4:29). For further discussion of the place of persecution within this letter, see Wilson (*Curse*, 79–89), Hardin (*Galatians*, 101–2), and Baasland ("Persecution," 144–47).

an important voice within this discussion. According to Jewett, the Galatian agitators were seeking to avoid reprisals from Judean Zealots attempting to purify Israel from pagan influence.[12] Given the widespread nationalistic concerns within first-century Judaism, Jewett's proposal aligns the concern of the agitators too closely with a specific group.[13] In light of the portrait Paul has already painted of his opponents in this letter, it is best to conclude that these Jewish Christians feared opposition from either individuals in the Jerusalem church or Jews in general (cf. Gal 2:3–12; 4:29).[14]

The presence of the phrase τῷ σταυρῷ τοῦ Χριστοῦ in v. 12c greatly aids in clarifying the nature of Paul's polemic in this context. The dative construction τῷ σταυρῷ in v. 12 is likely a dative of cause and suggests that Paul's opponents are striving to avoid persecution that might arise from unacceptable beliefs regarding the significance of Christ's death. Judging from Paul's prior statements in this letter, the agitators probably did not conclude that the death of Jesus "was a sufficient basis for acceptance into the inheritance of Israel" (cf. Gal 2:18–21; 3:1–2, 10–13; 5:2–6, 11).[15] According to Paul, these Jewish Christians preached a "different gospel" (Gal 1:6) in order to avoid persecution by requiring Gentile believers to undergo circumcision and essentially thus establishing them as proselytes to Judaism.[16]

Paul further castigates his opponents by questioning their commitment to Torah (v. 13a). Despite a long history of debate, most interpreters now argue on contextual grounds that the present participle περιτεμνόμενοι refers to the agitators.[17] Scholars have also understood Gal 6:13a in a variety of ways and have proposed a number of historical reconstructions to clarify

12. Jewett, "Agitators," 198–212. Cf. Longenecker, *Galatians*, xci–xciv, 291; Bruce, *Galatians*, 269; Weima, "Hermeneutical Key," 97; pace Nanos, *Irony*, 209–11; Matera, *Galatians*, 230; de Boer, "New Preachers," 48.

13. There are also a number of historical concerns related to Jewett's understanding of the Zealot movement. See Wright (*People of God*, 175–91) for further discussion.

14. Several scholars also argue that the agitators were compelling Gentile circumcision in order to avoid persecution from the Roman authorities by more closely aligning the Christ-faith with Judaism and thus benefiting from the latter's status as an official religion of the Roman Empire. Cf. Vouga, *Galater*, 155–56; Hardin, *Galatians*, 90, 113–15; Lührmann, *Galatians*, 101. While within the realm of possibility, it seems more likely that the primary threat to the Galatian agitators would have come from Jews or Jewish Christ-followers. Cf. Dunn, *Galatians*, 336.

15. Dunn, *Galatians*, 337.

16. Cf. Betz, *Galaterbrief*, 536.

17. Cf. Martyn, *Galatians*, 563; Matera, *Galatians*, 225; de Boer, "New Preachers," 47, 49; Longenecker, *Galatians*, 92–93; Schreiner, *Galatians*, 378. Note especially the introductory γάρ and the personal pronoun ὑμᾶς in v. 13.

Paul's rather enigmatic statement.[18] The terseness of Paul's charge suggests that rather than making a historical claim regarding the agitators' relationship to Torah, Paul is instead making a theological assertion regarding their ability to obey the Torah.[19] Though this is a matter of intense debate, Paul may have earlier implied in this letter that nomistic observance only has eternal benefit for those who faultlessly keep the divine law. Paul further demonstrates the primacy of faith over works-righteousness in Gal 3:10 by appealing to Deut 27:26, which suggests that those who do not flawlessly obey all the laws of Torah are cursed.[20] Furthermore, Paul informs his addressees in Gal 5:3 that anyone who undergoes the rite of circumcision is obligated to submit themselves to all of Torah's ethical obligations.[21] Underlying Paul's argument in these two texts is the implied premise that no one can perfectly obey the divine law.[22] When read in the light of Gal 3:10 and Gal 5:3, Paul's statement in Gal 6:13a thus encourages the Gentile Christ-followers in Galatia to consider the inevitable hypocrisy of the agitators.

Despite the ambiguity behind Paul's initial words in v. 13, it is clear that in his assessment, the agitators' mission was purely self-serving (v. 13b). The clause ἵνα ἐν τῇ ὑμετέρᾳ σαρκὶ καυχήσωνται in v. 13 again details another motivation of Paul's opponents and closely mirrors the introductory statement ὅσοι θέλουσιν εὐπροσωπῆσαι ἐν σαρκί in v. 12. The noun σαρκί

---

18. Of the conjectures offered regarding this statement, the following are worth mentioning: 1) the agitators engaged in the same form of selective obedience (cf. Gal 5:3) they permitted of their Gentile converts (so Martyn, *Galatians*, 563; de Boer, "New Preachers," 49-50); 2) Paul is comparing the agitators' paltry commitment to the ethical demands of Torah with his much stricter dedication when he was a Pharisee (so Barclay, *Obeying*, 65); and 3) they failed to grasp the ultimate intent of Torah in that they did not pursue the welfare of Gentiles (so Nanos, *Irony*, 228-29).

19. Betz (*Galaterbrief*, 537) similarly notes the challenge of knowing with certainty what form of historical claim Paul might be making in Gal 6:13a.

20. This traditional reading of Gal 3:10 is advocated by such scholars as Longenecker, *Galatians*, 118, 226-27; Longenecker, *Triumph*, 139-42; Das, *Law*, 145-70; Schreiner, "Perfect Obedience," 151-60; Hong, *Law*, 107-9. Recent years have seen concerted attempts to read Gal 3:10 in light of Paul's allusion to Deut 27:26 and the broader blessing/curse framework of Deut 27-30. See Morales (*Restoration of Israel*, 88-96) for further discussion of scholarly literature on this subject.

21. Galatians 5:3 plays an important role in Paul's argument in Gal 5:1-6 in that it supports his central claim that only two paths to right standing with God are available to all of humanity (παντὶ ἀνθρώπῳ) . . . faith in Jesus Christ alone (cf. Gal 2:16; 5:2, 4) or complete obedience to the whole Torah (ὅλον τὸν νόμον). Paul identifies the latter option (nomism) with a "yoke of slavery" and the former with "freedom" (Gal 5:1). On the continuity between Gal 5:3 and the understanding of obedience to the Law in Second Temple Judaism, see Das (*Law*, 12-69). Cf. *Jub.* 1:22-24; 5:19; 21:23; 23:16; 1QH 9:36; 1QS 3:6-12; Philo, *Deus* 162; *Migr.* 127-30.

22. Cf. Rom 3:9-26; 7:7-25; 11:32; Gal 3:22; Phil 3:6; Jas 2:10-11.

in v. 13b conceivably refers to the rite of circumcision.²³ The link between self-aggrandizement (καυχήσωνται) and circumcision in v. 13b strongly evokes the critique of works-righteousness elsewhere in the Pauline corpus (note also the use of the noun νόμος in v. 13a).²⁴ While it is possible that Paul is here condemning the agitators' attempt to curry favor with God by amassing Gentile converts, Longenecker's suggestion that their efforts to circumcise Gentile Christ-followers was an attempt to avoid persecution from adherents to Judaism deserves serious consideration (cf. v. 12).²⁵

New Creation in Galatians 6:14–16

At Gal 6:14, Paul begins to contrast himself sharply with the agitators. The first of these contrasts relates to their fundamental objectives (v. 14a).²⁶ Whereas the agitators gloried in the opinions of others (v. 12a) and in their missionary accomplishments (v. 13b), Paul gloried only in the cross of Christ (v. 14a).²⁷ Betz rightly notes, "solches 'Rühmen im Herrn' genau genommen gar kein Rühmen ist."²⁸ The noun σταυρός is employed in v. 14 as a metonym for Jesus' death and resurrection, and plays an important role in Paul's argument within this letter (cf. Gal 1:1, 4; 2:15–21; 3:1–3, 13–14, 23–26; 4:1–10; 5:11, 16–25).²⁹

The remainder of v. 14 then elaborates on the significance of the cross and clarifies the grounds of Paul's cruciform boasting.³⁰ The noun κόσμος carries a great deal of exegetical weight in Gal 6:14b (evidenced by its repetition). Given that this noun stands parallel to the expression καινὴ κτίσις in Gal 6:15b, its relevance to this project is heightened even further.³¹ Three

---

23. The phrase ἐν τῇ ὑμετέρᾳ in v. 13 points in this direction.

24. Cf. Rom 2:17–25; 3:20–27; 4:1–3; Eph 2:8–10; Phil 3:3–6. On the account of Paul's relationship to Torah offered by adherents to the "new perspective" on Paul, see below, p. 146.

25. Longenecker, *Galatians*, 293. The former option—Paul's opponents are seeking to merit right standing before God—represents the traditional account of v. 13 and is advocated by such scholars as Bruce (*Galatians*, 270).

26. Weima, "Hermeneutical Key," 93–94.

27. Cf. 1 Cor 1:31; 2 Cor 5:12–15; 10:17; Gal 1:10; 6:4; Phil 3:3–11. The repetition of the verb καυχάομαι in v. 14a makes it especially likely that Paul is seeking to draw a comparison between himself and the agitators.

28. Betz, *Galaterbrief*, 539. Cf. Martyn, *Galatians*, 563.

29. Cf. Weima, "Hermeneutical Key," 103–4.

30. The antecedent of the relative pronoun οὗ in v. 14b is probably the dative noun σταυρῷ (cf. Vouga, *Galater*, 156; Mussner, *Galaterbrief*, 414).

31. On the parallelism between κόσμος and καινὴ κτίσις in Gal 6:14–15, see Weima

literary contexts illuminate Paul's usage of the noun κόσμος in v. 14: 1) the apocalyptic eschatology of Second Temple Judaism; 2) the broader context of Paul's theology; and 3) Paul's earlier statements in Galatians.[32] Each of these contexts will be examined in the following analysis, though particular stress will be given to Paul's response to the Galatian crisis.

Since the apocalyptic eschatology of Second Temple Judaism comprises the primary background for understanding Paul's use of κόσμος in Gal 6:14, we will begin there. The relationship between the Pauline writings and these Jewish traditions is a well-known subject of debate. The portrait of an apocalyptic Paul goes as far back as Albert Schweitzer's monograph, *The Mysticism of St. Paul*.[33] Schweitzer's reading of Paul, however, was soon challenged by the demythologizing program of R. Bultmann. Bultmann's intensely anthropological interpretation of Paul was then shortly opposed by Käsemann, who famously described apocalyptic as "the mother of all Christian theology."[34] Käsemann's portrayal of Pauline theology has in turn exerted a strong degree of influence on recent interpreters, especially the important work of J. Beker and J. L. Martyn.[35] This enthusiasm for an "apoc-

---

("Hermeneutical Key," 101).

32. Prior to discussing the precise nature of the apocalyptic eschatology of Second Temple Judaism, it is necessary to make a few important terminological distinctions. First, the term "apocalypticism" refers to the worldview or set of beliefs associated with this particular eschatological understanding of the final stages of human history. Second, the term "apocalypse" refers to the genre of literature within Second Temple Judaism that particularly emphasizes the revelation of cosmic secrets and provides detailed portraits of the end (e.g., 1 Enoch). Third, the phrase "apocalyptic eschatology" is used to refer to the eschatology characteristic of these Jewish apocalypses. Fourth, the adjective "apocalyptic" is best reserved as a designation for the language, topics, and ideas associated with apocalyptic eschatology. Cf. Aune, "Apocalypticism," 25–26.

33. See Schweitzer, *Mysticism*, esp. 23–25, 36–40.

34. Käsemann, *Questions*, 102.

35. See especially Beker (*Paul*, 16–19, 143–59) and Martyn ("Apocalyptic Antinomies," 410–24). Martyn's apocalyptic reading of this letter requires further discussion because of the significance he assigns to Gal 6:13–15 for understanding the whole letter. According to Martyn (ibid., 114–15), within Gal 6:13–15 Paul appeals to the notion prevalent in the ancient world that "the structure of the cosmos lies in pairs of opposites" (what Martyn terms "antinomies"). His understanding of this passage heavily stresses the nature of the argument in vv. 14–15. Within vv. 14–15, Paul correlates the death of the world with: 1) the irrelevance of circumcision and uncircumcision (which Martyn describes as an antinomy); and 2) new creation. For Martyn (ibid., 117), the presence of this antinomy sandwiched in between two fundamentally cosmic statements suggests that "the letter [Galatians] is about the death of one world, and the advent of another." Cf. Martyn, *Galatians*, 22–23, 99–100, 102, 105, 570–74. Martyn's interpretation of Galatians helpfully highlights this letter's apocalyptic qualities, its stress on inaugurated eschatology, and serves as an important corrective to Beker's non-apocalyptic reading of Galatians (e.g., Beker, *Paul*, 57–58).

alyptic Paul," however, has been rightly criticized by B. Matlock.[36] It is particularly important to note that Matlock's concerns regarding an apocalyptic reading of Paul seem to have heavily influenced Hubbard and Y. Kwon, who both strongly question the place of inaugurated eschatology in Galatians.[37] With this discussion of the history of interpretation in mind, I will now briefly examine the relevance of apocalyptic eschatology for comprehending Paul's use of the noun κόσμος in Gal 6:14.

The primary aspect of Jewish apocalyptic eschatology that is pertinent to this discussion is its distinction between "the present age" and "the age to come." Within these ancient Jewish texts, the former notion depicts this present world as a time of evil, sin and suffering, while the latter portrays the world to come as an era of righteousness, truth, and eternal bliss (cf. *4 Ezra* 4:26-27; 6:7; 7:12-13, 50, 113; 8:1; *2 En.* 66:6; *L. A. B.* 3:9-10; 4Q215a 2:2-6). What is vital to consider when shifting from these apocalyptic texts to the Pauline corpus is that this two-part schema becomes altered to account for the eschatological significance of Christ's death and resurrection (cf. 1 Cor 1:20; 2:6, 8; 3:18; 10:11; Gal 1:4; 4:4; Eph 1:20-22; 2:7; 1 Tim 6:17; Titus 2:12). That is, while the apocalyptic eschatology of Second Temple Judaism anticipates a future act of divine intervention, Paul looked to the past and understood the Christ-event as God's response to the suffering of the present. Paul, however, still has room for a final act of divine intervention and does not contend that the consummation has arrived in its fullest sense (e.g., Rom 8:18-25; 1 Cor 15:20-28). For Paul, the present may thus be understood as an era of eschatological tension—a time in which believers now enjoy the benefits of God's inauguration of the future in the present, while at the same time anxiously awaiting the definitive completion of his redemptive plan (e.g., Rom 8:18-25).[38]

While there is much to appreciate about Martyn's reading of Galatians, it does present a few significant problems. First, appealing to this antinomy tradition seems unnecessary given that one is able to reach similar conclusions if sufficient weight is given to the Jewish apocalyptic traditions (traditions that Martyn himself emphasizes in his reading of Galatians) that inform Paul's eschatology. Second, Martyn (like Beker) unnecessarily separates Paul's apocalyptic gospel in Galatians from redemptive history and God's covenantal relationship with the people of Israel. According to Martyn ("Events in Galatia," 179), the Paul of Galatians does not "present as his theology a form of *Heilsgeschichte* in which Christ is interpreted in line with Israel's history" (cf. Beker, *Paul*, 51-56; pace Wright, *Climax*, 259-67).

36. Matlock, *Unveiling the Apocalyptic Paul*, esp. 11-19.

37. Cf. Kwon, *Eschatology*, 1-18; Hubbard, *New Creation*, 189, 225.

38. On this eschatological tension in Paul, see especially the important work of Cullmann (*Christ and Time*, esp. 32-33, 81-93).

While a thorough discussion of Paul's inaugurated eschatology outside of Galatians is beyond the scope of this present analysis, a few preliminary comments are nonetheless helpful.[39] First, it is clear that for Paul, the present may be aptly described as the beginning of the end (e.g., 1 Cor 10:11; 15:20-24; 2 Cor 6:2). Second, within his eschatological schema, Paul still has room for the cosmological renewal of reality as the clause "for the present form of this world is passing away" (παράγει γὰρ τὸ σχῆμα τοῦ κόσμου τούτου) in 1 Cor 7:31 indicates (cf. 1 John 2:17).[40] Third, it is apparent from Paul's critique of worldly wisdom in 1 Cor 1:20; 3:18-19 that the nouns αἰών and κόσμος are close synonyms in the Hauptbriefe (cf. 4 Ezra 7:112-13).

The presence of this inaugurated eschatology is evident at a number of key points in the letter to the Galatians. Paul, in fact, highlights the presence of the new age from the very opening of his response to the Galatian crisis.[41] The parenthetical reference to Christ's resurrection in Gal 1:1 (τοῦ ἐγείραντος αὐτὸν ἐκ νεκρῶν) introduces a motif that implicitly undergirds the remainder of the letter (cf. Rom 4:24; 8:11).[42] Paul's introductory statement in v. 1 thus suggests that through Christ's resurrection, "God the Father" has inaugurated the new age.[43] Another relevant parenthetical statement occurs in the letter opening at Gal 1:4. Paul here describes Christ's sacrificial death (τοῦ δόντος ἑαυτὸν ὑπὲρ τῶν ἁμαρτιῶν ἡμῶν) and then specifies its purpose (ὅπως). According to Gal 1:4, Christ died to free (ἐξέληται) humanity from the clutches of "the present evil age" (cf. Rom 12:2; 1 Cor 3:18; 2 Cor 4:4).[44] Gal 1:4 thus clearly places Paul's soteriology within this letter in strong continuity with the apocalyptic eschatology of early Judaism.[45]

---

39. See Dunn (*Theology*, 461-98) for further discussion of the eschatological structure of Paul's theology.

40. See Adams (*Constructing the World*, 130-36) for a discussion of Paul's apocalyptic *and* cosmological perspective in 1 Cor 7:29-31.

41. Pace Hubbard, *New Creation*, 192.

42. According to Wright (*Resurrection*, 219), "Resurrection is not a main theme in Galatians, but neither the overall argument nor the detail is comprehensible without it." The resurrection from the dead is an important feature of eschatological expectation in some elements of Second Temple Judaism (e.g., 2 Macc 7:9-36; *Apoc. Mos.* 13:3-4; 28:4; 41:3; 43:2). Cf. Ezek 37:1-14; Dan 12:1-3; Hos 6:1-2. Interestingly, the hope of resurrection is associated with an *Urzeit-Endzeit* eschatology and anthropological renewal ("for the evil heart shall be removed from them") in *Apoc. Mos.* 13:3-4.

43. Cf. Dunn, *Galatians*, 29; Schlier, *Galater*, 34.

44. The verb ἐξαιρέω is associated with the exodus in such texts as Exod 3:8; 18:4, 8-10. Paul thus implicitly portrays Christ's redemption of humanity as a second exodus (cf. Isa 60:16; Ezek 34:27; Bar 2:14). Cf. Kirchschläger, "Gal 1,4," 337.

45. Cf. Martyn, *Galatians*, 97-98, 101; pace Kwon, *Eschatology*, 156-61.

The presence of crucifixion imagery and the implicit discussion of Christ's resurrection in Gal 2:19 also shed light on Paul's statement in Gal 6:14. The clause ἐμοὶ κόσμος ἐσταύρωται in Gal 6:14 is frequently regarded as a parallel image to the clause Χριστῷ συνεσταύρωμαι in Gal 2:19.[46] As with Gal 5:24, there is a strong emphasis within this passage on the believing community's union with the risen Christ. This sense of solidarity is conveyed through the Χριστῷ συνεσταύρωμαι clause in v. 19 and the construction ζῶ δὲ οὐκέτι ἐγώ ζῇ δὲ ἐν ἐμοὶ Χριστός in v. 20. The clause Χριστῷ συνεσταύρωμαι in Gal 2:19 serves as a climactic summary of the death-life imagery (ἀπέθανον . . . ζήσω) in v. 19 and highlights the fundamental break with the old age. More specifically, the death-life imagery in Gal 2:19 situates Paul's statement directly within his old age/new age antithesis and contributes to his larger discussion in Galatians of the transient nature of the Mosaic law (cf. Gal 3:15—4:11).[47]

Though he leaves this unstated, Christ's resurrection remains a critical element within Paul's argument in Gal 2:19-20.[48] The purpose clause ἵνα θεῷ ζήσω in v. 19 indicates that a theocentric existence forms a critical element of Paul's rhetoric in this text. The remainder of Gal 2:19c-20 suggests that this theocentric existence is decisively grounded in the Christ-event. While Paul's focus in vv. 19-20 is clearly on death (both his and Christ's), the more positive aspect of the death-life metaphor presumably forms a crucial element in Paul's line of reasoning. The significance of Christ's resurrection in Rom 6:1-6 testifies to the relevance of the resurrection for understanding Paul's statements in Gal 2:19-20.[49] The manner in which Paul links Christ's resurrection in Rom 6:4 (ὥσπερ ἠγέρθη Χριστὸς ἐκ νεκρῶν) with a new mode of eschatological existence (καινότητι ζωῆς) particularly suggests that resurrection plays a critical role in Gal 2:19-20. As already noted, Christ's resurrection forms an important aspect of Paul's old age/new age antithesis.[50] The inauguration of the new age thus features strongly in Paul's argument in

---

46. Cf. Mell, *Neue Schöpfung*, 296-97, 316-17; Bruce, *Galatians*, 271; Mussner, *Galaterbrief*, 414.

47. The expression διὰ νόμου in Gal 2:19 is critical for understanding Paul's perspective on the role of Torah in that it suggests the law itself points to its own impermanence (cf. Rom 7:4; Gal 3:19-26). Cf. Schreiner, *Galatians*, 170-71.

48. Cf. Silva, "Galatians," 149.

49. The conceptual parallels between these two passages, especially with regard to the focus on ethics within both texts (cf. Rom 6:1-2; Gal 2:19ab) and the presence of the death-life metaphor, are worth observing.

50. The introductory clause ἐγὼ γὰρ διὰ νόμου νόμῳ ἀπέθανον in Gal 2:19 probably forms part of Paul's old age/new age antithesis (cf. Rom 6:2, 10-11; 7:2-6).

this letter and the parallelism between Gal 2:19–20 and Gal 6:14 has important implications for understanding new creation in Gal 6:15.

Paul also highlights the eschatological thrust of this letter in Gal 4:4. Here Paul places God's act of sending his son within an eschatological frame of reference by means of the phrase τὸ πλήρωμα τοῦ χρόνου. Through this phrase, Paul again aligns himself closely with ideas found in the apocalyptic writings of Second Temple Judaism.[51] With this apocalyptic worldview in mind, it is then likely that the sending of God's son in "the fullness of time" marks the dawn of the new age.[52]

Since Gal 6:15a fundamentally addresses the status of Torah, it is worth observing that Gal 4:4 also occurs in one of the main passages (Gal 3:15—4:11) within the letter in which Paul argues for the abrogation of the Mosaic law.[53] Gal 4:1–10 specifically contrasts the present freedom of Christ-followers with their former state of servitude to "the elemental spirits of the world" (cf. v. 3).[54] Furthermore, Gal 4:1–3 draws a comparison between the provisional nature of a tutor's supervision of an heir and the Christ-followers' (οὕτως καὶ ἡμεῖς [v. 3]) former enslavement to τὰ στοιχεῖα τοῦ κόσμου (v. 3). Paul's brief statement in v. 4 serves as the hinge upon which this existential transference from slavery to freedom is grounded. The use of an expression so strongly associated with early Jewish apocalyptic eschatology in v. 4 indicates that Paul is linking the coming of Christ with the dawn of the new era. We may thus conclude that a critical element in Paul's response to nomistic observance in Galatia is the equating of life under the dominion of the law with life in the old age and freedom from the law with participation in the new age.[55]

At this point, we now are able to discuss the use of the noun κόσμου in Gal 4:9. Arnold rightly suggests, "the whole phrase [τὰ στοιχεῖα τοῦ κόσμου]

---

51. Cf. 1QS 4:18–20; 1QpHab 7:2, 13. Similar ideas and language are also found elsewhere in the NT (e.g., Mark 1:15; Acts 7:17; Eph 1:10; Heb 1:2).

52. Cf. Schlier, *Galater*, 195; de Boer, *Galatians*, 211.

53. Galatians 4:1–11 represents one of Paul's more negative assessments of Torah. Christ is described as "born under the law" in v. 4. In v. 5, Paul provides the underlying purpose (ἵνα) behind Christ's incarnation (cf. v. 4b)—to liberate humanity from its enslavement to the law (ὑπὸ νόμον) and thereby shift the status of Christ-followers from that of slaves to that of children of God (cf. vv. 6–7). Furthermore, in close relation to his second use of the noun στοιχεῖα in v. 9, Paul also refers to various aspects of the Jewish religious calendar (ἡμέρας, μῆνας, καιρούς, ἐνιαυτούς) in Gal 4:10 (cf. Rom 14:5–6; Col 2:16–17; Josephus, *Ant.* 3:91; 11:294; 14:264; *Ag. Ap.* 2:282).

54. The identity of τὰ στοιχεῖα τοῦ κόσμου is a matter of intense debate (cf. Col 2:8, 20–21). See de Boer ("Meaning," 204–7) and Moses (*Practices*, 134–147) for helpful summaries of scholarly research on the meaning of this difficult phrase.

55. Longenecker, *Triumph*, 55; Hong, *Law*, 166–69.

is not a fixed title or expression" and this is the most plausible means of accounting for the use of the abbreviated expression τὰ στοιχεῖα in Gal 4:9.[56] If this is the case, one must evaluate the significance of the noun κόσμος in this rather perplexing expression. The genitive construction τοῦ κόσμου in Gal 4:3 is almost certainly a descriptive genitive and may be further classified as an attributive genitive (i.e., "the worldly elements"). Regardless of the specific nuance one attributes to the construction τοῦ κόσμου in Gal 4:3, it is likely that Paul is placing τὰ στοιχεῖα within his larger discussion of the eschatological significance of Christ's death (Gal 1:4; 2:19–21; 3:13–29; 4:21–31; 5:13–26).[57] In other words, Paul views τὰ στοιχεῖα in much the same light as the powers of sin and the flesh—as fundamental features of the old age that have succumbed to Christ's victorious death, yet remain active until Christ's reign is fully established at the culmination of human history.[58]

The use of the crucifixion metaphor in Gal 5:24 also clarifies Paul's statement in Gal 6:14b. Within Gal 5:24, Paul states that those who have been united with Christ (τοῦ Χριστοῦ) have also crucified the flesh (τὴν σάρκα

---

56. Arnold, "Returning," 65. With regard to the identity of the στοιχεῖα in Gal 4:3, 9, the clause ἐδουλεύσατε τοῖς φύσει μὴ οὖσιν θεοῖς in Gal 4:8 provides an important clue to its meaning. Several interpreters note the conceptual similarity between this clause and the clause εἴπερ εἰσὶν λεγόμενοι θεοί in 1 Cor 8:5 (e.g., Betz, *Galaterbrief*, 374; Bruce, *Galatians*, 201–2; Longenecker, *Triumph*, 50). Within the larger context of 1 Cor 8, Paul's assertion denies a genuine reality to the idols being worshiped in the pagan temples of Corinth (cf. Deut 6:4; 1 Cor 8:4). However, while Paul again denies that an "idol is anything" in 1 Cor 10:19, he nonetheless asserts these idols are in fact pawns of demonic forces (cf. Arnold, "Returning," 60).

The Jewish concept of territorial deities likely underlies Paul's discussion of the relationship between physical idols and cosmic evil in both Gal 4 and 1 Cor 8–10 (cf. Deut 32:8–9; Dan 10:13–14, 20–21; Sir 17:17; *1 En.* 20:5; *Jub.* 11:4–5; 15:31–32). According to Longenecker (*Triumph*, 51), these are angelic beings that were believed to "oversee the nations on behalf of God." Linking the στοιχεῖα in Gal 4 with these territorial spirits would explain why Paul uses the language of guardianship and administration (ἐπιτρόπους, οἰκονόμους) in v. 2 and enslavement (δεδουλωμένοι) in v. 3. The existence of evil angels within Paul's worldview then allows one to account for the assessment of the law presented in Gal 4:3–10. According to Arnold ("Returning," 69), while Paul does not equate the law with τὰ στοιχεῖα in this passage, he does nonetheless argue, "Just as sin and the flesh use the law as a base of operations, so do the evil principalities and powers" (i.e., τὰ στοιχεῖα). Cf. Woyke, "Paulus," 231.

The chief argument against the association of τὰ στοιχεῖα with "demonic forces" is the absence of texts from the first century CE that use the noun στοιχεῖα with that meaning (so for example, Schweizer, "Slaves," 455, 466). Arnold ("Returning," 57–59), however, argues the meaning "demonic forces" may be reflected in *T. Sol.* 8:1–2; 18:1–2 and *2 En.* 16:7.

57. The emphasis on provisionality and enslavement (both to the law and to evil cosmic forces) in Gal 4:1–9 confirms this suggestion.

58. Cf. Arnold, "Returning," 65, 67–70; Jackson, *New Creation*, 90–91; Adams, *Constructing the World*, 229–30.

ἐσταύρωσαν). This remark concerning the flesh's crucifixion in v. 24 summarizes Paul's discussion in Gal 5:13-23, where he issues a call for freedom grounded in love for others (vv. 13-15) and life in the Spirit (vv. 16-23). Paul's statements in Gal 5:24 also recall Gal 2:19-20, where Paul has already closely related participation in the Christ-event with crucifixion imagery.

The presence of the πνεῦμα/σάρξ antithesis in Gal 5:13-26 suggests that the noun σάρξ in v. 24 encompasses more than humanity's fallen nature and is also to be understood within an eschatological framework.[59] Paul's negative portrait of σάρξ in Gal 5:24 is strikingly similar to texts within Second Temple Judaism that associate humanity's evil inclination (*yēṣer*) with the activity of Belial/Satan (e.g., *T. Ash.* 1:8; *T. Jud.* 19:4—20:5; 1QH 15:2-3).[60] As with Gal 2:19-20, Paul's use of crucifixion imagery in v. 24 again positions this discussion within his old age/new age antithesis (cf. Gal 1:4; 2:19-20).[61] The image is used in Gal 5:24, however, to describe the Christ-follower's decisive break with the old age and participation (note the phrase οἱ δὲ τοῦ Χριστοῦ in v. 24) in the new.[62] For some scholars, the transcendent nature of the Spirit also suggests that σάρξ in this context is to be understood as a cosmic (in this case, demonic) power that is able to exert its influence upon the lives of Christ-followers (cf. Rom 8:6, 12).[63] Paul's brief remark regarding the flesh's crucifixion in v. 24 thus belongs within the framework of his inaugurated eschatology and may also resonate with his apocalyptic worldview.[64]

---

59. The importance of this contrast between the "Spirit" and the "flesh" within Paul's argument in Galatians is especially evident in Gal 3:3; 4:28-29; 5:13, 16 (cf. Rom 7:5-6; 8:1-13; Phil 3:3; 1QH 7:21-22; 12:29-33).

60. Cf. Marcus, "Evil Inclination," 17. On the evil *yēṣer* in early Jewish tradition, see esp. Gen 6:5; 8:21; 1QH 18:22-23; 1QS 4:19-21; 5:4-5; 11:9-10. See Frey ("Antithese," 54-67) for further discussion of the Jewish background of this theological construction.

61. Cf. Barclay, *Obeying*, 205-6.

62. Cf. Bruce, *Galatians*, 256; Dunn, *Galatians*, 314.

63. Cf. Käsemann, *Questions*, 135-36; Martyn, *Galatians*, 99-100, 483; de Boer, *Galatians*, 335-39; pace Longenecker, *Galatians*, 240-41, 245-46; Schnelle, *Anthropologie*, 73-75.

64. The continued threat of σάρξ suggests Paul's comment regarding the believer's crucifixion to the flesh must be understood from the perspective of the eschatological tension that qualifies his inaugurated eschatology (see above, p. 76). Cf. Rom 8:12-13; Gal 5:13, 16, 19-21. Finally, it is essential to appreciate the complexity of Paul's thought within the paraenetic discourse of Gal 5:13-26. There is undoubtedly a focus on ethics within this passage and Hubbard rightly highlights the significance of the death-life metaphor for understanding crucifixion to the flesh in v. 24, as well as the anthropological scope of this section of Galatians (Hubbard, *New Creation*, 191, 208-9). At the same time, Paul's ethical discussion is not unrelated to his complex eschatological understanding of Christ's death and resurrection and may also draw upon an apocalyptic

The preceding discussion of inaugurated eschatology in Galatians has important implications for understanding Paul's assertion ἐμοὶ κόσμος ἐσταύρωται in Gal 6:14. We have seen that Paul highlights the eschatological significance of Christ's death and resurrection from the very beginning of this letter (cf. Gal 1:1, 4). Christ's resurrection and the inauguration of the new age also implicitly form a crucial element in Paul's argument in Gal 2:19-20 (a text conceptually linked to Gal 6:14), where death to the law and theocentric existence (v. 19a) are grounded in the believer's eschatological participation in the Christ-event (cf. Gal 5:24). Paul also describes the coming of Christ in "fullness of time" at Gal 4:4a, a phrase that again evokes the apocalyptic worldview of early Judaism. When read within the context of Gal 4:1-10, Paul's use of this expression furthermore establishes a critical temporal contrast between the old age (a time of living under the custody of the law and slavery to τὰ στοιχεῖα) and the new age (a time of freedom from the law and the influence of τὰ στοιχεῖα).[65] Paul uses crucifixion imagery again in Gal 5:24 and the πνεῦμα/σάρξ contrast that runs throughout Gal 5:13-26 is firmly grounded in the belief that Christ's death and resurrection have not only defeated the (cosmic?) power of the flesh but also ushered in the new age and made possible life in the Spirit. In summary, Paul's statement in Gal 6:14 is closely related to preceding notions within this letter that greatly emphasize union with Christ and the eschatological participation in the new age.

Now that we have examined the nature of Paul's eschatology and Jewish background, we may consider the interpretation of the noun κόσμος in Gal 6:14. Hubbard has helpfully observed that scholars have generally advocated three readings of κόσμος in Gal 6:14: 1) cosmological; 2) ecclesiological; and 3) anthropological.[66] The prior discussion of κόσμος and crucifixion in Galatians revealed that both notions are strongly aligned with Paul's old age/new age antithesis. I have also observed that the nouns αἰών and κόσμος are close synonyms in 1 Cor 1:20; 3:18-19.[67] With these two factors in mind, it is likely the noun κόσμος in Gal 6:14 is a close synonym to the lexeme αἰών and belongs within Paul's inaugurated eschatology.[68] The very choice of

understanding of cosmic evil. These observations concerning the intricacy of Paul's thinking in this passage suggest one should at least be open to a similarly intricate reading of καινὴ κτίσις in Gal 6:15.

65. Cf. Gal 4:3, 9.

66. Hubbard, *New Creation*, 215-16. Hubbard further classifies the anthropological reading of κόσμος into three predominant lines of interpretation: 1) a worldly way of thinking; 2) the transience of the law; or 3) Paul's former life in Judaism.

67. See above, p. 76.

68. Cf. Adams, *Constructing the World*, 229-30; Jackson, *New Creation*, 98; Dunn,

the noun κόσμος in v. 14 suggests Paul's statement cannot be removed from the realm of cosmology, a subject that also belongs within his inaugurated eschatology (cf. 1 Cor 7:31). With this in mind, crucifixion to the "world" encompasses not only the believer's deliverance from the agents of the old age (e.g., sin, Torah, and the flesh) but also the reality that they "are in some proleptic sense already participating in the life of the new world."[69]

The clause οὔτε γὰρ περιτομή τί ἐστιν οὔτε ἀκροβυστία in Gal 6:15a also provides a vital clue to the meaning of the noun κόσμος in v. 14. The lexical and conceptual parallelism between Gal 6:15 and Gal 5:6 is worth noting at this point. The construction οὔτε περιτομή τι ἰσχύει οὔτε ἀκροβυστία ἀλλά in Gal 5:6 is virtually identical to the clause οὔτε γὰρ περιτομή τί ἐστιν οὔτε ἀκροβυστία ἀλλά in Gal 6:15 (cf. 1 Cor 7:19).[70] Both statements also build upon the Pauline notion of union with Christ.[71] The paramount importance of Gal 5:6 within Paul's argument in this letter to the Galatians should not be overlooked. According to Longenecker, Gal 5:6 may be understood as a "précis" of his central arguments in Gal 2:15—4:11 against nomistic observance.[72] Given Paul's earlier association of Torah with the old age which has passed away (e.g., Gal 4:3-10, 21—5:1), there is much to be said for closely aligning his statements in Gal 5:6 with his inaugurated eschatology.[73]

The concluding statement in Gal 5:6 (ἀλλὰ πίστις δι' ἀγάπης ἐνεργουμένη) suggests the need to offer a slightly more nuanced reading of κόσμος in Gal 6:14. Since this phrase summarizes Paul's law critique and emphasizes the priority of faith in Christ, the theological reach of Gal 5:6b

---

Galatians, 340; Longenecker, *Triumph*, 45.

69. Adams, *Constructing the World*, 227. It is helpful to distinguish here between internal and external participation in this "new world." In an internal sense, the believer primarily partakes in the life of the Spirit and the concomitant victory over sin and the flesh (cf. Gal 5:13-24; Rom 6:1-11; 8:1-9). See below, p. 85-86, for a discussion of the external character of the new world inaugurated by Christ's death and resurrection.

70. Galatians 5:6 and Gal 6:15a are generally considered parallel statements. E.g., Matera, "Gal 5:1—6:17," 83; Weima, "Hermeneutical Key," 101.

71. The phrase ἐν γὰρ Χριστῷ Ἰησοῦ in Gal 5:6 explicitly correlates Paul's assertion with his broader understanding of participation with Christ. While there is no explicit connection to such ideas in Gal 6:15a, such notions are immediately present in v. 14 (see above, p. 77).

72. Longenecker, *Galatians*, 228-29. In Gal 5:4, Paul stresses the attempt to be justified by Torah (specifically with regard to undergoing circumcision, vv. 2-3) separates oneself *from* Christ (ἀπὸ Χριστοῦ) and grace (χάριτος). In Gal 5:5, Paul then positively rephrases his negative assertions in vv. 2-5 by suggesting God will declare believers righteous solely on the basis of the work of the Spirit and on the basis of faith in Jesus Christ.

73. The mention of the work of the Spirit in v. 5 provides further warrant for this conclusion.

undoubtedly extends into the realm of anthropology. Hubbard, however, uses this observation to support an unjustifiable reading of κόσμος in Gal 6:14. According to Hubbard, the three antithetical statements in Gal 5:6, Gal 6:15, and 1 Cor 7:19 collectively express Paul's "insistence on the priority of internal versus external considerations."[74] On the basis of this emphasis on interiority in these three Pauline texts and the dominance of personal pronouns in Gal 6:14 (ἐμοί, ἐμοί, κἀγώ), Hubbard defines the noun κόσμος by stating, "the 'world' which ended for Paul was the only 'world' he had ever known: his 'former way of life in Judaism' (1:13)."[75]

Hubbard's purely anthropological understanding of κόσμος in Gal 6:14, however, is problematic on two fronts. First, as Jackson notes, equating Paul's use of this lexeme in v. 14 with his former adherence to Judaism assigns an atypical meaning to the noun κόσμος.[76] Second, Hubbard's interpretation of the noun κόσμος again assumes an unwarranted divorce between anthropology and cosmology within Paul's thought.[77] While Hubbard rightly criticizes some interpreters for suggesting the new world has been inaugurated in a definitive sense, he nonetheless too quickly dismisses the very real possibility that the newness Paul describes in this context extends beyond inward anthropological realities.[78] Principally, the external character of the new world is present in the believing community, an arena where the ecclesiological distinctions associated with the old age have been nullified (cf. Gal 3:28; Eph 2:11–15; Col 3:10–11).[79]

---

74. Hubbard, *New Creation*, 219. Hubbard (ibid., 219–21) cogently argues that Paul's stress on interiority derives from a close reading of Jer 9:22–25 LXX (note the reference to being "uncircumcised in heart" in v. 25) and also finds expression in Rom 2:23–29.

75. Hubbard, *New Creation*, 218. Hubbard (*New Creation*, 217) further clarifies his position on this issue by closely linking the noun κόσμος in v. 14 with Paul's "dismissal of the law" (in light of the reference to "circumcision" and "uncircumcision" in Gal 6:15a) and describing Paul's "'former life in Judaism' as one of people pleasing, religious ambition, and violent enforcement of a distinctively Jewish lifestyle (1:10–14)."

76. Jackson, *New Creation*, 89. Jackson states, "such an *individual* focus would represent a unique usage of κόσμος in the Pauline corpus" (emphasis mine).

77. Cf. ibid., 89. While Hubbard (*New Creation*, 218) rightly argues Gal 6:14 contains "an implicit plea for them [the Galatian believers] to reject the nomistic world which the opposing missionaries offered," he nonetheless fails to appreciate that Paul argues their understanding of reality is to be abandoned because of the dawn of the new age in Christ (see especially the above analysis of the τὰ στοιχεῖα τοῦ κόσμου in Gal 4:3, 9, p. 78–79).

78. Hubbard (ibid., 224) states, "From Paul's perspective, the newness of Christian experience was the Spirit's work within . . . so it is less accurate to speak of the believer entering the new age *than it is to speak of the new age entering the believer*."

79. Cf. Barclay, *Obeying*, 102. Scholars frequently associate the discussion of new

This discussion of the relationship between Gal 6:15a and Gal 5:6 has important implications for understanding Paul's crucifixion to the "world" in Gal 6:14. Once again, we see that Paul's discussion in Gal 6:11–16 evokes significant segments of his argument in this letter. In particular, Gal 6:15a draws upon Gal 5:6, a text that not only summarizes Paul's denunciation of Torah but also reiterates his emphasis on the necessity of faith in Jesus Christ. Galatians 5:6, in turn, also brings to mind Gal 3:28, where Paul succinctly describes the new world that has been instituted through the death and resurrection of Christ. Galatians 6:15a therefore forms part of a larger matrix of ideas within this letter that ultimately express the anthropological and cosmological scope of Paul's complex eschatology.

This finally brings us to the centerpiece of this larger discussion—Paul's use of the phrase καινὴ κτίσις in Gal 6:15. As with the noun κόσμος in v. 14, one may, generally speaking, distinguish among three interpretations of the expression καινὴ κτίσις in v. 15: 1) cosmological; 2) ecclesiological; and 3) anthropological.[80] As we saw earlier, the noun κόσμος in Galatians is closely identified with Paul's old age/new age antithesis (cf. Gal 4:3, 9). The correspondence between "the world" and καινὴ κτίσις in vv. 14–15 suggests that there is a strong sense in which new creation in Gal 6:15 must be understood cosmologically. The degree to which the noun κόσμος is associated with Paul's Torah-critique, both in Gal 4:3–10 and Gal 6:15, also points to a close correlation between καινὴ κτίσις in Gal 6:15 and his portrait of the new age that has dawned with the resurrection of Christ.[81]

Care should be taken at this point by fully considering the complex nature of Paul's eschatology. More specifically, a distinction must be made at this point between inaugurated eschatology and future eschatology. From the perspective of inaugurated eschatology, the new creation would be associated with such notions as freedom from the law and the gift of

---

creation in Gal 6:14–15 with Paul's statement in Gal 3:28. Cf. Jackson, *New Creation*, 109–11; Mell, *Neue Schöpfung*, 306–15; Weima, "Hermeneutical Key," 101; Stuhlmacher, "Erwägungen," 29; pace Hubbard, *New Creation*, 223. While Hubbard rightly notes the "logic and aim" of these two texts are different, he nonetheless fails to appreciate their conceptual correspondences (note the emphasis on the denunciation of Torah and union with Christ in both contexts). Cf. Jackson, *New Creation*, 110.

80. The anthropological reading of καινὴ κτίσις in Gal 6:15 is advocated by such scholars as: Hubbard, *New Creation*, 222–25; Betz, *Galaterbrief*, 541–43; Bruce, *Galatians*, 273; Kwon, *Eschatology*, 172–74; Mussner, *Galaterbrief*, 415. The ecclesiological scope of καινὴ κτίσις in Gal 6:15 is emphasized by such scholars as Matera, *Galatians*, 226; Barclay, *Obeying*, 101–2; Hong, *Law*, 148; Kraus, *Das Volk Gottes*, 251. Interpreters who lean toward a more cosmological understanding of καινὴ κτίσις include: Mell, *Neue Schöpfung*, 316–17; Jervis, *Galatians*, 159; Vouga, *Galater*, 157; Dunn, *Galatians*, 342–43.

81. Cf. Jackson, *New Creation*, 90–95; Adams, *Constructing the World*, 226–27.

the Spirit. Regarding Paul's future eschatology, Hubbard rightly chides interpreters who depict καινὴ κτίσις in Gal 6:15 as if *the* new creation has arrived.[82] Nonetheless, there is no need to conclude that καινὴ κτίσις in Gal 6:15—despite the absence of an allusion to Isaiah's "new heavens and new earth"—has no *future* cosmological implications (cf. 1 Cor 7:31b; 15:23-28, 51-55; Rom 8:18-25).[83] This reading of Paul's use of the phrase καινὴ κτίσις in v. 15 thus allows one to conclude that while "the cross has not brought about the expected cosmic transformation or re-creation . . . it has in some way started the ball rolling toward that end."[84]

Two significant contextual features that impinge on the meaning of καινὴ κτίσις in Gal 6:15 still need to be considered. First, there is Paul's negation of "circumcision" and "uncircumcision" in Gal 6:15a. Second, one must also account for Paul's designation of those who embrace the principle outlined in Gal 6:15 as "the Israel of God" in v. 16b.[85] In my analysis of Gal 6:14-15a, I argued that the noun κόσμῳ and the clause οὔτε γὰρ περιτομή τί ἐστιν οὔτε ἀκροβυστία (Gal 5:6; 6:15a) must be read in light of the complex interaction between eschatology and soteriology that Paul outlines in the main body of this letter. The central place of ecclesiology within Gal 3:28 and Gal 5:6, nonetheless, warrants additional comment. For Paul to assert "[t]here is no longer Jew or Greek" in Christ (Gal 3:28) is to speak not only of the inauguration of a new world, but also (perhaps even more so) to express the fundamental eradication of ecclesiological distinctions which divided the old age.[86] Furthermore, Paul's statement οὔτε περιτομή τι ἰσχύει οὔτε ἀκροβυστία in Gal 5:6a also speaks of the absolution of identity markers that distinguished the "not my people" from God's "people" (cf. Hos 2:23). Returning to Gal 6:15, the closely related declaration οὔτε γὰρ περιτομή τί ἐστιν οὔτε ἀκροβυστία ultimately points to the abrogation of the law and cannot be separated from Paul's larger ecclesiological interest in explaining the redefinition of the people of God that has transpired with the dawn of the new age.[87]

---

82. Hubbard, *New Creation*, 223-24.

83. Cf. Jackson, *New Creation*, 89, 92. Paul's use of the noun κόσμῳ (as opposed to αἰών) in v. 14 would point strongly in this direction. The strong association between anthropology and cosmology in Isaiah would also support this conclusion (e.g., Isa 40:1-5).

84. Adams, *Constructing the World*, 227.

85. The preposition καί and the expression τῷ κανόνι τούτῳ both directly link the subsequent statements in v. 16 with Gal 6:15. Cf. Martyn, *Galatians*, 566-67.

86. Cf. Mell, *Neue Schöpfung*, 316-17.

87. According to Hubbard (*New Creation*, 201), "the question of who constitutes the people of God is an important but subsidiary corollary issuing from the more

Paul's statements in Gal 6:16 confirm a close association between ecclesiology and new creation in v. 15. As already noted, the blessing Paul pronounces in v. 16 is directly related to his account of new creation in v. 15 (see above, p. 85). For our purposes, it is critical to determine whether Paul is declaring this blessing of "peace" and "mercy" in v. 16 upon two groups of people or one group. Longenecker's treatment of this issue is worth quoting at length:

> All of the views that take "the Israel of God" to refer to Jews and not Gentiles, while supportable by reference to Paul's wider usage (or nonusage) of terms and expressions, fail to take seriously enough the context of the Galatian letter itself. For in a letter where Paul is concerned to treat as indifferent the distinctions that separate Jewish and Gentile Christians and to argue for the equality of Gentile believers with Jewish believers, it is difficult to see him at the very end of that letter pronouncing a benediction (or benedictions) that would serve to separate groups within his churches.[88]

If the phrase Ἰσραὴλ τοῦ θεοῦ in Gal 6:16 does point to the union of Jew and Gentile in Christ as I have argued above, this will have important implications for understanding καινὴ κτίσις in v. 15. The syntax of Gal 6:16 indicates that Paul's statements regarding "the Israel of God" are closely related to the discussion of new creation in v. 15. One may therefore conclude that "the Israel of God" forms an integral aspect of Paul's new creation theology.[89] If this is the case, it remains difficult to detach Paul's understanding of new creation from ecclesiological concerns.

---

crucial question, the 'truth of the gospel' question: *what now demarcates the people of God—νόμος or πίστις?*" (cf. Acts 15:1). Hubbard concludes that the central issue within Galatians is anthropology not ecclesiology. Cf. ibid., 199–201. While there is a strong measure of validity to his conclusion, his overall analysis fails to give sufficient weight to the clear interrelationship between anthropology, cosmology, and ecclesiology within this letter (see especially Gal 1:4; 2:1–3, 7–21; 3:6–14, 27—4:6; 5:4–6). Jackson (*New Creation*, 114) offers a more appropriate assessment of the place of anthropology, cosmology, and ecclesiology in this letter when he states, "Paul's soteriology is seen as a function of that event [the cross] which should not be spoken of in isolation as cosmological, anthropological or ecclesiological. Rather, a Christological focus holds together these mutually *inclusive* emphases which Paul would not have imagined as *exclusive* categories."

88. Longenecker, *Galatians*, 298. Cf. Martyn, *Galatians*, 574–75; Weima, "Hermeneutical Key," 105; Schreiner, *Galatians*, 381–83.

89. Looking more broadly at the *corpus Paulinum*, the discussion of new creation in Gal 6:15-16 would therefore closely parallel the depiction of new creation in Eph 2:11–22 and possibly also Col 3:10–11.

However, not only is new creation here thus closely related to the identity of the people of God, it may also be reasonably linked with an *Urzeit-Endzeit* schema. Paul's description of the incorporation of the Gentiles within the people of God in Gal 6:16 may also indicate that his understanding of new creation draws upon Isaiah's prophecy (cf. Isa 66:18–24) and stands within the same stream of tradition as other early Jewish accounts of new creation.[90] Given how frequently these Second Temple traditions correlate their apocalyptic eschatology with an *Urzeit-Endzeit* typology, it is possible that Paul is likewise placing his portrait of ecclesiological unity ("the Israel of God") within the same interpretative framework.[91]

Summary of New Creation in Galatians 6:14–16

This analysis of Gal 6:14–16 indicates the phrase καινὴ κτίσις v. 15b is found within a passage that exhibits a complex interaction between anthropology, cosmology, and ecclesiology. However, it is difficult to ascertain which of these three theological categories predominates in this passage. This challenge presents itself chiefly because the phrase καινὴ κτίσις in Gal 6:15b not only forms a direct contrast to the clause οὔτε γὰρ περιτομή τί ἐστιν οὔτε ἀκροβυστία in Gal 6:15a, but is also paralleled by the "crucified world" of Gal 6:14b and is closely related to "the Israel of God" of Gal 6:16. If a decision must be made on this issue, it would be most fitting to conclude that cosmology dominates the depiction of new creation in Gal 6:15.[92] The noun κόσμῳ in v. 14 is likely used as a close synonym for the noun αἰών and thus once again relates Paul's discussion of new creation with his old age/new age antithesis. When read in this light, Paul's statement in Gal 6:15 ultimately

---

90. See above, chapters 2 and 3. Cf. Kraus, *Das Volk Gottes*, 248–51; Jackson, *New Creation*, 112–13. While Kraus and Jackson both appreciate the conceptual parallelism between Gal 6:16 and Isa 66:18–24, neither of these scholars recognize that Isaiah's new exodus represents the intertextual link between these texts nor the likelihood that "the Israel of God" may be read through an *Urzeit-Endzeit* typological lens.

91. This linking of new creation with ecclesiological unity in Gal 6:15–16 would essentially point to the fulfillment of the Abrahamic covenant, a subject that plays a significant role with this letter (cf. Gal 3:6–29; 4:21–31). See above, p. 4, on the relationship between ecclesiology and the *Urzeit-Endzeit* typology.

92. Recent research in Galatians has tended to read this letter through the purview of three distinct questions: 1) "what time is it?" (e.g., Martyn); 2) "what must I do to be right with God?" (e.g., Hubbard); and 3) "who are the people of God?" (e.g., Dunn, Kraus). I would argue that while the first of these questions dominates the content of this letter, these are ultimately closely associated questions (e.g., Gal 1:4; 2:11–16, 19–21; 3:21–29). Finally, it is natural to find these three issues brought together in this letter's postscript.

points to the irrelevance of "circumcision" and "uncircumcision" and the centrality of participation in the new world inaugurated by the death and resurrection of Christ. This matter is further complicated by the need to recognize that Gal 6:15-16 ultimately also touches another significant issue within this letter—the identity of the people of God. Finally, a variety of factors (both within Gal 6:14-16 and the body of the letter) also give a measure of credence to reading new creation anthropologically in this text (cf. Gal 2:19-20; 5:6).[93]

New Creation in 2 Corinthians 5:14–17

While it is generally agreed that Paul's letter to the Galatians was composed before 2 Corinthians, 2 Cor 5:17b is the only point in the undisputed letters where Paul explicitly links new creation with the OT. The allusion to Isaianic tradition in 2 Cor 5:17b thus provides us with an important clue for grasping the nature of new creation in this passage. Nonetheless, it is not without its own set of exegetical challenges.[94] It is therefore important to understand 2 Cor 5:17 within both the wider context of 2 Cor 1:1—5:13 and the immediate context of 2 Cor 5:11-21.

Apostolic Defense in 2 Corinthians 1:1—5:13

The discussion of new creation in 2 Cor 5:14-17 occurs within a section of 2 Corinthians (2 Cor 1:1—7:16) that may be understood as a sustained defense of Paul's apostolic ministry. Despite the presence of a number of lofty theological concepts in 2 Cor 5:11-21, this text fundamentally functions as part of Paul's larger apology. A significant segment of Paul's actual defense in 2 Cor 1:1—7:16 occurs within 2 Cor 3:1—4:6. This passage is especially important for this present investigation because of the extent to which Paul draws upon the OT to buttress his apostolic authority. Furthermore, this text gives the reader a relatively clear window into the nature of Paul's complex soteriology. The combination of these two factors points to the need to examine 2 Cor 3:1—4:6 and consider how it might set the stage for Paul's discussion of new creation in 2 Cor 5:17.

---

93. The use of personal pronouns in Gal 6:14 also indicates the scope of new creation in v. 15 extends to anthropology.

94. See p. 15 and chapter 2 above on the nature of the allusion to Isaianic tradition in 2 Cor 5:17b and the complex nature of Isaiah's new exodus.

Second Corinthians 3:1—4:6 begins by clarifying in v. 1a (ἀρχόμεθα πάλιν ἑαυτοὺς συνιστάνειν) the nature of Paul's self-commendation in 2 Cor 2:17. Paul then indicates that rather than needing to rely on letters of commendation (συστατικῶν ἐπιστολῶν) from other believing communities as his opponents do, the validation of his apostleship may be discerned in the lives of those who have been impacted by his ministry (2 Cor 3:1b-3).[95] The reference to the Spirit in v. 3 is then expanded upon in 2 Cor 3:4-6 in such a way that it is clear the catalyst underlying Paul's ministry is none other than God himself (cf. 1 Cor 3:5-7).[96] Paul's description of himself and his traveling companions as "ministers of a new covenant" in v. 6 then gives rise to an extended "allusive homily based on biblical incidents" that mainly interacts with Exod 34:29-35 (2 Cor 3:7-18).[97] Within this segment of 2 Cor 3, Paul: 1) demonstrates that the glory of the new covenant (identified with the "ministry of the Spirit" in v. 8) surpasses the glory attendant with the old covenant (vv. 7-11);[98] and 2) suggests that the inward transformation associated with the new covenant allows him to pursue his ministry with "boldness" (vv. 12-18).

The letter/Spirit and old covenant/new covenant antitheses are fundamental to Paul's defense within this section of 2 Corinthians. Hubbard rightly notes that there is "a clear pneumatological drift to Paul's thought which betrays a salvation-historical framework issuing from the theology of the latter prophets—particularly Jeremiah and Ezekiel."[99] One need only consider the clause κάλυμμα ἐπὶ τὴν καρδίαν αὐτῶν κεῖται in v. 15 to realize that as with his predecessors Jeremiah and Ezekiel, Paul situates the plight of those under the old covenant firmly within their hearts.[100] Hubbard also correctly argues that the solution Paul offers within the argument of 2 Cor 3:16, 18 is inward transformation (cf. 2 Cor 4:4, 6).[101] It is thus evident from this discussion that anthropology plays an important role within this passage.

95. The construction ὡς οἱ πολλοί in 2 Cor 2:17 is expanded upon in 2 Cor 3:1b (note the use of the expression ὥς τινες).

96. The phrase ἡ ἱκανότης ἡμῶν ἐκ τοῦ θεοῦ in 2 Cor 3:5 may answer the question, "Who is sufficient for these things?" in 2 Cor 2:16. Cf. Belleville, *Reflections of Glory*, 143.

97. Hays, *Echoes*, 132.

98. According to Hafemann (*Moses*, 334), "Paul offers [in vv. 7-11] an argument *from the events surrounding the giving of the Law itself* for his prior assertion that 'the letters kills' and its corollary that, with the dawning of the new covenant, the old is brought to an end."

99. Hubbard, *New Creation*, 151.

100. Cf. ibid., 153. On the importance of the heart within the new covenant prophecies of Jeremiah and Ezekiel, see chapter 3 above.

101. Ibid., 153-61. See Collange (*Énigmes*, 141) on the parallel nature of 2 Cor 3:18;

Limiting the scope of this passage to the theological realm of anthropology, however, does not do sufficient justice to the depth of Paul's defense. In particular, the eschatological import of the Spirit must not be overlooked (cf. Ezek 11:19; 36:25-27; 37:1-14; Joel 2:28-32; Acts 2:14-21; 10:5; Gal 3:1-5; 1 Macc 4:46; 9:27; 14:41). While there is undoubtedly an emphasis on the inward work of the Spirit within this text, one must still consider that the presence of the Spirit in Paul's thought is a token of the presence of the new age.[102] Hubbard's appeal to the allusions to the new covenant promises of Jeremiah and Ezekiel within this text also deserves further comment. In particular, though interiority is stressed within the new covenant traditions of Jeremiah and Ezekiel, the scope of restoration within these passages extends beyond inward renewal and also encompasses cosmological concerns.[103]

The allusions to Gen 1-2 within 2 Cor 3:18—4:6 also help clarify the theological scope of Paul's discussion in 2 Cor 3-4. It is generally agreed that the portrait of Christ as the "image of God" in 2 Cor 4:4 evokes the description of Adam in Gen 1:26-27 (cf. Col 1:15; Wis 7:25-26).[104] There is also a growing consensus that the clause ὁ θεὸς ὁ εἰπών ἐκ σκότους φῶς λάμψει in 2 Cor 4:6 represents a conflation of Gen 1:3 and Isa 9:1 LXX.[105] Finally, a number of interpreters suggest the confluence of image and glory terminology in 2 Cor 3:18 and 2 Cor 4:4 builds upon traditions from the Second Temple period that associated the new age with the restoration of Adam's lost glory.[106]

The presence of these allusions to the creation narrative of Gen 1-2 has important implications for understanding the nature of conversion within 2 Cor 3-4. As Hubbard notes, "What is significant about [2 Cor] 4:6 is that Paul views conversion through the lens of Genesis and deems

---

4:4, 6. Cf. Stockhausen, *Moses' Veil*, 158-59.

102. Cf. Hafemann, *Moses*, 428-30.

103. See my analysis of Jeremiah and Ezekiel above.

104. Cf. Newman, *Paul's Glory-Christology*, 221-22; Matera, *II Corinthians*, 102; Thrall, *Corinthians*, 310-11.

105. Cf. Barnett, *Corinthians*, 225; Stockhausen, *Moses' Veil*, 161-62; Kim, *Origin*, 8-9; Wilk, *Jesajabuches*, 269-70. The presence of the construction φῶς λάμψει in Isa 9:1 LXX establishes a particularly strong link with 2 Cor 4:6. According to Collange (*Énigmes*, 138-39), 2 Cor 4:4 only alludes to Isa 9:1.

106. Cf. Hubbard, *New Creation*, 157; Stockhausen, *Moses' Veil*, 296; Thrall, *Corinthians*, 310-11. *Jub.* 23:22-31 contains a similar discussion of the restoration of Adam's glory (see above, p. 65-66). Cf. *Apoc. Mos.* 20:2; 21:6; 2 *Bar.* 51:1, 3; 54:15, 21; CD 3:20; 1QH 4:15; 1QS 4:23; 4Q171 3:1-2. Interestingly, the divine gift of the "glory of Adam" is associated with the forgiveness of sins in 1QH 4:15. Finally, see Fletcher-Louis (*Adam*, 97) for the suggestion that "the life-setting for this expression is Israel's Temple theology," which is especially evident in Sir 49:16—50:21 and CD 3:12—4:4

the initial creation to be a fitting analogy to God's new covenant work in the hearts of believers."[107] Hubbard also rightly observes that in 2 Cor 4:6 Paul "merges the primordial events of Genesis with the eschatological vision of Isaiah and considers both to be realized Christologically (ἐν προσώπῳ Χριστοῦ) in conversion."[108] However, Hubbard is mistaken in his conclusion that the presence of these allusions to Genesis and Isaiah in 2 Cor 3:18—4:6 requires a rigorously anthropological reading of new creation in 2 Cor 5:17.[109] As already noted, a unified reading of Isaiah speaks strongly against a strict separation between anthropology and cosmology within his proclamation of a new exodus.[110] Furthermore, the use of Genesis traditions in this passage suggests that Paul is here describing conversion through the lens of an *Urzeit-Endzeit* typology.[111]

In summary, 2 Cor 3:1—4:6 is relevant to this larger discussion on a number of levels. Despite the presence of explicit links between 2 Cor 3:1—4:6 and 2 Cor 5:11-21, both these passages represent sustained defenses of Paul's ministry and provide a glimpse into his understanding of the gospel. Second Corinthians 3:1—4:6 undoubtedly exhibits a strong emphasis on anthropology (cf. 2 Cor 3:3, 6, 14-18; 4:3-6). Nonetheless, a number of factors suggest that Paul's statements in this context should also be understood within a broader eschatological framework. First, one must consider that Paul's discussion of the ministry of the Spirit in 2 Cor 3:3, 6, 8, 17-18 places this passage within his old age/new age antithesis. Second, Paul's association of conversion with imagery from Gen 1-2 suggests that the transformation depicted in 2 Cor 3:1—4:6 should be understood as God's act of beginning the process of restoring humanity to its primordial state. Third, the cosmological interest within the new covenant promises of Jeremiah and Ezekiel also calls into question any attempt to limit the breadth of 2 Cor 3:1—4:6 solely to anthropology.

---

107. Hubbard, *New Creation*, 160. Dunn (*Theology*, 468) also reads 2 Cor 3:18; 4:4, 6 within the framework of Second Temple traditions related to the eschatological restoration of Adam's glory and states, "Salvation is the completion of the original goal of creation—to renew that image [of God], to bring humanity to that fuller share of divine glory which Adam forfeited." Cf. ibid., 101-7.

108. Hubbard, *New Creation*, 160.

109. Ibid., 185-86.

110. See chapter 2 above.

111. Cf. Hafemann, *Moses*, 430-31.

The Immediate Context of 2 Corinthians 5:14–17

As with much of the preceding context of 2 Corinthians, the discussion of new creation in 2 Cor 5:14–17 occurs within a passage that focuses on buttressing Paul's apostolic claims. The introductory οὖν in v. 11 indicates that Paul is here drawing conclusions from the reality of an impending judgment according to works in v. 10. The phrase εἰδότες οὖν τὸν φόβον τοῦ κυρίου in v. 11 points to the seriousness with which the apostle views this looming eschatological event, while the phrase ἀνθρώπους πείθομεν summarizes his response (cf. Gal 1:10). The construction ἀνθρώπους πείθομεν may be understood as a précis of Paul's conception of his ministry. Taken together, the general nature of this statement and the concluding clause ἐλπίζω δὲ καὶ ἐν ταῖς συνειδήσεσιν ὑμῶν πεφανερῶσθαι in v. 11 suggest that he is referring to both his evangelistic efforts and his ministry within established communities of Christ-followers.[112]

The remainder of v. 11 expresses Paul's confidence in his moral integrity before God and the Corinthians (cf. 2 Cor 2:17). Paul's use of the verb πεφανερώμεθα and the infinitive πεφανερῶσθαι in 2 Cor 5:11b probably builds upon the earlier discussion of his transparency in 2 Cor 3:12, 18; 4:2.[113] Paul first conveys his assurance of righteousness before God (θεῷ δὲ πεφανερώμεθα). He then communicates his desire that the Corinthians would likewise discern his lack of duplicity in his dealings with them (ἐλπίζω δὲ καὶ ἐν ταῖς συνειδήσεσιν ὑμῶν πεφανερῶσθαι).

Second Corinthians 5:12 primarily functions as a qualification of v. 11 and details Paul's underlying motivations. Paul first indicates that his confident assertions in v. 11 are not to be understood as self-glorifying praise (v. 12a).[114] Instead, Paul suggests that his prior statements are intended to encourage the Corinthians to rally around him and his ministry (ἀλλὰ ἀφορμὴν διδόντες ὑμῖν καυχήματος ὑπὲρ ἡμῶν).[115] The remainder of v. 12 expands upon 2 Cor 5:12b and conveys the reason (ἵνα) Paul desires the Corinthians would have an "opportunity to boast" (v. 12c). Paul essentially hopes

---

112. Harris, *Corinthians*, 413. The verb πείθω is a somewhat unconventional word for describing Paul's apostolic ministry. Some scholars conclude that the verb formed part of the polemic of Paul's opponents and that 2 Cor 5:11a represents Paul's counterattack. Cf. Thrall, *Corinthians*, 402–3. The verb πείθω, however, is employed to describe Paul's missionary activity in such texts as Acts 18:4; 19:8, 26; 28:23. Nonetheless, the verb is also used in Gal 1:10 and a strong case can be made in that context for seeing it as part of the accusations of Paul's antagonists.

113. Cf. Harris, *Corinthians*, 414.

114. Cf. 2 Cor 3:1.

115. Cf. Rom 5:2–3, 11; 15:17; 1 Cor 1:31; 3:21; 9:1–17; 2 Cor 1:12, 14; 10:8—12:12; Gal 6:1–4; Eph 2:8–10; Phil 1:25–26; 2:16; 3:3; 1 Thess 2:19.

to present the Corinthians with a means of answering those who would mount misguided challenges to his leadership and ministry. Paul also offers his own critique of his opponents by representing them as individuals who pride themselves in their external achievements (ἐν προσώπῳ καυχωμένους) rather than their internal virtues (μὴ ἐν καρδίᾳ).[116]

Paul next presents a terse statement that expresses a fundamental guiding principle for his apostolic ministry (v. 13). While it is clear that this text continues Paul's defense of his ministry, 2 Cor 5:13 nonetheless poses a number of interpretative dilemmas for the exegete. The introductory γάρ is best understood in an explanatory sense, but it is unclear precisely how much of the preceding context it elucidates.[117] This question may be best answered by considering the meaning of the verb ἐξέστημεν in v. 13a. According to the scholarly consensus, Paul uses the verb ἐξίστημι to describe experiences of religious ecstasy.[118] On this reading of the clause εἴτε γὰρ ἐξέστημεν θεῷ in 2 Cor 5:13a, Paul is giving an explanation of 2 Cor 5:12c.[119]

This interpretation of 2 Cor 5:12c–13, however, does not provide a satisfactory account of Paul's statements. Perhaps the most telling problem associated with the consensus view is the assumption that v. 13 is making an implicit contrast between Paul and his opponents. If Paul were articulating such a comparison, one could reasonably expect him to use the personal pronoun ἡμεῖς, as he does in a number of other texts where he distinguishes between himself (along with his traveling companions) and his opponents.[120] The consensus view also assigns a specific sense to the verb ἐξίστημι outside the lexeme's typical range of meaning in the LXX and NT.[121]

If 2 Cor 5:13 must be understood in the light of vv. 11–12 as I have suggested above, then Paul's ἐξέστημεν/σωφρονοῦμεν contrast functions as

116. Cf. 1 Sam 16:7; 2 Cor 3:1–6; 4:18; 5:16; 11:17–22; 12:1–7.

117. Some interpreters suggest the conjunction is related to vv. 11–12. Cf. Barnett, *Corinthians*, 283; Matera, *II Corinthians*, 131. Others argue the conjunction only expands upon 2 Cor 5:12b (e.g., Furnish, *2 Corinthians*, 308).

118. Cf. Barrett, *Corinthians*, 166–67; Bultmann, *Korinther*, 150–52; Martin, *2 Corinthians*, 126–27; Wolff, "Knowledge," 120–21; Gräßer, *Korinther*, 212–13; Georgi, *Opponents*, 280–81. On this reading, the ἐξίστημι/σωφρονέω contrast in v. 13 is equivalent to the ἐξίστημι/μαίνομαι antithesis in 1 Cor 14:23.

119. According to some of the proponents of this interpretation, the phrase ἐν προσώπῳ in 2 Cor 5:12c refers to the visible facial contortions evident during incidences of spiritual fervour. Cf. Georgi, *Opponents*, 282; Furnish, *2 Corinthians*, 324.

120. Hubbard, *New Creation*, 164. Cf. 1 Cor 1:22–23; 2 Cor 10:12–13; Phil 3:2–3; 1 Thess 5:6–8.

121. The verb ἐξίστημι is associated with ecstatic experiences in Philo. Cf. Philo, *Leg.* 2:31; *Her.* 1:249–51. The brevity of 2 Cor 5:13, however, makes it difficult to link the use of ἐξίστημι in that context with such phenomena in other texts.

part of his apostolic defense. It is at this point that it is helpful to consider the meaning of the datives θεῷ and ὑμῖν. The balanced nature of the two segments of v. 13 suggests that these two datives are to be interpreted in parallel terms. One should also consider the elliptical character of v. 13 and determine what verbal notion is implicitly expressed in Paul's statement. Interpreters generally read the two datives in 2 Cor 5:13 as datives of advantage and supply the verb εἰμί.[122] Lambrecht, however, suggests θεῷ and ὑμῖν are simple datives and argues the verb φανερόω should be supplied from v. 11 (i.e., my actions are open to God and to you).[123] While this is an attractive solution, the traditional reading establishes a more natural connection with the ensuing clause ἡ γὰρ ἀγάπη τοῦ Χριστοῦ συνέχει ἡμᾶς in 2 Cor 5:14 and is thus to be preferred.

In summary, 2 Cor 5:11–13 continues Paul's sustained defense of his apostolic ministry in 2 Cor 2:14—7:4. This passage builds directly upon the description of the divine judgment in v. 10 and addresses Paul's response to God's eschatological scrutiny of his life and conduct. Second Corinthians 5:11a indicates that Paul's reaction to this impending event is one of reverent awe and the use of effective rhetorical practices. Second Corinthians 5:11 also conceivably expands upon the thought of v. 10 by implying that the integrity of Paul's actions is apparent not only to God, but also the Corinthians. Paul then suggests that his claim of blamelessness in v. 11 is not an act of self-aggrandizement, but is intended to furnish the Corinthians with a rejoinder to his opponents who overemphasize superficial qualities and achievements to the detriment of weightier considerations (v. 12). This section concludes with a cryptic statement in v. 13 that summarizes vv. 11–12 and suggests that all of Paul's actions serve either God or his fellow believers.[124]

Apostolic Defense and New Creation in 2 Corinthians 5:14–17

The statement ἡ γὰρ ἀγάπη τοῦ Χριστοῦ συνέχει ἡμᾶς in 2 Cor 5:14 has been aptly described by one scholar as "das Wie und die Wozu seines [Paul's]

---

122. Cf. Wallace, *Greek Grammar*, 144; Gräßer, *Korinther*, 213.

123. Lambrecht, "Reconcile," 365–66, 374–75. This is a plausible proposal given: 1) the presence of the clauses θεῷ δὲ πεφανερώμεθα and ὑμῶν πεφανερῶσθαι in v. 11; and 2) the likelihood that 2 Cor 5:13 functions as a summary of vv. 11–12.

124. See Webb (*Returning Home*, 113) for the suggestion that the verb ἐξέστημεν in 2 Cor 5:13a "forms a merism with σωφρονοῦμεν to say, 'whatever state I am in . . . it is for God or for you.'"

apostolisches Dienstes."[125] With this clause, Paul expresses the ultimate motivation that drives his apostolic service.[126] The genitive construction τοῦ Χριστοῦ in v. 14 is widely construed as a subjective genitive that points to Christ's love for humanity (cf. Rom 5:8; 8:35; Gal 2:20).[127] The verb συνέχω in this context characterizes the effect of Christ's benevolence on Paul's life and ministry (cf. Phil 1:23). While this verb is capable of a fairly wide range of meaning, the connotation "to control" best fits within the context of vv. 11-13. On this reading of the verb, v. 14 is implying that "Christ's self-sacrificing love restrains Paul from self-seeking."[128]

In the remainder of v. 14, Paul expresses the reason Christ's love affects him so profoundly. The aorist participle κρίναντας is best understood causally and may refer to a settled conviction that Paul formed around the time of his conversion (v. 14b).[129] The ὅτι εἷς ὑπὲρ πάντων ἀπέθανεν clause in 2 Cor 5:14c (which specifies the content of the pronoun τοῦτο in v. 14b) then correlates Paul's life-defining conviction with the death of Jesus Christ. While some have understood the phrase εἷς ὑπὲρ πάντων ἀπέθανεν in a substitutionary sense, it nonetheless is strongly reminiscent of Paul's first Adam/second Adam typology (note the corollary assertion ἄρα οἱ πάντες ἀπέθανον in 2 Cor 5:14d) and suggests that Christ is here portrayed as a corporate figure whose life affects all of humanity as Adam's did (cf. Rom 5:12-19; 1 Cor 15:20-22, 44-49).[130]

---

125. Gräßer, *Korinther*, 213. Martin (*2 Corinthians*, 127) states, "This verse marks an end to Paul's explicit proof that he is not commending himself, and the beginning of his manifesto on reconciliation." Cf. Lambrecht, "Reconcile," 376. While the rich depth of Paul's thought in 2 Cor 5:14-21 should not be missed, there is nonetheless an inherent pragmatic quality to these statements (in that these verses largely continue Paul's defense of his apostleship, especially in vv. 15-16, 20) which should likewise not be downplayed.

126. Cf. Collange, *Énigmes*, 253.

127. So for example Furnish, *2 Corinthians*, 309; Schmeller, *Korinther*, 321; Dinkler, *Zeichen*, 179. There are, however, a number of voices who argue that the notion of Paul's love for Christ (an objective genitive) cannot be completely removed from this context. Cf. Barrett, *Corinthians*, 167-68; Martin, *2 Corinthians*, 128; Wallace, *Greek Grammar*, 120; Collange, *Énigmes*, 253. Given that Paul is addressing the principal reality that motivates his ministry, this suggestion warrants serious consideration. Nonetheless, since the statements in 2 Cor 5:14b-15 focus on the significance of Christ's death, the primary emphasis is on the sacrificial love Christ demonstrated for humanity in his death.

128. Thrall, *Corinthians*, 408.

129. Harris, *Corinthians*, 419-20; pace Furnish, *2 Corinthians*, 310.

130. Cf. Pate, *Adam*, 139-40; Wolff, "Knowledge," 122; Dunn, *Theology*, 210-11; pace Martin, *2 Corinthians*, 129-33; Bultmann, *Korinther*, 153. This is not to deny a substitutionary approach to the atonement is taught elsewhere in the Pauline tradition (cf. 1 Cor 5:7; 2 Cor 5:21; Gal 3:13; 1 Tim 2:6).

The presence of the clause εἷς ὑπὲρ πάντων ἀπέθανεν in v. 14 presents a serious obstacle for a purely anthropological (i.e., individualized) understanding of new creation in 2 Cor 5:17. As Jackson notes, 2 Cor 5:14 "provides a clue that Paul's understanding of new creation is not limited to an individual experience."[131] The Adam-Christ antithesis in Paul is frequently used in connection with eschatological notions, and this likely has implications for understanding how καινὴ κτίσις in 2 Cor 5:17 is to be comprehended (cf. 1 Cor 15:20–24, 35–50; 2 Cor 4:4–6).[132]

Paul's use of this contrast in Rom 6:6 is especially helpful in this regard. Romans 6:1–11 is essentially a response to the hypothetical objection that Paul's statements in Rom 5:20–21 promote a law-free gospel. In Rom 6:6, Paul uses the construction ὁ παλαιὸς ἡμῶν ἄνθρωπος to describe humanity's former existence within the old age (cf. Col 3:9; Eph 4:22).[133] Paul suggests that this "old self" was crucified with Christ (συνεσταυρώθη) so that "the body of sin" might be destroyed and believers might be freed from their subservience to sin and the old age.[134]

The thought of Rom 6:6 is strikingly close to that of 2 Cor 5:14. The central concern in both texts is the grounds for ethical behavior (cf. Rom 5:20–21; 2 Cor 5:13). In these two passages, Paul draws upon his Adam Christology and depicts Christ as the inaugurator of the new age. For Paul, those in Christ participate in this new existence and are free from the power of sin and self-centeredness. The presence of this new Adam Christology in 2 Cor 5:14 has important implications for understanding the nature of new creation in v. 17 and calls into question attempts to limit the meaning of καινὴ κτίσις.[135] More specifically, the close association between Paul's comments on the termination of the old age in v. 14 and his discussion of new creation in v. 17 indicates that the latter notion is not devoid of eschatological import. Given the place of cosmological renewal within Paul's inaugurated eschatology (cf. 1 Cor 7:31), this observation suggests that the allusion to Isaianic tradition in v. 15 encompasses more than anthropological restoration.

The appeal to his Adam Christology in 2 Cor 5:14 also places Paul's discussion of new creation in v. 17 within the context of an *Urzeit-Endzeit* typology. As already noted, there was the expectation within some segments

---

131. Jackson, *New Creation*, 137–38.

132. Ibid., 139–45; Matera, *II Corinthians*, 137.

133. The use of the verb συνεσταυρώθη in Rom 6:6 strongly evokes the thought of Gal 2:20; 6:14. These statements provide further proof that Paul's new creation theology is tightly connected with the thought of participation in Christ (cf. Eph 2:5–6).

134. Cf. Moo, *Romans*, 374–75.

135. Cf. Jackson, *New Creation*, 143.

of Second Temple Judaism that the sin of Adam would someday be reversed (cf. 2 *Bar.* 51:1–3; 54:15, 21; *Apoc. Mos.* 20:2; 21:6). Paul's statements in 2 Cor 4:4 have already placed him in continuity with this hope. In 2 Cor 4:4, Paul uses language drawn from the creation account (τὸν φωτισμὸν τοῦ εὐαγγελίου τῆς δόξης τοῦ Χριστοῦ) to describe the experience of conversion (see above, p. 90–91). The association of Adam Christology and creation imagery in 2 Cor 4:4 suggests that Paul is depicting the conversion of "the unbelievers" as an act of new creation and Christ as the representative head of the new age.[136] Thus, the new creation is once again depicted using imagery and concepts drawn from the creation narrative of Gen 1–3. Given the use of Adam Christology in 2 Cor 5:14 and the degree to which 2 Cor 5:17–21 focuses on conversion and reconciliation, it is likely that an *Urzeit-Endzeit* typology underlies 2 Cor 5:14–21.[137]

Paul then expresses in 2 Cor 5:15 the ethical implications of Christ's representative death (v. 14) for those who participate in the new eschatological era. The clause καὶ ὑπὲρ πάντων ἀπέθανεν recalls the principal thought of v. 14 and directly links the ensuing statements in 2 Cor 5:15bc with the preceding theological truths. The remainder of v. 15 then expresses the underlying purpose (ἵνα) that motivated Christ's death.[138]

The identity of those referred to as "those who live" in v. 15b is a fairly contested issue (cf. 1 Cor 15:22). According to some interpreters, the phrase οἱ ζῶντες is a designation for all of humanity.[139] Others suggest this group are best understood as a segment of the "all" in vv. 14–15 and specifically refers to those who are united in Christ's death and resurrection.[140] Three points of evidence speak in favor of the latter interpretation. First, the extension of this discussion to include Christ's resurrection (καὶ ἐγερθέντι) in v. 15c suggests that Paul is drawing upon his understanding of union

---

136. Hafemann, "Comfort," 301.

137. Cf. Scroggs, *Last Adam*, 96. The allusion to Isaianic tradition in 2 Cor 5:17b also confirms this suggestion. Finally, while Hubbard (*New Creation*, 172–73) discerns the presence of this redemptive-historical perspective within 2 Cor 5:14–17, he nonetheless fails to consider fully its implications for understanding the nature of new creation in this context.

138. There are instances in the NT when the ἵνα plus subjunctive construction is used in such a way that the semantic boundary between purpose and result is imperceptible (e.g., Rom 7:13; Phil 2:9–11). Cf. Wallace, *Greek Grammar*, 473–74. Since there is a tacit hortatory force behind 2 Cor 5:15, the ἵνα clause may in fact convey intent and consequence.

139. Cf. Lambrecht, "Reconcile," 378; Mell, *Neue Schöpfung*, 360; Matera, *II Corinthians*, 135; Thrall, *Corinthians*, 412.

140. Cf. Furnish, *2 Corinthians*, 311, 328; Hubbard, *New Creation*, 173; Bultmann, *Korinther*, 154.

with Christ, a reality that is limited only to genuine Christ-followers (cf. Rom 5:15-17; 6:1-11; Eph 2:4-6, 8).[141] Second, as Hubbard notes, the experience of life within the wider context of 2 Corinthians is strictly limited to believers (cf. 2 Cor 2:15-16; 4:11).[142] Third, the very substitution from derivatives of the adjective πᾶς to the phrase οἱ ζῶντες in v. 15 suggests that Paul is describing two distinct groups of individuals.[143] Paul then specifies the negative (μηκέτι) and positive (ἀλλὰ τῷ) impact of Christ's death on believers (v. 16). More specifically, the clause μηκέτι ἑαυτοῖς ζῶσιν intimates that Christ's death has brought an end to the sinful self-seeking associated with Adamic existence and "makes possible a new kind of existence with the risen Christ at the center."[144]

Paul then expresses two significant consequences in 2 Cor 5:16-17 of the theological truths expressed in vv. 14-15.[145] Three closely related questions arise from 2 Cor 5:16. First, should the phrase κατὰ σάρκα be understood adverbially (modifying οἴδαμεν and γινώσκομεν) or adjectively (modifying οὐδένα and Χριστόν)? Second, what are the meaning and significance of the κατὰ σάρκα phrases in the protasis and apodosis of 2 Cor 5:16? Third, what is one to make of the possibility that 2 Cor 5:16b describes Paul's knowledge of the earthly Jesus?

We may profitably begin our analysis of 2 Cor 5:16a by considering the significance of the phrase ἀπὸ τοῦ νῦν.[146] The debate surrounding the meaning of this phrase concerns whether it is related to Paul's conversion, eschatology, or a combination of both. That the inauguration of the new age in Christ forms at least part of the grounds for Paul's outlook in v. 16 may be seen in the close relationship between 2 Cor 5:14-15 (with its portrait of Christ as the second Adam) and v. 16.[147] Despite the eschatological referent

---

141. Cf. Martin, *2 Corinthians*, 132.

142. Hubbard, *New Creation*, 173; pace Matera, *II Corinthians*, 135.

143. Cf. Harris, *Corinthians*, 421. One could certainly argue, however, that the expression οἱ ζῶντες is simply an instance of stylistic variation. This, nonetheless, seems unlikely when one accounts for the other points of evidence.

144. Thrall, *Corinthians*, 411-12. Cf. Barnett, *Corinthians*, 292-93.

145. That the conjunction ὥστε in v. 16 and v. 17 is to be understood in an inferential sense is argued by such scholars as Wolff ("Knowledge," 87) and Furnish (*2 Corinthians*, 311). The parallelism between v. 16 and v. 17 is seen in the use of the introductory conjunction ὥστε.

146. On the paradigmatic nature of v. 16, see Bultmann (*Korinther*, 155), Martin (*2 Corinthians*, 151), and Gräßer (*Korinther*, 219); pace Wolff ("Knowledge," 87) and Thrall (*Corinthians*, 412-13).

147. So Bultmann, *Korinther*, 156; Gräßer, *Korinther*, 219; Martyn, "Epistemology," 274; Kim, *Origin*, 13-14. Martyn's discussion of the relationship between eschatology and epistemology in 2 Cor 2-6 is especially helpful. Cf. Martyn, "Epistemology, 271-74.

of this construction, the voices of those who would link this phrase with Paul's conversion certainly offer a plausible alternative reading.[148] Hubbard, in particular, advances a number of arguments in favor of limiting the phrase ἀπὸ τοῦ νῦν to Paul's conversion and thus to the theological realm of Paul's anthropology.[149] Nonetheless, Jackson rightly notes that since conversion and anthropology cannot be separated from eschatology within Paul's thought, Hubbard's reading of ἀπὸ τοῦ νῦν in v. 16 creates an unjustifiable detachment of anthropology from eschatology (cf. 2 Cor 6:2).[150] In the final analysis, it thus remains difficult to separate the phrase ἀπὸ τοῦ νῦν in v. 16 from Paul's eschatology *and* conversion experience; this, in turn, provides further proof that the discussion of new creation in 2 Cor 5:17 encompasses a broad range of theological realities.

The remainder of 2 Cor 5:16a suggests that the dawn of the new age has liberated those in Christ from the sinful propensity to assess others according to worldly criteria. The verb οὐδένα carries a wide range of meaning but in this context probably means "to evaluate" or "to value" (cf. 1 Thess 5:12).[151] By means of the κατὰ σάρκα construction, Paul then clarifies how his perception of others has been altered.[152] The noun σάρξ carries a great deal of theological weight in the Pauline corpus and significantly impinges on the meaning of 2 Cor 5:16. The meaning of κατὰ σάρκα in v. 16 may be helpfully clarified if one observes that Paul employs this phrase in either a morally neutral (Rom 1:3; 4:1; 9:3, 5; 10:18; Gal 4:23, 29) or negative sense (Rom 8:4-5, 12-13; 1 Cor 1:26; 2 Cor 1:17; 10:2-3; 11:18).[153] The immediate

---

148. So Hubbard, *New Creation*, 173-74; Barrett, *Corinthians*, 170; Lambrecht, "Reconcile," 379. Stuhlmacher ("Erwägungen," 6) suggests that v. 16 depicts "die paulinische Bekehrung als ein eschatologisches Ereignis." Cf. Gignilliat, *Paul*, 98.

149. Hubbard, *New Creation*, 174. Hubbard mainly appeals to: 1) the wider import of Paul's conversion in 2 Cor 2-7 (cf. 3:16, 4:4-6; 5:5); 2) the likelihood that the phrase ἀπὸ τοῦ νῦν is directly related to the participle κρίναντας in v. 14; 3) the strongly soteriological emphasis within Paul's death-life conception of Christian existence; and 4) the parallelism between 2 Cor 5:16a and 2 Cor 5:17a. Of these four points, the second is particularly compelling.

150. Jackson, *New Creation*, 132-33. Cf. Stuhlmacher, "Erwägungen," 4-6; Collange, *Énigmes*, 258.

151. Furnish, *2 Corinthians*, 312; Harris, *Corinthians*, 427.

152. There is a strong sense of agreement that the phrase κατὰ σάρκα modifies the verb οἴδαμεν. Cf. Barnett, *Corinthians*, 294-95; Fraser, "Paul's Knowledge," 297-98; Schmeller, *Korinther*, 324-25; Wolff, "Knowledge," 87; Furnish, *2 Corinthians*, 312; Martyn, "Epistemology," 270-74; Collange, *Énigmes*, 258-59; pace Georgi, *Opponents*, 252-53; Mell, *Neue Schöpfung*, 350-52.

153. The former usage of the expression predominantly refers to physical descent, while the latter according to Dunn (*Theology*, 68) points to "a morally culpable quality of social living."

context of 2 Cor 5:16a almost certainly excludes a neutral connotation to the phrase κατὰ σάρκα; therefore, it is best to conclude that Paul is here rejecting "worldly criteria as a basis for understanding and evaluating other people."[154] The wider context of this passage also suggests that the phrase κατὰ σάρκα in 2 Cor 5:16a modifies the verb οὐδένα rather than the pronoun οὐδένα.[155]

Paul then employs his past as a negative example in 2 Cor 5:16b to illuminate what it means to know someone in a fleshly way. The introductory clause εἰ καί may express either a real condition that introduces an actual event in Paul's past or refers to a hypothetical means of assessing Jesus Christ.[156] Given the degree to which 2 Cor 5:14-16 evokes Paul's conversion experience (especially by means of the phrase ἀπὸ τοῦ νῦν in v. 16a), the construction εἰς καί almost certainly refers to that climactic event in Paul's life. Given the parallelism between 2 Cor 5:16a and 2 Cor 5:16b, the phrase κατὰ σάρκα is best understood adverbially modifying the verb ἐγνώκαμεν and points to a fleshly evaluation of Christ.[157] The brevity of 2 Cor 5:16b prevents one from knowing precisely what kind of knowledge of Christ Paul is here describing. It is nonetheless likely that "Paul is repudiating . . . as totally erroneous his sincere yet superficial preconversion estimate of Jesus as a misguided messianic pretender, a crucified heretic, whose followers must be extirpated."[158]

---

154. Thrall, *Corinthians*, 413. Thrall goes on to propose that Paul is repudiating two ways of relating to other people: 1) evaluating others on the basis of their wealth, social status, or religious position; and 2) evaluating others on the basis of how one might benefit from forming a relationship with them.

155. Two features within 2 Cor 5:11-15 are worth noting here. First, as already noted, this passage represents a defense of Paul's apostolic ministry. Especially important in this regard is Paul's claim to actively seek the profit of God and others (v. 13, 15). Second, Martyn's appeal ("Epistemology," 271-74) to Paul's discussion of the relationship between eschatology and epistemology in 2 Cor 2-6 is also relevant here in light of the presence of Adam Christology in vv. 14-15 and the phrase ἀπὸ τοῦ νῦν in v. 16 (see above, p. 98-99).

156. The former option is advocated by Martyn, "Epistemology," 274; Barrett, *Corinthians*, 170-71; Wolff, "Knowledge," 88; Barnett, *Corinthians*, 295; Breytenbach, *Versöhnung*, 130. Scholars who argue 2 Cor 5:16b refers to a hypothetical knowledge of Christ include Furnish, *2 Corinthians*, 313; Georgi, *Opponents*, 252-53, 276.

157. Cf. Furnish, *2 Corinthians*, 313; Lambrecht, "Reconcile," 379; Martyn, "Epistemology," 274; Wolff, "Knowledge," 88-91; Fraser, "Paul's Knowledge," 297-98; pace Georgi, *Opponents*, 254-57, 290-92.

158. Harris, *Corinthians*, 429. Cf. C. Wolff, "Knowledge," 88. While it is possible (though impossible to confirm) that Paul physically encountered the earthly Jesus, the parallelism with v. 16a suggests that this is not the primary notion underlying v. 16b. On this reading, Paul's statements in v. 16b are thus not intended to counter the claims of his opponents (pace Georgi).

Second Corinthians 5:16 is thus primarily concerned with how Paul interacts with others. These statements are closely related (ὥστε) to Paul's preceding apologia in vv. 14–15. While most strongly associated with his Damascus road experience, the wider context suggests that his eschatological understanding of Christ's death and resurrection nonetheless lies near. The clause οὐδένα οὐδένα κατὰ σάρκα in 2 Cor 5:16a expresses the primary thought of v. 16 and suggests that for Paul, his conversion (and the inauguration of the new age in Christ) negates the possibility of judging any other individual on fleshly or worldly grounds.[159] The remainder of v. 16 contrasts Paul's present ethic of human relationships with his prior conception of Jesus' messiahship (v. 16b). The controversial statement εἰ καὶ ἐγνώκαμεν κατὰ σάρκα Χριστόν in v. 16b in all likelihood does not point to Paul's knowledge of the earthly Jesus or represent some sort of rejoinder to Paul's opponents. Instead, this phrase is to be read in close relationship to v. 16a and functions as an admission of Paul's prior failure to acknowledge Jesus Christ as God's promised Messiah.[160]

Paul then presents in 2 Cor 5:17 a second consequence (ὥστε) derived from his portrait of Christ as a second Adam in vv. 14–15.[161] The principal thought in v. 17a is that those who participate in Christ's death and resurrection (cf. vv. 14–15) are now caught up in the new age. Given the tendency of some scholars to overemphasize the anthropological aspect of new creation in Paul, the use of the singular pronoun τις in v. 17 requires special consideration.[162] While Stuhlmacher rightly describes the pronoun as a "gnomischen Verallgemeinerung," it is nonetheless problematic to conclude that this observation precludes an anthropological reading.[163] As already noted, 2 Cor 5:17 is closely related to v. 16 and the pronoun τις in the former text parallels the singular pronoun οὐδένα in the latter. With a number of

---

159. See Martyn ("Epistemology," 285) for the suggestion that the converse of knowledge κατὰ σάρκα is knowledge κατὰ σταυρόν.

160. While it is clear that 2 Cor 5:16a and 2 Cor 5:16b are to be understood as parallel statements, it is nonetheless difficult to grasp why Paul expands upon the former statement and refers to his egregious (and likely well-known) past. The underlying mimetic function of this passage may have factored into this statement.

161. See Wolff (*Korinther*, 127) and Matera (*II Corinthians*, 136) for the suggestion that v. 16 and v. 17 are negative and positive restatements (respectively) of the same truth. Cf. Schmeller, *Korinther*, 326.

162. The presence of this singular pronoun is viewed as significant evidence for an anthropological interpretation of καινὴ κτίσις by such scholars as Thrall, *Corinthians*, 427; Hubbard, *New Creation*, 177, 179; Wolff, *Korinther*, 127; pace Lambrecht, "Reconcile," 380; Furnish, *2 Corinthians*, 314.

163. Stuhlmacher, "Erwägungen," 4. Cf. Martin, *2 Corinthians*, 152.

scholars, it is therefore difficult to avoid the conclusion that the pronoun τις in 2 Cor 5:17a should be understood individualistically.[164]

Nonetheless, one should not overlook the fact that the construction ἐν Χριστῷ modifies the pronoun τις in v. 17. By means of this statement, Paul expresses one of the most profound aspects of his Christology—participation in Christ. This rich theological construction is expressed by means of a number of formulations in the Pauline corpus and is employed in a variety of ways.[165] Within the context of 2 Cor 5:17, this phrase is employed to describe the new mode of existence in which believers have found themselves as a result of the salvific work God has effected through Christ's death and resurrection.[166] While the emphasis in the ἐν Χριστῷ phrase is firmly on the individual and anthropology, the presence of Paul's Adam Christology in vv. 14-15 suggests that the significance of this construction also encompasses the eschatological scope of the atonement.[167] When read in light of 2 Cor 5:14-15, the notion of being in Christ thus also depicts the believer's participation in the new age that Christ has inaugurated by means of his representative death.[168] Several scholars also suggest that the phrase ἐν Χριστῷ in 2 Cor 5:17a carries corporate/ecclesiological connotations, and this reading should be taken seriously in light of the πᾶς language in vv. 14-15.[169]

This now brings us to the troublesome expression καινὴ κτίσις in 2 Cor 5:17a. The phrase forms the apodosis of the conditional sentence in 2 Cor 5:17a (εἴ τις) and is dependent upon the locution ἐν Χριστῷ within the protasis. The central concerns for this present analysis are twofold. First, I will assess the theological scope of this expression.[170] Second, I will determine the degree of Paul's dependence upon early Jewish traditions.

---

164. Cf. Adams, *Constructing the World*, 235; Webb, *Returning Home*, 127; Dinkler, *Zeichen*, 183.

165. Paul's notion of participation in Christ is also conveyed through the constructions ἐν κυρίῳ (e.g., Rom 14:14; 1 Cor 4:17), σὺν Χριστῷ (e.g., Rom 6:8), εἰς Χριστόν (e.g., Rom 6:3; Gal 3:27), διὰ Χριστοῦ (e.g., 2 Cor 1:5; 5:18) and even the simple noun Χριστοῦ (e.g., Rom 8:9; Gal 3:29).

166. This understanding of ἐν Χριστῷ makes the most sense of the preceding singular pronoun τις. Cf. Hubbard, *New Creation*, 178-80; Matera, *II Corinthians*, 137; Schmeller, *Korinther*, 326.

167. Cf. Jackson, *New Creation*, 144; Bultmann, *Korinther*, 158; Gräßer, *Korinther*, 222.

168. Cf. Gräßer, *Korinther*, 222; Adams, *Constructing the World*, 235.

169. Cf. Jackson, *New Creation*, 143-46; Adams, *Constructing the World*, 235. Jackson helpfully notes that restoration within the Jewish worldview was conceived in strongly ecclesiological terms.

170. That is, is the expression anthropological, cosmological, ecclesiological, or some combination of the three categories?

Regarding the connotation of καινὴ κτίσις in 2 Cor 5:17a, our analysis of the preceding context indicates that this concept must be understood in fairly expansive terms. Admittedly, the immediate context of v. 17a places strong emphasis on anthropology.[171] As I have already noted, both the pronoun τις and the phrase ἐν Χριστῷ in v. 17a suggest that Paul's chief interest in the immediate context is on elucidating the individual transformation of the believer. Furthermore, if 2 Cor 5:17 is a positive reformulation of v. 16, the personal and ethical foci of v. 16 would then bear upon the meaning of καινὴ κτίσις in v. 17. Nonetheless, despite the anthropological emphasis within 2 Cor 5:16–17a, the context of 2 Cor 5:14–15 should not be discounted (especially since vv. 16–17 is semantically dependent upon vv. 14–15). The presence of Paul's Adam Christology in vv. 14–15 prevents one from completely limiting the meaning of καινὴ κτίσις to anthropology and points to the need to also view this expression through the lens of Paul's inaugurated eschatology.[172] The full scope of eschatological restoration in the OT and Second Temple Judaism should not be overlooked at this point.[173] Given the breadth with which renewal is depicted in Paul's Jewish background (especially in Isaiah's prophecy), the depiction of Christ as a new Adam in vv. 14–15 suggests that Paul is placing himself firmly within the framework of these eschatological expectations. One may thus conclude that while anthropology is stressed in 2 Cor 5:17, sufficient contextual grounds are present for not limiting the significance of new creation solely to the individual.

With regard to the traditions that underlie Paul's understanding of καινὴ κτίσις in 2 Cor 5:17a, it is helpful to begin by recalling the nature of restoration in the OT and Second Temple Judaism. In my analysis of the conception of restoration within these texts, I demonstrated that this concept is a fairly broad notion and encompasses a number of expectations.[174] This is not to say all of these texts portray restoration in precisely the same way or that later texts that draw upon the early Jewish conception of restoration (such as 2 Cor 5:14–17) incorporate the full range of convictions associated with this concept. Nonetheless, the fact that restoration is portrayed in these Jewish texts in such a far-reaching manner makes any attempt to limit the scope of καινὴ κτίσις in 2 Cor 5:17a suspect.

---

171. This aspect of καινὴ κτίσις is emphasized by such scholars as Hubbard, *New Creation*, 177–83; Wolf, *Korinther*, 127; Thrall, *2 Corinthians*, 420–28; Baumgarten, *Paulus*, 166–70; Schneider, "Die Idee der Neuschöpfung," 264–65.

172. Cf. Jackson, *New Creation*, 145–46.

173. On this subject, see chapters 2 and 3 above.

174. See chapters 3 and 4.

These observations with respect to the early Jewish depiction of restoration have important implications for understanding the phrase καινὴ κτίσις in 2 Cor 5:17a. More specifically, the degree to which this expression (and the larger notion of restoration) is associated with cosmological renewal in early Judaism makes it difficult to exclude such notions from Paul's understanding of new creation (cf. *1 En.* 10:18-19; 11:1; 72:1; 90:37-38; 91:16; *Jub.* 4:26; 23:25-29; 1QS 4:25).[175] On its own, this argument carries very little weight since Paul could have employed this expression in a unique way. Nonetheless, the presence of Adam Christology in 2 Cor 5:14-15 suggests that Paul remains in strong continuity with the Jewish expectations of his day.

The allusion to Isaianic tradition in 2 Cor 5:17b provides further support for this reading of καινὴ κτίσις in v. 17a. As already noted, the clause τὰ ἀρχαῖα παρῆλθεν ἰδοὺ γέγονεν καινά is best understood as an allusion to Isaiah's larger new exodus theme rather than a specific text (or texts) within Isaiah.[176] The meaning of καινὴ κτίσις in v. 17a may be helpfully clarified by in turn considering the referent of the adjectives ἀρχαῖα and καινά in v. 17b. As Webb notes, the old/new contrast plays an integral role in Isaiah's new exodus and encompasses both supra-individual and individual notions.[177] Not only does Isaiah's new exodus clearly give rise to the salvation of God's people, but also a number of texts (even within Isa 40-55) indicate

---

175. A cosmological reading of καινὴ κτίσις is favored by such scholars as Barrett, *Corinthians*, 173-74; Gignilliat, *Paul*, 97-99; Martin, *2 Corinthians*, 152; Mell, *Neue Schöpfung*, 370-71; Adams, *Constructing the World*, 226-27.

176. See my analysis in chapter 2 on new creation in Isaiah.

177. Webb, *Returning Home*, 121-25; pace Hubbard, *New Creation*, 180-82. The principal problem with Hubbard's analysis of Isaiah's new things/former things and new exodus themes is his failure to appreciate the unity of Isaiah's message, which leads him to distinguish sharply between the content of Isa 40-55 and Isa 56-66. Cf. Jackson, *New Creation*, 120-21. Hubbard (*New Creation*, 182) also argues, "the Isaianic oracles contain important and memorable cosmologically framed statements relating to the 'new heavens' and the 'new earth,' and it is arguably clear that Paul could have cited these texts had they been conducive to his argument." While admittedly true on one level, Hubbard's statement not only fails to appreciate the "polytextual" nature of Paul's evocation of Isaianic tradition in 2 Cor 5:17b, but also disregards recent scholarly advances in our understanding of how Paul appropriates the OT. Finally, Hubbard's identification (ibid., 183) of the phrase τὰ ἀρχαῖα with "boasting in appearances (5:12), living for self (5:14-15), and judging others κατὰ σάρκα (5:16)" largely ignores the Isaianic context of Paul's allusion in v. 17b.

Mell (*Neue Schöpfung*, 364-67) offers another extreme account of the Isaianic material. His reading of such texts as Isa 43:18-19; 65:17; 66:22 overemphasizes the cosmological nature of these texts and does not do sufficient justice to the complexity that is Isaiah's new exodus. In general, the nuanced approaches to Isaiah's new exodus found in the works of Webb (*Returning Home*, 121-25), Beale ("Reconciliation," 553-59), and Jackson (*New Creation*, 17-32), provide a more helpful means of understanding Paul's conception of new creation in 2 Cor 5:17.

God's new act of deliverance will directly impinge on the created order (e.g., Isa 40:3-4; 43:16, 19-20). Once again, the salvation of the Gentiles is also depicted in several new exodus passages within Isaiah.[178] This raises the question of the degree that καινὴ κτίσις carries an ecclesiological force in 2 Cor 5:17.[179] Paul's discussion of the universal scope of Christ's representative death in vv. 14-15 certainly indicates that the soteriological emphasis within this passage is not limited to the individual. Additional corporate overtones are also present in 2 Cor 5:18-21 (see below, esp. p. 109-110).

In summary, in 2 Cor 5:17 Paul expands upon Christ's representative death in vv. 14-15 by positively describing its consequences. Within the apodosis of 2 Cor 5:17b, both the singular pronoun τις and the construction ἐν Χριστῷ place a decided emphasis on the anthropological significance of the cross. Nonetheless, despite the stress placed on the individual in v. 17b, a number of factors suggest that Paul's account of new creation in this context should also be understood eschatologically and corporately.[180] First, the Adam Christology underlying vv. 14-15 aligns the account of new creation in v. 17 with Paul's inaugurated eschatology.[181] Second, the degree to which the expression καινὴ κτίσις (and the Jewish understanding of restoration) is used cosmologically in Second Temple Judaism also speaks against limiting the sense of new creation in v. 17 to anthropology. Finally, the allusion to Isaianic tradition in 2 Cor 5:17b (τὰ ἀρχαῖα παρῆλθεν ἰδοὺ γέγονεν καινά) suggests Paul is closely linking new creation with Isaiah's new exodus, a complex motif which encompasses anthropological, cosmological, and ecclesiological renewal.

New Creation and Reconciliation in 2 Corinthians 5:18–21

The preceding analysis of 2 Cor 5:14-17 chiefly addressed the meaning of καινὴ κτίσις in v. 17a. In my analysis of this text, I demonstrated that while the term καινὴ κτίσις undoubtedly must be understood as an expression of Paul's anthropology, it nonetheless should not be separated from his cosmology and ecclesiology. In other words, in contrast to scholars such as Mell, Hubbard, and Kraus, who argue for a rather narrow conception of

---

178. See my analysis in chapter 2 for a closer analysis of the complex nature of Isaiah's new exodus.

179. As I have already noted, this is a very real possibility with regard to the use of the term καινὴ κτίσις in Gal 6:15 (see above, p. 85–87). The expression καινὴ κτίσις in 2 Cor 5:17 is interpreted ecclesiologically by Kraus (*Das Volk Gottes*, 260–61).

180. Paul, in fact, effortlessly transitions from corporate language in vv. 14–16 to individualistic in v. 17, and then back to corporate in vv. 18–21.

181. Note also the frequent use of the adjective πᾶς in vv. 14–15.

new creation in this passage, it is my contention that the meaning of καινὴ κτίσις is not limited to a single theological category and instead captures the complexity of Paul's understanding of the Christ-event. In the following section, I will address how Paul's statements in vv. 18–21 contribute to our understanding of the significance of new creation.

Second Corinthians 5:18–21 follows on naturally from Paul's discussion of Christ's representative death in vv. 14–17. Within the context of this passage, 2 Cor 5:18–21 functions as a climactic summary of Paul's apostolic defense.[182] The introductory wording τὰ δὲ πάντα in v. 18 directly connects the ensuing statements with the entire discussion within 2 Cor 5:14–17.[183] The use of the introductory phrase ὡς ὅτι in v. 19, in turn, suggests that the ensuing statements explicate the precise content of Paul's understanding of τὴν διακονίαν τῆς καταλλαγῆς (cf. v. 18).[184] While there is a sense in which v. 20 follows logically (οὖν) from v. 19c, Paul's description of himself and his traveling companions as "ambassadors" in v. 20 also expands upon the portrait of God in v. 18 as the one who has given (δόντος) to them τὴν διακονίαν τῆς καταλλαγῆς.[185] Finally, the discussion of Christ's death in 2 Cor 5:21 likely elaborates on the plea to the Corinthians in v. 20b to "be reconciled to God."[186] I will now consider the significance of this passage for our understanding of καινὴ κτίσις in 2 Cor 5:17.

First, the degree to which 2 Cor 5:18–21 depicts the work of Christ as an act of reconciliation (καταλλάξαντος) between God and humanity indicates that new creation in v. 17 carries a strong anthropological emphasis. The phrase τὰ δὲ πάντα ἐκ τοῦ θεοῦ directly links the ensuing statements with vv. 14–17 and depicts the Father as "the primary actor in this drama of salvation."[187] The notion of reconciliation in this passage encompasses God's

---

182. According to Barnett (*Corinthians*, 300), "This passage is the crux of the exposition of the apostolic office (2:14—7:4) and of the entire letter."

183. The dependence of vv. 18–21 on the general message of vv. 14–17 is the most viable conclusion when one considers the logical dependence of vv. 16–17 on vv. 14–15. Cf. Gräßer, *Korinther*, 223; Schmeller, *Korinther*, 328; Lambrecht, "Reconcile," 384–85; pace Bultmann, *Korinther*, 159; Wolff, *Korinther*, 128; Martin, *2 Corinthians*, 152–53.

184. Cf. Barnett, *Corinthians*, 305–6; Harris, *Corinthians*, 439–40.

185. Similarly Lambrecht, "Reconcile," 387.

186. Harris (*Corinthians*, 434–35) helpfully notes that 2 Cor 5:18–21 focuses on two issues, God's redemptive work in Christ and the nature of Paul's apostolic ministry. He also suggests that while both these topics are addressed in vv. 18–19, the former is at the heart of v. 20 and the latter comes to the forefront at v. 21. This account of the content of 2 Cor 5:18–21 allows for a balanced appreciation of the scope of theology and apostolic defense in this text.

187. Matera, *II Corinthians*, 138. Cf. Breytenbach, *Versöhnung*, 132.

objective act of effecting peace with humanity.[188] The object of God's reconciling work is specified by means of the plural pronoun ἡμᾶς in v. 18 and the noun κόσμον in v. 19. As with the singular pronoun τις in v. 17, the presence of the pronoun ἡμᾶς in v. 18 indicates that reconciliation in this context focuses on the realm of humanity.[189] Finally, the phrase μὴ λογιζόμενος αὐτοῖς τὰ παραπτώματα αὐτῶν in 2 Cor 5:19b demands an anthropological reading of the noun κόσμον in v. 19a.[190] In summary, the description of reconciliation in 2 Cor 5:18–19 must primarily be understood within an anthropological framework.[191]

This now brings us to the troublesome question of the meaning of the clause ἵνα ἡμεῖς γενώμεθα δικαιοσύνη θεοῦ ἐν αὐτῷ in 2 Cor 5:21. Several scholars closely link this statement with Paul's discussion of new creation in v. 17 and some go so far as to equate καινὴ κτίσις in v. 17 with the clause γενώμεθα δικαιοσύνη θεοῦ in v. 21.[192] While directly associating these two theological concepts is problematic, the presence of the "in Christ" formulation in v. 17 and v. 21 does suggest that they are nonetheless related.[193]

Before discussing the meaning of the statement "we might become the righteousness of God" in 2 Cor 5:21b, we must make a few observations regarding Paul's statements in v. 21a. First, the absence of a linking particle indicates that v. 21a is directly related to the declaration "be reconciled to God" in v. 20c (see above, p. 106). Second, the presence of the conjunction ἵνα at the beginning of v. 21b suggests that the notion of becoming the righteousness of God (γενώμεθα δικαιοσύνη θεοῦ) is logically dependent on the divine act of making Christ the personification of sin (ἁμαρτίαν ἐποίησεν).[194]

188. Cf. Martin, 2 Corinthians, 146.

189. Cf. Thrall, Corinthians, 430.

190. Cf. Hubbard, New Creation, 181; Wolff, "Knowledge," 129; Adams, Constructing the World, 235; pace Furnish, 2 Corinthians, 319.

191. At the same time, Jackson (New Creation, 124) suggests, "If Paul picks up the Isaianic understanding of the connection between creation and redemption, there is [sic] strong likelihood that his use of κόσμος here [in v. 19] would have reverberated with these associations, especially in the context of his discussion of καινὴ κτίσις." Once again, cogent reasons exist for not strongly bifurcating anthropology and cosmology within the context of 2 Cor 5:14–21. Nonetheless, an ecclesiological reading of κόσμος in v. 19 is probably preferable (see below, p. 109–110).

192. Kraus, Das Volk Gottes, 259-61; Breytenbach, Versöhung, 141.

193. Cf. Hubbard, New Creation, 178; Barrett, Corinthians, 181.

194. Two main lines of interpretation have developed around the clause ἁμαρτίαν ἐποίησεν in 2 Cor 5:21a: 1) Christ is portrayed as a sin-offering; and 2) Christ is depicted as the personification of sin. Of these two, the final reading best comports with the use of the verb ποιέω in this context (cf. Lambrecht, "Reconcile," 388; Harris, Corinthians, 452-54; pace Martin, 2 Corinthians, 157; Barnett, Corinthians, 314). In truth, there seems to be little need to separate these two approaches to the meaning of this clause

Third, there is an implicit contrast and parallelism between these two actions, which further indicates that the clause ἁμαρτίαν ἐποίησεν in v. 21a strongly influences the meaning of the clause γενώμεθα δικαιοσύνη θεοῦ in v. 21b.[195]

The construction δικαιοσύνη θεοῦ in 2 Cor 5:21b has traditionally been understood to refer to the act of being justified by God (Rom 2:13; 3:20, 24, 28, 30; 4:1-8; 1 Cor 6:11; Gal 2:16-17; 3:3-14, 24).[196] However, beginning with the work of E. Käsemann, a number of scholars have understood the genitive noun θεοῦ in this construction as a subjective genitive (i.e., God's own character or activity) and have closely linked this expression with a variety of divine attributes.[197] Two points of evidence within the immediate context, however, point to the need to understand the genitive θεοῦ in v. 21b as a genitive of origin (i.e., righteousness that comes from God). First, if 2 Cor 5:21 expands upon the καταλλάγητε τῷ θεῷ clause in v. 20c as I have argued above, it is natural to understand v. 21 within the framework of Paul's broader understanding of salvation and justification (cf. Rom 4:1-25; 5:9-10; 9:30-32; 10:4-10; Gal 3:5-14).[198] Second, if the converse of "righ-

---

since both allow Christ's death to be understood in substitutionary and representative terms. Furthermore, even with the use of the preposition ὑπέρ instead of περί (cf. Isa 53:10), Paul's depiction of Christ's work in 2 Cor 5:21 may nonetheless be understood as an allusion to the portrait of Isaiah's "suffering servant" (note especially the use of the verb δικαιόω in Isa 53:11). Barnett's suggestion (*Corinthians*, 314) that "Paul's words [in 2 Cor 5:21a] summarize without explaining Isa 52:13—53:12" provide a helpful description of the use of Isaianic tradition in 2 Cor 5:21. See Gignilliat (*Paul*, 103-6) for further discussion of the relationship between the "servant" of Isa 53 and Paul's statement in 2 Cor 5:21.

195. Cf. Thrall, *Corinthians*, 443-44; Matera, *II Corinthians*, 143; Barrett, *Corinthians*, 179.

196. Paul's statement in 2 Cor 5:21b has also played an important role in the debate surrounding the doctrine of the imputation of Christ's righteousness to the believer. There is a growing sense of agreement that while this doctrine is not explicitly taught in Scripture, it is nonetheless a conclusion that is implicitly found in the biblical material. See Bird ("Incorporated Righteousness," 253-75) for the suggestion that the believer's justification is best understood in close relation to Paul's understanding of union with Christ. Cf. Gignilliat, *Paul*, 104-5.

197. Käsemann himself argued that Paul's use of the phrase "the righteousness of God" draws upon apocalyptic Judaism and suggested it refers not just to God's gift, but also his power (cf. 1QS 11:12). Cf. Käsemann, *Questions*, 168-82; Käsemann, *Perspectives*, 74, 77-78.

198. Hooker's ("Interchange," 353) observation regarding the flow of thought in this passage is relevant at this point: "As Paul is dealing here with reconciliation, it is natural that he should write in terms of 'sin' and 'righteousness.'" Thus, while there is a distinct absence of the faith/works terminology in 2 Cor 5:21 so characteristic of his treatment of justification in Romans and Galatians, the fact that Paul is dealing with a theological concept (reconciliation) so strongly aligned with soteriological concerns makes it natural to link the "righteousness" referred to in v. 21 with his particular understanding

teousness" in v. 21b is "sin" in v. 21a, this would further suggest that the "righteousness of God" in v. 21b should be interpreted within the realm of Paul's soteriology.[199] In summary, while the phrase "righteousness of God" may constitute explicit "God-talk" elsewhere in the Pauline corpus (cf. Rom 1:17; 3:21–22, 26), close examination of 2 Cor 5:20c–21 reveals that the central concern in this context is on Paul's understanding of the atonement, which would obviate a subjective reading of the clause δικαιοσύνη θεοῦ in v. 21 (cf. Phil 3:9).[200]

Paul's statements in 2 Cor 5:18–21 therefore confirm that his conception of new creation in v. 17 must be strongly aligned with anthropology. Much of vv. 18–21 describes Paul's understanding of divine reconciliation. According to v. 19a, the object of God's reconciling work is the "world" and the remainder of v. 19 verifies that the sphere of this activity is the realm of humanity. Furthermore, the construction δικαιοσύνη θεοῦ in 2 Cor 5:21b closely links Christ's death with the believer's justification and, as with καινὴ κτίσις in v. 17, is grounded in the believer's participation in Christ (ἐν Χριστῷ/ἐν αὐτῷ). The strong correlation between salvation and the renewal of the created order in Paul's Jewish heritage also suggests that 2 Cor 5:18–21 is not entirely removed from cosmological concerns. In the same vein, the very use of the noun κόσμος in the context of v. 19 indicates that Paul's thinking here on reconciliation should be understood corporately rather than individualistically.

The degree to which the salvation of the nations plays an important role in portraits of the end in the OT and Second Temple Judaism is also relevant here. Even though the noun κόσμον in 2 Cor 5:19 is to be understood chiefly in an anthropological sense, it must not be overlooked that humanity within a Jewish framework is composed of Jew and Gentile and that for Paul, these two formerly estranged parties have been united in Christ (cf. Gal 3:28; 6:15–16). Paul's discussion of reconciliation in 2 Cor 5:18–21 may thus constitute an important part of his ecclesiology.

---

of soteriology.

199. Cf. Dinkler, *Zeichen*, 189.

200. Thrall (*Corinthians*, 443) helpfully notes that a significant problem with interpreting δικαιοσύνη θεοῦ as a subjective genitive in this text is the assumption that this expression must have "a unitary meaning in all its Pauline occurrences."

New Creation and Isaiah's New Exodus in 2 Corinthians 6:1–18

It is generally agreed that there are two quotations from Isaiah's prophecy in 2 Cor 6:1–18. Paul first quotes Isa 49:8 in v. 2a and then Isa 52:11 in v. 17abc.[201] The tendency to interpret new creation in the Hauptbriefe via the *traditionsgeschichtliche* method, however, has meant that these intertextual references have largely been ignored. The work of Hubbard and Jackson, however, are important exceptions. Hubbard's interest in 2 Cor 6:2 is primarily limited to making sense of the phrase ἀπό τοῦ νῦν in 2 Cor 5:16.[202] Jackson's discussion of 2 Cor 6:2 forms part of his analysis of Paul's use of Isaianic traditions within 2 Cor 5. His treatment of the quotation of Isa 49:8 in 2 Cor 6:2 mainly focuses on the referent of the pronouns σου and σοι in 2 Cor 6:2.[203] The wider contours of the second servant song in Isa 49, however, have been generally disregarded.[204] Paul's appeal to Isa 52:11 in v. 17abc (closely related to his designation of believers as the "temple of the living God" in 2 Cor 6:16) has also been neglected within this debate. Since these statements in v. 2 and vv. 16–17 are directly related to Paul's earlier treatment of new creation and reconciliation in 2 Cor 5:14–21, they could shed a great deal of light on the significance of the phrase καινὴ κτίσις in 2 Cor 5:17.[205]

---

201. Cf. Stanley, *Paul and the Language of Scripture*, 216–17; Webb, *Returning Home*, 40–41, 131–33; Harris, *Corinthians*, 459, 495; Barnett, *Corinthians*, 318, 353; Beale, "Reconciliation," 561, 571. Second Corinthians 6:2a is a verbatim quotation of Isa 49:8 LXX. While the statements in 2 Cor 6:17abc closely follow Isa 52:11 LXX (particularly the constructions ἐξέλθατε ἐκ μέσου αὐτῶν, ἀφορίσθητε, and καὶ ἀκαθάρτου μὴ ἅπτεσθε), Paul nonetheless has altered his *Vorlage* for rhetorical and grammatical reasons. In particular, the use of the masculine pronoun αὐτῶν in 2 Cor 6:17a corresponds to the masculine noun ἀπίστοις in v. 14a, while the addition of the conjunction διό indicates v. 17abc expresses a logical inference derived from the statements in v. 16. Paul's inversion of the clauses καὶ ἀκαθάρτου μὴ ἅπτεσθε and ἐξέλθατε ἐκ μέσου αὐτῆς from Isa 52:11 LXX may be intended to highlight the importance of separation from pagan influences for his addressees.

202. Hubbard, *New Creation*, 174.

203. Building upon Gignilliat's work on this subject, Jackson (*New Creation*, 127) appropriately concludes, "Paul's purpose is not to make a particular identification with these pronouns but rather to emphasize that the work of Christ has brought about an eschatological fulfillment to the Isaianic prophecies." See below, p. 112, for a fuller discussion of the referent of the pronouns σου and σοι in 2 Cor 6:2.

204. While Jackson (ibid., 125) briefly comments on the presence of universalistic statements in Isa 49:5–6, 8 and the indications of renewal of the created order in Isa 49:8, further work could still be done to explore the extent to which Paul might be drawing upon Isa 49 in other ways. I intend to investigate this issue in my analysis of 2 Cor 6:2.

205. Regarding 2 Cor 6:2, Koch (*Die Schrift*, 263) argues for a strong degree of

At 2 Cor 6:1, Paul seems to revisit the description of himself and his traveling companions as "ambassadors for Christ" in 2 Cor 5:20. The use of the verb παρακαλέω strongly links 2 Cor 6:2 with his statements in 2 Cor 5:20-21.[206] The referent of the participle συνεργοῦντες in 2 Cor 6:1 is generally interpreted in one of three ways: 1) other teachers; 2) the Corinthian believers; and 3) God himself.[207] On the basis of the repetition of the verb παρακαλέω from 2 Cor 5:20, the latter option is to be preferred and is accepted by the majority of scholars.[208] The appeal implicit in the verb παρακαλοῦμεν is almost certainly addressed to the Corinthian believers.[209] The phrase μὴ εἰς κενὸν τὴν χάριν τοῦ θεοῦ δέξασθαι in 2 Cor 6:1b then specifies the exact content of Paul's exhortation.

The precise meaning of "the grace of God" in v. 1 is probably dependent upon Paul's prior statements in 2 Cor 5:14-21. When read in this light, the "grace of God" would then refer to all the benefits (e.g., participation in Christ's representative death and in the new age) outlined in the preceding context.[210] The broader content of Paul's apostolic defense in 2 Cor 2-7 is also relevant to this question. Paul's plea in 2 Cor 6:1 fundamentally exhorts the Corinthians to recognize the divine authority (implied in the participle συνεργοῦντες) that underlies his ministry as one of God's ambassadors (cf.

---

parallelism between 2 Cor 5:17 and 2 Cor 6:2 on the basis of: 1) the common "Hervorhebung der Gegenwärtigkeit des eschatologischen Heils"; 2) their mutual appeal to Isaiah; and 3) the use of the interjection ἰδού in both verses. To these observations could be added the fact that both texts appeal to Isaianic new exodus passages. Commenting on 2 Cor 6:16-18, Beale ("Reconciliation," 369) notes, "the six generally agreed upon OT references refer in their respective contexts to God's promise to restore exiled Israel to their land." He suggests this observation has significant implications for appreciating Paul's argument, "since it allows us to view vv. 16-18 as a continuation of the restoration promises to Israel quoted by Paul in 6:2 and even earlier in 5:17." Further remarks regarding the flow of Paul's argument in 2 Cor 6:1-18 will be made throughout this present discussion.

206. Cf. Barnett, *Corinthians*, 316. Thrall (*Corinthians*, 451) argues that: 1) the introductory καί in 2 Cor 6:1 suggests this passage is something of an expansion of 2 Cor 5:20; and 2) the use of the personal pronoun ὑμᾶς indicates that these comments are directly addressed to the Corinthian believers.

207. See Martin (*2 Corinthians*, 164-65) for a brief discussion of scholarly literature on this subject.

208. Cf. Furnish, *2 Corinthians*, 341; Martin, *2 Corinthians*, 164-65; Lambrecht, "Favorable Time," 382; Matera, *II Corinthians*, 149; Schmeller, *Korinther*, 346.

209. The personal pronoun ὑμᾶς in v. 1 and the wider context of 2 Cor 2-7 would support this understanding of the verb παρακαλοῦμεν.

210. This reading of the clause τὴν χάριν τοῦ θεοῦ in v. 1 builds upon the close correlation between apostolic defense and Christology/soteriology in 2 Cor 5:14-21, themes which are present in 2 Cor 6:1. Cf. Harris, *Corinthians*, 457-58; Beale, "Reconciliation," 560.

2 Cor 5:20). Given the apologetic nature of 2 Cor 2–7, Paul's exhortation in v. 1 thus implicitly calls upon the Corinthians to reject the theological program advocated by his opponents ... to do otherwise would be to "accept the grace of God in vain" (cf. 2 Cor 2:17—3:1; 5:11–13; 11:13–23).

Paul's allusion to Isa 49:8 in 2 Cor 6:2 also clarifies the nature of the exhortation in v. 1.[211] The introductory γάρ in v. 2 indicates that Paul is employing this Isaianic text to establish the grounds of the plea in v. 1. Isaiah 49:8 speaks of a future "time of favor" (καιρῷ δεκτῷ) and "day of salvation" (ἡμέρᾳ σωτηρίας). In 2 Cor 6:2b, Paul proclaims that "acceptable time" (καιρὸς εὐπρόσδεκτος) and "day of salvation" (ἡμέρα σωτηρίας) have now arrived (ἰδοὺ νῦν)! The presence of this evocation of Isaianic tradition in 2 Cor 6:2 invites the reader to consider how closely Paul links his apostolic defense here with the message of Isa 49. An examination of the broader context of Isa 49:8 will now follow that explores: 1) the new exodus imagery in Isa 49:8–13; 2) the scope of the restoration envisioned in Isa 49:1–13; and 3) the relationship between the new exodus imagery in Isa 49:8–13 and the description of the restored Zion in Isa 49:14–26. I will begin, however, by explaining how Isa 49:8 functions within the context of Isa 49:1–7.

Isaiah 49:8 is closely related to the second servant song in Isa 49:1–6.[212] More specifically, the divine proclamation of restoration in v. 8 is to be understood as YHWH's response to the servant's expression of despair (κενῶς ἐκοπίασα καὶ εἰς μάταιον καὶ εἰς οὐδὲν ἔδωκα τὴν ἰσχύν μου) in Isa 49:4.[213] Thus, while the servant evaluates his mission as a failure (v. 4), in v. 8 YHWH suggests the story is not yet finished and there will come a day when he will respond (ἐπήκουσά) and help (ἐβοήθησά) his servant. The remainder of Isa 49:8b then explains the specific manner in which YHWH will aid his servant.

Looking now more broadly at Isa 49:8–13, we see that the servant's ministry gives rise to a new exodus. The servant's cry ἐξέλθατε in Isa 49:9a evokes Isa 48:20 where YHWH (cf. v. 17) proclaims to his people "go out from Babylon."[214] The reference to Babylon in Isa 48:20 largely envisions

---

211. Regarding the referent of the pronouns σου and σοι, Beale ("Reconciliation," 561–66) and Webb (*Returning Home*, 128–31) have argued that Paul is here typologically identifying himself with Isaiah's servant. While Paul certainly links his ministry with that of the servant (cf. Gal 1:10, 15; Phil 1:1), Gignilliat's more subtle approach to this issue is preferable. According to Gignilliat (*Paul*, 60–107), there is a thematic movement within Isaiah 40–66 from the servant in Isa 40–55 to the "servants of the servant" (Isa 56–66) and it is this latter group that Paul identifies himself with in 2 Cor 6:2.

212. On the identity of the servant in Isaiah, see Watts (*Isaiah 34–66*, 116–18) for a summary of scholarly views on this issue.

213. So Beale, "Reconciliation," 561. Cf. Oswalt, *Isaiah 40–66*, 297. These scholars also note that the universalistic promises in Isa 49:6 function in a similar manner.

214. Cf. Jer 51:45; Rev 18:4. See Webb (*Returning Home*, 134) for the suggestion

the backdrop of the Babylonian exile in Isa 40–55 and is then followed by clear evocations of the exodus tradition in v. 21 (cf. Exod 17:6; Deut 8:15; Ps 77:15–16 LXX; 104:41 LXX).²¹⁵ In much the same way, Isa 49:9–12 employs imagery associated with the exodus from Egypt and Isaiah's new exodus.²¹⁶ This is especially clear in Isa 49:11, which evokes the ecological degradation and way imagery (ὁδόν, τρίβον) of such Isaianic new exodus texts as Isa 40:3–4; 42:15–16; 43:16, 19; 57:14.²¹⁷ Furthermore, as in Isa 40:10–11, Isa 49:9b depicts YHWH as a shepherd caring for his flock of sheep (cf. Ps 76:18–20 LXX).²¹⁸ One can also conclude that the manner in which YHWH is portrayed as a benevolent shepherd in Isa 49:10a envisions a journey through the desert so often associated with Isaiah's new exodus (e.g., Isa 40:3–4; 43:19–20).²¹⁹

Concerning the scope of restoration in Isa 49:1–13, it is evident that this concept in vv. 1–13 encompasses the salvation of the nations. This passage begins in Isa 49:1 by addressing the "islands" (νῆσοι) and "nations" (ἔθνη). At Isa 49:6, YHWH (cf. v. 5) declares that the servant's mission is to extend beyond the deliverance of God's covenant people and will also embrace the nations.²²⁰ Isa 49:7 may also point to the same notion given the worshipful response (προσκυνήσουσιν αὐτῷ) of these "Kings" and "princes" to YHWH's glorious presence.²²¹ Furthermore, the clause ἔδωκά σε εἰς

---

that the Hebrew expression יצא מן, "became almost a formulaic expression to describe the first exodus out of Egypt" (e.g., Exod 32:11; Lev 19:36; Dan 9:15; Hag 2:5).

215. As with other new exodus texts in Isaiah, there are problems with understanding Isa 49:8–13 solely within the framework of the return from the Babylonian exile. Cf. Lund, *Way*, 236–46.

216. E.g., Exod 15:13; Ps 77:52 LXX; Isa 40:3–4, 10–11; 41:18; 43:19–20; 48:21; 63:11–14. Cf. Webb, *Returning Home*, 133–34.

217. Way imagery (ὁδοῖς, τρίβοις) is also present in Isa 49:9b.

218. Lund, *Way*, 239–40. These two passages seem to be primarily linked on a conceptual level, though the MT and LXX both exhibit linguistic connections (e.g., Isa 40:11 MT: ינהל // Isa 49:10 MT: ינהלם; Isa 40:10 LXX: παρακαλέσει// Isa 49:10 LXX: παρακαλέσει). Goldingay (*Message*, 381) goes so far as to suggest, "What [Isa] 49:1–12 has been confessing, portraying and promising is indeed the fulfillment of the opening vision in [Isa] 40:1–11."

219. Note the references to hunger, thirst, and springs of water in v. 10.

220. The purpose clause εἶναί σε εἰς σωτηρίαν ἕως ἐσχάτου τῆς γῆς especially points to the redemption of the Gentiles in v. 6. In discussing Isa 49:6 LXX, Ekblad (*Isaiah's Servant Poems*, 123–24) suggests, "while the MT emphasizes liberation for Israel, the LXX stresses salvation for the nations."

221. The use of the future verb ὄψονται and the personal pronoun αὐτόν in v. 7 may suggest a conscious attempt on the part of the LXX translator/s to link this passage explicitly with the theophany imagery in Isa 40:3–5 (cf. Isa 52:8, 10; 66:18). The presence of new exodus imagery in Isa 49:9–12 strengthens this possibility.

διαθήκην ἐθνῶν τοῦ in Isa 49:8 depicts the servant as a mediator of the new covenant and foresees the participation of Gentiles in this new covenant.[222] As with other new exodus texts in Isaiah, Isa 49:12 also suggests that the deliverance depicted in this passage will extend throughout the world (cf. Isa 40:5; 43:5–6; 52:10).[223]

Further analysis of Isa 49:1–13 also indicates that the divine renewal depicted in this passage is to extend to the created order. The infinitive construction καταστῆσαι τὴν γῆν in Isa 49:8b indicates that a key aspect of the servant's mission is related to the restoration of the land.[224] According to Goldingay, the universalistic scope of Isa 49:1–7 suggests that "the land" in v. 8 should not be limited to Palestine and the restoration envisioned in v. 8 is closely related to the renewal of Zion in vv. 14–26.[225] The new exodus imagery in v. 11 also once again closely links this act of redemption with cosmological renewal (cf. Isa 40:3–5; 43:19–20). Finally, the call issued to the "heavens," "earth," "mountains," and the "hills" to praise YHWH in Isa 49:13 implies that the created order somehow participates in and is benefited by the new exodus depicted in Isa 49:8–12 (cf. Isa 43:20; 44:23; Rom 8:19–22).[226]

One can also conclude that the goal of the new exodus in Isa 49:1–13 is the restored Zion/Jerusalem. It is clear that vv. 9–12 depicts the exiles being led by YHWH on a journey.[227] While it is not explicitly stated in vv. 9–12, when read within the light of the remainder of Isa 40–66, this trek

---

222. Cf. Webb, *Returning Home*, 135, 138–39.

223. The pronoun οὗτοι would then refer to those individuals who traverse through the metaphorical desert depicted in Isa 49:9–12. While it is difficult to determine the specific geographic location referred to by the MT's סינים, the LXX suggests some (ἄλλοι) of the exiles will come ἐκ γῆς Περσῶν (i.e., the east).

224. That Isa 49:8b envisions the restoration of the land is particularly evident in the MT, which uses a verb (קום) frequently associated with the re-establishment of Zion/Jerusalem (e.g., Isa 58:12; 60:1; 61:4). Furthermore, the verb is also used in Isa 49:6 (in the very same infinitival form) to describe the restoration of God's people (להקים את־שבטי יעקב). Finally, the presence of new exodus imagery in vv. 9–12 also suggests the notion of restoration is in view in v. 8b.

225. Goldingay, *Message*, 377–78. Cf. Oswalt, *Isaiah 40–66*, 298. Goldingay's observations provide further proof that Isaiah's new exodus is not limited to the return from Babylon and ultimately looks ahead to a far greater act of deliverance.

226. The presence of the verb παρακάλεσεν (on the verb ἠλέησεν, see above, p. 27) in Isa 49:13 indicates this passage is closely related to Isa 40:1–11.

227. This is evident not only from the imperative ἐξέλθατε in v. 9a, but also in the infinitive construction κληρονομῆσαι κληρονομίαν ἐρήμου in v. 8b. One could go so far as to suggest that vv. 9–12 describes the outworking of this aspect (and to a lesser extent, the first infinitival construction καταστῆσαι τὴν γῆν in v. 8) of the servant's mission in v. 8

presumably leads to the restored Zion/Jerusalem (cf. Isa 40:9-11; 43:21; 51:9-11; 52:7-11; 66:18-24).²²⁸ This conclusion is supported by the fact that Isa 49:1-13 is immediately followed by an extended portrait of the restored Zion/Jerusalem in vv. 14-26. Isaiah 49:18, in particular, describes a sea of humanity gathering (συνήχθησαν) around the desolated city intent on entering its gates (cf. Isa 11:12; 43:5; 60:14; 66:18; Tob 13:5, 13-15). Isaiah 49:19-20 then presents a picture of the massive extent of Zion's repopulation. YHWH is also depicted in v. 22a calling to the nations to bring his covenant people home (cf. Isa 11:10, 12; 62:10). Isaiah 49:19-22 may thus be understood as the outworking of YHWH's promise in Isa 49:12.

This analysis of Isa 49:1-26 has important implications for understanding the significance of Paul's quotation in 2 Cor 6:2a. This is especially true if Paul's declaration ἰδοὺ νῦν καιρὸς εὐπρόσδεκτος ἰδοὺ νῦν ἡμέρα σωτηρίας in 2 Cor 6:2b is related to and builds upon his discussion of new creation and reconciliation in 2 Cor 5:14-21 as I have argued above.²²⁹ First and foremost, it is evident from Isa 49:9-13 that the "acceptable time" and "day of salvation" Paul refers to in 2 Cor 6:2a are to be understood as the inaugurated fulfillment of Isaiah's prophecy of a new exodus. According to Webb, "It is a deliverance and acceptance/welcoming to the homeland *patterned after the exilic return*, a return which finds it roots deep in the movements of salvation-history."²³⁰ Further analysis of Isa 49 suggests that more can be said about this "acceptable time" and "day of salvation." On the basis of Isa 49:1-26, we can conclude that the expected act of deliverance is universalistic in scope (vv. 6-8, 12, 22), directly affects the created order (vv. 8, 11, 13), and culminates in the restoration of Zion/Jerusalem (vv. 14-26). This reading of 2 Cor 6:2 confirms the need to interpret new creation in 2 Cor 5:17 as a sweeping concept that takes in anthropological, cosmological, and ecclesiological realities. Furthermore, in light of the prominence of the restored Zion/Jerusalem in Isa 52:7-11, it is likely that new creation in 2 Cor 5:17 is to be closely aligned with this important motif in Isaiah and the *Urzeit-Endzeit* typology that undergirds it.

The next significant evocation of Isaianic tradition occurs in 2 Cor 6:17abc (διὸ ἐξέλθατε . . . μὴ ἅπτεσθε).²³¹ Second Corinthians 6:17abc is

---

228. Cf. Lund, *Way*, 237, 243-46. Interestingly, Isa 40:1-2 links YHWH's act of comforting his people with the restoration of "Jerusalem." In much the same way, Isa 49:13 speaks of YHWH comforting his people and is followed by a description of the restoration of Zion/Jerusalem.

229. See above, pp. 110-11.

230. Webb, *Returning Home*, 145.

231. The text of 2 Cor 6:17abc forms part of Paul's defense of his apostolic ministry within 2 Cor 1:1—7:16 and is ultimately closely related to his argument in 2 Cor

the second within a series of four quotations from the OT (cf. 2 Cor 6:16d–18). According to Scott, "there can be no doubt that the function of these citations is to substantiate v. 14a."[232] There is also a sense, however, in which these citations are meant to validate the clause ἡμεῖς γὰρ ναὸς θεοῦ ἐσμεν ζῶντος in v. 16b.[233] As already noted, there is a strong consensus that there is a modified citation of Isa 52:11 in 2 Cor 6:17abc.[234]

5:11—6:16. While it may seem that 2 Cor 6:3-10 is only loosely connected to the preceding context, further examination reveals that this passage actually continues the thought of 2 Cor 5:11—6:2 (Fitzgerald, *Cracks*, 184-88; Harris, *Corinthians*, 464; pace Collange, *Énigmes*, 282-83).

Paul's statements in 2 Cor 6:11-13 also form part of his overall apostolic defense in 2 Cor 1:1—7:16. There is admittedly an absence of lexical links with the preceding sections in 2 Cor 5:11—6:10. Nonetheless, the direct address to the Corinthians in v. 11 and the frequent use of second person personal pronouns in vv. 11-13 (ὑμας, ὑμῶν, ὑμεῖς) suggest this passage has the larger issue of Paul's relationship with the Corinthians in view. Paul's plea πλατύνθητε καὶ ὑμεῖς in v. 13c (cf. 2 Cor 6:11) also is reminiscent of his admonishment to them to "not receive the grace of God in vain" in 2 Cor 6:1, especially when one considers his portrait of himself as God's ambassador and a servant of the servant (cf. 2 Cor 5:20; 6:2). Cf. Beale, "Reconciliation," 566.

This now brings us to 2 Cor 6:14—7:1, a passage whose authenticity has been widely debated among scholars (e.g., Fitzmeyer, "Qumran," 271-80; Gnilka, "2 Kor 6,14-71," 86-99; Walker Jr., *Interpolations*, 199-209). See Webb (*Returning Home*, 159-75) for a helpful overview of scholarly discussion of this issue. Paul's statements in v. 14 indeed are abrupt and the absence of an introductory connective only heightens the sense that this passage was originally contained within a separate composition and later incorporated into the document we now know as 2 Corinthians. There are also a relatively high number of *hapax legomena* within this passage (e.g., Βελιάρ in v. 15). Nonetheless, interpolation theories raise more questions than answers, especially with regard to why this passage would have been inserted after 2 Cor 6:13. See Scott ("2 Corinthians 6:16c-18," 88-96), Fee ("II Corinthians VI.14-VII.1," 140-62), and Thrall ("Problem," 132-48) for helpful defenses of the integrity of this passage. A logical link between 2 Cor 6:14a and the preceding context may be satisfactorily discerned via Paul's petition πλατύνθητε καὶ ὑμεῖς in v. 13c. When read in the light of v. 13c, the charge μὴ γίνεσθε ἑτεροζυγοῦντες ἀπίστοις in v. 14a explains *how* Paul envisions the Corinthian believers are to open their hearts to God's minister of reconciliation. Since the ἄπιστοι of v. 14 are probably unbelievers and the principal concern Paul is addressing in this passage relates to participation in pagan idolatry (cf. v. 16), then, "[w]ithdrawal from the Gentile cults will be their way of responding to his call to them" in v. 13c (Barnett, *Corinthians*, 341). For an extensive discussion of the meaning of the verb ἑτεροζυγοῦντες and the noun ἀπίστοις in v. 14a, see Webb (*Returning Home*, 184-215).

232. Scott, "2 Corinthians 6:16c-18," 75. In other words, like the rhetorical questions in 2 Cor 6:14b-16b, the catena of quotations in vv. 16c-18 is meant to corroborate Paul's plea to the Corinthians in v. 14a to "not be mismatched with unbelievers."

233. The conjunction καθώς in v. 16c suggests that the catena of quotations in 2 Cor 6:16c-18 provide a biblical commentary on the assertion ἡμεῖς γὰρ ναὸς θεοῦ ἐσμεν ζῶντος in v. 16b. The conjunction διό in v. 17a, in turn, suggests that the quotation of Isa 52:11 presents a logical deduction of the statements in v. 16.

234. See above, p. 110.

A brief review of Isa 52:7-12 will set the stage for considering how this Isaianic text functions within Paul's argument.[235] As noted earlier, Isa 52:7-12 depicts YHWH's salvation of his people as a new exodus.[236] For the purposes of this present discussion, it is especially important to note that Isa 52:7-12 again presents this new exodus as an act of divine temple-building and describes the restoration of Zion/Jerusalem (cf. vv. 7-9). Finally, when read in light of the overall message of Isaiah's prophecy, the clause ὄψονται πάντα τὰ ἄκρα τῆς γῆς τὴν σωτηρίαν τὴν παρὰ τοῦ θεοῦ in v. 10 contributes to the universalistic scope of salvation within the prophet's message (cf. Isa 2:1-3; 40:5; 66:18-24).

These observations have important implications for understanding how Isa 52:11 functions within Paul's argument in 2 Cor 6:14-18. The citation of Isa 52:11 in 2 Cor 6:17abc at a minimum describes the ethical response Paul deems appropriate to the reality that the believing community is to be identified with the "temple of the living God" (v. 16b).[237] The rhetorical questions in 2 Cor 6:14b-16a place a strong emphasis on moral separation from pagan influences. The modified quotation of Isa 52:11 in v. 17abc thus continues this line of thought from vv. 14b-16a. However, the extent that new exodus and new covenant imagery pervade both the immediate context of v. 16cd and the wider context of 2 Cor 2:14—7:4 should not be overlooked.[238] The mixed citation of Lev 26:11-12 and Ezek 37:27 in 2 Cor 6:16cd particularly places Paul's discussion of the believing community as a temple within a new covenant framework and suggests that he is drawing upon a broad set of traditions.[239] In light of the dominance of new exodus and new covenant thought within this section of 2 Corinthians, Paul's appeal to Isa 52:11 in v. 17abc probably goes beyond the ethical imperatives of Isa 52:11 and draws upon the thought of Isa 52:7-11 as a whole. There is thus sufficient basis to conclude that the citation of Isaianic tradition in 2

---

235. See above, pp. 26-29, for a fuller treatment of this passage.

236. Once again, new exodus imagery is particularly pronounced in vv. 9-10 (see above, pp. 27-28).

237. Cf. Scott, "2 Corinthians 6:16c-18," 84-85.

238. On the use of new exodus and new covenant traditions in 2 Cor 2:14—7:4, see Webb (*Returning Home*, 31-158).

239. Scott (*Restoration*, 79-80) helpfully notes that the covenant formula cited in 2 Cor 6:16cd is used in two primary ways within the OT: 1) protologically in close relation to the exodus from Egypt and the *establishment* of God's covenant relationship with Israel (cf. Exod 6:3-7; 2 Sam 7:23-24; 1 Chron 17:21-22; Jer 7:22-23; 11:3-5); and 2) eschatologically to describe the *restoration* of that covenant relationship after Israel has been judged through the exile for their covenant unfaithfulness (e.g., Jer 31:31-33; Ezek 11:17-20; Zech 8:7-8).

Cor 6:17abc may be understood as yet another instance of metalepsis within the Pauline corpus.

Reading 2 Cor 6:17abc as an example of the phenomenon of metalepsis has significant implications for appreciating Paul's description of the church as "the temple of the living God" in v. 16b. At the very least, Paul is again pointing to the fulfillment of Isaiah's vision of a new exodus (cf. 2 Cor 5:17; 6:2; Gal 6:15). The prominence of the restoration of Zion/Jerusalem in Isa 52:7–11 (and other Isaianic new exodus texts) may also suggest that Paul is presenting the nascent Christian community as the inaugural realization of Isaiah's restored Zion/Jerusalem.[240] This reading of 2 Cor 6:16b–17c indicates that Paul views the church within an *Urzeit-Endzeit* frame of reference and as a visible testimony to the reality that God has acted to restore his creation. Finally, given the association of YHWH's return to Zion with this new exodus in Isa 52:8 MT (בשוב יהוה ציון יראו), Paul may envision God's presence with his people (via the Spirit) as the initial fulfillment of that aspect of Isaiah's prophecy.[241]

Summary of New Creation in 2 Corinthians 5:11–21

Despite recent scholarly attempts to do so, it is evident that the essence of new creation in 2 Cor 5:11–21 cannot be strictly confined to anthropology, cosmology, or ecclesiology. One should, no doubt, concede that there is a strong emphasis on anthropology within the context of this passage. Second Corinthians 5:15 fundamentally describes the shift in lordship that has resulted with Christ's death. Furthermore, v. 16 suggests Paul's newfound outlook drives him to refrain from evaluating others in a fleshly way. Finally, the extended discussion of reconciliation in 2 Cor 5:18–21 also indicates new creation in v. 17 is weighted heavily in an anthropological direction.[242]

Several factors, however, indicate Paul's conception of new creation in 2 Cor 5:14–17 also reaches into the realms of cosmology and ecclesiology. Most significantly, the allusion to Isaianic tradition in 2 Cor 5:17b directly fixes new creation within Isaiah's proclamation of a new exodus, a prophetic expectation which ultimately culminates in a "new heavens and new earth"

---

240. Once again, the restored Zion/Jerusalem is clearly depicted as a cultic notion in Isa 66:18–24 (see above, p. 40).

241. As already noted, there is no direct equivalent to the clause יראו בשוב יהוה ציון in the LXX, which instead uses a less anthropomorphic verb (ἐλεέω) for the MT's שוב (see above, p. 27–28).

242. Note especially Paul's use of the phrase μὴ λογιζόμενος αὐτοῖς τὰ παραπτώματα αὐτῶν in v. 19.

(cf. Isa 65:17–25; 66:18–24). Paul's second Adam typology in vv. 14–15 also suggests that new creation in v. 17 forms part of his inaugurated eschatology. The use of the noun κόσμος in v. 19 additionally indicates that new creation should not be understood on a purely individualistic plane. The corporate nature of new creation may, in turn, point to the diverse nature of the believing community, composed of both Jew and Gentile. An ecclesiological understanding of καινὴ κτίσις in v. 17 and κόσμον in v. 19 is also plausible when one considers the degree to which the salvation of the nations encompasses Isaiah's message of a new exodus and the depiction of the "new heavens and new earth" in Isaiah 66 (see above, esp. p. 18–19, 39–40).

We should also consider the extent to which new creation in 2 Cor 5:14–17 evokes an *Urzeit-Endzeit* typology. It is helpful to recall at this point that Paul has already associated conversion with this hermeneutical structure (cf. 2 Cor 3:18; 4:4, 6) within the context of a lengthy contrast between his new covenant ministry and the old covenant ministry of Moses (2 Cor 3:1–18).[243] The presence of new Adam imagery in 2 Cor 5:14–15 also opens the door for καινὴ κτίσις in v. 17 to be understood within an *Urzeit-Endzeit* framework. Moreover, the notion of reconciliation in 2 Cor 5:18–21 implies a past breach in *shalom* between God and humanity. For Paul to speak of the reconciliation of the world thus evokes the fall narrative of Gen 3 and points to God's definitive resolution of that crisis in the Messiah. Finally, the extent to which an *Urzeit-Endzeit* typology forms part of Isaiah's new exodus allows for a similar conception of new creation in 2 Cor 5:17.[244]

A particularly unique feature of the preceding analysis of new creation in 2 Corinthians is the investigation of 2 Cor 6:1–18. The Isaianic quotations in 2 Cor 6:2b and 2 Cor 6:17abc, in particular, have significant implications for grasping the significance of new creation in this letter. As with 2 Cor 5:17, both of these texts clearly link Paul's argument with Isaiah's new exodus (cf. Isa 49:9–13; 52:7–11). Significantly, these two Isaianic passages suggest the new exodus is associated with the restored Zion/Jerusalem and the redemption of the nations (cf. Isa 49:1, 6–8, 12, 14–26; 52:7–10). In the case of Isa 49:9–13, it is also evident that the new exodus impacts creation itself (vv. 11, 13). While the search for Paul's logic in 2 Cor 6:1–17 may be arduous at times, there are ample grounds to presume that this passage builds upon his statements in 2 Cor 5:11–21. The prominence of new exodus/new covenant traditions within Paul's argument throughout 2 Cor 2:14—7:4 is also relevant at this point as it is apparent that Paul is drawing upon a matrix

---

243. See above, pp. 90–91.

244. See chapter 2 on the place of the *Urzeit-Endzeit* typology within the Isaianic tradition.

of ideas within 2 Cor 2:14—7:4 that is closely related to the notion of new creation. On the strength of these two factors, the quotations of Isa 49:9 and Isa 52:11 in 2 Cor 6:2b, 17abc corroborate a fairly broad reading of new creation in 2 Cor 5:17. That is, the presence of ecclesiological and cosmological overtones in the wider context of Isa 49:9–13 and Isa 52:7–11 confirm the likelihood that καινὴ κτίσις in 2 Cor 5:17 embraces anthropological, ecclesiological, and cosmological renewal. Finally, if the designation of believers as the "temple of the living God" in 2 Cor 6:16 is to be understood in the light of Isaiah's restored Zion/Jerusalem, new creation in 2 Cor 5:17 may then be related to the eschatological temple and *Urzeit-Endzeit* typology so prominent in Second Temple Jewish traditions.

Conclusion

The foregoing analysis of new creation in 2 Cor 5:14–17 and Gal 6:14–16 has demonstrated that this concept intersects with several major thoroughfares within Paul's complex understanding of what God has accomplished in Christ. In contrast to scholars such as Hubbard, Mell, and Kraus, I have maintained that though these two texts emphasize different aspects of new creation (in 2 Cor 5:14–17, anthropology predominates the discussion, while cosmology receives the greatest stress in Gal 6:14–16), one may reasonably conclude that Paul understands new creation in cosmological, anthropological, and ecclesiological terms. I have also demonstrated that a strong case can be made for linking 2 Cor 5:14–17 with an *Urzeit-Endzeit* typology (cf. 2 Cor 6:2, 16). Finally, it must be directly admitted that the absence of temple imagery in Gal 6:14–16 makes it difficult to detect the presence of an *Urzeit-Endzeit* typological scheme in this text. Nonetheless, since v. 16 links new creation with the ecclesiological unity (a subject naturally associated with the *Urzeit-Endzeit* pattern) achieved through the Christ-event, it is evident that Paul once again has depicted new creation as the restoration of the Creator's original intentions for the cosmos.

5

New Creation in Ephesians 1–2

Introduction

THE PREVIOUS THREE CHAPTERS have principally discussed the background of new creation in the Hebrew Bible and Second Temple Judaism, as well as the complex portraits of new creation in Galatians and 2 Corinthians. Regarding the former topic, we have seen that new creation encompasses anthropological, cosmological, and ecclesiological restoration. We have also seen that new creation in these ancient Jewish traditions is depicted within an *Urzeit-Endzeit* framework. Regarding the latter topic, the preceding analysis of Galatians and 2 Corinthians has shown that new creation in these Pauline texts closely follows the pattern set forth by these Jewish traditions.

This chapter has two principal objectives. First, I will assess the nature of new creation in Eph 1–2 and consider the degree to which new creation is presented in anthropological, cosmological, and ecclesiological terms within this text. Second, I will examine how the OT shapes the author's conception of new creation in Eph 1–2. The presence of a new creation motif in Eph 1–2 is not a new observation. Nor have scholars overlooked the fact that AE directly links his discussion of new creation in Eph 2:15 with Isaiah's new exodus (cf. Eph 2:13, 17).[1] This close correlation between new exodus and new creation in Eph 2:13–17 forms a strong degree of congruity between new creation in Ephesians and 2 Corinthians (cf. 2 Cor 5:17). The allusions to the OT in Eph 1:20–22 (cf. Ps 8:7 LXX; 109:1 LXX) and the description of the community of Christ-followers as an expanding temple in Eph 2:19–22, however, have been overlooked in this discussion.[2] These two

---

1. Beale, "Reconciliation," 578; Webb, *Returning Home*, 117–20.

2. My treatment of Eph 1–2 will draw upon Gombis' ("Ephesians 2," 403–18) general analysis, with some modification, of ANE temple-building traditions in Eph 1:20—2:22.

textual features in Eph 1-2 are significant in that they establish further links with Isaiah's depiction of a new exodus.³ Other important Jewish traditions lie latent within Eph 1-2 (e.g., Eph 2:15). The following analysis of Eph 1-2 will expand upon these observations by considering the significance of the OT for understanding the author's conception of new creation. Interpreting Eph 1-2 intertextually may in turn clarify the degree of continuity and discontinuity between new creation in Ephesians and the Hauptbriefe.

New Creation and Ephesians 1:9-10

The Ephesian Mysterion in Ephesians 1:9-10a

AE's discussion of new creation in Eph 1:9-10 is set within the letter's theological introduction and constitutes part of the author's delineation of the spiritual blessings believers have received through their union with Christ.⁴ This section immediately follows the letter opening (vv. 1-2) and is best understood on a formal level as a eulogy drawing upon traditions associated with liturgical texts in the OT and Second Temple Judaism.⁵ Despite uncertainty regarding the precise structure of this eulogy, the primary blessings identified in Eph 1:3-10 are fairly evident: 1) election in Christ (v. 4); 2) adoption in Christ (vv. 5-6); and 3) redemption in Christ (vv. 7-10).

A number of interpreters have suggested the *anakephalaiōsis* of Eph 1:10 is related to the letter's new creation theme.⁶ The same cannot be said for the author's discussion of the revelation of God's mystery in v. 9.⁷ The close linking of these two central ideas within vv. 9-10, however, opens the door for this possibility.⁸

---

3. The significance of divine warrior and temple-building traditions within Isaiah's new exodus has been extensively treated in chapter 2 (see above, esp. pp. 20-24, 26-27).

4. On Eph 1:3-14 as a theological introduction, see O'Brien ("Ephesians 1," 504-16).

5. E.g., 1 Kgs 8:15, 56; Ps 71:18 LXX; 105:48 LXX; 1QS 11:15-20; 1QH 5:20; 10:14; 12:32; 19:29; 1QM 10:5. Cf. Caragounis, *Mysterion*, 40; Kuhn, "Ephesians," 116-17; Van Roon, *Ephesians*, 184-88.

6. These scholars primarily suggest that the infinitive ἀνακεφαλαιώσασθαι in Eph 1:10 carries a recapitulatory sense. Cf. Lincoln, *Ephesians*, 33-34; Hartin, "ANAKE-ΦΑΛΑΙΩΣΑΣΘΑΙ," 231-34; Turner, "Mission and Meaning," 139-40; McHugh, "Reconsideration," 302-9; pace Barth, *Ephesians 1-3*, 91-92.

7. Caragounis (*Mysterion*, 118), however, is an important exception.

8. The clauses γνωρίσας ἡμῖν τὸ μυστήριον τοῦ θελήματος αὐτοῦ (v. 9a) and ἀνακεφαλαιώσασθαι τὰ πάντα ἐν τῷ Χριστῷ (v. 10 b) are linked syntactically through the phrase εἰς οἰκονομίαν τοῦ πληρώματος τῶν καιρῶν (v. 10a). The clause ἀνακεφαλαιώσασθαι τὰ πάντα ἐν τῷ Χριστῷ also expresses the subject matter of the mystery in v. 9. Cf. Martin, *Adamica*, 88; Thielman, *Ephesians*, 65.

The background of the noun μυστήριον sheds a great deal of light on its usage in Eph 1:9. During the first half of the twentieth century, scholars generally linked this noun with Hellenistic traditions. More specifically, the noun μυστήριον was frequently associated with the initiatory rites of Greco-Roman mystery religions and Gnostic traditions.[9] Owing principally to the work of R. Brown, scholars now have a greater appreciation of the importance of Jewish traditions for understanding the use of μυστήριον in the NT.[10] Especially important in this regard is the usage of μυστήριον as a translation of the Aramaic noun רז in Dan 2:19, 27, 30, 47 LXX. Within Dan 2:19-47 LXX, the noun μυστήριον is employed to describe divine secrets previously hidden, but now revealed to King Nebuchadnezzar by means of Daniel's vision. The mysteries disclosed and interpreted to Nebuchadnezzar pertain to eschatological events that will occur "at the end of days" (cf. Dan 2:28-29, 45 LXX). The noun retains this meaning within later Jewish apocalyptic texts such as *4 Ezra* 14:5 and *1 En.* 9:6; 38:3; 83:7; 103:2-4. Several interpreters also note that the noun μυστήριον is used in starkly similar ways in Daniel and Ephesians to describe God's eschatological plan to renew the cosmos.[11] In summary, the noun μυστήριον likely builds upon traditions found in the OT and Second Temple Judaism and AE may be "conscious of standing in the Danielic tradition and carrying on what Dan has bequeathed."[12]

The noun μυστήριον occurs in Eph 1:9 within a participial phrase beginning with the participle γνωρίσας. The LXX frequently uses the verb γνωρίζω in connection with divine disclosures, and the NT and Ephesians maintain the same connotation.[13] For a number of scholars, this adverbial participle of manner likely further describes how God lavished his grace upon believers and represents an action contemporaneous with the verb ἐπερίσσευσεν in v. 8.[14] The participle is followed by the dative pronoun ἡμῖν,

9. See Gladd (*Mysterion*, 8-16) for a recent summary of the history of interpretation of this noun.

10. According to Brown ("Semitic," 87), "Paul and the NT writers could have written everything they did about *mysterion* if there had never been pagan mystery religions."

11. Cf. Caragounis, *Mysterion*, 123-26; Lincoln, *Ephesians*, 30; Arnold, *Ephesians*, 86-87.

12. Caragounis, *Mysterion*, 135.

13. Cf. 2 Sam 7:21; Neh 9:14; Ps 97:2 LXX; 102:7 LXX; Dan Θ' 2:23, 28, 29, 30, 45; Rom 9:22-23; 16:26; Eph 3:3, 5; Col 1:27.

14. Cf. Hoehner, *Ephesians*, 214; Wallace, *Greek Grammar*, 625; pace Best, *Ephesians*, 133; Caragounis, *Mysterion*, 93. According to Best and Caragounis, the participle expresses an independent action. Given the logical flow of the eulogy to this point (in particular with regard to the likelihood that the phrase ἐν πάσῃ σοφίᾳ καὶ φρονήσει in v. 8b semantically prepares for the thought of v. 9), it does seem best to view the statements in v. 9 as part of the unit which began in v. 7.

which clearly identifies the recipients of this revelation as the same individuals who have received the spiritual blessings outlined in this passage. The author, therefore, makes clear that knowledge of the mystery is not a product of human creativity or ingenuity, but of divine revelation and suggests it is directly related to the same grace conferred upon believers in v. 8.

This statement in v. 9 linking redemption in Christ with the revelation of God's eternal plan is followed by another prepositional phrase beginning with the preposition κατά (v. 9b).[15] The construction κατὰ τὴν εὐδοκίαν αὐτοῦ ἥν προέθετο ἐν αὐτῷ in Eph 1:9b parallels Eph 1:5 in both content and function. As in v. 5, this prepositional phrase describes the standard or norm upon which the divine decision to grant the revelation of the mystery was based.[16] This phrase may also (as in v. 5) express the reason God revealed the mystery to those in Christ.[17] Eph 1:9b, therefore, further qualifies the notion of revelation in the previous clause by suggesting that the basis of this disclosure lies in God's benevolent character and eternal decree.

The statement pertaining to the divine will in Eph 1:9b is, in fact, part of a larger unit of thought which ends at Eph 1:10a (εἰς οἰκονομίαν τοῦ πληρώματος τῶν καιρῶν). The significance and meaning of this phrase are strongly dependent upon two related issues: 1) the sense of the preposition εἰς; and 2) the meaning of the noun οἰκονομίαν. With a number of scholars, the preposition εἰς in this context conveys the purpose of God's decision to center the redemption of believers around Jesus Christ (v. 9b).[18] The meaning of the noun οἰκονομίαν in this context also presents challenges to the interpreter. Once again, there does seem to be something of a consensus that the noun is used here to describe God's activity of administering.[19] If the construction εἰς οἰκονομίαν in Eph 1:10a refers to the divine action of governing, the phrase τοῦ πληρώματος τῶν καιρῶν then specifies what is being governed. The noun πληρώματος here is not used in the theological sense found in such texts as Eph 1:23; 3:19; 4:13 and Col 1:19. Instead, the noun carries the meaning of "climax" or "completion."[20] There is general agreement among commentators that the plural noun καιρῶν draws upon apocalyptic traditions which divide world history into a series of epochs

---

15. Syntactically, the phrase κατὰ τὴν εὐδοκίαν modifies the participle γνωρίσας. Cf. Schlier, *Epheser*, 62.

16. Cf. Hoehner, *Ephesians*, 215.

17. Cf. Caragounis, *Mysterion*, 94.

18. Cf. Muddiman, *Ephesians*, 75; Lincoln, *Ephesians*, 31; Caragounis, *Mysterion*, 94–95.

19. Cf. Thielman, *Ephesians*, 64; Bruce, *Ephesians*, 262; Muddiman, *Ephesians*, 75; pace Barth, *Ephesians 1–3*, 87.

20. Cf. Lincoln, *Ephesians*, 32; Barth, *Ephesians 1–3*, 88.

(e.g., *Tob* 14:5; *4 Ezra* 4:37; 1QpHab 7:2; *2 Bar.* 14:1).[21] When taken together, the phrase τοῦ πληρώματος τῶν καιρῶν thus points to "den Höhepunkt aller irdischen Zeiten . . . die (eschatologische) Zeit Christi."[22]

The author's discussion of the "mystery of Christ" in Eph 3:3–5 helps to clarify the significance of Eph 1:9–10a for understanding the nature of new creation in Eph 1–2. Ephesians 3:3–5 forms part of the author's larger treatment of the Apostle Paul's ministry to the Gentiles in Eph 3:2–13. Within Eph 3:3–5, two important points are made that shed light on the meaning of the author's statements in Eph 1:9–10a. First, Eph 3:4 identifies the content of the "mystery" in Eph 1:9 with Christ (cf. Col 2:2; 4:3).[23] Second, Eph 3:6 links this "mystery" with the equal participation of Jew and Gentile in the redemptive work of Christ.[24] Regarding this first point, Eph 3:4 and Eph 1:9b (ἣν προέθετο ἐν αὐτῷ) both stress that Christ is the focal point of the divine mystery. Regarding the latter point, the close connection between Eph 3:6 and Eph 2:19–22 suggests that Eph 1:9–10a prepares for the author's further discussion of the union of Jew and Gentile in the remainder of this letter (cf. Eph 2:11–22).[25]

In summary, the discussion of the divine mystery in Eph 1:9–10a introduces the author's discussion of new creation in Eph 1–2 in several ways. First, the use of the noun μυστήριον in Eph 1:9 evokes Dan 2:19–47 LXX and closely correlates new creation with God's plan for the consummation of human history. This is made explicit in Eph 1:10 through the use of the phrase εἰς οἰκονομίαν τοῦ πληρώματος τῶν καιρῶν. Second, the noun μυστήριον in Eph 1:9 also foreshadows the author's treatment of the union of Jew and Gentile, not only in Eph 3:3–6, but also in Eph 2:11–22. The subject of the cessation of hostility between Jew and Gentile is, in fact, strongly associated

21. Cf. Schnackenburg, *Epheser*, 57. According to Hoehner (*Ephesians*, 219), "the plural appears to point to the fullness or totality of the times or epochs of history."

22. Schnackenburg, *Epheser*, 58. Cf. Mussner, *Christus*, 68. According to Lindemann (*Die Aufhebung*, 96), the construction τοῦ πληρώματος τῶν καιρῶν points to the "Zusammenfassung aller 'Zeitpunkte' . . . das Ende aller Zeit, der Augenblick, an dem die Anakephalaiosis des Alls manifest wird." Lindemann's understanding of Eph 1:10, however, is especially problematic given his equating of the "fullness of time" with the gathering up of "all things" in Christ (cf. Eph 2:2; 6:12).

23. The genitive construction τοῦ Χριστοῦ in Eph 3:4 is best understood as a genitive of apposition. Cf. Arnold, *Ephesians*, 188; Barth, *Ephesians 1–3*, 331.

24. While the noun μυστήριον is absent in Eph 3:5–6, there is, nonetheless, a logical relationship between v. 4 and vv. 5–6 because of: 1) the relative pronoun ὅ and the revelatory language (ἐγνωρίσθη and ἀπεκαλύφθη) in v. 5; and 2) the likelihood that the infinitive εἶναι is used in an epexegetical sense. Cf. Best, *Ephesians*, 311.

25. The frequent use of the σύν prefix in Eph 2:19–22 and Eph 3:6 establishes a significant connection between these two texts.

with new creation imagery in Eph 2:11–22. The author's treatment of the divine mystery in Eph 1:9–10a therefore directly links this topic with God's eschatological action in history and foreshadows an ecclesiological concern that is depicted as an act of new creation in Eph 2:11–22.

The Anakephalaiōsis of All Things in Ephesians 1:10b

The following discussion will mainly explore the meaning of the infinitive ἀνακεφαλαιώσασθαι in Eph 1:10b by means of the linguistic distinction between a lexeme's denotation and its connotation.[26] I will begin by first making a few general comments regarding the morphological components of the verb ἀνακεφαλαιόω and the verb's range of meaning. I will then give careful attention to the verb's denotation and connotation. I will then conclude this discussion by exploring how the gathering up of "all things" in Christ in Eph 1:10 is related to the new creation theme in this letter.[27]

A brief morphological discussion of the lexeme ἀνακεφαλαιόω allows for a valuable entry point into the larger discussion of the significance of this phrase. Essentially, this verb is probably derived from a combination of the preposition ἀνά and the noun κεφάλαιον ("summary," "main point"), not κεφαλή ("head").[28] For some scholars, the prefix ἀνά when associated with the noun κεφάλαιον carries the meaning "again" and expresses the idea of recapitulation.[29] Best, however, rightly notes the presence of the prefix may simply be intended to amplify the meaning of the root.[30] That the verb ἀνακεφαλαιόω stems from the noun κεφάλαιον and not κεφαλή makes the most sense of the manner in which it is employed in Rom 13:9 and other rel-

---

26. See Cotterell and Turner (*Linguistics*, 45–47) for a useful treatment of the difference between denotation and connotation.

27. Given the programmatic nature of Eph 1:10, it is helpful to distinguish between the *anakephalaiōsis* of Eph 1:10 and the *anakephalaiōsis* concept in the remainder of this letter. This distinction will allow us to account for the introductory nature of Eph 1:10. By the *anakephalaiōsis* concept, I am referring to the outworking of the author's statement in Eph 1:10 as it primarily relates to the church and the powers. Cf. Caragounis, *Mysterion*, 143–46; O'Brien, *Ephesians*, 112–13. A demarcation between the significance of the construction ἀνακεφαλαιώσασθαι τὰ πάντα ἐν τῷ Χριστῷ in Eph 1:10 and the *anakephalaiōsis* concept in this letter would also provide a helpful means of addressing the thorny question of how the portrait of Christ as "head" in Ephesians is related to Eph 1:10 (cf. Eph 1:22; 4:15). On the meaning of the noun κεφαλή, see Bedale ("Meaning," 211–16) and Grudem ("ΚΕΦΑΛΗ," 38–59).

28. Cf. Turner, "Mission and Meaning," 139; Hartin, "ΑΝΑΚΕΦΑΛΑΙΩΣΑΣΘΑΙ," 230; Schlier, "ἀνακεφαλαιόομαι," *TDNT* 3:681–82; Usami, *Somatic*, 117.

29. Cf. Arnold, *Ephesians*, 89; Sellin, *Epheser*, 107.

30. Best, *Ephesians*, 140. Cf. Thielman, *Ephesians*, 65.

evant primary sources.³¹ Several scholars, nonetheless, argue the discussion of Christ's headship in Eph 1:22 is closely related to the ἀνακεφαλαιώσασθαι τὰ πάντα ἐν τῷ Χριστῷ in Eph 1:10b.³²

The verb ἀνακεφαλαιόω carries a range of meaning corresponding to the sense of the noun κεφάλαιον. Classical writers used the verb in discussions of rhetoric to describe the act of summarizing an argument.³³ The only other occurrence of the verb ἀνακεφαλαιόω in the NT outside of Eph 1:10 is found in Rom 13:9. Here Paul summarizes the commandments contained in the second section of the Decalogue under the rubric of the command ἀγαπήσεις τὸν πλησίον σου ὡς σεαυτόν. In the post-apostolic era, the verb carries the meaning "to end" in the Epistle of Barnabas and "to recapitulate" in the writings of Irenaeus.³⁴ In summary, the verb ἀνακεφαλαιόω exhibits the following range of meaning within the ancient world: 1) "to summarize an argument"; 2) "to sum up"; 3) "to conclude" or "to end"; and 4) "to recapitulate."

Having considered the lexical components that comprise the verb ἀνακεφαλαιόω and established its range of meaning, we are now in a position to analyze its denotative sense in Eph 1:10. Aside from its use in the Epistle of Barnabas (and possibly the Psalter), a common feature of each of the meanings associated with ἀνακεφαλαιόω in Classical Greek, Romans, and Irenaeus, is the notion that distinguishable parts (whether of an argument, the Decalogue, or segments of human history) are somehow acted upon. More specifically, in each of these three literary corpora, separate elements are brought together under the rubric of a singular entity.

---

31. LSJ (κεφάλαιος, 944), however, notes that the nouns κεφάλαιος and κεφαλή are synonymous in secular Greek literature.

32. Cf. Schlier, *Epheser*, 65; Usami, *Unity*, 148; Kitchen, ἀνακεφαλαίωσις, 74, 76–77; Schnackenburg, *Epheser*, 58; Dawes, *Body in Question*, 142–44; Van Kooten, *Cosmic Christology*, 151; Lona, *Eschatologie*, 274–75; pace Sellin, *Epheser*, 107; Thielman, *Ephesians*, 66.

Barth (*Ephesians 1–3*, 91) describes such an approach as "an unwarranted etymological adventure." See Barr (*Semantics*, 237–38) for further critique of this methodology. Nonetheless, the phrase ἐν τῷ Χριστῷ in Eph 1:10 implies "all things" will be placed in a subordinate position to Christ. There is thus a sense in which Eph 1:10 *prepares* for the fuller treatment of Christ's headship in Eph 1:22 and Eph 4:15. In the end, it is prudent to fall back on a distinction between the meaning of the construction ἀνακεφαλαιώσασθαι τὰ πάντα ἐν τῷ Χριστῷ in Eph 1:10b and the *anakephalaiōsis* motif in Ephesians. That is, despite the linguistic complexity of adjudicating the relationship between the lexemes ἀνακεφαλαιόω, κεφάλαιον, and κεφαλή, there is little need to deny that the portrait of Christ as "head" over all things forms an integral part of this letter's *anakephalaiōsis* theme.

33. Kitchen, ἀνακεφαλαίωσις, 72–73.

34. Cf. *Barn.* 5:11; *Adv. Haer.* 1:10:1; 3:16:6; 3:18:1, 7; 3:21:10; 5:20:2; 5:21:1.

Further scrutiny, however, indicates that the meaning of the verb ἀνακεφαλαιόω expands in the writings of Irenaeus. As McHugh notes, the act of working from beginning to end does establish an important similarity between the use of the verb ἀνακεφαλαιόω in Irenaeus' notion of recapitulation and the use of the verb in Classical literature.[35] However, it is problematic to conclude with McHugh that the verbal idea of reenacting, restoring, or making anew is related to the act of summarizing or summing up.[36] One may therefore conclude that while there is some degree of similarity between the manner in which the verb ἀνακεφαλαιόω is used in Classical Greek and Irenaeus, there is nonetheless an important difference that suggests the verb experienced a significant expansion in meaning at the hand of Irenaeus. I will now assess the degree to which that progression in meaning represents a legitimate reading of Eph 1:10.

The conclusions I have reached concerning the denotative meaning of the infinitive ἀνακεφαλαιώσασθαι do not negate the possibility that AE coined a new meaning. It is at this point that an analysis of the verb's connotation in Eph 1:10 becomes helpful. As one considers the phrases linked to the infinitive ἀνακεφαλαιώσασθαι in Eph 1:10, it becomes clear that while AE uses the verb with a slightly different sense, its denotative meaning, nonetheless, remains largely unchanged.

The first phrase that impinges upon the connotative meaning of ἀνακεφαλαιόω in this context identifies the object of the infinitive as "all things in Christ" (cf. Eph 3:9; 4:10). The presence of the phrase ἐν τῷ Χριστῷ in v. 10 likely builds upon the thought of Eph 1:9b and indicates that the scope of the action expressed by the infinitive ἀνακεφαλαιώσασθαι occurs in the Messiah.[37] The phrase τὰ πάντα ἐν τῷ Χριστῷ in v. 10 is, in turn, modified by the phrase τὰ ἐπὶ τοῖς οὐρανοῖς καὶ τὰ ἐπὶ τῆς γῆς ἐν αὐτῷ (cf. Col 1:16, 20). With this latter phrase, AE identifies the πάντα of the preceding phrase with the "things in heaven and things on earth."

Thanks to the work of Caragounis on this subject, it is now generally recognized that the phrase τὰ ἐπὶ τοῖς οὐρανοῖς καὶ τὰ ἐπὶ τῆς γῆς in v. 10 refers to the representatives of two distinct realms of existence that feature

---

35. McHugh, "Reconsideration," 307.

36. Cf. ibid., 307–8.

37. Hoehner (*Ephesians*, 222) helpfully notes that the article before the noun Χριστῷ points to the titular rather than personal use of the noun and suggests that the author is arguing the *anakephalaiōsis* "of all things will occur in Israel's promised Messiah." While Best (*Ephesians*, 143) sees "little in Jewish messianic speculation to connect the Messiah to the consummation of the cosmos," such notions are drawn together in Isa 11:1–12 (especially when read in close relation to Isa 65:17–25).

prominently in this letter.³⁸ Specifically, the construction τὰ ἐπὶ τοῖς οὐρανοῖς is commonly viewed as a reference to the heavenly powers, while the construction τὰ ἐπὶ τῆς γῆς is predominantly understood to refer to the church composed of Jews and Gentiles.³⁹ Regarding his reading of the phrase τὰ ἐπὶ τοῖς οὐρανοῖς, Caragounis appeals to the portrait of the powers in Ephesians as spiritual beings who while hostile to the divine purpose, have been subjugated by Christ (Eph 1:21-22; 2:2; 6:12).⁴⁰ Caragounis finds support for his reading of the phrase τὰ ἐπὶ τῆς γῆς by appealing to: 1) the general discussion in Eph 1-2 of the believing community's forgiveness, redemption, and heavenly status (cf. Eph 1:7, 14, 22-23; 2:1-10); 2) the detailed treatment of the union of Jew and Gentile in Eph 2:11-22; and 3) the coalescing of all these issues in Eph 3:1-13 in direct connection with the "mystery" of Eph 1:9.⁴¹

The preceding discussion has revealed that the verb ἀνακεφαλαιόω generally refers to the action of bringing together distinguishable elements under the rubric of a single entity. As one examines Eph 1:10, it becomes clear this denotative meaning remains largely unchanged. According to this text, the *anakephalaiōsis* somehow concerns τὰ πάντα (further defined as τὰ ἐπὶ τοῖς οὐρανοῖς καὶ τὰ ἐπὶ τῆς γῆς), and the deed expressed by means of the infinitive ἀνακεφαλαιώσασθαι is said to occur "in Christ." All the essential features (separate elements . . . τὰ πάντα; the action of bringing these separate elements together into a single entity . . . the Messiah) associated with the conventional denotative meaning of ἀνακεφαλαιόω are, therefore, present in Eph 1:10.

Now that we have examined the denotation and connotation of the infinitive ἀνακεφαλαιώσασθαι in Eph 1:10, we are in a better position to consider the degree to which the statements in Eph 1:10 may be legitimately understood within the framework of an *Urzeit-Endzeit* typology.⁴²

---

38. Several scholars suggest that the phrase simply refers to the animate and inanimate parts of creation. Cf. Hoehner, *Ephesians*, 223; Barth, *Ephesians 1-3*, 91-92. While true in a general sense, this interpretation fails to account for the critical role these ideas play in the remainder of the letter.

39. Caragounis, *Mysterion*, 96, 144-46. Cf. Bruce, *Ephesians*, 261-62; Barth, *Ephesians 1-3*, 91-92.

40. Caragounis, *Mysterion*, 144-45.

41. Ibid., 139-45. According to Caragounis (ibid., 142), "The strain begun at 1:9 f. [sic] is brought to its proper conclusion at 3:1-13 in the context of Gentile participation in the Body of Christ." Caragounis' interpretation of the phrase τὰ ἐπὶ τῆς γῆς confirms my earlier suggestion that the divine mystery of Eph 1:9: 1) foreshadows the author's later discussion of the union of Jew and Gentile; and 2) forms part of the author's new creation theme.

42. Such a reading of Eph 1:10 has a long history that goes back as far as Irenaeus (see above, p. 128).

Further study of Eph 1:3–10 suggests the infinitive ἀνακεφαλαιώσασθαι in Eph 1:10 may indeed be understood through the lens of this typology. As already noted, the first spiritual blessing identified in this passage is election in Christ (cf. Eph 1:4). Especially pertinent for this present discussion is the prepositional phrase πρὸ καταβολῆς κόσμου in v. 4 which places the act of divine election "before the foundation of the world." The remainder of Eph 1:3–14 describes a series of other blessings, which have been graciously given to believers. Ephesians 1:5–10 in particular focuses on two metaphors that describe the salvation, adoption, and redemption of Christ-followers. Ephesians 1:7 mentions τὴν ἄφεσιν τῶν παραπτωμάτων, which would implicitly draw upon the narrative of Adam's sin in Gen 3:1–24. Since the divine action in v. 10 is closely associated with the notion of God's governing of history towards a climactic goal, the author has, therefore linked this notion in v. 10 with a constellation of ideas that look backward to the beginning of history *and* forward to its eschatological fulfillment. Ephesians 1:3–10 thus depicts a chronological movement from "eternity past" to the consummation, and the salvation of believers is placed between these two poles of reality.[43]

Summary

This analysis of Eph 1:9–10 has explored the nature of new creation in this text and assessed the significance of the OT for understanding this concept. Ephesians 1:9–10 occurs within the letter's theological introduction and forms part of the author's description of the spiritual blessings that believers have received through their union with Christ (vv. 3–14). Despite the absence of quotations, vv. 9–10 draws upon the OT in subtle ways. The divine μυστήριον in v. 9 is not only derived from terminology in Dan 2:19, 27, 30, 47 LXX but also is developed in Eph 1:9–10a in such a way that both texts express the same underlying idea—God's plan to redeem humanity and the rest of creation. The specific content of this mystery is outlined in Eph 1:10b. Here the author indicates that the goal of Christ's victorious death is the

---

43. A distinction between the lexeme ἀνακεφαλαιώσασθαι in Eph 1:10 and the development of the *anakephalaiōsis* motif in this letter is again useful at this point as it allows one to avoid what linguists have termed the root fallacy (see Cotterell and Turner, *Linguistics*, 130–33; Louw, *Semantics*, 25–29, for helpful discussions of the root fallacy). In other words, in contrast to scholars such as Lincoln and McHugh, I would not argue the infinitive ἀνακεφαλαιώσασθαι in Eph 1:10 itself evokes an *Urzeit-Endzeit* typology. I would argue, nonetheless, that the wider context of Eph 1:3–10 and the unfolding of the *anakephalaiōsis* motif in such texts as Eph 1:20—2:22 support such a reading.

restoration of the original unity of creation.[44] Finally, the plan unfolded in Eph 1:9–10 implicitly presents a condensed summary of Scripture's grand metanarrative of creation-fall-redemption-new creation.[45]

This reading of Eph 1:9–10 has important implications for understanding the nature of new creation in Ephesians. First, since Eph 1:9–10 prepares for the author's fuller discussion of the bringing together of Jew and Gentile in Christ, it is evident that new creation in Ephesians ultimately takes on a distinct ecclesiological force. Second, when read in the light of the overarching plot line of creation-fall-redemption-new creation that underlies Eph 1:3–10, the phrase ἀνακεφαλαιώσασθαι τὰ πάντα ἐν τῷ Χριστῷ in Eph 1:10 takes on an *Urzeit-Endzeit* typology. AE thus depicts the final eschatological goal of human history very much in keeping with other Jewish traditions, while nonetheless offering a distinctively Christological slant.[46]

New Creation in Ephesians 1:20—2:22

Introductory Remarks

For some scholars, the presence of the introductory καί in Eph 2:1 demands a strict separation between Eph 1:20–23 and Eph 2:1–23.[47] One must readily admit that the author does shift his focus in Eph 2:1 towards describing the salvific work of Christ. Nonetheless, the discussion of the addressees' deliverance from τὸν ἄρχοντα τῆς ἐξουσίας τοῦ ἀέρος in Eph 2:1–7 assumes the author's prior treatment of Christ's supremacy in Eph 1:20–23.[48] In this regard, the parallelism between Eph 1:20 and Eph 2:5–6 should be especially accounted for, which directly links Christ's exaltation with the

---

44. This reading of the phrase ἀνακεφαλαιώσασθαι τὰ πάντα ἐν τῷ Χριστῷ in Eph 1:10 goes back as far as Irenaeus. However, I have sought to support this interpretation through a more rigorous methodology. Finally, the complexity of Irenaeus' doctrine of recapitulation suggests his writings postdate the letter to the Ephesians.

45. On the significance of this plot for understanding Pauline thought, see Witherington (*Paul's Narrative Thought World*, 3–5).

46. Cf. *1 En.* 90:28–38; 91:11–17; 4Q174 2:12—3:13; IQS 4:23–26; 11QTemple 29:7–10; *Jub.* 1:28–29; 4:26.

47. Cf. Hoehner, *Ephesians*, 305–6; Lincoln, *Ephesians*, 84; Barth, *Ephesians 1-3*, 212.

48. Cf. Schnackenburg, *Epheser*, 86–88; Best, "Dead," 14; Allen, "Exaltation," 103–4; Jeal, *Ephesians*, 100–1. Of the parallels between these two passages suggested by Allen, the following are especially significant: 1) ἐκ νεκρῶν//ὑμᾶς ὄντας νεκρούς . . . ὄντας ἡμᾶς νεκρούς (Eph 1:20; 2:1, 5); and 2) ἐν τῷ αἰῶνι τούτῳ ἀλλὰ καὶ ἐν τῷ μέλλοντι//ἐν τοῖς αἰῶσιν τοῖς ἐπερχομένοις (Eph 1:21; 2:7).

spiritual existence of Christ-followers in the heavenly realm.[49] By giving sufficient weight to the relationship between Christ's defeat of the powers in Eph 1:20–23 and the redemption of believers in Eph 2:1–7, we are able to address the significance of the introductory καί in Eph 2:1 and appreciate the close relationship between these two texts.[50] What remains is to consider how the account of Christ's cosmic victory in Eph 1:20–23 is related to the author's description of the new creation of humanity in Eph 2:1–10 and the union of Jew and Gentile into one new humanity/new temple in Eph 2:11–22. In the ensuing analysis, I will attempt to establish a unified reading of Eph 1:20—2:22 by accounting for the relationship between the author's extended discussion of new creation in Eph 2:1–22 and his appeal to the OT in Eph 1:20, 22; 2:13, 15, 17, 20.

Ephesians 1:20–23 as an Introduction to Ephesians 2:1–22

Ephesians 1:15–19 constitutes the author's prayer for the letter's recipients.[51] The content of Eph 1:20–23 expands upon the final request within Eph 1:15–19 related to the greatness of the divine power in v. 19. More specifically, this section of the prayer report identifies four ways in which the power mentioned in v. 19 has manifested itself in the Messiah (ἐν τῷ Χριστῷ): 1) it was instrumental in Christ's resurrection (v. 20a); 2) it placed him in a position of supreme authority within the heavenly realms (v. 20b); 3) it placed everything in the cosmos in submission to Christ (v. 22a); and finally, 4) it made him ruler of the cosmos on behalf of the church (v. 22b).[52] Importantly, the second and third assertions are expressed by means of allusions to Ps 109 LXX and Ps 8 LXX (cf. Rom 8:34, 38–39; 1 Cor 15:21–22, 24–27; Phil 3:20–21).

According to some scholars, the use of Ps 109 LXX and Ps 8 LXX in Eph 1:20, 22 derives from early Christian traditions related to Christ's death and resurrection.[53] T. Moritz, however, has cogently argued that the use

---

49. Cf. O'Brien, *Ephesians*, 170; Allen, "Exaltation," 105.

50. See Fee (*God's Empowering Presence*, 672) for the suggestion that the καί in Eph 2:1 is to be understood grammatically as a paratactic καί.

51. The construction διὰ τοῦτο in v. 15 may directly connect this passage with the entire berakah.

52. Technically speaking, Eph 1:20–23 is structured around three finite verbs (ἐνήργησεν, v. 20a; ὑπέταξεν, v. 22a; ἔδωκεν, v. 22b) and two participles (ἐγείρας, v. 20b; καθίσας, v. 20c). Since the content of Eph 1:20b–23 focuses on how God has mightily acted in Christ, it is best to view the two participles and final two finite verbs as parallel statements subordinate to the verb ἐνήργησεν in v. 20a. Cf. Best, *Ephesians*, 170.

53. Hay, *Glory*, 40, 42; Loader, "Ps. CX.1," 199–217; Lincoln, "Use," 40–42.

of these two texts in Eph 1:20, 22 stems from the author's own personal contemplation of these two texts.[54] Moritz builds upon this proposal and concludes, "If the claim that Eph 1:20–23 may well result from the author's own reflection on Pss 110:1 [109:1 LXX] and 8:7 is correct, it follows that we must pay close attention to the OT texts themselves in order to recover the author's logic in employing them."[55] In the ensuing analysis, I will build upon Moritz's work on Eph 1:20, 22 by demonstrating how AE's appeal to these two psalms sets the stage for Eph 2:1–22 and introduces the author's fuller elaboration of new creation.

Psalm 109 LXX may be broadly described as a royal song that focuses on YHWH's military support of the Davidic King.[56] Careful consideration of the internal evidence suggests that Ps 109 LXX is best divided into two strophes.[57] The first strophe begins with a divine promise to place the Davidic king in a position of authority and grant him aid in military conflicts with his foes (v. 1).[58] The remainder of the strophe explains how God will conquer the king's enemies (vv. 2–3).[59] The second strophe of Ps 109 LXX also begins with an oracular statement; this declaration, however, portrays the Davidic king in priestly terms in much the same manner that Melchizedek functioned as a priest-king (cf. Gen 14:17–20; Heb 5:6, 10; 6:20; 7:1–17). As with the first strophe, the divine oracle is followed by a description of the process by which the promise is effected. However, whereas vv. 2–3 primarily attributes the victory to the Davidic king, in vv. 5–7 it is YHWH himself who fights on behalf of Israel's monarch.

Returning to Eph 1:20–23, one is able to discern that AE is primarily using Ps 109 LXX in order to connect Jesus' Messiahship with his defeat of cosmic evil. The use of the noun Χριστός in Eph 1:20a identifies Jesus as the expected Messiah in much the same way that the noun functions in Eph 1:10, 12.[60] Since the main verb in Eph 1:20–21 is probably the lexeme

54. Moritz, *Profound Mystery*, 9–14.

55. Ibid., 14.

56. Allen, *Psalms 101–150*, 83; Kraus, *Psalmen*, 936–37.

57. Allen, *Psalms 101–150*, 85; Goldingay, *Psalms 90–150*, 291; pace Kraus, *Psalmen*, 928–29.

58. The NT undoubtedly interprets Ps 109 LXX in a messianic direction (cf. Matt 22:44; Mark 12:36; Luke 20:42; Acts 2:34; Heb 1:34). However, within the original historical context of this psalm, the speaker seems to portray himself as a prophet or member of the royal court who refers to the Davidic king as "my Lord" (v. 1). Cf. Goldingay, *Psalms 90–150*, 291, 293; Allen, *Psalms 101–150*, 86.

59. According to Schaper (*Eschatology*, 101), "One of the most remarkable messianic interpretations in the Greek Psalter is provided by Ps [sic] 109 (110), 3."

60. See above, p. 128.

ἐνήργησεν in Eph 1:20a, the participial phrase καθίσας ἐν δεξιᾷ αὐτοῦ must be understood as an additional manner in which God worked in the Messiah. For AE, Jesus is the ultimate Davidic king whom God grants victory over not earthly enemies as in Ps 109 LXX, but over the spiritual forces of evil (cf. Eph 1:21).[61]

Psalm 8 LXX is a hymn of praise to the universal splendor of God's name (vv. 2, 9). This psalm is best divided into three sections. The first section begins with an introductory statement of praise to God (v. 2). This is followed by an enigmatic declaration that contrasts the divergent ways in which God relates to newborns and his enemies (v. 3).[62] The next section (vv. 4–8) primarily focuses on the significance of the *imago dei* for humanity's worth (cf. 1QS 11:20–22).[63] The poet concludes that despite our seeming insignificance when compared to the heavenly bodies (v. 4), since God has created humanity in his image and established us as vice-regents over creation (vv. 5–9), he is to be praised (v. 10).[64]

Looking now at the use of Ps 8 LXX in Eph 1:22, it is reasonable to deduce that this psalm played a more significant role in formulating AE's understanding of the Christ-event than Ps 109 LXX.[65] That is, whereas AE seems to employ Ps 109 LXX primarily as a means of describing Christ as a divine warrior, reflection on Ps 8 LXX may have led AE to understand the significance of Christ on a grander scale (cf. 1 Cor 15:27). I have al-

---

61. Moritz (*Profound Mystery*, 15) helpfully suggests that one of the reasons the author appropriates Ps 8 LXX is because of the presence of the clause καὶ κατέστησας αὐτὸν ἐπὶ τὰ ἔργα τῶν χειρῶν σου πάντα in v. 7. In alluding to Ps 8 LXX, AE thus expands the focus of the Davidic king's victory from the earthly "enemies" of Ps 109:1 LXX to encompass all who are hostile to the divine will.

Finally, the portrait of YHWH in Ps 109:5–7 LXX as a divine warrior conquering the Davidic king's enemies is also relevant at this point. Since AE ultimately attributes Christ's defeat of the powers in Eph 1:20b–21 to divine agency in Eph 1:20a, it does not seem out of the realm of possibility to suggest Ps 109:5–7 LXX also influenced AE's understanding of Jesus' Messiahship. Albl (*Testimonia*, 236), however, contends that only Ps 109:1, 4 LXX "received Christian attention . . . before the time of Justin." If the divine warrior imagery in vv. 5–7 influenced AE's argument in Eph 1:20–21, Moritz's argument for conscious reflection of Ps 109 LXX on the part of AE (over against early Christian traditions) would be strengthened. It may not be necessary, however, to exclude the possibility that AE interacted with early Christian traditions on some level.

62. On the complex questions of the textual difficulty and meaning of Ps 8:3, see Craigie (*Psalms 1–50*, 105, 107).

63. There is sufficient basis to conclude that Ps 8:6–8 LXX alludes to Gen 1:26–28. Cf. Broyles, *Psalms*, 73; Moritz, *Profound Mystery*, 17–18.

64. See Jónsson (*Image of God*, 10–191) for an extensive discussion of the history of interpretation of the image of God concept.

65. Pace Martin, *Adamica*, 89–91. According to Martin, the allusion to Ps 8 LXX in Eph 1:22 simply restates the content of the allusion to Ps 109:1 LXX in Eph 1:20.

ready noted Moritz's suggestion that AE alluded to Ps 8 LXX because the presence of the adjective πάντα in v. 7 allowed him to shift the sphere of Christ's victory away from the earthly (emphasized in Ps 109 LXX) towards the cosmic. What needs to be further considered is that the allusion to Ps 8 LXX also allows AE to portray Christ as a new Adam and thereby implicitly introduces his discussion of new creation in Eph 2:1–22.[66]

The portrayal of Christ as a new Adam in Eph 1:22 is significant on a number of levels. First, if Ps 8 LXX exhibits "eschatological potential" because of its use of the creation narrative and implicit description of Adam's pre-fall state as Moritz suggests, then it is reasonable to presume that the portrayal of Christ as a new Adam is correlated with an *Urzeit-Endzeit* typology.[67] This proposal finds support in the description of Christ in Eph 1:20 as one who has overcome death by the power of God (cf. Rom 5:12–21).[68] Further verification of this suggestion may be found in the wider context of Eph 2:1–22, which is directly related to Eph 1:20–23 (see above, p. 131–32) and presents an extensive elaboration of the significance of Christ's inauguration of the new creation for humanity.[69]

The allusions to Ps 8 LXX and Ps 109 LXX in Eph 1:20, 22 thus suggest that AE employed these liturgical texts as a means of describing Christ as a divine warrior and pioneer of the new creation. It is helpful at this point to consider now how the portrait of Christ as a divine warrior is related to the development of new creation theology in Eph 2:1–22. In a recent article, T. Gombis has argued that Eph 1:20—2:22 can be understood against the backdrop of ANE traditions related to cosmic conflict. According to Gombis, Eph 1:20—2:22 may be read as a unified whole that conforms to the "narrative pattern of divine warfare" and exhibits the following structural similarities to ANE myths such as *Enuma Elish*:

---

66. See Martin (*Adamica*, 93–94), Lincoln ("Use," 41), and Dunn (*Christology*, 108–9) on the portrait of Christ as a new Adam in Eph 1:22 (pace Sellin, *Epheser*, 144).

67. Moritz, *Profound Mystery*, 18.

68. According to Moritz (ibid., 21), "Ephesians . . . sees Christ as the victor over death (1:20) and as the agent of the restoration of pre-Fall conditions." Dunn (*Christology*, 101–13) also understands Paul's Adam-Christ typology via the creation-fall-redemption-new creation metanarrative within Scripture.

69. One finds a similar use of Genesis traditions in Col 1:15–20, which describes Christ as the "image of the invisible God" (v. 15), the divine agent of creation (v. 16), and the inaugurator of the new creation (v. 18). Cf. Gordley, *The Colossian Hymn*, 213–14, 223–24.

Eph 1:20–23: Lordship

Eph 2:1–16: Conflict-victory

Eph 2:17: Victory Shout

Eph 2:18: Celebration

Eph 2:20–22: House-building[70]

Gombis' proposal, however, presents two significant difficulties. First, Gombis' suggestion that Eph 2:17 is to be correlated with the victory shout within the ANE narrative pattern of divine warfare does not account for: 1) the significance of the allusion to Isa 52:7 in v. 17; and 2) the use of the participle ἐλθών in v. 17.[71] Second, while Eph 2:18 does contain cultic imagery as Gombis suggests, the reverberations of ANE mythological traditions related to cosmic conflict are not particularly strong in this portion of Eph 1:20—2:22.[72] Given these problems, it is prudent to abandon Gombis' suggestion that Eph 1:20—2:22 reflects the narrative *pattern* of divine warfare.[73] Nonetheless, since divine warrior traditions are evoked in Eph 1:20–23 and Eph 2 does conclude with the description of the church as a temple (vv. 19–22), Gombis' general thesis does provide a helpful means of accounting for the unity of Eph 1:20—2:22.

Instead of reflecting the narrative pattern of divine warfare within ANE mythology, it is more reasonable to conclude Eph 1:20—2:22 mirrors the simplified version of this pattern one encounters in Isaiah. In my discussion of Isaiah's new exodus, I noted that a number of Isaianic texts exhibit links with ANE temple-building traditions (cf. Isa 11:1–12; 40:3–5, 9–11; 43:16–21; 51:9–11; 52:7–10; 66:15–24).[74] Within these passages, YHWH is depicted as a victorious warrior fighting against the enemies of his people and his triumph gives rise to the establishment of the restored Zion/Jerusalem (see above, esp. p. 16–17). Furthermore, there are no links within

---

70. Gombis, "Ephesians 2," 407–18.

71. Ibid., 415. The precise referent of the participle ἐλθών is a notorious interpretative difficulty within this passage. If the author were referring to Christ's heavenly enthronement, one would expect a verb that less strongly evoked the incarnation. See below, p. 161, for further discussion of these two issues.

72. Gombis (ibid., 416) notes that allusions to ANE cosmic conflict traditions in the Old Testament frequently describe worshipers celebrating the divine victory in the temple (cf. Ps 23:3–6 LXX; 47:8–14 LXX) and concludes that these traditions are evoked in v. 18 by means of the noun προσαγωγήν. This intertextual echo seems too subtle and it is instead best to view v. 18 as simply expressing the result of the statements in v. 17.

73. It is, therefore, more appropriate to conclude that vv. 17–18 should be linked with the treatment of the divine warrior's victory in Eph 2:1–16.

74. It is worth observing that a similar condensing of the ANE pattern of divine warfare occurs in 1QM 12:9–18 (see below, pp. 184–85).

these passages to other formal features of ANE temple-building traditions. As already noted, the presence of allusions to Isa 52:7; 57:19 in Eph 2:13, 17 opens up the possibility of reading Eph 1:20—2:22 as a description of the fulfillment of Isaiah's new exodus. The close relationship between the portrait of Christ as a divine warrior in Eph 1:20-23 and the description of new creation in Eph 2:1-22 may thus be best explained on the basis of the author's close reflection on Isaiah's proclamation of a new exodus.

Eph 1:20-22 thus betrays a complex interaction between various OT and ANE traditions. More specifically, if one probes the wider context of Ps 8 LXX and Ps 109 LXX it becomes evident that these Jewish traditions seem to have played a formative role in AE's understanding of Christ not only as a divine warrior, but also as one who inaugurates the new creation. The stress in Eph 2:1-22 on new creation (vv. 1-7, 10, 15, 19-22) raises the possibility that the allusion to Ps 8:7 LXX in Eph 1:22 may thus play an introductory role within the context of this passage. Finally, the conceptual similarity between the church as τὸ πλήρωμα in Eph 1:23 and a temple in Eph 2:19-22 provides further evidence for the relevance of temple-building traditions in this context and to this I now turn.

The statement τὸ πλήρωμα τοῦ τὰ πάντα ἐν πᾶσιν πληρουμένου presents the would-be interpreter with a number of difficult lexical, grammatical, and theological problems. Much ink has been spilled in attempting to address these complex exegetical issues. The following analysis of this text will attempt to give sufficient weight to the following features of the wider context: 1) Eph 1:23b forms part of a thanksgiving prayer in which the author expresses the desire that the addressees know the greatness of God's power (Eph 1:18-19); 2) the allusion to Ps 8 LXX in Eph 1:22 portrays Christ as a new Adam and inaugurator of the new creation; 3) the pervasive presence of new creation imagery in Eph 2:1-22; and 4) Eph 2:1-22 may be understood as an elaboration of Eph 1:20-23. Given the complexity of this portion of AE's thanksgiving prayer, it is best to begin this analysis by evaluating a few of the significant words within this statement.

The first lexeme we will consider is the noun σῶμα (v. 23a). With this word, AE provides a further description of the "church" of v. 22.[75] As with almost every other use of the noun σῶμα in Ephesians, here it metaphorically describes the organic relationship between Christ and his people (cf. Eph 2:16; 4:4, 12, 16; 5:23, 28, 30).[76] Whereas this theological concept is used in the Hauptbriefe to emphasize the presence of "multiformity within

---

75. Cf. Barth, *Ephesians 1-3*, 158; Sellin, *Epheser*, 153, 155-56.

76. The only literal use of the noun σῶμα occurs in Eph 5:23. The lexeme σῶμα is used with a similar sense in Rom 12:4-5; 1 Cor 12:12, 27.

uniformity," the stress in Ephesians and Colossians falls on the unity of the church (cf. Eph 2:16; 4:4; Col 3:15).[77] Finally, the body's growth is another important idea related to this metaphor within Ephesians and Colossians (cf. Eph 4:12, 16; Col 2:19).[78]

The next significant word to be examined is the noun πλήρωμα. With a number of scholars, it is best to conclude that the antecedent of the noun πλήρωμα in this context is the noun σῶμα in v. 23a.[79] The meaning of the noun in this context is a much more perplexing issue. The verb πληρόω generally means "to fill" or "to complete."[80] For some interpreters, the use of the nominal form πλήρωμα in this context of Eph 1:23 is best comprehended by means of the Gnostic redeemer myth, which pictured the *Urmensch* as both redeemer and head of the universe.[81] However, the lateness of these Gnostic traditions and the differences they exhibit when compared to the material in Ephesians have led a number of scholars to question the validity of this background.[82]

Beginning with the work of G. Münderlein, scholars have sought to explicate the meaning of the noun πλήρωμα on the basis of the OT.[83] While the noun form of the root πληρ– is employed in a number of texts within the OT to denote the creatures that inhabit the earth and the sea, it is the use of the verbal and adjectival forms of this root that likely provided the catalyst for this theological concept in the Pauline tradition.[84] More specifically, verbal and adjectival forms of πληρ– are associated in these Jewish traditions with a variety of divine attributes, yet with a particular emphasis on God's glory.[85] These traditions are then taken up in Colossians as a means of describing something akin to the notion found within the OT of God's shekina (his presence, power, and glory) and expressed by means of the nominal

77. Cf. Fung, "Body of Christ," 79. See Fung (ibid., 77–78) for a helpful discussion of the development of this concept in Paul.

78. Since both of these issues—the body's oneness and expansion—are important ideas within Eph 2:11–22, there is further reason to believe that Eph 1:23 serves as an introduction to the ensuing discussion of new creation in Eph 2 (cf. Eph 2:21; 4:4, 15–16).

79. This seems to be the most plausible conclusion given the nearness and grammatical agreement of these two nouns. Cf. Dawes, *Body in Question*, 238; Arnold, *Ephesians*, 116; Best, *Ephesians*, 183–84; pace Muddiman, *Ephesians*, 95–97.

80. BDAG, πληρόω, 827–29.

81. Cf. Schlier, *Epheser*, 96–99.

82. Cf. Best, *Ephesians*, 186; Barth, *Ephesians 1–3*, 201–3.

83. Münderlein, "Pleroma," 264–76. Cf. O'Brien, *Ephesians*, 149; Arnold, *Power and Magic*, 83–84.

84. Cf. Ps 23:1 LXX; 49:12 LXX; 88:12 LXX.

85. Cf. Ps 118:64 LXX; Isa 6:3; Jer 23:23–24; Ezek 43:5; 44:4; Hag 2:7; Wis 1:7.

form πλήρωμα (cf. Col 1:19; 2:9).⁸⁶ AE, in turn, seems to have shifted the Christological emphasis associated with the noun in Colossians and given it a more ecclesiological force.⁸⁷ In conclusion, the particular use of the noun πλήρωμα found in Ephesians and Colossians represents a development of Jewish traditions and relates in various ways to the divine presence either in Christ (Colossians) or in the church (Ephesians).

I will now examine the meaning of the participle πληρουμένου in Eph 1:23. The principal issue surrounding this participle is its voice. Generally speaking, scholars have interpreted the voice of this participle in one of three ways: 1) the participle is passive (i.e., Christ is being filled by the church); 2) the participle is a true middle (i.e., Christ fills the church and the cosmos for himself); and 3) the participle is a middle with an active sense (i.e., Christ fills the church and the cosmos).⁸⁸ If one assumes with Barth that the noun πλήρωμα and the participle πληρουμένου (whether passive, reflexive, or active) cannot have the same grammatical voice, a great deal of progress can be made towards solving this troublesome exegetical issue.⁸⁹ Thus, if the noun πλήρωμα is understood passively, the participle πληρουμένου must then be a true middle or be in the active voice. Likewise, if the participle is understood passively, the noun must then carry an active sense.

When Barth's point is given sufficient emphasis, it is the third option that provides the most viable account of this statement.⁹⁰ First, in a more perspicuous text, AE elsewhere *prays* that the addressees would grow in their understanding of Christ's love "so that [they] may be filled with all the fullness of God" (Eph 3:19; cf. Eph 1:15-17). Second, as already noted,

---

86. Arnold, *Power and Magic*, 83-84; Meyer, *Kirche und Mission*, 44; Münderlein, "Pleroma," 274.

87. This reconstruction obviously assumes knowledge of Colossians on the part of AE, yet need not imply literary dependence of Ephesians upon Colossians.

88. See Hoehner (*Ephesians*, 296-99) for an extensive survey of secondary literature related to the meaning of the participle πληρουμένου in Eph 1:23. See BDF §316 (1) on the use of the middle voice with an active sense.

89. Barth, *Ephesians 1-3*, 159; pace Dawes, *Body in Question*, 242. Dawes bases his critique of Barth on the suggestion that he ignores a third possible reading of the participle πληρουμένου—God is the implicit subject and he "fills" Christ. See Dawes (ibid., 243-45) for a defense of this position. Dawes' attempt to counter Lincoln's (*Ephesians*, 76) critique by appealing to present participles in the Pauline tradition that do not carry a continuous sense places too much interpretative weight on grammatical considerations (cf. 1 Cor 7:17-24; 1 Thess 1:10; 2:12; 5:24). In general, those who argue πληρουμένου carries a passive force should give greater stress to more lucent texts which expressly describe Christ as *already* the "fullness of God (cf. Col 1:19; 2:9) and the immediate context of Eph 1:20-23 which focuses on Christ's victory over the powers.

90. Cf. Barth, *Ephesians 1-3*, 205-9; Arnold, *Power and Magic*, 82-85; Muddiman, *Ephesians*, 96; Schnackenburg, *Epheser*, 79-83.

if one can assume AE's familiarity with Colossians, it would be problematic for him to suggest the church fills Christ when Col 1:19 and Col 2:9–10 state that he is already "the fullness of God" and the church has come "to fullness [πεπληρωμένοι] in him."[91] Third, since Eph 1:23 occurs within the context of a thanksgiving-prayer, it is reasonable to assume the church is the one filled with the divine attributes described in Eph 1:17–19.[92] Fourth, and perhaps most telling, if the phrase τὰ πάντα in Eph 1:23 carries a cosmic force as it does in a number of texts within Ephesians, to argue the noun πλήρωμα carries an active force in Eph 1:23 would advance a radical ecclesiology in opposition to Eph 4:10, 13.[93]

Eph 1:23 thus presents the reader with an interesting amalgamation of ecclesiology and Christology. On the one hand, the church is depicted as the locus of Christ's presence and a recipient of the divine presence. On the other hand, Eph 1:23 also develops the description of Christ's cosmic victory in Eph 1:20–22 by describing him as a sovereign ruler whose triumph will extend throughout the universe.[94]

This ecclesiological reading of the noun πλήρωμα in v. 23 also conceivably forms part of AE's transformation of ANE temple-building traditions. I have already argued that the unit Eph 2:1–22 follows naturally from Eph 1:20–23 and the use of ANE temple-building traditions constitutes one of the principal means by which Eph 1:20—2:22 is unified (see above, p. 131-142). Further links to ANE temple-building traditions may be discerned if the description of the church in Eph 1:23 as σῶμα and πλήρωμα is ultimately related to its portrait as a temple in Eph 2:19–22.[95] Beale has

---

91. Cf. Eph 1:10; 3:19; 4:10.

92. Cf. O'Brien, *Ephesians*, 150.

93. Pace Yates, "Ephesians 1:23," 149–51; Overfield, "Pleroma," 393. The reading of Eph 1:23 advocated by these scholars originated with Robinson (*Ephesians*, 42–45). That the phrase τὰ πάντα does convey a cosmic sense is plausible when one considers the stress in Eph 1:20–22 on Christ's supremacy over the powers. Cf. Muddiman, *Ephesians*, 96.

94. If the phrase τὸ πλήρωμα τοῦ τὰ πάντα ἐν πᾶσιν πληρουμένου is read in the light of Eph 1:20–22 it also becomes evident that there is a significant commingling of inaugurated and future eschatology in vv. 20–23. That is, while the description of Christ's defeat of the powers in vv. 20–22 strikes a note of inaugurated eschatology, v. 23b could be viewed as something of a theological corrective that draws the reader back to the emphasis on future eschatology found in Eph 1:10.

95. Lincoln (*Ephesians*, 75) helpfully notes that since "in the OT God's glorious presence could be seen as permeating not only the creation but also the temple . . . it should not be surprising that in an epistle which calls the Church 'a holy temple in the Lord . . . a dwelling place of God in the Spirit' (2:21, 22) it should also be seen as the place of the dynamic fullness of God in Christ." See Beetham (*Echoes*, 154–55) for a similar assessment regarding the use of Ps 67:17 LXX in Col 1:19 and its implications

observed that the statements in Eph 2:21–22 regarding the growth and expansion of the temple follow conventions found in ANE cosmologies that likewise describe creation as a garden-temple whose boundaries are to expand by means of the service of the priest-king (cf. 1 Cor 3:6–17).[96] If Eph 1:23 is connected to the depiction of the church as an expanding temple in Eph 2:19–22, the latter text may shed light on the author's designation of the church as Christ's σῶμα and πλήρωμα. That is, as Christ's σῶμα, the church may be understood as his earthly representative and its growth is a visible manifestation of Christ's victory over the powers.[97] Furthermore, as Christ's fullness, the church receives (individually and corporately) greater manifestations of the Spirit, which extend its capacity to serve as the earthly locus of the divine presence.[98]

In conclusion, Eph 1:20–23 forms an introduction to the author's treatment of new creation in Eph 2:1–22 by portraying Christ as a divine warrior (and thus evoking ANE temple-building traditions) and inaugurator of the new creation. This portrait of Christ is found in Eph 1:20–22 and is accomplished by means of allusions to Ps 109:1 LXX and Ps 8:7 LXX in v. 20 and v. 22, respectively. Significantly, an intertextual reading of Ps 8:7 LXX suggests that the declaration of Christ's supremacy over "all things" in v. 22 foreshadows the more extended discussion of new creation in Eph 2:1–22. Finally, Eph 1:23 also presents a subtle amalgamation of ecclesiology and Christology by describing the church as the earthly focal point of the divine presence (πλήρωμα) and suggesting that Christ is engaged in the process of extending his triumph (πληρουμένου) throughout the cosmos (τὰ πάντα). This association of the church with the divine presence in v. 23 serves as a prelude to the fuller portrayal of the church as a temple in Eph 2:19–22

---

for understanding the presence of fullness imagery in Col 2:9–10.

96. Beale, *Temple*, 263. See Beale (ibid., 81–167) for an analysis of the development of this theme in the OT.

97. Meyer, *Kirche und Mission*, 140–41, 144–45.

98. Regarding this point, it is important to note the presence of the phrase πνεῦμα σοφίας καὶ ἀποκαλύψεως ἐν ἐπιγνώσει αὐτοῦ in Eph 1:17. With this phrase, the author expresses the central content of his prayer for the addressees in vv. 17–23. If the noun πλήρωμα is best understood in a passive sense, it is plausible that v. 17 ultimately identifies what the church receives (i.e., the church is further endowed with the divine Spirit). In his discussion of the Old Testament background of the noun πλήρωμα, Münderlein ("Pleroma," 272) suggests the noun represents a way of referring to the Spirit. While this proposal has rightly been criticized because of the absence of explicit connections between these concepts in the Old Testament, Arnold (*Power and Magic*, 198) notes it is certainly possible that AE has developed notions which are latent in the OT and made them somewhat more overt.

and strengthens the links between this passage and ANE temple-building traditions.

This reading of Eph 1:20–23 has two significant implications for understanding the conception of new creation in Ephesians. First, it further demonstrates that new creation in the Pauline tradition is closely aligned with Isaiah's prophetic message. As noted in chapter 2, temple-building traditions play an important role in Isaiah's new exodus. Nonetheless, since Isaiah's descriptions of temple-building do not exhibit the complex formal patterns found in ANE traditions that describe cosmic conflict and temple-building, insufficient evidence exists within this text to conclude that the author is evoking the "narrative pattern of divine warfare" as Gombis concludes.[99] Instead, it is more reasonable to conclude that the author is reflecting the strong association between portraits of YHWH as a divine warrior and the restoration of Zion/Jerusalem in Isaiah's new exodus. The presence of allusions to Isaianic new exodus traditions in Eph 2:13, 17 strengthens this suggestion. Second, the evocation of ANE temple-building traditions in Eph 1:20–23 once again indicates that new creation in Ephesians is closely aligned with an *Urzeit-Endzeit* typology. In other words, as the original creation is depicted as an act of temple-building in Gen 1–2, so too is the new creation of Eph 1:20—2:22.

New Creation, Anthropology, and Cosmology in Ephesians 2:1–10

According to Gombis, Eph 2:1–10 describes "the triumph of God in Christ over the powers that rule the present evil age."[100] Eph 2:1–10 consists of three sections: 1) the immoral past of the addressees (vv. 1–3); 2) the divine action that remedied their sinful condition (vv. 4–7); and 3) an elaboration on the declaration χάριτί ἐστε σεσῳμένοι in Eph 2:5c (vv. 8–10).[101] In the preceding section, I argued that though there is a distinct shift in content at Eph 2:1, Eph 2:1–10, nonetheless, expands upon the description of Christ's victory over the powers in Eph 1:20–23 and outlines the eschatological significance of the Christ-event. In the ensuing analysis, I will demonstrate that Eph 2:1–10 builds upon the prior discussion of Christ's cosmic victory by describing the renewal of humanity and creation as an act of new creation.

---

99. See above, chapter 2. One can reach similar conclusions regarding the use of temple-building traditions in Second Temple Judaism (see below, pp. 184–85).

100. Gombis, "Ephesians 2," 410.

101. Cf. O'Brien, *Ephesians*, 154; Best, *Ephesians*, 198–99; Schnackenburg, *Epheser*, 88–89.

The author's primary means of describing humanity's transformation in Eph 2:1–10 is the death-life metaphor. In Eph 2:1, the pre-conversion *spiritual* condition of the author's audience is summarized by means of the phrase ὄντας νεκρούς (cf. Eph 2:5; 5:14). The remainder of vv. 1–3 consists of a series of subordinate clauses that further elaborate on this bleak state of affairs. Ephesians 2:1b makes clear that the principal factor that gave rise to their spiritual deadness was their immoral behavior. Yet Eph 2:2 also suggests that factors external to the individual are also at play. Specifically, by way of two κατά phrases which comment on the construction ἐν αἷς ποτε περιεπατήσατε, AE suggests that: 1) the readers formerly conformed their lives to the ethical norms associated with this evil earthly realm (v. 2b); and 2) the readers formerly lived under the influence of cosmic evil (v. 2cd).[102] AE then elaborates on the comments in v. 2 by indicating that Jewish believers also (καὶ ἡμεῖς πάντες) lived under the dominance of supernatural evil (v. 3).[103] However, whereas v. 2 placed great emphasis on forces outside the believer, v. 3 stresses the internal influence of fleshly desires (ἀνεστράφημέν ποτε ταῖς ἐπιθυμίαις τῆς σαρκὸς ἡμῶν ποιοῦντες τὰ θελήματα τῆς σαρκὸς καὶ τῶν διανοιῶν).

Beginning in v. 4, the author changes course from describing their state of death to their new life in Christ. This discussion commences in v. 4 by stating that the transfer from death to life is to be entirely attributed to divine agency (ὁ δὲ θεός) and charity (cf. 2 Cor 5:18).[104] This new life is described in vv. 5–6 by means of three finite verbs that begin with the preposition σύν, thus emphasizing the relationship between their eschatologi-

---

102. There is some question regarding how best to understand the noun αἰῶνα in the first κατά phrase in v. 2. Some see the use of this noun as a reference to the personal God "Aeon." E.g., Best, *Ephesians*, 203–4 (cf. 1 Cor 2:6, 8; 2 Cor 4:4). In light of the typical usage of this noun in the NT and AE's pleonastic style, it is best to view the construction τὸν αἰῶνα τοῦ κόσμου τούτου in Eph 2:2 in temporal-spatial terms (cf. Rom 12:2; 1 Cor 1:20; 2:6–8; Gal 1:4; Eph 1:21; 3:9, 11; 1 Tim 6:17). Cf. Arnold, *Power and Magic*, 59–60; Carr, *Angels and Principalities*, 100–101; Schwindt, *Das Weltbild des Epheserbriefes*, 379–83.

103. According to some scholars, the personal pronoun ἡμεῖς in v. 3 does more than simply distinguish between author and reader and vv. 1–3 actually differentiates between Gentile believers (v. 1) and Jewish believers (v. 3). Cf. O'Brien, *Ephesians*, 161; Muddiman, *Ephesians*, 105–6; Barth, *Ephesians 1–3*, 212. Given the programmatic significance of Eph 1:10 and the degree to which the relationship between Jew and Gentile is addressed in Eph 2:11–22, a distinction between Gentile Christ-followers and Jewish Christ-followers in Eph 2:1–3 seems to make the most sense of the shift in personal pronouns in this text.

104. The stress on divine action in inaugurating the believer's new existence parallels the statements in Eph 1:19–20, which similarly indicate it was God's power which effected Christ's resurrection and ascension.

cal existence and solidarity with Christ (τῷ Χριστῷ . . . ἐν Χριστῷ Ἰησοῦ). Given the emphasis in vv. 1-3 on their spiritual death, it is natural that the first of these finite verbs (συνεζωοποίησεν) describes their transfer to a state of spiritual vitality (cf. Col 2:12-13). The next two metaphors presumably describe consequent actions (καί . . . καί) and depict the convert's new life as a spiritual existence in the heavenly realm (v. 6). More specifically, Eph 2:6 suggests that believers have been exalted with Christ (συνήγειρεν) and been given a position of authority with Christ (συνεκάθισεν).[105]

The connection between death-life symbolism and anthropological renewal in Eph 2:1-7 requires further comment. The relationship between these two theological realities in the Hauptbriefe has already been closely analyzed by Hubbard. According to Hubbard, the close association between baptism and death-life imagery in Rom 6:1-11 forms part of the general human tendency to use such language to explicate the significance of initiatory rites.[106] Hubbard further argues that the use of the death-life metaphor in Rom 6:1-11; 7:1-6; and Gal 2:19-20 is consistently "anthropologically oriented and maintains a clear focus on the individual."[107] Another significant aspect of Hubbard's discussion of this theme within the undisputed Pauline epistles is his treatment of the Spirit's role within this motif. For Hubbard, the work of the Spirit in this regard draws upon the new covenant prophecies of Jeremiah and Ezekiel and depicts the Spirit as the driving-force behind the believer's new existence.[108]

Returning to Eph 2:1-7, we see that the death-life metaphor is also employed with a strong anthropological emphasis. As with the three texts Hubbard discusses in the Hauptbriefe, Eph 2:1-7 also stresses the ethical implications of the believer's union with Christ.[109] There is need for caution at this point, however, since these texts are not devoid of eschatological notions. Hubbard's own analysis of Rom 6:1-11 and Rom 7:1-6 exhibits an awareness of these eschatological underpinnings.[110] Eschatology is certainly

---

105. Cf. Eph 1:20; Col 2:12; 3:1.

106. Hubbard, *New Creation*, 79-92. Cf. Wedderburn, *Baptism and Resurrection*, 363-92.

107. Hubbard, *New Creation*, 129. For Hubbard's analysis of these texts within the Hauptbriefe, see ibid., 91-112, 123-28.

108. Ibid., 113-22. Cf. Jer 31:31-34; 32:36-40; Ezek 36:25-27; 37:14.

109. Particularly strong parallels between these passages within the Pauline tradition can be observed in: 1) the use of the verb περιπατέω in Rom 6:4 to describe ethical conduct (cf. Eph 2:2, 10); and 2) the description of the believer's former bondage to sin in Rom 6:6, 9, 12-14; 7:5-6 (cf. Eph 2:2-3).

110. In discussing Paul's treatment of the new life in Rom 6:1-11, Hubbard (ibid., 101) argues that while the verb ἐσόμεθα in v. 5 is best understood temporally, "there would be no denial that a presently experienced 'newness of life' (v. 4) mediated

not absent in Eph 2:1–7 and is particularly robust in v. 6, which speaks of the believer's new life in terms of a heavenly existence.[111] The presence of an eschatological substructure within the death-life symbolism in the Pauline corpus, therefore, should not be ignored.

Eph 2:8–10 is a parenthetical elaboration on the phrase χάριτί ἐστε σεσωσμένοι in Eph 2:5c. This text not only continues AE's discussion of new creation but also depicts new creation in anthropological *and* cosmological terms. This portrait of new creation is chiefly found in v. 10.

Eph 2:8–10 begins by returning to the grace mentioned in v. 5 and v. 7. The addition of the phrase διὰ πίστεως in v. 8a, however, expands upon the statement in v. 5 and indicates that the concept of faith plays an important role in the ensuing statements.[112] The remainder of v. 8 (καί . . . δῶρον) clarifies that the salvation described in vv. 4–8a does not derive from human effort but instead from the benevolent character of God.[113] AE then explains the οὐκ ἐξ ὑμῶν construction of v. 8 in Eph 2:9a by suggesting that salvation cannot be

---

through death (v. 13) is one of the central points of this passage" (cf. Rom 6:8). Cf. Jewett, *Romans*, 402. As already noted, Hubbard (*New Creation*, 122) strongly emphasizes the eschatological import of the Spirit in Paul's death-life metaphor (see above, p. 3) and concludes that Paul directly connects "the Spirit with the *new age* and life from death" (emphasis mine). Cf. Jewett, *Romans*, 401–2.

There is indeed much to be said for Hubbard's stress on the importance of Paul's death-life theology for understanding new creation. Cf. Mell, *Neue Schöpfung*, 13. Hubbard (*New Creation*, 107–8) observes a number of structural parallels between Rom 7:1–6 and 2 Cor 5:14–17 and deduces that these two texts "are members of that group of passages in which the physiomorphic imagery of dying and rising with Christ constitutes the dominant soteriological metaphor." Given his firmly anthropological reading of the latter, however, one should question the degree to which Hubbard has sufficiently incorporated the Spirit's eschatological import in his analysis of new creation in Paul (see above, pp. 89–90). Admittedly, anthropology does receive a great deal of stress within these texts. The heavily soteriological significance of the Spirit in the new covenant promises of Jeremiah and Ezekiel must also not be overlooked. Nonetheless, Hubbard's treatment of 2 Cor 5:14–17 and Gal 6:12–18 raises questions regarding the degree to which he has overemphasized the importance of the death-life metaphor and failed to interpret these texts on their own terms (see below, pp. 80–86, 95–105).

111. Cf. O'Brien, "Church," 94. In commenting on Eph 2:4–10, Arnold (*Power and Magic*, 147) notes, "There is surely no doubt that the author has emphasized the present aspect of salvation to a degree unparalleled in Paul."

112. The central place the noun πίστις plays within the discussion of Eph 2:8–10 is evident when one considers the degree to which its theological antithesis ("works") is discussed in vv. 9–10.

113. Thus, while the noun πίστεως implicitly plays an important role in vv. 9–10, there is no need to conclude with scholars such as Caird that the noun πίστεως is the antecedent of the pronoun τοῦτο in v. 8. Cf. Caird, *Letters*, 53. Given that the lexeme τοῦτο is a neuter pronoun and πίστεως a feminine noun, it is more likely that the pronoun refers to all of Eph 2:8a (and possibly vv. 4–7 as well). Cf. Arnold, *Ephesians*, 139; Hoehner, *Ephesians*, 342–43; Bruce, *Ephesians*, 289–90.

earned on the basis of moral achievements (οὐκ ἐξ ἔργων).¹¹⁴ Following his exclusion of works as a means of acquiring salvation, AE then indicates that God's underlying purpose (ἵνα) is to withhold the possibility of human boasting (καυχήσηται) in so ultimate a concern as redemption (v. 9b).¹¹⁵

Within its immediate context, Eph 2:10 serves as an explanatory statement clarifying Eph 2:8-9. What must be accounted for in this discussion is AE's use of the noun ποίημα and the participle κτισθέντες. The noun ποίημα is a rare word in the NT corpus. Its only other occurrence is in Rom 1:20. In that context, the noun is used to describe the material aspects of the created order that reveal the divine nature and is generally translated something like "the things he has made" (cf. NRSV). As one examines the use of this noun in the LXX it becomes evident that it is used in two main ways in connection with the divine being: 1) to refer to something God has

---

114. With the rise of the "new perspective on Paul," AE's statement in v. 9 has attracted a fair amount of attention from those who perceive differences between the theology of Ephesians and that of the Hauptbriefe. With the publication of his work *Paul and Palestinian Judaism*, Sanders has challenged the traditional perspective of Palestinian Judaism as a religion of legalistic merit. Sanders argues that the soteriology of Palestinian Judaism: 1) is best described by the phrase "covenantal nomism"; 2) focuses on God's gracious election of Israel through the Abrahamic covenant; and 3) perceived the Mosaic law not as a means of *getting in* the covenant but of *staying in*. Cf. Sanders, *Paul*, 419-27. Dunn, in turn, has built upon Sanders' reading of Paul's opponents and argued that the phrase "works of the law" in the Hauptbriefe specifically refers to markers of Jewish identity such as circumcision, dietary laws, and the observance of religious festivals. Cf. Dunn, "Works," 523-42. On the basis of this reading of the undisputed Pauline epistles, some scholars have argued that the noun ἔργον in Eph 2:9 represents a generalization of the Pauline terminology by a later disciple and reflects the predominantly Gentile audience of this text. Cf. Best, *Ephesians*, 228; Lincoln, "Ephesians 2:8-10," 622-23; Räisänen, *Paul*, 197-98. This is, of course, a debate with a long history. See Westerholm (*Perspectives*, 101-258) for an extensive review of scholarly material on this subject within the twentieth century.

To the degree that this attempt to separate the theology of Ephesians from the theology of the Hauptbriefe is dependent upon Dunn's proposal, then it should not go unchallenged. A number of scholars have, in fact, mounted serious objections to Dunn's views regarding the phrase "works of the law" in the *undisputed* Pauline letters. Perhaps most problematic for Dunn's position is Paul's argument in Rom 4:1-5, which uses the example of Abraham as proof that justification is not dependent upon "works of the law" (cf. Rom 3:20, 28) since Abraham was justified prior to the giving of the Mosaic law. Since Rom 4:1-5 is a logical development of Rom 3:20-31, the use of the simple noun ἔργων and the participle ἐργαζομένῳ in Rom 4:1-5 suggests that the phrase "works of the law" cannot have the specific meaning Dunn and others who challenge the traditional interpretation of this phrase wish to attribute to it. Further problems for Dunn's reading of the "works of the law" are raised by the use of the nouns ἔργων and νόμος in Rom 9:11-12; Gal 3:11-12, 21. Cf. Westerholm, *Perspectives*, 300-21; Schreiner, "'Works of Law,'" 217-44; Jewett, *Romans*, 297-98, 309-10.

115. Cf. Rom 3:27; 4:2, 4; 1 Cor 1:28-31; Gal 6:13-14; Phil 3:3.

made or created; and 2) to refer to an action or deed of God within history.[116] Scholars generally appeal to Ps 91:5 LXX and Ps 142:5 LXX to clarify the background of ποίημα in Eph 2:10.[117] The linking of the noun ποίημα with the noun χείρ in these two texts provides a strong degree of confirmation for this suggestion.[118] Other texts within the LXX which seem to use the noun ποίημα to depict divine *creative* activity include Eccl 3:11; 7:13 and Isa 29:16.[119] The remaining texts in the LXX which use the noun ποίημα and have God as its complement all generally refer to God's providential acts.[120]

Within the Pseudepigrapha, there is a more distinct tendency to use the noun ποίημα in connection with the physical creation. In *T. Job* 49:2, after she "had her heart changed," Job's daughter Kasia is described speaking in the dialect of the "archons" and praising God for "the creation (τὸ ποίημα) of the heights." *T. Job* 49:3 consequently states, "If anyone wishes to know the creation (τὸ ποίημα) of the heavens" they should consult "the hymns of Kasia." In *T. Ab.* 9:6, the construction τὰ ποιήματα is used synonymously with the noun οἰκουμένην. The presence of the relative clause ἅ διὰ λόγου ἑνὸς συνέστησας ("which God established through one word") indicates that Abraham's request pertains to the created order.[121]

---

116. Cf. Ps 63:10 LXX; 91:5 LXX; 142:5 LXX; Eccl 3:11; 7:13; 8:17; 11:5; Isa 29:16.

117. Cf. Gnilka, *Epheserbrief*, 130; Lincoln, *Ephesians*, 130; O'Brien, *Ephesians*, 178; Hoehner, *Ephesians*, 347.

118. The nouns ἔργον and ποίημα in Ps 63:10 LXX; 91:5 LXX; 142:5 LXX exhibit a parallel relationship in these texts. Within the LXX, the nouns ἔργον and χείρ are frequently used in the LXX to describe the creative activity of God (e.g., Job 10:3; 14:15; Ps 8:7 LXX; 101:26 LXX; 138:8 LXX; Isa 64:7). The noun ποίημα in these two psalms thus seems to be used as a synonym for ἔργον.

119. Regarding Eccl 3:11, the presence of the verb ἐποίησεν and the phrase ἀπ' ἀρχῆς καὶ μέχρι τέλους shifts the meaning of ποίημα in this direction. Similar conclusions can be drawn about Isa 29:16. Finally, the logical relationship between the phrases τὰ ποιήματα τοῦ θεοῦ and ὃν ἂν ὁ θεὸς διαστέψῃ αὐτόν in Eccl 7:13 allows for this reading.

120. The description of the ruin of the Psalmist's enemies in Ps 63:8–9 LXX indicates that the use of the noun ποίημα in Ps 63:10 LXX refers to God's acts of deliverance. The parallelism between the phrases τὰ ποιήματα τοῦ θεοῦ and τὸ ποίημα τὸ πεποιημένον ὑπὸ τὸν ἥλιον in Eccl 8:17 indicates that the former phrase refers to divine actions within the realm of human history. While the phrase ὅσα ποιήσει σὺν τὰ πάντα in Eccl 11:5 undoubtedly describes God as creator, the remaining content of v. 5 is too general to conclude the phrase τὰ ποιήματα τοῦ θεοῦ in this context explicitly refers to divine creative activity.

121. Given the temporal proximity of *T. Job* and *T. Ab.* to Ephesians (and Romans), one can presume all four texts participated in the same stream of tradition which closely linked the noun ποίημα with creation. *Gk. Apoc. Ezra* 2:24 also uses the noun ποίημα as a close synonym for the nouns πλάσιν and ἔργα in v. 23. Interestingly, since v. 23 ultimately refers to humanity, there is a degree of similarity between this text and Eph 2:10. The uncertainty regarding the date of *Gk. Apoc. Ezra* and the presence of

In summary, when viewed historically, there does seem to be a gradual development in the use of the noun ποίημα. Within the OT, when used in connection with God the noun generally refers to God's actions in history but also occasionally describes his creative acts (cf. Ps 91:5 LXX; 142:5 LXX; Eccl 3:11; 7:13; Isa 29:16). However, the word is never associated directly with the physical creation. The lexeme does become more explicitly aligned with the created order in the Pseudepigrapha. This raises the question, "With which sense does AE use the noun ποίημα in Eph 2:10?" Given the presence of the participle κτισθέντες immediately following the noun ποίημα in Eph 2:10, it is best to conclude that AE is using the noun with the more specific connotation of something God has made or created. That the noun ποίημα is also used with the same meaning elsewhere in the Pauline corpus also speaks heavily in favor of this reading (cf. Rom 1:20).

It is also helpful to consider the function of the participle κτισθέντες within the wider context of Eph 2:1–10. Within v. 10, κτισθέντες is an adjectival participle that further describes the believer's identity as God's creation. The participle also seems to encapsulate the movement from death to life in vv. 1–7. This state of new life is described using the verbs συνεζωοποίησεν, συνήγειρεν, and συνεκάθισεν (vv. 5–6). With the participle κτισθέντες, AE summarizes this new state of existence as a new creation that is to be understood in analogous but not equivalent terms to the creation account in Gen 1–2.[122] This close linking of v. 10 with vv. 1–7 is confirmed when one observes the repetition of the "in Christ" motif with the phrase κτισθέντες ἐν Χριστῷ Ἰησοῦ in v. 10.

In conclusion, Eph 2:8–10 continues the author's discussion of new creation in vv. 1–7 by means of the noun ποίημα and the participle κτισθέντες (cf. Eph 2:10). It is difficult to deny that there is a strong degree of emphasis placed on the anthropological component of new creation within Eph 2:1–10. This passage not only employs death-life imagery to describe the believer's deliverance from the dominion of cosmic evil and σάρξ in vv. 1–7 but also links new creation imagery in v. 10 with the performance of "good works." One must not, however, overlook the highly eschatological depiction of salvation in Eph 2:6. The author's choice of new creation imagery in v. 10 is also relevant to this discussion. Specifically, the lexemes ποίημα and κτίζω both evoke the original creation and do not allow for a strict demarcation between anthropology and cosmology.

Christian interpolations in v. 25, however, suggests the need for exercising caution in appealing to this text within the present discussion.

122. Cf. Miletic, *One Flesh*, 63.

The Use of Scripture in Eph 2:13, 15, 17

New creation is clearly a noteworthy motif within Eph 2:1–10. I have suggested that while this passage emphasizes the anthropological scope of new creation (vv. 1–6), it is also depicted in cosmological terms (v. 10). New creation is no less a significant concept in Eph 2:11–22. However, there is some measure of debate regarding the extent to which this treatment of new creation is intertextually related to the OT. Prior to assessing the nature of new creation in Eph 2:11–22, I will examine the use of Scripture in Eph 2:13, 15, 17. That the author uses new creation imagery in Eph 2:15 is not a new insight.[123] Further work on the new creation theme in Eph 2:11–18, nevertheless, needs to be done. More specifically, the relationship between the creation of "one new humanity" in Eph 2:15b and the abrogation of the law in Eph 2:15a has yet to be fully explored. The explicit linking of these two notions has important implications for understanding the nature of new creation in Ephesians and demands a careful analysis of Eph 2:11–15. The import of Isaianic traditions in Eph 2:13, 17 also requires careful consideration. Before tackling these two issues, however, I will briefly address the presence of traditional material in vv. 13–18.

The presence of common language within Eph 2:13 and Eph 2:17 raises the question of the importance of Isaianic traditions in Eph 2:11–18. More specifically, while interpreters generally agree that v. 17 is to be understood as a conflated allusion to Isa 52:7 and Isa 57:19, some scholars contend that AE has been influenced by a preexisting hymn.[124] The diversity of hymnic reconstructions related to these proposals should call into question their viability as a solution to this problem.[125]

Lincoln's proposal that the far/near metaphor in Eph 2:13 derives from Jewish proselyte traditions (rather than Isa 57:19) is also relevant to this discussion (cf. Deut 28:49; 29:22; Isa 5:26; *Mek. Exod.* 18:5; *Num. Rab.* 8:4).[126] While this suggestion is more plausible than the argument that vv. 13–16 is

---

123. Cf. Arnold, *Ephesians*, 164; O'Brien, *Ephesians*, 200; Jackson, *New Creation*, 184.

124. According to some scholars, Eph 2:14–18 betrays the influence of a hymn related to the Gnostic redeemer myth. Cf. Pokorný, *Gnosis*, 114–15. Others suggest that Eph 2:14–18 stems from an early Christian hymn (e.g., Gnilka, *Epheserbrief*, 147–52). Still others suggest that this text is derived from the author's reflection on Col 1:15–23 (e.g., Lincoln, "Use," 25–26). See Yee (*Ethnic Reconciliation*, 127–33) for a helpful summary of literature related to this subject.

125. Cf. Best, *Ephesians*, 245, 247–50.

126. Lincoln, "Use," 26–28. Cf. Kirby, *Ephesians*, 157. Other scholars are more willing to accept a tacit allusion to Isa 57:19 in v. 13, which is then expressly fleshed out in v. 17. Cf. Best, *Ephesians*, 245; Schnackenburg, *Epheser*, 111; Stuhlmacher, "Friede," 347; Moritz, *Profound Mystery*, 46–47.

developed from a preexisting hymn, Lincoln's objection to the possibility that Eph 2:13 constitutes an allusion to Isa 57:19 is unwarranted. According to Lincoln, the absence of any notion in Isa 57:19 of the "far off becoming near" speaks against this suggestion.[127] While Lincoln's challenge to this reading of v. 13 is undoubtedly accurate, it nonetheless faces a significant methodological problem. More specifically, Lincoln's opposition to seeing Eph 2:13 as an allusion to Isa 57:19 fails to consider the significance of the wider context of this Isaianic text for understanding the message of v. 13.[128]

If one examines the surrounding statement of Isa 57:19, it does become reasonable to conclude that there is a literary relationship between Eph 2:13 and Isa 57:19. I have already noted that Isa 57:14-21 forms part of Isaiah's new exodus theme (see above, p. 29-33). I have also argued that one of the focuses of the Isaianic new exodus is the redemption of the nations. Returning to Eph 2:13, it is evident this text employs the far/near imagery to explicate the vertical reconciliation of God and Gentiles.[129] If this is the case, it becomes plausible to view Eph 2:13 as an interpretation of Isaianic tradition that focuses on the prophet's universalistic message (e.g., Isa 40:5; 52:8-10; 66:18-24). This approach to the development of v. 13 may also account for its conceptual parallelism with v. 18.[130] More specifically, since the explicit allusion to Isa 57:19 in Eph 2:17 is followed by a declaration of humanity's new found "access" (προσαγωγήν) to God (v. 18), the far/near imagery in v. 13 may then also represent an allusion to Isa 57:19 since it likewise points to the inauguration of the same new reality.[131] In summary,

---

127. Lincoln, "Use," 26.

128. It is perhaps not coincidental that Lincoln's article was written a few years prior to Hays's groundbreaking study on the use of the OT in the Pauline corpus, *Echoes of Scripture in the Letters of Paul*.

129. Cf. Schnackenburg, *Epheser*, 111.

130. The clauses ἐγενήθητε ἐγγὺς ἐν τῷ αἵματι τοῦ Χριστοῦ in v. 13 and δι' αὐτοῦ ἔχομεν τὴν προσαγωγήν in v. 18 both: 1) point to the reconciliation of God and humanity; and 2) suggest that this new reality has occurred by the agency of Christ.

131. Regarding the question of whether the noun προσαγωγήν should be interpreted transitively (i.e., "introduction") or intransitively (i.e., "access"), the emphasis on Christ's work in this passage (vv. 13-17) makes the latter option more plausible. Cf. Sellin, *Epheser*, 229. Lincoln (*Ephesians*, 149) notes that the combination of this reference to the divine Spirit and the cultic imagery in v. 18 indicates that the author is here suggesting the ability to approach the Father "is not confined to a specific locality such as the temple" (cf. John 4:20-24; 1 Pet 2:4-10). Cf. Mussner, *Epheser*, 87. The redemptive-historical shift implicit in Eph 2:11-18 and the description of the church as a temple in vv. 19-22 provide further confirmation for this reading of v. 18. See Adai (*Geist*, 170-71) for the suggestion that the noun πνεύματι in v. 18 refers to the divine Spirit.

the most plausible means of accounting for the far/near imagery in Eph 2:13 is to conclude that it comprises an allusion to Isa 57:19.

It is necessary at this point to consider the nature of the author's appeal to Isaiah's proclamation of a new exodus. According to Stuhlmacher, Eph 2:13–18 is "eine christologische Exegese von Jes 9, [sic] 5; 52, [sic] 7; 57, [sic] 19."¹³² Stuhlmacher also argues that AE's use of Scripture in Eph 2:13–18 follows rabbinic exegetical methods and the noun εἰρήνη functions as a catchword that allows for the bringing together of these three Isaianic texts.¹³³ Moritz also suggests that AE engaged in careful reflection of Isaiah's prophecy. According to Moritz, AE's "argument in Eph 2:13–18 is closely tied up with the Prophet's vision."¹³⁴ Yet neither Stuhlmacher nor Moritz fully develop just how closely AE's message in Eph 2:11–22 has been shaped by Isaianic traditions. In the ensuing analysis of Eph 2:11–22, I will attempt to clarify just how fully AE presents the portrait of new creation in this passage as the fulfillment of Isaiah's portrait of divine salvation and deliverance.

The verb κτίσῃ and the phrase ἕνα καινὸν ἄνθρωπον in Eph 2:15b also seem to constitute deliberate allusions to the OT. In contrast to Moritz, I would argue the use of the verb κτίσῃ in v. 15 reflects interaction with the creation narrative of Gen 1–2.¹³⁵ According to Moritz, the verb κτίσῃ in Eph 2:15 is best explained on the basis of the use of the verb ברא in Isa 57:19a MT.¹³⁶ The textual difficulties present in Isa 57:19—specifically, the fact that the LXX begins with the word εἰρήνην and does not include an equivalent of the first phrase of the MT, בּוֹרֵא נוּב שְׂפָתָיִם—while recognized by Moritz, create a serious problem for his argument.¹³⁷ Interestingly, Moritz argues that the phrase "one new humanity" in v. 15b comprises an allusion to Gen 1–2.¹³⁸ If this is the case, the linking of creation terminology with new Adam imagery provides strong evidence that the verb κτίσῃ echoes back to Gen 1–2. A reverberation of the creation narrative becomes more plausible

---

132. Stuhlmacher, "Friede," 347. Cf. Mussner, *Christus*, 100–101.

133. Stuhlmacher, "Friede," 347. Cf. Schnackenburg, *Epheser*, 112.

134. Moritz, *Profound Mystery*, 55.

135. Cf. Miletic, *One Flesh*, 63; Martin, *Adamica*, 163–65.

136. Moritz, *Profound Mystery*, 42–43. Moritz (ibid., 43), states, "It is preferable to see Eph 2:15 as being based on Isa 57 which was already on the author's mind in v. 13." He thus views the creation of the "new humanity" in close relation to the allusion to Isa 57:19 in Eph 2:13, 17. Moritz's account of the author's intertextual matrix is in some ways a simpler proposal than the one I am proposing. Nonetheless, the primary data does not allow for a neat and tidy solution to this problem.

137. In other words, Moritz assumes that AE was working from a tradition that is reflected in the MT, yet is absent in the LXX. While this is not implausible, his proposal at this point offers a more complex solution than is ultimately warranted

138. Ibid., 43.

when one considers the degree to which new creation thought pervades Eph 1:20—2:22 and the likelihood that the programmatic *anakephalaiōsis* in Eph 1:10 should be understood within an *Urzeit-Endzeit* framework.[139]

In summary, there are sufficient reasons to conclude that the discussion of new creation in Eph 2:11–17 is closely related to traditions in the OT. More specifically, the far/near language in v. 13, the verb κτίσῃ and the phrase ἕνα καινὸν ἄνθρωπον in Eph 2:15b, and the conflated allusion to Isa 52:7 and Isa 57:19 in v. 17, all probably represent deliberate appeals to the OT. It now remains to consider the interpretative significance of these appeals to the OT.

New Creation in Ephesians 2:11–18

In the preceding section, I considered the author's use of the OT in Eph 2:13, 15, 17. There I argued that the author grounds his portrait of new creation in the creation narrative of Gen 1–2 and Isaianic new exodus traditions. I will now more closely consider the nature of new creation in this passage and how the OT shapes its meaning and content. Special attention will be given in this analysis to considering the relationship between the abrogation of the law in Eph 2:15a and the creation of "one new humanity" in Eph 2:15b. The explicit linking of these two notions has important implications for understanding the nature of new creation in Ephesians and demands a careful analysis of Eph 2:11–15.

Eph 2:11–12 chiefly functions as a call to the Gentile addressees (τὰ ἔθνη) to consider their former state of estrangement. Some degree of debate surrounds the qualifying construction ἐν σαρκί in v. 11. This construction is best read as a reference to the ethnic status of these believers because

---

139. Cf. Muddiman, *Ephesians*, 133. The evocation of Gen 1:27 in Eph 4:24 is also relevant at this point. While the similarities between Eph 4:24 and Gen 1:27 are not strong enough to classify Eph 4:24 as an explicit quotation of the Genesis text, the degree of correspondence between these two texts does confirm the presence of some form of intertextual link. One does, however, have to account for the absence of the noun εἰκών (which explains the use of the accusative θεόν in Eph 4:24). In this regard, it is helpful to note the similarity between Eph 4:24 and Col 3:10 and the presence of the noun εἰκών in the latter text. Cf. Beetham, *Echoes*, 231–32; Watson, *Text and Truth*, 281–82; Lincoln, *Ephesians*, 287; Hoehner, *Ephesians*, 611; pace O'Brien, *Ephesians*, 333. For his part, O'Brien seems to overemphasize the differences between Eph 4:24 and Col 3:10. Finally, the presence of the phrase καινὸν ἄνθρωπον in Eph 2:15 again raises interesting questions when one considers Col 3:11 (which is directly connected to Col 3:10 through the preposition ὅπου) also addresses the Jew-Gentile question that dominates Eph 2:11–21. The parallelism between Col 3:11 and Gal 3:28 should again lead one to wonder just how strongly new creation theology is linked with the question of the identity of the people of God within the Pauline tradition.

of the manner in which it is further modified by the participial phrase οἱ λεγόμενοι ἀκροβυστία ὑπὸ τῆς λεγομένης περιτομῆς.[140] Finally, the designation ἀκροβυστία describes the Gentile believers from a Jewish perspective and points to their perceived inferiority relative to ethnic Jews.[141]

Ephesians 2:12 then specifies the author's main concern by describing the former estrangement of these Gentile Christ-followers from the covenantal privileges associated with belonging to the nation of Israel (cf. Rom 3:1–2; 9:4).[142] This alienation from the people of God is presented by means of five phrases that express their separation: 1) from the promised Messiah (χωρὶς Χριστοῦ); 2) from the realm of God's religious/political activity with Israel[143] (ἀπηλλοτριωμένοι τῆς πολιτείας τοῦ Ἰσραήλ); 3) from the sphere of God's covenantal relationship with Israel (ξένοι τῶν διαθηκῶν τῆς ἐπαγγελίας); 4) from God's redemptive purposes orchestrated through Israel (ἐλπίδα μὴ ἔχοντες); and 5) from genuine worship of God[144] (ἄθεοι ἐν τῷ κόσμῳ).

---

140. Cf. O'Brien, *Ephesians*, 186; Best, *Ephesians*, 238.

141. Cf. Best, *Ephesians*, 238. A number of scholars have suggested the participle λεγομένης and the adjective χειροποιήτου in v. 11 indicate that the author is strongly distancing himself from his Jewish religious heritage. According to these scholars, the former lexeme is best translated with the expression "so-called" and the latter points to the Pauline distinction between physical circumcision and spiritual circumcision (cf. Rom 2:28–29; Gal 6:12–15; Phil 3:3–5; Col 2:11). Cf. Schnackenburg, *Epheser*, 108; Barth, *Ephesians 1–3*, 255; Dahl, *Studies in Ephesians,* 445; pace Muddiman, *Ephesians*, 117; Best, "Ephesians 2:11–22, 60; Yee, *Ethnic Reconciliation*, 83–87. While this reading of v. 11 is plausible, it must be admitted that the brevity of the author's discussion of circumcision makes it difficult to arrive at a definitive position on this question. Nonetheless, AE's statement regarding Christ's nullification of the law in v. 15 indicates that his attitude towards Judaism is certainly not entirely positive.

142. The introductory ὅτι in v. 12 probably recommences the initial thought of v. 11 (διὸ μνημονεύετε ὅτι ποτέ) and indicates that v. 12 supplies the principal content of what the readers are admonished to recall.

143. The range of meaning associated with the noun πολιτεία is somewhat broad but generally (in keeping with the sense of its root πολι–) leans toward political connotations. Best's observation (*Ephesians*, 241) that "our rigid separation between politics and religion was unknown in the ancient world" is helpful at this point. The integration of civic and religious life in pre-modern society makes the largely political reading of the phrase τῆς πολιτείας τοῦ Ἰσραήλ advocated by some scholars problematic. Cf. Lincoln, *Ephesians*, 137. Given the tight linking of this phrase (note the ensuing καί) in v. 12 with the strongly religious notion of the "covenants of promise," a fairly general interpretation seems most viable. While it is difficult to encompass this notion in an appropriate English lexeme, the phrase τῆς πολιτείας τοῦ Ἰσραήλ almost certainly refers to the various religio-political institutions associated with the Israelite nation that developed from its election by God (cf. 2 Macc 4:11; 8:17; 4 Macc 8:7; 17:9). Cf. Yee, *Ethnic Reconciliation*, 95.

144. The principal charge associated with the adjective ἄθεοι in Eph 2:12c is the

Eph 2:13 marks the point (νυνὶ δέν) at which the author shifts from describing the addressees' past state to expressing their present condition (cf. Eph 2:4). This new mode of religious existence is firmly placed within a Christological framework (ἐν Χριστῷ 'Ιησοῦ). Imagery from Isa 57:19 is then employed to render the past (ὑμεῖς οἵ ποτε ὄντες μακράν) and present (ἐγενήθητε ἐγγύς) situation of these Gentile Christ-followers. As already noted, the allusion to Isa 57:19 in v. 13 draws upon the universalistic message of Isaiah's new exodus and points to the fulfillment of these texts in the death and resurrection of Christ. Ephesians 2:13 then closes with a prepositional phrase (ἐν τῷ αἵματα τοῦ Χριστοῦ) that identifies the death of Jesus as the means by which this new state of affairs is inaugurated.

Beginning at Eph 2:14, the author then proceeds to describe the social ramifications of Christ's death.[145] Eph 2:14 begins by personifying Christ as the embodiment of peace (εἰρήνη).[146] The personal pronoun ἡμῶν and the adjective ἀμφότερα indicate AE is pointing to the once divided (yet now united) parties described in vv. 11–12. The participial phrase ὁ ποιήσας τὰ ἀμφότερα ἕν explains the nature of Christ's peace-making activity and encapsulates it in the notion of establishing harmony between Jew and Gentile. The next participial phrase (τὸ μεσότοιχον τοῦ φραγμοῦ λύσας) is somewhat parallel to the first phrase and further explicates how Christ is to be understood as the embodiment of peace between Jew and Gentile.[147] Interpreters have offered a variety of proposals to explain the nature of the "dividing wall" of v. 14. There is now a growing consensus that the following

---

distinction between the monotheistic worship of Judaism and the various manifestations of polytheism associated with ancient pagan religions (cf. Deut 6:4; 1 Cor 8:5–6; Gal 4:8; 1 Thess 4:5, 13).

145. The introductory clause αὐτὸς γάρ ἐστιν ἡ εἰρήνη ἡμῶν in v. 14 expands upon the comment on Christ's death in v. 13. The participial phrases in vv. 14a–16 that elaborate on this initial phrase are thus *semantically* subordinate to vv. 11–13.

146. Cf. Isa 9:6–7; Mic 5:5.

147. There is some debate regarding how best to understand the syntactical relationships between the various clauses which comprise Eph 2:14c–15a (καί . . . καταργήσας). Perhaps the simplest means of addressing this question is to focus on the final six lexemes in v. 14 (τὴν ἔχθραν ἐν τῇ σαρκὶ αὐτοῦ). While some critical texts (NA[26, 27]; UBS[3corr., 4]) do link these words together, it is hard to discern how the "dividing wall" could be identified with hostility in Christ's body. Cf. Best, *Ephesians*, 258. It is therefore prudent to split these six words into two clauses (τὴν ἔχθραν and ἐν τῇ σαρκὶ αὐτοῦ) and determine how they relate to the two participial phrases within Eph 2:14c–15a. It is perfectly natural to view the clause τὴν ἔχθραν as an appositional expansion of τὸ μεσότοιχον τοῦ φραγμοῦ λύσας that identifies the "dividing wall" as the source of hostility between Jew and Gentile. This leaves the phrase ἐν τῇ σαρκὶ αὐτοῦ, which could modify the construction τὸ μεσότοιχον τοῦ φραγμοῦ λύσας. It is, however, much more natural to link the phrase ἐν τῇ σαρκὶ αὐτοῦ with the ensuing statement in v. 15. Cf. Hoehner, *Ephesians*, 371–74; Schnackenburg, *Epheser*, 115; Gnilka, *Epheserbrief*, 141.

participial phrase τὸν νόμον τῶν ἐντολῶν ἐν δόγμασιν καταργήσας (v. 15a) functions as an explanation of the phrase τὸ μεσότοιχον τοῦ φραγμοῦ in v. 14. On the basis of this evidence, scholars now generally argue that the "dividing wall" refers to the Mosaic law, which engendered enmity between Jew and Gentile.[148]

The author continues his discussion of the horizontal reconciliation of Jew and Gentile in vv. 14d-15a by commenting on the present validity of Torah. As already observed, the phrase ἐν τῇ σαρκὶ αὐτοῦ in v .14 is likely syntactically linked with the ensuing participial phrase (τὸν νόμον τῶν ἐντολῶν ἐν δόγμασιν καταργήσας) in v. 15a.[149] This statement in v. 15a has sparked a great deal of debate regarding AE's attitude toward the Mosaic law (cf. Rom 3:31; 7:1-6; 2 Cor 3:11-18). In general, two primary solutions have been offered in response to this question: 1) the death of Christ has nullified those laws within the Mosaic law code which generated hostility between Jew and Gentile (e.g., circumcision); and 2) the death of Christ has nullified the entire Mosaic law.

A number of points of evidence speak in favor of the first interpretation. It is helpful to begin considering this issue by noting the significance of Eph 6:2. Within this text, AE explicitly cites the fifth commandment in the Decalogue in order to support his injunction to children to submit to parental authority (cf. Exod 20:12; Deut 5:16). This appeal to the Mosaic law indicates that it still has some relevance for AE.[150] Further analysis of Eph 2:11-15 also supports a more limited assessment of Christ's abrogation of the law in Eph 2:15. Specifically, the construction τῶν ἐντολῶν ἐν δόγμασιν in v. 15a may be read as a qualification of the noun νόμον and suggests that the author is focusing on a specific feature of the Mosaic law, its "commandments and ordinances" (cf. Col 2:14).[151] A number of interpreters place great weight on the presence of the nouns ἐντολή and δόγμα within this

---

148. Cf. Martin, *Reconciliation*, 179-87; Hoehner, *Ephesians*, 368-71; O'Brien, *Ephesians*, 195-96; Schnackenburg, *Epheser*, 113-14; Talbert, *Ephesians*, 79-81; Lincoln, *Ephesians*, 141-42; Barth, *Ephesians 1-3*, 283-87, 290-91; Roetzel, "Ephesians 2:15a," 82-84.

149. The noun σαρκί in this context probably refers to Christ's physical death (cf. Col 1:22) and according to Yee (*Ethnic Reconciliation*, 154) "is closely associated with the 'flesh' by which Jews used to make a clear-cut ethnic and national division between Jews and Gentiles."

150. Cf. Muddiman, *Ephesians*, 132.

151. With Hoehner (*Ephesians*, 375), it is best to view the genitive construction τῶν ἐντολῶν appositionally to the construction τὸν νόμον and the prepositional phrase ἐν δόγμασιν as a modification of the noun ἐντολῶν which further specifies its general character.

context (v. 15) and conclude that it is not the entire Torah that is abolished but some particular aspect of its "commandments and ordinances."[152]

This limited account of the phrase τὸν νόμον τῶν ἐντολῶν ἐν δόγμασιν καταργήσας in Eph 2:15a is not without some significant problems. First, as Muddiman notes, the construction τῶν ἐντολῶν ἐν δόγμασιν may either emphasize *or* diminish the stress placed on Christ's abrogation of the law.[153] In other words, while this construction possibly specifies the nature of the noun νόμον in v. 15, it may also communicate "a sense of the oppressiveness of the law's commandments."[154] Perhaps most significantly, Eph 2:11–14 is not simply concerned with the estrangement of Jew and Gentile. Within this text, there is also a clear emphasis on the vertical alienation of God and Gentile. According to vv. 12–13, these Gentile believers once had "no hope and [were] without God in the world, yet have now "been brought near by the blood of Christ." Accounting for the vertical significance of Eph 2:11–14 diminishes the likelihood that Eph 2:15a merely refers to the annulment of those commandments that separated Jew and Gentile.

Despite the complexity of this issue, a way through this exegetical quagmire, nonetheless, may be discerned. The stress placed on Gentile exclusion from the divine economy within Eph 2:11–13 and the explicit mention of "the covenant or promise" in v. 12 help clarify the author's attitude towards the law. While this passage is devoid of an overt reference to the Abrahamic covenant, it is, nonetheless, likely that the construction τῶν διαθηκῶν τῆς ἐπαγγελίας in v. 12 encompasses the underlying narrative of God's promises to Abraham within the Pentateuch.[155] If this is the case, the prospect of blessing for the nations within the Abrahamic covenant must not be overlooked (cf. Gen 12:2; 17:1–6). Returning to Eph 2:11–13, I have already noted that v. 13 points to a fundamental shift in God's dealings with humanity, which would involve a reversal of the bleak circumstances

---

152. Adherents of this limited reading of Eph 2:15a may generally be divided into three camps: 1) those who argue that Christ's death has abolished the ceremonial requirements of the Mosaic law (e.g., Faust, *Pax Christi*, 120–21); 2) those who argue that Christ has annulled those commandments such as circumcision which separated Jew from Gentile (e.g., Schnackenburg, *Epheser*, 115; Barth, *Ephesians 1–3*, 290–91; Yee, *Ethnic Reconciliation*, 154–61; Thielman, *Ephesians*, 170); and 3) those who argue Christ has abolished the legalistic and "precept-centric" use of Torah (e.g., Roetzel, "Ephesians 2:15a," 84–86; Schlier, *Epheser*, 126).

153. Muddiman, *Ephesians*, 132–33.

154. Lincoln, *Ephesians*, 142. Cf. O'Brien, *Ephesians*, 197.

155. Cf. Thielman, *Ephesians*, 154. The Abrahamic covenant, after all, is the first in a series of covenants with the descendants of Abraham that regulated the relationship between God and his people. On the importance of the covenant theme within Paul's theology, see Wright (*Climax*, xi, 137–56, 203, 265–66; *Paul*, 485–505).

(viewed from a Gentile perspective) depicted in v. 12. I previously also suggested that when considering the status of the law in Eph 2:11–15, one must not overlook that this passage is concerned with both horizontal *and* vertical reconciliation. In light of the foregoing considerations, Eph 2:11–13 thus points to the fulfillment of God's promise to make Abraham an agent of divine favor for all of humanity.

These observations on the place of universalism within the Abrahamic covenant help shed light on the construction τὸν νόμον τῶν ἐντολῶν ἐν δόγμασιν in Eph 2:15a. The use of the lexemes ἐντολῶν and δόγμασιν in Eph 2:15a as modifiers of the noun νόμον in v. 15a strongly evokes the law code characteristic of YHWH's covenant with Moses.[156] If Eph 2:11–14 implicitly links the death and resurrection of Christ with the realization of God's promises to Abraham, the reference to the nullification of the law in v. 15a would then assume an underlying contrast between the Abrahamic and Mosaic covenants. In Gal 3:1–19, Paul directly discusses the inclusion of Gentiles into the divine economy and there also contrasts the permanence of the Abrahamic covenant with the transience of the law (cf. Rom 15:8–12). One may discern additional links with the undisputed Pauline epistles if Eph 2:15a implicitly points to the inauguration of the new covenant as a number of scholars have proposed (cf. 2 Cor 3:1–18; Gal 4:21–31).[157]

In summary, one seems forced to conclude with Schreiner's suggestion that "one cannot give an unqualified 'yes' or 'no' answer regarding the cessation of the law" in the Pauline tradition.[158] If Eph 2:11–15 implicitly describes the fulfillment of the Abrahamic covenant and the abrogation of the Mosaic covenant as I have suggested, AE's relationship to the OT certainly cannot be subsumed under the simplistic rubric of either continuity *or* discontinuity. Instead, we see that while AE affirms the permanency of God's promise to make Abraham a blessing to the nations, he also insists on the annulment of the Mosaic covenant. Nonetheless, the appeal to the Decalogue in Eph 6:2 makes it clear that AE does not advocate an antinomian approach to ethics and thus the law in some sense remains valid.[159]

---

156. Cf. Talbert, *Ephesians and Colossians*, 81.

157. Best, *Ephesians*, 261; O'Brien, *Ephesians*, 199; Bruce, *Ephesians*, 298–99.

158. Schreiner, *Law*, 160–61. Cf. Rom 3:31; 7:6; 2 Cor 3:1–18; Gal 4:1–10.

159. AE would more than likely distinguish between the Torah and something like what is referred to as "the law of Christ" (i.e., a Christological appropriation of the Mosaic law) in the Hauptbriefe (cf. Gal 6:2; 1 Cor 9:20–21). Cf. Hoehner, *Ephesians*, 377; Thielman, *Ephesians*, 170. Dunn (*Theology*, 653–55) suggests that the notion of the law of Christ cannot be entirely removed from obedience to the Mosaic law and the discussion of Torah in Ephesians supports his argument (cf. Rom 13:8–10; 15:1–3; Gal 5:14).

The remainder of Eph 2:15–16 provides two reasons for Christ's abolishment of the law. These reasons are expressed by means of two parallel and related subjunctive clauses.¹⁶⁰ According to v. 15b, Christ nullified the law in order to establish Jew and Gentile together as a new entity (ἕνα καινὸν ἄνθρωπον). Eph 2:16 additionally suggests Christ abrogated the law in order to establish harmony between Jew and Gentile (ἐν ἑνὶ σώματι) and between God and humanity (τῷ θεῷ).¹⁶¹

If Eph 2:15b constitutes an allusion to the creation narrative, this would strengthen the sense in which new creation in Ephesians should be understood by means of an *Urzeit-Endzeit* typology.¹⁶² I have already noted that Eph 2:11–15a draws upon the narrative of Abraham's election in Gen 12–17 and implicitly describes the fulfillment of God's promise to make him a conduit of blessing for the nations (see above, p. 156–57). Within the Pentateuch, the Abraham cycle marks the point at which the Creator begins to focus almost exclusively on Abraham and his descendants, giving rise to a series of covenants that regulate the relationship between God and his people (cf. Gen 11:27; 12:1–3; 15:1–21; 17:1–14; 2 Sam 7:11–16; Eph 2:11–12). Furthermore, Abraham is portrayed in the Pentateuch as the one through whom God will address the dilemma produced by Adam's sin.¹⁶³ Eph 2:13–15 in turn points to the inclusion of Gentiles within this divine economy, and the author's use of new creation imagery to describe this new ecclesiological reality in Eph 2:15 suggests he is establishing a connection between the creation account and the promise of blessing for all people within the covenant of Gen 17:1–6. If Eph 2:11–15 points to the fulfillment of the Abrahamic covenant, the presence of new Adam imagery in v. 15 would suggest God's original design for humanity has been achieved and his creation is in the process of being restored. AE is thus reading the primeval

---

160. The presence of terminology from v. 14 within Eph 2:15b–16 (ποιῶν εἰρήνην, τοὺς ἀμφοτέρους, τὴν ἔχθραν) also suggests this section of Eph 2:11–18 develops the portrait of Christ as peacemaker in v. 14.

161. The introductory καί in v. 16 is syntactically connected to the ἵνα conjunction in v. 15. Furthermore, the subjunctive finite verb ἀποκαταλλάξῃ in v. 16 is probably used to convey an additional purpose-result of Eph 2:14–15a.

162. Cf. Miletic, *One Flesh*, 62–65.

163. In this regard, one should observe the following movement within Genesis: 1) God's initial *command* to Adam to "be fruitful and multiply" is later issued to Abraham and his descendants; and 2) God's initial *blessing* to Adam is later bestowed upon Abraham and his offspring (cf. Gen 1:28; 12:2–3; 17:2, 6, 8; 22:16–18; 26:3–4, 24; 28:3; 35:11–12; 47:27; 48:3–4). Cf. Wright, *Paul*, 783–95; Wright, *People of God*, 260–66; Wenham, *Genesis 1–15*, 274–75; Clines, *Pentateuch*, 77–79.

history in close relation to God's covenant with Abraham and sees the latter as the solution to the crisis that began during the former.[164]

There is some debate surrounding the precise nature of the "one new humanity" in v. 15. For some scholars, this "new humanity" must be construed in corporate terms.[165] Other scholars argue that the "new humanity" of v. 15 should be apprehended on an individual level.[166] As we have seen, this is a question that also relates to the conception of new creation in the undisputed Pauline epistles. It is helpful to begin considering this issue by noting the presence of the phrase καινὸν ἄνθρωπον in Eph 4:24. While the wider context of Eph 4:24 is strongly paraenetic in nature and the exhortations expressed in Eph 4:17–24 are to be performed by individual Christ-followers, the use of the plural pronouns in this passage adds a corporate dimension to the nature of this καινὸν ἄνθρωπον.[167] Furthermore, Eph 2:15 occurs within the context of an ecclesiological discussion of the union of Jew and Gentile. An individualized reading of the phrase καινὸν ἄνθρωπον in v. 15 is also obviated by the parallel description of this new entity in Eph 2:16 as "one body." Despite the grammatical considerations within Eph 2:14–16 that Best appeals to in support of an individual reading of "the new humanity," these larger contextual factors should be given greater weight. The phrase καινὸν ἄνθρωπον is thus a fairly complex notion in Ephesians that carries corporate overtones in Eph 2:15, yet may be understood corporately and individualistically in Eph 4:24.

AE next depicts the union of Jew and Gentile as the formation of "one body" (v. 16).[168] Throughout Eph 2:11–15, the author stresses the effect of Christ's death on the relationship between Jew and Gentile. While this issue is not ignored in the preceding statements, v. 16 explicitly clarifies the significance of Christ's death for the vertical relationship (τῷ θεῷ διὰ τοῦ σταυροῦ) between God and humanity (cf. vv. 12–13).[169] This new state of

---

164. Ephesians 2:11–15 thus exhibits a linkage between ecclesiology and the *Urzeit-Endzeit* scheme that is starkly similar to what one encounters in Paul's letter to the Galatians (see above, page 129–30). Cf. Gal 3:6–29; 4:21–31; 6:15–16.

165. Cf. Yee, *Ethnic Reconciliation*, 166; Talbert, *Ephesians and Colossians*, 81; Barth, *Ephesians 1–3*, 310; Lindemann, *Aufhebung*, 167; Thielman, *Ephesians*, 170–71.

166. Cf. Best, *One Body*, 152–54; Moritz, *Profound Mystery*, 42. Interestingly, Moritz and Best both presume an individualized account of new creation in 2 Cor 5:17 and Gal 6:15 supports their reading of the "new humanity" in Eph 2:15.

167. Cf. O'Brien, *Ephesians*, 331; Lincoln, *Ephesians*, 287.

168. The presence of the introductory καί in v. 16 suggests this statement is closely related to the creation of a new humanity in v. 15b and forms part of the author's larger account of the consequences of Christ's nullification of the law in v. 15a. Cf. Best, *Ephesians*, 263–64.

169. Yee (*Ethnic Reconciliation*, 171–73) helpfully notes that the horizontal

affairs among all three parties (God, Jew, and Gentile) is depicted in v. 16 by means of the body metaphor (σῶμα).[170] The concluding phrase ἀποκτείνας τὴν ἔχθραν ἐν αὐτῷ brings this section to a climax by returning to the passage's *Hauptmotiv* (hostility) and explicitly stating the consequences of Christ's death for the dual relationships between: 1) Jew and Gentile; and 2) God and humanity.[171]

Given the essential unity of Eph 1:20—2:22, it is important to note the use of the noun σῶμα in Eph 1:23. Mayer rightly notes that the image is shifted in Eph 2:16; nonetheless, the metaphor is used in the typical Pauline manner in v. 16 to convey a sense of "unity within diversity" (see above, p. 137-38).[172] I have already noted that the phrase τὸ πλήρωμα in Eph 1:23 further describes the church as Christ's σῶμα and is to be understood in close relation to the portrait of the church as a new temple in Eph 2:19-22 (see above, p. 140-42). Returning to Eph 2:16, we may now consider how this text expands upon Eph 1:23 by continuing the development of the divine μυστήριον of Eph 1:9-10. Within Eph 1:20-22a, there is a strong emphasis on Christ's defeat of evil cosmic forces. This is in clear contrast to the decided interest in earthly concerns in Eph 2:1-22.[173] Eph 1:22b-23 may nonetheless be understood as a transitional bridge that marks the shift

---

dimension is not entirely absent in v. 16 and the notion of "one body" has implications for ethnic enmity between Jew and Gentile. Reading v. 16 (and Eph 2:11-22) within the context of Eph 1:20—2:10 thus indicates that the author's vision of restoration must be understood on a much grander scale (cf. Eph 1:10).

The use of the compound verb ἀποκαταλλάσσω in v. 16 to explicate the peacemaking nature of Christ's work requires further comment. The only other use of this verbal construction in the NT occurs in Col 1:20, 22. Interestingly, Col 1:20 exhibits a number of other correspondences (εἰρηνοποιήσας, τοῦ αἵματος τοῦ σταυροῦ αὐτοῦ) with Eph 2:15-16. For some scholars, these similarities constitute evidence of AE's dependence on Colossians. Cf. Sellin, *Epheser*, 222; Martin, *Reconciliation*, 172; Lincoln, *Ephesians*, 128-30, 145. The conceptual differences between these two texts, however, speak against the plausibility of this reconstruction. Cf. Muddiman, *Ephesians*, 135; Best, "Who," 90.

170. With the majority of interpreters, the σῶμα metaphor is used here to describe the unity of Jew and Gentile in Christ, not Christ's physical body. Cf. Lincoln, *Ephesians*, 144; Mayer, *Einheit*, 131; Schnackenburg, *Epheser*, 117; pace Barth, *Ephesians 1-3*, 298. The parallelism between v. 15b and v. 16 would give compelling support to the consensus reading.

171. Cf. Stuhlmacher, "Friede," 351; Schnackenburg, *Epheser*, 118; Pokorný, *Epheser*, 127-28; pace Best, *Ephesians*, 266; Yee, *Ethnic Reconciliation*, 178-79.

172. Mayer, *Einheit*, 131.

173. This is not to imply that the ensuing discussion in Eph 2:1-22 has no concern with the metaphysical (cf. Eph 1:23b; 2:2, 19-22). Nonetheless, Eph 2:1-22 is patently focused on explicating the import of Christ's death on humanity (both individually and corporately).

from the transcendent to the physical. Within Eph 1:22b-23, the presence of the adjective πάντα and the phrase τὰ πάντα evokes the programmatic statement in Eph 1:10 and hints at the possibility that the "church" is directly involved in the *anakephalaiōsis*. This prospect is confirmed in Eph 2:1-22 through the author's explanation of the significance of Christ's death for humanity, both individually (vv. 1-10) and corporately (vv. 11-22).[174] The formation of "one body" in Eph 2:16 thus forms part of a larger matrix of ideas introduced in Eph 1:9-10 and indicates that the σῶμα of Eph 1:23 constitutes a multi-ethnic community.[175]

AE then summarizes this Christological discussion of rapprochement in v. 17 by explicitly grounding Christ's peace-making ministry in Isaiah's proclamation of a new exodus (cf. v. 13). The intertextual significance of the allusion to Isa 57:19 in Eph 2:17 (εἰρήνην ὑμῖν τοῖς μακρὰν καὶ εἰρήνην τοῖς ἐγγύς) has already been discussed (see above, p. 31-33). The troublesome construction καὶ ἐλθών and the allusion to Isa 52:7 (εὐηγγελίσατο) in v. 17, however, have yet to be fully treated.[176] While the use of the verb ἔρχομαι in v. 17 makes it somewhat natural to read this statement in the light of Jesus' incarnation, the emphasis in vv. 13-16 is decidedly on Jesus' sacrificial death.[177] It is thus plausible to construe the participle ἐλθών as a reference to the incarnation, but the stress placed on Jesus' death in the wider context suggests that his proclamation of peace must be read in close connection to his earthly ministry *and* the proclamation of victory in Isa 52:7.[178]

The significance of the verb εὐηγγελίσατο may also be helpfully interpreted in the light of its background in Isa 52:7.[179] As already noted, Isa 52:7 introduces a passage (vv. 7-12) which describes the restoration of Zion. Within Isa 52:7, the announcement of peace (εὐαγγελιζομένου ἀκοὴν εἰρήνης) represents a declaration of YHWH's victory and universal reign. When this Isaianic background is accounted for, it is evident that the verb εὐηγγελίσατο in Eph 2:17 does not refer to a specific proclamation of peace to Jew and

---

174. The identification of "the mystery of Christ" with the salvation of the Gentiles in Eph 3:4-6 corroborates my suggestion that Eph 2:11-22 is related to the divine "mystery" and *anakephalaiōsis* of Eph 1:9-10.

175. Cf. Caragounis, *Mysterion*, 139.

176. See Best (*Ephesians*, 271-73) for a helpful summary of the varied interpretations of the expression καὶ ἐλθών in v. 17.

177. Cf. Lincoln, "Use," 30; Moritz, *Profound Mystery*, 44-45. The more literal interpretation of ἐλθών is adopted by such scholars as Muddiman (*Ephesians*, 137) and Stuhlmacher ("Friede," 353).

178. See Barth (*Ephesians 1-3*, 285, 294-95), Lindemann (*Aufhebung*, 176-77) and Moritz (*Profound Mystery*, 50, 53) for the suggestion that it is difficult to limit the referent of this participle to any single period in Jesus' ministry.

179. Cf. Moritz, *Profound Mystery*, 444.

Gentile during Jesus' earthly ministry but must instead be understood in the light of his final victory over cosmic evil on the cross (cf. Eph 1:20–22).[180] If this is the case, the verb εὐηγγελίσατο in v. 17 does not so much relate to a verbal declaration of peace to Jew and Gentile but instead represents the author's means of identifying his earlier personification of Jesus as peacemaker in v. 14 (αὐτὸς γάρ ἐστιν ἡ εἰρήνη ἡμῶν) with the fulfillment of Isaiah's proclamation of a new exodus.[181]

In conclusion, the depiction of new creation in Eph 2:11–18 exhibits strong interaction with the OT. Despite the absence of explicit quotations or allusions in vv. 11–14, it is nonetheless evident that the author is drawing upon a careful reading of the OT that ultimately points to the fulfillment of the Abrahamic covenant and the inauguration of the new covenant. The use of new Adam imagery in v. 15 thus not only suggests that new creation in Ephesians is to be understood within an *Urzeit-Endzeit* framework, but also that this concept forms part of a canonical reading of Scripture that incorporates material from Isaiah's prophecy. A variety of factors also indicate that the author's understanding of new creation extends beyond the largely anthropocentric focus of Eph 2:1–10 and additionally is to be apprehended on a corporate (specifically, an ecclesiological) level. Regarding the use of Isaianic tradition in Eph 2:11–18, for now it is sufficient to note that v. 13 and v. 17 point to the fulfillment of Isaiah's proclamation of restoration and the salvation of the nations.

New Creation in Ephesians 2:19–22

The preceding section focused on exploring the use of Scripture in Eph 2:11–18 and its implications for understanding the author's portrait of new creation. I primarily argued that there is an underlying narrative within this passage that correlates new creation with the inauguration of the new covenant and the fulfillment of God's covenant with Abraham. I will now consider how the portrait of the church as a temple in vv. 19–22 fits within the author's larger discussion of new creation in Eph 1:20—2:22 and draws upon the OT. More specifically, I will discuss how Eph 2:19–22 continues the intertextual reading of vv. 11–18 by: 1) examining the newfound identity

---

180. It is helpful at this point to recall my earlier suggestion that Eph 1:20—2:22 is best read as a unitary whole. There is a sense in which Gombis' ("Ephesians 2," 415) description of the statement in Eph 2:17 as a "victory shout" accurately conveys the author's thought in this context. Nonetheless, I would prefer to give greater stress to the Isaianic material rather than the ANE narrative pattern of cosmic conflict.

181. On the promise-fulfillment framework of Eph 2:17, see Moritz (*Profound Mystery*, 44); pace Yee (*Ethnic Reconciliation*, 181) and Lincoln ("Use," 29).

of Christ-followers in vv. 19–22; and 2) examining how v. 20 grounds this new reality in Isaianic tradition.[182]

The author begins his treatment of the new identity of believers by first reorienting the status of Gentile Christ-followers (v. 19). The nouns ξένοι and πάροικοι in v. 19 are likely synonymous terms that hark back to the description of Gentile exclusion from the privileges associated with participation in God's covenant community in vv. 11–12.[183] These two nouns are predominantly used in the LXX to describe individuals living in a foreign land and their coordination in this context prepares for the alteration in the status of Gentile believers implicit in the second half of v. 19 (ἀλλά . . . θεοῦ).[184] The new standing assigned to these Gentile believers is expressed by means of the compound noun συμπολῖται, which conveys their essential equality with Jewish Christ-followers.[185]

The significance of the noun συμπολῖται depends greatly on the referent of the clauses τῶν ἁγίων and οἰκεῖοι τοῦ θεοῦ in v. 19. Scholars have offered a variety of proposals for the meaning of the noun ἁγίων in v. 19. Noting the use of the noun πολιτεία in v. 12, some have argued that the noun ἁγίων refers to either Jewish believers or the nation of Israel and AE is thus continuing his discussion in vv. 19–22 by again reiterating the union of Jew and Gentile that has been achieved through Christ's death.[186] Other scholars note the adjective ἁγίων is employed in the Qumran literature and in Eph 1:18 to describe angelic beings. They thereby conclude that v. 19 de-

182. Since the construction ἄρα οὖν at the beginning of v. 19 is used in a consequential sense, vv. 19–22 essentially describes in greater detail the outcome of the author's argument in Eph 2:11–18. Cf. Pokorný, *Epheser*, 129–30; Best, *Ephesians*, 276. The use of the adverb οὐκέτι in v. 19 also points to a close relationship between vv. 11–18 and vv. 19–22 and indicates that the once-now schema of vv. 11–13 is resumed (cf. Eph 2:1–7). Finally, the repetition of the noun ξένοι and the root πολιτ– in v. 19 also links vv. 19–22 with vv. 11–18 (cf. v. 12).

183. Cf. Lincoln, *Ephesians*, 150; Schnackenburg, *Epheser*, 121.

184. Cf. Gen 15:13; 23:4; Exod 2:22; 18:3; Ruth 2:10; Ps 118:19 LXX; Jer 14:8; Lam 5:2; *Pss. Sol.* 17:28; 1 Macc 11:38; *Ant.* 7:335.

185. The noun πολίτης undoubtedly has political connotations of citizenship (cf. Acts 21:39; Phil 3:20; Josephus, *Ant.* 2:101; 12:46; Philo, *Opif.* 1:143; *Cher.* 1:121).

186. See Rantzow (*Christus Victor Temporis*, 196), Faust (*Pax Christi*, 184–87), and Caird (*Letters*, 60) for the suggestion that the noun ἁγίων refers to Jewish believers. See Barth (*Ephesians 1–3*, 269–70) and Yee (*Ethnic Reconciliation*, 195–98) for the suggestion that the noun points to ethnic Jews. The Israelites are described as "holy ones" in such texts as Exod 19:6; Deut 7:6; Ps 15:3 LXX; Dan 7:27; 12:7; Wis 3:9; 10:15, 17; 11Q 48:7, 10. This reading of ἁγίων, however, does not sufficiently account for the presence of the expression ἄρα οὖν, which indicates that the author is here presenting a new stage in his argument. To identify the noun ἁγίων with historical Israel would also fail to account for the close relationship between the constructions τῶν ἁγίων and οἰκεῖοι τοῦ θεοῦ (note the presence of the καί). Cf. Schlier, *Epheser*, 140.

scribes the participation of all believers in the heavenly realm (cf. CD 20:8; 1QH 11:21-23; 14:10-14; 1QS 11:7-9; 1QM 12:1-7).[187] Still other scholars observe that Eph 2:6 has already described the heavenly existence of believers and conclude that v. 19 presents a picture of the believing community's involvement in the heavenly temple with angels and other deceased believers (cf. Gal 4:26; Phil 3:20; Heb 12:18-24).[188] While there is little difference between the second and third interpretations, the latter seems to account best for the development of notions related to heavenly existence in Eph 1–2.

The new status of believers is further described by means of the phrase οἰκεῖοι τοῦ θεοῦ in v. 19 (cf. Gal 6:10; 1 Tim 5:8). According to some interpreters, the phrase οἰκεῖος τοῦ θεοῦ has cultic overtones and suggests that the author is here again referring to the participation of Jew and Gentile believers in the heavenly temple.[189] Others, however, make a distinction between the expression οἰκεῖος τοῦ θεοῦ and the expression οἶκος τοῦ θεοῦ.[190] These scholars conclude the latter expression is limited to the realm of kinship and thereby suggest Eph 2:19 describes the church in familial terms and thus again depicts the vertical reconciliation accomplished in Christ.[191] Some interpreters, nonetheless, note that the notion of a household forms part of the same conceptual field as the divine dwelling place and conclude that the phrase οἰκεῖοι τοῦ θεοῦ also conveys the thought of fellowship with God.[192]

In summary, Eph 2:19 portrays the new status of believers using a complex blending of political, cultic, and familial imagery. Importantly, two of these experiential realms are associated with the notion of divine communion within the biblical worldview. There is thus a strong sense in which Eph 2:19 prepares for the more explicit description of the church as a temple in Eph 2:20-22. I will now more closely examine the portrait of the church in vv. 21-22.

Eph 2:21-22 provides the reader with a more explicit description of the nature of the church.[193] Eph 2:21 continues the architectural imagery

187. Gnilka, *Epheserbrief*, 154; O'Brien, "Heavenly," 101-2; Gärtner, *Temple*, 63-64; McKelvey, *New Temple*, 111.

188. Schlier, *Epheser*, 140-41. Cf. Lincoln, *Paradise*, 151-54.

189. O'Brien, *Ephesians*, 102-3. Cf. Muddiman, *Ephesians*, 140.

190. Cf. Lev 18:6, 12, 13; Isa 3:6; Amos 6:10.

191. Gnilka, *Epheserbrief*, 154; Lincoln, "Church and Israel," 608; Schnackenburg, *Epheser*, 122; Hoehner, *Ephesians*, 394.

192. Cf. Schnackenburg, *Epheser*, 122; Pokorný, *Epheser*, 130; Arnold, *Ephesians*, 169.

193. The repetition of the ἐν ᾧ phrase in v. 22 not only suggests that v. 21 and v. 22 are parallel statements but also indicates that the central focus in this section of Eph

from v. 20 by suggesting the development of the church is dependent upon Christ and has the construction of a "holy temple" ναὸν ἅγιον as its ultimate goal. The anarthrous construction πᾶσα οἰκοδομή is probably a designation for the universal church ("the whole structure"), rather than individual local congregations.[194] The use of this building imagery again serves to emphasize the unity of Jew and Gentile in Christ and prepares the reader for the description of the church as an expanding temple in v. 21b.[195] The process of expansion is expressed through the participle συναρμολογουμένη in v. 21, which further heightens the sense that the building imagery rhetorically functions as a means of relating the unity of the church.[196] The expansion of this "structure" is conveyed through the finite verb αὔξει (cf. 1 Cor 3:6-7; Col 1:6, 10; Eph 4:15; 2 Pet 2:3-6). The growth expressed through this verb is likely numerical and spiritual in nature (cf. Eph 4:11-16; Col 2:18-19).[197] The phrase εἰς ναὸν ἅγιον in v. 21b then indicates that the focus of this growth is the creation of a holy temple.[198] Given the degree to which Isaiah's new exodus forms the backdrop to Eph 1:20—2:22 and incorporates ANE temple-building traditions, the description of the multi-ethnic community becoming a "holy temple" may be understood in close relation to

---

2:11-22 is on describing Christ's pre-eminent status within the community of faith.

194. Cf. Bruce, *Ephesians*, 307; Thielman, *Ephesians*, 183; Hoehner, *Ephesians*, 407-8. See Best, (*Ephesians*, 286), Lincoln (*Ephesians*, 124), and Sellin (*Epheser*, 239) on the textual difficulty πᾶσα ἡ οἰκοδομή in such textual witnesses as ℵ[a], A, C and P. The reading πᾶσα οἰκοδομή is the more difficult reading—it is possible to explain the addition of the definite article before the noun as an attempt to exclude the possibility of reading the phrase πᾶσα οἰκοδομή as "every building"—and is also to be preferred on external grounds.

195. Cf. McKelvey, *New Temple*, 119. Generally speaking, the noun οἰκοδομή carries three distinct meanings: 1) a building or temple (1 Chr 29:1; Ezek 40:2; Matt 24:1; Mar 13:1-2; 1 Cor 3:9; 2 Cor 5:1; 1 Esd 5:60, 73; Philo, *Abr.* 1:139); 2) metaphorically to describe the notion of edification (Rom 14:19; 15:2; 1 Cor 14:3, 5, 12, 26; 2 Cor 10:8; 12:19; 13:10; Eph 4:12, 16, 29); and 3) the act of repairing or constructing a building (1 Chr 26:27; Ezek 17:17; 1 Esd 2:26; 4:51; 6:6; Josephus, *Ant.* 11:59).

196. The verb συναρμολογέω is used with a sharply similar sense in Eph 4:16. The fact that the participle συναρμολογούμενον in v. 16 is modified by the participle συμβιβαζόμενον ("to bring together, unite") confirms this suggestion.

197. Cf. Best, *Ephesians*, 287; Beale, *Temple*, 263. Given the degree to which the mystery motif is related to the union of Jew and Gentile in this letter, the enlargement of the church depicted in this passage is probably related to the *anakephalaiōsis* of Eph 1:10.

198 McKelvey (*New Temple*, 119) helpfully notes, "The image of the temple approximates very closely to that of the body, and . . . the idea of the building (οἰκοδομή) provides the link." Cf. Eph 4:15-16.

Isaiah's eschatological temple (cf. Isa 2:1-4; 40:5; 66:18-24; 1 En. 90:28-38; 91:12-13; 11QTemple 29:7-10).[199]

This passage concludes with a climactic statement in v. 22 that points back to the author's earlier discussion of God's plan to restore "all things" (cf. Eph 1:10). While v. 22 remains closely parallel to v. 21, the addition of the phrase καὶ ὑμεῖς may function as the author's final effort to convey the eschatological significance of Christ's death for his Gentile audience. As with the participle συναρμολογουμένη in v. 21, the passive verb συνοικοδομεῖσθε in v. 22 continues the reconciliation theme that so strongly governs this passage (cf. 1 Pet 2:5; 1 Esd 5:65; Philo, Spec. 1:274; Praem. 1:120). The construction κατοικητήριον τοῦ θεοῦ constitutes the object of this main verb in v. 22 and provides an additional characterization of the church. This phrase is directly parallel to the "holy temple" in v. 21 and also draws upon language from Jewish traditions used to describe the temple (cf. Exod 15:17; 1 Kgs 8:39, 43, 49; 2 Chr 6:30, 33, 39; 30:27; Ps32:14 LXX; 75:3 LXX; 3 Macc 2:15). By describing Gentile believers in this way, the author incorporates his depiction of the church into his *Urzeit-Endzeit* framework and again presents a measure of confirmation that the Jew/Gentile divide is a fundamental aspect of this eschatological pattern (see above, p. 4). As already noted, the programmatic *anakephalaiōsis* of Eph 1:10 is to be understood within this same conceptual structure. If the plural pronoun ὑμεῖς in Eph 2:22 refers to Gentile believers as a number of scholars conclude, then the author is here informing the reader that the divine plan to unify the cosmos has been partially accomplished in the oneness of the church.[200]

The author's description of Christ as the "cornerstone" in Eph 2:20 supports this reading of v. 22.[201] The phrase ὄντος ἀκρογωνιαίου αὐτοῦ Χριστοῦ Ἰησοῦ in v. 20b qualifies the lofty position assigned to the apostles and prophets in v. 20a (cf. Ps 117:22 LXX; Matt 16:18; 2 Tim 2:19; Gal 2:9; 1 Pet

---

199. Beale (*Temple*, 263) suggests that ANE temple-building traditions are additionally evoked by means of this passage's portrait of the church as an expanding temple.

200. That the pronoun ὑμεῖς refers to Gentile Christ-followers seems likely on the basis of: 1) the strong parallelism between v. 21 and v. 22; and 2) the presence of the conjunction καί. Cf. Lincoln, *Ephesians*, 158; Schlier, *Epheser*, 145; pace Muddiman, *Ephesians*, 144.

201. Ephesians 2:20 fundamentally explains the ideological basis of the church. According to v. 20, the church is constructed upon the ministry and teaching of the apostles and prophets. While the "apostles" of v. 20 are likely the authoritative leaders within the early church (cf. 1 Cor 12:28; 14:29-32; Eph 1:1; 3:5; 4:11), the identity of the "prophets" is a more challenging issue. The presence of the nouns ἀπόστολος and προφήτης in Eph 3:5 creates a particularly strong parallel to Eph 2:20 and makes it probable that the "apostles and prophets" in the latter text refers to NT prophets. Cf. Muddiman, *Ephesians*, 142; Schnackenburg, *Epheser*, 122-23.

2:4–8; Rev 21:14). Whether one chooses to interpret the noun ἀκρογωνιαίου as a capstone or cornerstone, it is clear that the authority of the "apostles and prophets" is of a limited nature (cf. Eph 1:22; Col 1:18). Regarding the first interpretation, a number of scholars suggest that the noun ἀκρογωνιαίου refers to a stone at the top of a building or arch on the basis of the use of the noun ἀκρογωνιαῖος in such texts as *T. Sol.* 22:7—23:4; 2 Kgs 25:17; Ps 117:22 LXX.[202] Identifying the "cornerstone" of Eph 2:20b with a stone placed at the top of a building, however, raises a number of significant problems. First, the texts appealed to in support of the capstone interpretation in Eph 2:20 are relatively late.[203] Second, Eph 2:20 presents a close relationship between this "cornerstone" and the "apostles and prophets," suggesting the "cornerstone" forms part of the building's structural foundation.[204] Third, and perhaps most importantly, viewing the "cornerstone" of Eph 2:20b as a stone found at the top of a structure fails to account for the likelihood that this statement constitutes an allusion to Isa 28:16.[205]

If Christ's description as a "cornerstone" in Eph 2:20 represents an intertextual allusion to Isa 28:16, this would strengthen the possibility that vv. 21–22 is to be understood in connection with an *Urzeit-Endzeit* typology. Isaiah 28:16 forms the central statement within a text unit (vv. 14–22) that revolves around the question, "Where can one find genuine hope?" Two features of Isa 28:16 are particularly worth observing in order to understand how this Isaianic text is being used in Eph 2:20. First, the fact that the "cornerstone" of Isa 28:16 is laid in "Zion" and is being portrayed as a symbol of hope suggests that this text is related to Isaiah's discussion of the restoration of Zion/Jerusalem.[206] Second, if Eph 2:20 alludes to Isa 28:16 and identifies Jesus with this "cornerstone," then AE is here offering a messianic reading

202. This reading of the noun ἀκρογωνιαίου is attributed to the work of Jeremias ("Der Eckstein," 65–70). Other recent scholars who have followed this interpretation include: Gnilka, *Epheserbrief*, 158; Best, *Ephesians*, 284–86; Barth, *Ephesians 1–3*, 317–19; Patzia, *Ephesians*, 201–2, 204. Finally, the noun ἀκρογωνιαίου is used in Symmachus' Greek translation of 2 Kgs 25:17 and Ps 117:22 LXX.

203. Yee, *Ethnic Reconciliation*, 204–5.

204. Cf. Schnackenburg, "Bau," 263. Gaston (*No Stone*, 195, 214) rightly observes that the noun θεμελίῳ in Eph 2:20 forms part of broader semantic field (comprised of such lexemes as λίθος and πέτρα) that is used to describe concepts associated with the temple in the NT.

205 Cf. Thielman, *Ephesians*, 182; Schnackenburg, "Bau," 263–64; Yee, *Ethnic Reconciliation*, 206–7; McKelvey, *New Temple*, 405–6; pace Lincoln, *Ephesians*, 155–56. That the phrase ὄντος ἀκρογωνιαίου αὐτοῦ Χριστοῦ Ἰησοῦ in Eph 2:20 constitutes an allusion to Isa 28:16 seems a plausible conclusion on the basis of the presence of the nouns θεμέλια and ἀκρογωνιαῖον in the latter text.

206. Cf. Muddiman, *Ephesians*, 142.

of Isa 28:16 which conforms to renderings found in the LXX and the Isaiah Targum.[207]

These observations have important implications for understanding how AE is using Isa 28:16 within the context of his portrait of the church in Eph 2:21-22. If Isaianic traditions provide the intertextual framework for understanding AE's discussion of new creation in Eph 1:20—2:22 as I have argued above, the description of Christ as a "cornerstone" in Eph 2:20 serves to specify the link between these traditions and the temple of Eph 2:19-22. It is important to recall at this point that the restored Zion/Jerusalem is a central theme within Isaiah's prophecy (and Second Temple Judaism) and is the goal of the new exodus theme in Isaiah (see above, esp. p. 16-17). The phrase ὄντος ἀκρογωνιαίου αὐτοῦ Χριστοῦ Ἰησοῦ in Eph 2:20 thus does more than present a messianic interpretation of Isa 28:16. Rather, when one accounts for the larger appropriation of Isaianic tradition in Eph 1:20—2:22, the identification of Christ with the "cornerstone" of Isa 28:16 suggests that Isaiah's restored Zion/Jerusalem has drawn nigh in an inaugurated sense.[208] To paraphrase the language of Isa 28:16, "a stone has been laid in Zion" and the temple that is being constructed is intricately related to Jesus Christ and is to be understood in close relation to Isaiah's restored Zion/Jerusalem.[209]

In conclusion, Eph 2:19-22 essentially provides a more detailed description of the church and correlates this portrait with the author's eschatological vision of Christ's work. This passage builds upon the preceding discussion in vv. 11-18 by emphasizing the unity of the multi-ethnic community of Christ-followers by means of architectural, cultic, and domestic imagery. Several factors also suggest that the portrait of new creation in vv. 19-22 is closely aligned with an *Urzeit-Endzeit* typology. First, the use of cultic imagery in vv. 19-22 allows the larger discussion of new creation in Eph 1:20—2:22 to conclude by implicitly evoking the ANE temple-building traditions that are featured so strongly in Gen 1-2 and Isaianic new exodus traditions.[210] Second, Eph 2:22 evokes Eph 1:10 (a governing statement within

---

207. Note the presence of the expression ὁ πιστεύων ἐπ' αὐτῷ in Isa 28:16 LXX (cf. *Tg. Isa* 28:16). The use of the phrase εἰς τὰ θεμέλια αὐτῆς in Isa 28:16 LXX also suggests that a foundation stone is in view.

208. Cf. Thielman, *Ephesians*, 184; Beale, *Temple*, 259-63.

209. Regarding the relationship between the "foundation of the apostles and prophets" and the description of Christ as the "cornerstone," AE would probably have the reader perceive the "cornerstone" as the initial stone laid in the construction of a building that functions as a guide in placing the other stones that comprise the foundation. Cf. Schnackenburg, *Epheser*, 124; McKelvey, *New Temple*, 198. On this basis, one need not conclude Eph 2:20 contradicts 1 Cor 3:11.

210. My earlier discussion regarding the primacy of Isaianic tradition over the "narrative pattern of divine warfare" in Eph 1:20—2:22 is worth recalling at this point (see

this letter that directly connects the goal of the Christ-event with an *Urzeit-Endzeit* typology) by describing the Gentile addressees as a "dwelling place for God" in v. 22 and again pointing to the unity of the church. Third, since the description of Christ as a "cornerstone" alludes to Isa 28:16, this portrait of the church is firmly fixed within Isaiah's proclamation of a restored Zion/Jerusalem and new exodus. These two sets of tradition are ultimately closely intertwined and are to be understood within an *Urzeit-Endzeit* typology.

Summary

In this section of my analysis of new creation in Eph 1–2, I have again sought to understand the nature of new creation in Eph 1:20—2:22 by means of an intertextual analysis. In comparison to Eph 1:3-14, the use of the OT in Eph 1:20—2:22 is much more overt. At a number of points, the author quotes and alludes to the OT and in doing so frames the Christ-event as the fulfillment of God's promises to the people of Israel (cf. Eph 1:20, 22; 2:13, 17, 20). There are several points in Eph 1–2, however, where the author also implicitly evokes the OT and places new creation within God's plan to address the dilemma narrated in Gen 3 (cf. Eph 1:9-10; 2:11-15).

This intertextual reading of Eph 1:20—2:22 has clarified the nature of new creation in this passage in a number of ways. First, the allusions to Ps 109:1 LXX and Ps 8:7 LXX in Eph 1:20, 22 set the stage for the author's fuller discussion of new creation in Eph 1–2 by evoking the divine warrior traditions that feature so strongly in Isaiah's depiction of a new exodus and recalling Jewish expectations that God would tackle the problem presented in Gen 3. Second, the coordination of death-life imagery in Eph 2:1-6 and creation imagery in Eph 2:10 (ποίημα, κτισθέντες) draws upon Jewish traditions which closely link the renewal of the cosmos with the restoration of humanity. Third, several literary elements within Eph 2:11-16 suggest that the author is implicitly appealing to Scripture's grand story of redemption by directly correlating the fulfillment of the Abrahamic covenant with the inauguration of the new covenant and new creation (cf. v. 12, 14–15). Fourth, the intertextual references to Isa 52:7 and Isa 57:19 in Eph 2:13, 17 suggest that AE is depicting new creation as the fulfillment of Isaiah's prophecy of a new exodus.[211] Fifth, the use of the phrase καινὸν ἄνθρωπον in Eph 2:15 is widely understood as an allusion to Gen 1–2 and not only depicts new creation in corporate terms but again indicates that the author

---

above, p. 135–37).

211. See chapter 2 for an extensive discussion of the relationship between new creation and new exodus in Isaiah.

is placing new creation within an *Urzeit-Endzeit* framework. Sixth, the allusion to Isa 28:16 in Eph 2:20 closely relates the description of the church as a temple in Eph 2:19–22 with Isaiah's restored Zion/Jerusalem motif (a theme that is strongly connected to Isaiah's proclamation of a new exodus) and suggests that the temple in Eph 2:19–22 is being portrayed as the inaugural fulfillment of the "new heavens and new earth" of Isa 65–66.

Conclusion

It is evident from this analysis of Eph 1–2 that any attempt to pigeonhole AE's understanding of new creation into a single theological category (whether anthropology, cosmology, or ecclesiology) would simply not do adequate justice to the genius of his vision of what God has done in Christ. This raises serious problems for Hubbard's appeal to Ephesians in support of his anthropological understanding of new creation in 2 Corinthians and Galatians.[212] If one takes a myopic view of Eph 1–2, it is evident that individual passages within this text sequence focus on different aspects of the author's larger understanding of new creation. Nonetheless, a detailed examination of Eph 1–2 reveals that the author's depiction of new creation accords to a greater degree with Jackson's conception of new creation in the Hauptbriefe as a cosmological, anthropological, and ecclesiological reality.

---

212. Cf. Hubbard, *New Creation*, 7.

6

Conclusion

Summary

THE PRIMARY GOAL OF this research project has been to explore the degree of continuity and discontinuity between the portraits of new creation in the Hauptbriefe (specifically, in 2 Corinthians and Galatians) and the letter to the Ephesians. Up to this present point in the history of scholarship, the bulk of the work on new creation in the Pauline corpus has concentrated on the meaning of new creation in 2 Corinthians and Galatians, while the new creation theme in Ephesians has been largely ignored. Furthermore, the precise significance of new creation in the Hauptbriefe remains clouded in debate. Despite the lack of unanimity concerning the authorship of the letter to the Ephesians, this analysis explores the relationship between the conceptions of new creation in these two sets of texts in order to bring a measure of clarity to this ongoing discussion.

The allusions to Isaianic tradition in 2 Cor 5:17b and Eph 2:13, 17 constituted an important launching point for this present investigation. In keeping with recent studies on the use of the OT in the *corpus Paulinum*, I argued that these evocations of Isaianic tradition in 2 Corinthians and Ephesians are not to be viewed as mere proof-texts that are entirely unrelated to their original contexts. Instead, I proposed these reverberations of Isaiah's prophecy of a new exodus depict new creation in the Pauline tradition as the fulfillment of Isaiah's grand vision of divine deliverance.

The first major component of my argument was an analysis of Isaiah's new exodus theme. Two important presuppositions undergirded this treatment of Isaiah: 1) Paul and AE would have read and interpreted Isaiah as a unified whole; and 2) the allusion to Isaianic tradition in 2 Cor 5:17b entrenches new creation within the entire framework of Isaiah's new exodus rather than specific texts in Isaiah. With these premises in mind, I engaged in an extensive analysis of texts related to Isaiah's new exodus theme and considered the extent to which these texts correlated God's act of restoration with anthropological, cosmological, and ecclesiological concerns. As a result of this study, it is evident that Isaiah's new exodus is closely associated with anthropological and cosmological renewal, as well as the salvation of the Gentiles (cf. Isa 40:1–5, 9–11; 43:16–21; 51:3–5, 9–11; 52:7–10; 57:14–19; 62:10–12; 65:17–25; 66:18–24). A particularly significant feature of this analysis was my observation that a number of Isaianic new exodus texts also strongly draw upon ANE temple-building traditions (cf. Isa 40:3–5, 9–11; 43:16–21; 51:9–11; 52:7–10).

This observation suggests Isaiah's vision of restoration is aligned with an *Urzeit-Endzeit* typology, in which the end of human history is strongly related to its beginning. This also has important implications for understanding the nature of the restored Zion/Jerusalem in Isaiah, as well as the significance of the divine warrior and temple imagery in Eph 1:20–22 and Eph 2:19–22. With regard to this *Urzeit-Endzeit* typology, it is likely that Isaiah's restored Zion/Jerusalem is to be understood in close relation to the garden-temple of Gen 1–3.[1] Concerning the divine warrior and temple imagery in Eph 1:20–22; 2:19–22, the prominence of ANE temple-building traditions in Isaiah's new exodus suggests that AE is: 1) presenting Eph 1:20—2:22 as a distinct textual unit; and 2) depicting the account of new creation in Eph 1:20—2:22 as the fulfillment of Isaiah's new exodus.

My discussion of new creation in Isaiah was followed by a broad analysis of the nature of new creation and restoration in Ezekiel, Jeremiah, 1 Enoch, and Jubilees. Once again, this chapter primarily explored the scope of new creation and restoration in these texts by assessing how these two related concepts are associated with anthropological, cosmological, and ecclesiological realities. A secondary focus of this chapter was examining how the "new heavens and new earth" of Isa 65–66 was read by elements within Second Temple Judaism. My analysis of these texts has demonstrated the presence of a number of common threads within these four texts. More specifically, new creation and restoration in Jeremiah, Ezekiel, *1 Enoch*, and *Jubilees* are frequently connected with: 1) the appearance of an eschatological temple (Jer 30[37]:18–22; 38:40 LXX; Ezek 37:26–28; 40–48; *1 En.* 25:3–6; 90:28–29; 91:13; *Jub.* 1:17, 27–29; 4:26a); 2) inward, anthropological renewal (cf. Jer 31[38]:31–34; Ezek 36:26; *1 En.* 10:21; 90:32–33; *Jub.* 1:17–29; 4:26); 3) cosmological restoration (Ezek 36:29–30, 34–35; *1 En.* 10:18–19; 11:1; *Jub.* 1:29); 4) the redemption of the Gentiles (cf. Ezek 47:21–23; *1 En.* 10:16, 21;

---

1. The presence of allusions to Gen 1–3 in Isa 65:17–25 and the cultic imagery in Isa 66:18–24 further strengthens this hypothesis.

90:37–38; 91:14); and 5) an *Urzeit-Endzeit* typology (Ezek 36:35; *1 En.* 10:3, 18–19; 25:6; *Jub.* 23:22–32). The complexity of new creation and restoration in these texts does not require an analogous reading of new creation in the Pauline tradition. Nonetheless, the complex manner in which new creation and restoration are depicted in Jeremiah, Ezekiel, *1 Enoch*, and *Jubilees* presents a considerable challenge to the relatively neat and tidy representations of new creation in the Hauptbriefe offered by Mell, Hubbard, and Kraus.[2]

The next major step in my argument was an examination of new creation in the Hauptbriefe. This analysis began by considering the extent to which Paul portrays new creation in Gal 6:11–16 as an anthropological, cosmological, and ecclesiological concept. Here I argued that new creation in Gal 6:11–16 resonates more strongly with Paul's eschatological understanding of Christ's death and resurrection. The close association between the crucified "world" of v. 14 (a noun strongly aligned with Paul's inaugurated eschatology) and the expression καινὴ κτίσις in v. 15, in turn, suggests the latter should primarily be interpreted cosmologically (cf. 1 Cor 7:31).[3] Paul's depiction of new creation in this passage, however, is complicated by the need to consider the close intersection between inaugurated eschatology and soteriology within this letter (cf. Gal 3:1–29; 4:1–10; 5:5–6). When this "eschatologically-infused soteriology" is accounted for, Paul's negation of circumcision and uncircumcision in v. 15 also comes to express the conviction that salvation is found through faith in Christ and not nomistic observance.[4] Finally, the direct correlation between καινὴ κτίσις in v. 15 and "the Israel of God" in v. 16 also indicates that new creation in Galatians captures an essential element of what God has done in Christ—the abolishment of the ecclesiological divisions associated with the old age (cf. Gal 3:28). In conclusion, new creation in Galatians is a concise summary of Paul's complex understanding of the significance of Christ's death and resurrection and brings together aspects of his cosmology, anthropology, and ecclesiology.

I then examined the portrait of new creation in 2 Cor 5:11–21. I began this analysis by exploring the nature of Paul's apostolic defense in 2 Cor 1–5. I noted there that in 2 Cor 3:1–18, Paul not only aligns genuine apostolic ministry with the work of the Spirit and the new covenant, but also 2 Cor 3:18—4:6 describes conversion using imagery drawn from Gen 1–2.

---

2. This point is particularly valid since the portrayals of new creation and restoration in these texts within the OT, Second Temple Judaism, and the Pauline corpus are frequently connected with the same traditions in Genesis and Isaiah (e.g., Gen 1–2; Isa 65:17–25).

3. The crucified "world" in Gal 6:14 likely forms part of Paul's old age/new age antithesis.

4. Cf. Jackson, *New Creation*, 6, 173–82.

On the basis of these observations, I concluded that while Paul undoubtedly emphasizes anthropology within 2 Cor 3:1—4:6, he nonetheless does so in such a way that the eschatological significance of Christ's death is not downplayed.

As with much of this project, my analysis of 2 Cor 5:11–21 was primarily concerned with exploring the relationship between the description of new creation in this passage and relevant elements of anthropology, cosmology, and ecclesiology. I concluded that while there is a definite emphasis on anthropology within this context, Paul's description of new creation also bears the imprint of his cosmology and ecclesiology. The clearest evidence of a close correlation between new creation and anthropology in this passage may be discerned in: 1) the hortatory thrust of vv. 14–16; 2) Paul's fluid shift from new creation in v. 17 to a discussion of the vertical reconciliation of God and humanity in v. 18–21; and 3) the parallelism between the phrase θεὸς ἦν ἐν Χριστῷ κόσμον καταλλάσσων ἑαυτῷ and the phrase μὴ λογιζόμενος αὐτοῖς τὰ παραπτώματα αὐτῶν in v. 19. However, the new Adam typology in vv. 14–15 suggests that the treatment of new creation in vv. 11–21 must also be understood through Paul's inaugurated eschatology. This correlation between Paul's inaugurated eschatology and new creation in vv. 14–17 makes it reasonable to conclude that new creation is to be understood as the initial fulfillment of Isaiah's "new heavens and new earth" and thus encompasses cosmological restoration. Finally, Paul's description of the object of the divine work of reconciliation in v. 19 as the "world" at a minimum indicates that new creation is not an entirely individualistic concept. Furthermore, since new creation in the OT and Second Temple Judaism is so frequently linked with the salvation of the Gentiles (especially within Isaiah's new exodus), Paul's use of this noun evokes these traditions and points to the ecclesiological scope of new creation.

A unique feature of my analysis of new creation in 2 Corinthians was a discussion of 2 Cor 6:1–18. Paul links his argument with Isaiah's new exodus at two points in this section of the letter (cf. Isa 49:9–13; 52:7–11; 2 Cor 6:2, 17abc). These depictions of a new exodus are not only correlated with Isaiah's restored Zion/Jerusalem motif, but also present an image of divine renewal that reaches into the theological spheres of anthropology, cosmology, and ecclesiology (cf. Isa 49:1, 6–8, 11–26; 52:7–10). Paul's statements in 2 Cor 6:1–18 thus confirm a broad reading of καινὴ κτίσις. Furthermore, Paul's description of the believing community as the "temple of the living God" in v. 16 also provides additional proof that new creation in 2 Corinthians is related to an *Urzeit-Endzeit* typology (cf. 2 Cor 3:18; 4:4, 6) and may also portray the church as the inaugural fulfillment of Isaiah's restored Zion/Jerusalem.[5]

The final significant element of this analysis was an examination of new creation in Eph 1–2. I began this discussion by exploring the introductory nature of Eph 1:9–10. There I argued that the use of the noun μυστήριον in v. 9 develops the new creation motif in Ephesians by linking it with the universal gospel for all nations (cf. Eph 2:11–22; 3:3–6). I also suggested that the *anakephalaiōsis* of Eph 1:10 is an eschatological concept that strongly aligns new creation in Ephesians with an *Urzeit-Endzeit* typology.

The crux of my discussion of new creation in Eph 1–2 addressed the author's statements in Eph 1:20—2:22. A particularly salient feature of this section of my analysis is the proposal that Eph 1:20—2:22 is to be read as a unitary whole that mirrors the prominent role given to ANE temple-building traditions within Isaiah's new exodus (cf. Isa 11:1–12; 40:3–5, 9–11; 43:16–21; 51:9–11; 52:7–10; 66:15–24). I also argued that Eph 1:20–23 has an introductory role within Eph 1:20—2:22 by: 1) portraying Christ as a divine warrior in v. 20 (cf. Ps 109:1 LXX); 2) implicitly evoking the notion of new creation through the allusion to Ps 8:7 LXX in v. 22; and 3) foreshadowing the description of the church as a growing temple in Eph 2:19–22 through the noun πλήρωμα in v. 23.

Eph 2:1–10 also played a significant role in my overall discussion of new creation in Eph 1:20–22. There I argued that while the death-life imagery in vv. 1–6 places great stress on the anthropological quality of new creation, the author also sets new creation within an eschatological framework. The eschatological component of new creation is evident in v. 6, where the author links new life in Christ with heavenly existence, thus correlating the death-life imagery in vv. 1–6 with an inaugurated eschatology. Furthermore, cosmological overtones are present in the use of the noun ποίημα (a noun elsewhere associated with creation in the OT, the NT, and the Pseudepigrapha) and the participle κτισθέντες in v. 10.[6] We can thus conclude that the discussion in Eph 2:1–10 leans heavily towards the anthropological side of new creation, yet does not neglect the cosmological quality of AE's inaugurated eschatology.

---

5. A relationship between 2 Cor 6:16b and the *Urzeit-Endzeit* eschatological scheme seems especially plausible when one accounts for the frequency with which the OT and early Jewish texts correlate an eschatological temple with the new age (see above, chapters 2 and 3). Finally, 2 Cor 6:16b expresses an understanding of the church that is rather similar to the self-understanding of the Qumran community in 4Q174 3:6 (see below, p. 189).

6. Cf. Ps 91:5 LXX; 142:5 LXX; Eccl 3:11; 7:13; Isa 29:16; Rom 1:20; *T. Ab.* 9:6; *T. Job* 49:3.

The focus of my analysis of Eph 2:11–18 concerned understanding the relationship between new creation and the abrogation of Torah in v. 15. I made the case there that the phrase διαθηκῶν τῆς ἐπαγγελίας in v. 12 fixes the author's discussion of horizontal and vertical reconciliation within the context of God's covenantal relationship with the Israelite people and particularly stresses the universalistic promises of the Abrahamic covenant (cf. Gen 12:2; 17:1–6). When read within the context of this narrative in the OT, the author's discussion of the inclusion of Gentiles in the divine economy in vv. 13–18 points to the fulfillment of God's promises to Abraham. Understanding Eph 2:11–18 in this light suggests that v. 15 not only implicitly announces the inauguration of the new covenant but also further confirms that new creation in Ephesians is intimately associated with an *Urzeit-Endzeit* typology.[7]

My analysis of Eph 2:19–22 primarily concentrated on apprehending its portrait of the believing community and the significance of the noun ἀκρογωνιαίου in v. 20. Regarding the former, I argued that the use of cultic imagery in vv. 21–22 and the stress on the unity of the church again evoke an *Urzeit-Endzeit* typology (cf. Eph 1:10). Regarding the latter, I maintained that the noun ἀκρογωνιαίου in v. 20 represents a deliberate allusion to Isa 28:16. This allusion to Isaianic tradition allows the temple of Eph 2:19–22 to be closely aligned with the restored Zion/Jerusalem theme in Isaiah (a motif closely related to Isaiah's new exodus theme) and thus portrays the church as the initial realization of Isaiah's "new heavens and new earth."[8]

It is now appropriate to offer a suitable definition of new creation in the Pauline tradition. I have purposely avoided this issue up to this point, largely because of the methodological concern of accounting for the arguments against the Pauline authorship of Ephesians. In light of the correspondences between new creation in these three texts, new creation in the Pauline tradition may be defined as, *a pithy summary (resulting from an intertextual reading of Scripture) of the redemptive-historical significance of Christ's death and resurrection that encompasses the anthropological, cosmological, and ecclesiological scope of divine restoration within the conceptual framework of an Urzeit-Endzeit typology.*

---

7. The portrait of Abraham in the Pentateuch as God's means of addressing the sin of Adam and restoring creation is important to consider in this discussion.

8. This, of course, should be apprehended within the conceptual structure of the author's inaugurated eschatology, much like the account of heavenly existence in Eph 2:6.

Implications

The primary question this research project has sought to resolve concerns the degree of continuity and discontinuity between the presentations of new creation in 2 Corinthians and Galatians and that of Ephesians. As a result of this analysis, one may conclude that there is a strong degree of continuity between the portraits of new creation within these three texts. With regard to the depiction of new creation in 2 Corinthians and Galatians, a composite view of 2 Cor 5:11–21 and Gal 6:11–16 suggests that new creation is aligned with anthropology, cosmology, and ecclesiology.[9] Turning now to Ephesians, it is evident that new creation in Eph 1–2 is also closely linked with anthropological, cosmological, and ecclesiological notions. The presence of an *Urzeit-Endzeit* typology within both these sets of texts also adds an additional conceptual similarity. A significant correspondence that seems to have been overlooked to this point in the history of scholarship is the firm association between new creation and the abrogation of the law in both Gal 6:15 and Eph 2:15.[10] The linkage between ecclesiology and an *Urzeit-Endzeit* typological pattern in Gal 6:15–16 and Eph 2:11–22 would establish an additional correspondence between the portrait of new creation in the Hauptbriefe and that of the letter to the Ephesians. Yet another point of similarity between these two sets of texts involves the close association between new creation and the portrait of the church as a temple (cf. 2 Cor 6:16; Eph 2:19–22). A final note of congruence within these texts that is worth observing is the manner in which new creation in 2 Cor 5:14–21 and Eph 2:1–22 seamlessly transitions between individualistic and corporate categories.

It is natural to consider now the significance of this study for the debate over the authorship of Ephesians. While the presence of such strong agreement between these texts strengthens the case for the Pauline authorship of Ephesians, it is not sufficient evidence to prove definitively that Ephesians was indeed written by the Apostle Paul. Caution at this point is especially advisable since Ephesians exhibits a more complex use of Isaianic tradition and its *Urzeit-Endzeit* typology is more pronounced. While it is possible to attribute these developments to a later disciple, since they are a natural augmentation of the conception of new creation in 2 Corinthians and Galatians, it is equally likely that the amplified portrait of new creation in Eph 1–2 is the work of the Apostle Paul himself.

---

9. Jackson (*New Creation*, 155–67) rightly notes that cosmology and anthropology are closely aligned in the portrait of new creation in Rom 8:18–25.

10. Note also that the once-now schema in Eph 2:11–13, 19 also points to the new ecclesiological world that has arisen with Christ's death and resurrection (cf. Gal 3:28; 6:15–16).

With this perspective on the authorship of Ephesians in mind, it is now possible to explore the significance of this project for the new creation debate in the Hauptbriefe. Whether written by the Apostle Paul or a later disciple, the likelihood that Ephesians was penned after 2 Corinthians and Galatians suggests that the portrait of new creation in Eph 1–2 can bring a measure of clarity to the meaning of new creation in these two undisputed texts.[11] With this framework in mind, it is difficult to avoid the conclusion that a simplistic account of new creation in 2 Cor 5:11–21 and Gal 6:11–16 does not do justice to the complex manner in which Paul portrays new creation in these two texts. Furthermore, while there are minor problems with his description of new creation as an expression of Paul's "eschatologically-infused soteriology," Jackson's understanding of new creation is closer to the meaning of new creation in the Hauptbriefe than the more restricted proposals offered by Mell, Hubbard, and Kraus.[12]

The preceding study also clarifies the place of apocalyptic eschatology and salvation history in the Pauline corpus. This issue constitutes the center of a debate largely initiated by K. Stendahl and E. Käsemann concerning the doctrine of justification by faith.[13] While there is a definite absence of justification *terminology* in Eph 1–2, the *concept* is nonetheless present in Eph 2:8–10 (see above, p. 145–46). The parallelism between Eph 2:1–10 and Eph 2:11–22 indicates that this implicit treatment of justification by faith is placed within a salvation-historical framework that is strongly aligned with God's dealings with (and promises to) the people of Israel (cf. Eph 2:11–12, 19–22). At the same time, the apocalyptic quality of new creation is evident in such textual features as the once-now schema and the believing community's deliverance from cosmic evil (cf. vv. 1–4, 11–13, 19). The discussion of new creation in Eph 1–2 thus exhibits no simple bifurcation between apocalyptic eschatology and salvation history. Instead, there is a distinct merging of these two theological horizons that places new creation (and

---

11. See Best (*Ephesians*, 44–46) on the dating of the letter to the Ephesians. Even if one adopts a skeptical position on the Pauline authorship of Ephesians, there is still a strong sense in which this letter can function as an interpretative guide for the undisputed Pauline epistles. Viewed in this way, the letter to the Ephesians at the very least demonstrates the semantic potential of the Hauptbriefe in much the same manner that texts from Second Temple Judaism reveal how the OT might be interpreted.

12. This study, however, expands on Jackson's (and that of Adams) account of new creation in the undisputed Pauline epistles by: 1) demonstrating the link between new creation and an *Urzeit-Endzeit* typology; 2) clarifying the significance of new creation's ecclesiological scope; 3) shedding light on how Paul's understanding of new creation is derived from an intertextual reading of Scripture; and 4) correlating the temple imagery in 2 Cor 6:16 with Paul's understanding of new creation.

13. Cf. Stendahl, "Apostle Paul," 199–215; Käsemann, *Perspectives*, 60–78.

justification) within the framework of continuity *and* discontinuity with the past.[14] Such a heated debate certainly cannot be settled on the basis of these observations from Eph 1-2. Nonetheless, these comments on this text suggest that one need not keep these two theological constructs at arm's length.

Areas for Further Research

Perhaps the most significant avenue for further research this project has opened up is the need to examine the new creation theme in the entire letter to the Ephesians. My analysis of Eph 1-2 has laid some important groundwork for such a project.

It would also be worthwhile to consider the extent to which the multifaceted portrait of new creation I have detected in the Pauline corpus is present in other texts within the NT. The letter to the Colossians is particularly suited to such a project. Jackson has already made a number of valuable observations regarding Colossians that pave the way for a rich analysis of this letter's new creation theme.[15] Nonetheless, he fails to note the linking of new creation and ecclesiology in Col 3:10-11. The possibility of reading Col 1:15-20 through an *Urzeit-Endzeit* typology is also relevant to this discussion.

Finally, it could also be profitable to explore the relationship between the portrait of new creation in the Pauline corpus and the portrayal of the "new heavens and new earth" in Rev 21-22. Since the author of the Apocalypse seems to be drawing upon the same streams of tradition in the OT (Genesis and Isaiah) to express his understanding of the "new heavens and new earth," further study of Rev 21-22 could help validate the reading of new creation presented in this analysis.

---

14. See Barclay (*Obeying*, 104-5) for the suggestion that Paul's letter to the Galatians also exhibits a coalescing of apocalyptic eschatology and salvation history. Jackson (*New Creation*, 182-83) reaches similar conclusions in his analysis of new creation in the undisputed Pauline epistles.

15. Jackson, *New Creation*, 184.

Appendix One

The Use of ANE Temple-building Traditions outside of Isaiah's Prophecy

THE PRECEDING DISCUSSION HAS noted several points at which ANE temple-building traditions are evoked in Isa 43:16–21 and Exod 15:1–19. These allusions to ANE temple-building traditions suggest that the migration of the Israelites from Egypt and the new exodus of Isaiah ultimately lead to the formation of a worshiping community and the construction of a place of worship. In associating these two "creative" events—the creation of Israel in the former and the inauguration of the new creation in the latter—with ANE temple-building traditions, the authors of these two sets of tradition are ultimately closely aligning these two events with the creation narrative of Gen 1–2. I will now briefly discuss the nature of these ANE temple-building traditions and their use in the OT and Second Temple Judaism.

In essence, ANE temple-building traditions are a prominent feature of cosmogonic texts from the ANE that link the creation of the universe with the building of a temple. Generally speaking, these mythical traditions from the ANE follow a fairly typical narrative pattern that correlates creation with conflict between the gods and the construction of a temple in honor of the victorious god's conquest and kingship.[1] This narrative pattern may be helpfully illustrated from *Enuma Elish* 1:73–76, which recounts the god Ea's defeat of his adversaries:

> After Ea had vanquished (and) subdued his enemies,
>
> Had established his victory over his foes,

---

1. Cf. Cross, *Canaanite Myth*, 112–20; Hanson, *Dawn*, 292–304; Batto, *Mythmaking*, 33–35, 75–79.

(And) had peacefully rested in his abode,

He named it *Apsu* and appointed (it) for shrines.[2]

Three features of *Enuma Elish* 1:73–76 are worth highlighting: 1) the description of Ea's victory in lines 73–74; 2) the description of his act of resting in his "abode" in line 75; and 3) the description of this "abode" as a sanctuary.

While one should resist the temptation to overstress the force of these parallels, this ANE background nonetheless remains useful for understanding the creation narrative of Gen 1–2.[3] The danger of what S. Sandmel has referred to as "parallelomania" is especially real when evaluating possible evocations of ANE cosmologies in Gen 1:1–31, especially with regard to vv. 1–2, 6–7.[4] One can be reasonably confident, however, that the description of divine rest in Gen 2:1–3 is somehow related to these ANE traditions. Seen through the lens of temple-building traditions, God's rest on the seventh day in Gen 2:1–3 is best grasped as a symbolic act demonstrating his universal reign and the completion of his cosmic temple.[5] Later portrayals of the construction of the tabernacle and the Jerusalem temple also follow this mythic pattern of divine conflict, victory, and temple-building, and to this I now turn.

The narrator of the Pentateuch establishes a close correspondence between the creation narrative of Gen 1–2 and the building of the tabernacle (cf. Exod 25–40), primarily in two ways. First, God's instructions to Moses concerning the construction of the tabernacle in Exod 25–31 are structured around a sequence of seven speeches that each begin with the divine pronouncement, "The Lord spoke to Moses" (cf. Gen 1:3, 6, 9, 14, 20, 24, 26; Exod 25:1; 30:11, 17, 22, 34; 31:1, 12).[6] Perhaps most telling, the seventh speech, in Exod 31:12–17, discusses the celebration of the Sabbath, which strongly parallels the seventh day of creation on which God rested from his

---

2. Cf. *Enuma Elish* 1:37–40; 6:1–70.

3. This word of caution is particularly relevant as one approaches the text of Gen 1:2 LXX. While the language of that text undoubtedly brings to mind notions from within Platonic philosophy (note especially the use of the adjectives ἀόρατος and ἀκατασκεύαστος), such dependence is nonetheless problematic. See Cook ("Greek Philosophy," 182–83) and Rosel (*Übersetzung*, 251) for further discussion of this issue.

4. Sandmel, "Parallelomania," 1–13. On the relationship between Gen 1–2 and ANE cosmologies more broadly, see Arnold (*Genesis*, 31–34, 40–42, 45–48).

5. See Beale (*Temple*, 62–76) and Wenham ("Sanctuary Symbolism," 19–23) for further discussion of the portrait of Eden as a garden-temple in Gen 1–2.

6. Weinfeld, "Sabbath," 502–3.

labor (cf. Gen 2:1–3).⁷ Second, the narrator's account of the completion of the tabernacle in Exod 39:42–43 also closely corresponds to Gen 1:31—2:3, which similarly describes the completion of creation. Scholars generally argue that the following verses parallel one another and again establish a literary/conceptual link between the creation of the universe and the building of the tabernacle: Gen 1:31//Exod 39:43; Gen 2:1//Exod 39:32; Gen 2:2//Exod 40:33; Gen 2:3//Exod 39:43.⁸

The OT traditions related to the construction of the Solomonic temple are also relevant to this discussion. In particular, 2 Sam 7:1–6 notes that David determined to build a temple after "the Lord had given him *rest* from all his enemies around him" (emphasis added). Within that same context, God promises David: 1) he will give him "rest" from his enemies (v. 11); and 2) one of his descendants will be the one to construct a temple (v. 12; cf. 1 Chr 22:8–10, 18–19; 23:25–26; 28:3). As with the creation narrative and the exodus from Egypt, the building of a temple thus follows conflict and victory over one's adversaries.⁹ J. Levenson also argues one can discern analogous patterns between Gen 1–2 and the construction of Solomon's temple when one considers that the latter also took seven years to build and was dedicated by Solomon on the seventh month during the festival of tabernacles (a seven day feast), by means of a speech structured around a sevenfold appeal (cf. Lev 23:34–36; 1 Kgs 6:38; 8:2, 31–55, 65; 2 Chr 7:9).¹⁰ The narrator of Kings therefore seems to be making a deliberate attempt to model the construction of the Solomonic temple after the creation of the world and establish a direct relationship between temple-building and divine conquest.¹¹

---

7. Cf. Sailhamer, *Pentateuch*, 298–99; Blenkinsopp, "Structure," 279, 281; Beale, *Temple*, 60–61.

8. Cf. Blenkinsopp, "Structure," 275–81; Fishbane, *Text and Texture*, 12; Beale, *Temple*, 61. Cf. Ps 132:7–8, 13–14 LXX.

The tabernacle and temple are also associated with the creation narrative of Gen 1–2 in Sir 24. This passage primarily extols the greatness of Wisdom and describes her presence at creation (vv. 3–6) and seeking a "resting place" (ἀνάπαυσιν) in v. 7. Sir 24:8–12 then describes YHWH placing Wisdom among his covenant people and specifically allowing her to dwell in the tabernacle and the temple (vv. 10–11). According to Fletcher-Louis (*Adam*, 75), Sir 24:13–17 draws on the Genesis creation narrative in the following ways: "(1) fecundity of nature suggestive of the trees of life (vv. 13–17), (2) freedom from shame and the curse upon labour (v. 22), (3) the rivers of Eden (vv. 25–27), (4) comparison to the 'first man' (v. 28) who (5) was supposed to be Eden's gardener (vv. 30–31, cf. Gen 2:15)."

9. Cf. Beale, *Temple*, 62–63; Levenson, *Creation*," 107–8.

10. Levenson, *Creation*, 78–79.

11. Cf. Exod 15:17; 1 Kgs 5:4–5; Ps 28:3, 10 LXX; 88:4–15 LXX; 92:1–5 LXX; 98:1–5 LXX; 131:7–8, 13–14 LXX. The frequent use of language and imagery from Gen 2–3

If we shift our attention from the biblical material to texts associated with Second Temple Judaism, we see that the correlation between divine conflict and temple-building continues. The use of this narrative pattern from ANE cosmologies, however, is not without a significant adaptation. More specifically, rather than associating divine conflict and the construction of a temple with protology, these actions are linked with eschatological portraits of the defeat of cosmic evil and the inauguration of the new creation.[12]

4Q174 2:12—3:13 provides a useful starting point for discussing the place of temple-building traditions in the Second Temple period. This text is primarily a midrash on 2 Sam 7:10-14, with an accompanying discussion of Exod 15:17-18 and Amos 9:11 (cf. Acts 15:13-18). As already noted, the broader contexts of 2 Sam 7 and Exod 15:1-17 both draw on temple-building traditions.[13] The quotation of Exod 15:18 ("the Lord will reign forever and ever") in line 3 especially evokes temple-building traditions and when read in conjunction with the explanation of 2 Sam 7:10-11a ("This 'place' is the house that [they shall build for Him] *in the Last Days*") indicates that this text envisions the construction of an eschatological temple that is to be built after YHWH defeats his enemies (cf. 11Q19 29:9-10).[14] After a commentary on Exod 15:17-18, the interpreter then quotes God's promise to give David "rest" from his enemies, which he explains as "rest" from the "sons of Belial" (4Q174 3:7-8). YHWH's conflict and victory over "Belial" and the "sons of Belial" are implicit behind this explanation in lines 7-8 (cf. 4Q174 2:14). Admittedly, the literary form of 4Q174 2:12—3:13 breaks up the close linking of divine conflict, conquest, and temple-building that is found in ANE cosmologies and traditions from the OT. Nonetheless, the presence of these three themes within 4Q174 2:12—3:13 is apparent enough that it is reasonable to conclude the author is correlating his depiction of the new age with temple-building traditions.

Temple-building traditions also play a role in the depiction of the eschatological war in 1QM 12:9-18 (cf. 1QM 19:1-8). The "Hero of War" is clearly portrayed as a victorious divine warrior in 1QM 12:10-12. The victory of the "Hero" is particularly evident in: 1) the instruction for him to take his "captives" and "plunder" in lines 10-11; and 2) the command to place his hand on his enemies' neck and his foot "upon the back of the

---

in descriptions of the tabernacle and Jerusalem temple suggests that later writers also viewed Eden as the first temple (e.g., Exod 25:7; 28:9-12; 1 Kgs 6:18, 29, 32; 7:20; Ps 35:9-10 LXX; Ezek 28:13-18; 47:1-12; *Jub.* 4:25-26; 8:19).

12. Cf. Batto, *Mythmaking*, 174-75.
13. See above, pp. 23-24, 183.
14. Emphasis added.

slain" in line 11. The text of 1QM 12:9–18 also evokes imagery from Gen 1–2 in a variety of ways.[15] Lines 13–15 also suggest that the conquest of the "Hero" leads to the restoration of Zion/Jerusalem. This is not only apparent through the statement in line 13, "O Zion, rejoice greatly, and shine with joyful songs, O Jerusalem," but also by means of the conflated allusion to Isa 49:23 and Isa 60:14 in lines 14–15.[16] 1QM 12:9–18 thus creatively describes the outcome of the divine warrior's victory through an intertextual web spanning Gen 1–2 and the prophecy of Isaiah. Given the cultic nature of Eden and Isaiah's restored Zion/Jerusalem, 1QM 12:9–18 seems to closely follow the ANE pattern of cosmic conflict ... victory ... temple-building.[17]

This analysis has revealed that ANE temple-building traditions play a significant role within several texts outside the prophecy of Isaiah. All of the passages from the OT and the Dead Sea scrolls probed in this excursus focus on either protology or eschatology.[18] One can also conclude that it is the presence of temple-building traditions that allows these eschatological texts to be aligned with an *Urzeit-Endzeit* typology. Thus, the use of temple-building traditions in the prophecy of Isaiah not only suggests that the new exodus is to be understood as a creative act comparable to the creation of the cosmos and the nation of Israel, but also that Isaiah participates in a stream of tradition running through Second Temple Judaism that links the new age with the primeval age by means of temple-building traditions.

15. According to Fletcher-Louis (*Adam*, 435–36), the following features of 1QM 12:9–18 allude to Gen 1:1—2:1) the "mist covering" the earth in line 9 (cf. Gen 1:2; 2:6; Sir 24:3b); 2) the "abundance of cattle" in line 12, which implies a restoration of primordial conditions; 3) the statement "rule [רדה] over the kingdoms" in line 15, which evokes Adam's command to "have dominion [רדה]" over creation in Gen 1:28; 4) the promise that Israel will "reign eternally" in line 15; and 5) the use of the verb עדה in line 15, which is likely a play on the noun עדן ("Eden"). On the basis of these parallels, Fletcher-Louis (ibid., 436) concludes that this text places Israel "in the position of the true Adam in consequence of the divine warrior's eschatological victory and recapitulation of creation."

16. Both Isa 49:14–26 and Isa 60 clearly depict the restoration of Zion/Jerusalem.

17. Cf. Ibid., 436.

18. While the temple-building texts from Exodus, Samuel, Kings and Chronicles do not focus on protology in the same manner as Gen 1–2, one still can conclude that they implicitly deal with this topic given the association between the cosmos and the temple.

Appendix Two

Isaiah's New Exodus in the Writings of Second Temple Judaism

THE SECOND TEMPLE PERIOD was a time of great angst and uncertainty for the Jewish people. Although the exiles had returned from Babylon and Jerusalem was rebuilt, the full scope of restoration promised in the OT had not come to pass. Furthermore, the Jewish people lived under the dominion of foreign powers throughout much of this era. In response to these trying times, various texts were written to give hope and comfort to those yearning for restoration. These documents often drew on the OT to depict the longings of God's covenant people. Isaiah's prophecy, in particular, was an important resource for these early Jewish theologians.[1] The following analysis will explore several texts from the Second Temple era with a view to understanding how Isaiah's new exodus was read and interpreted around the time of the writing of the NT.

T. Dan 5:8–13 is a particularly helpful text for appreciating how Isaiah's new exodus was interpreted within Second Temple Judaism.[2] Much of this particular testament focuses on warning the reader of the dangers of the "spirit of falsehood and anger" (cf. *T. Dan* 2:1). The author then shifts in *T. Dan* 5:4–7 to describing the "last days" as a time when the Jewish people "will turn from the Lord" (ἀποστήσεσθε τοῦ κυρίου). As a result of

1. Cf. Blenkinsopp, *Opening*, esp. 89–128, 222–50.

2. The *Testament of Dan* forms part of the *Testaments of the Twelve Patriarchs*, a document whose date of composition is a subject of intense debate. The primary question surrounding this dispute is whether the text's final form is the result of a reworking of an earlier Jewish document (the consensus opinion) or an entirely Christian composition (a view especially associated with M. de Jonge). See Kugler (*Testaments*, 31–38) for a helpful summary of this debate. The scholarly consensus holds that this document was written around the time of the Maccabean revolt. Since the chief concern of this analysis is understanding how Isaiah's new exodus was interpreted around the first century CE, *T. Dan* 5:8–13 may then be reasonably appealed to in this discussion.

this apostasy, God will punish his people with exile from the land (*T. Dan* 5:8; cf. *T. Zeb.* 9:5-6; *Pss. Sol.* 9:1). The remainder of *T. Dan* 5:9-13ab then focuses on describing the restoration that will occur when the covenant people "turn back to the Lord" (*T. Dan* 5:9a).

Importantly, the restoration depicted in *T. Dan* 5:9-13ab draws heavily upon Isaiah's proclamation of a new exodus. The clause ἐπιστρέψαντες πρὸς κύριον ἐλεηθήσεσθε in *T. Dan* 5:9a is likely an allusion to Isa 55:7b (ἐπιστραφήτω ἐπὶ κύριον καὶ ἐλεηθήσεται), which also describes God's response to the repentant exiles.[3] Reverberations of Isaianic tradition are also present in *T. Dan* 5:9b, where the author describes God leading his people "into his holy place" and "proclaiming peace" to them (καὶ ἄξει ὑμᾶς εἰς τὸ ἁγίασμα αὐτοῦ βοῶν ὑμῖν εἰρήνην). Here the author probably: 1) draws upon the frequent association between theophany imagery and new exodus imagery in Isaiah (cf. Isa 40:3-5, 9-10; 49:9-10; 52:7-10); and 2) develops a conflated allusion to Isa 40:3 (βοῶντος//βοῶν) and Isa 52:7 (εὐαγγελιζομένου ἀκοὴν εἰρήνης). The presence of divine warrior imagery in *T. Dan* 5:10-11a strengthens this reading of v. 9b, as the theophanic imagery in such texts as Isa 40:10; 49:10; 52:7-10 specifically functions as a means of depicting YHWH as a victorious warrior leading his people home.[4] It is also evident from *T. Dan* 5:12-13 that the author has merged temple, Eden, and restored Zion/Jerusalem traditions into a grand vision of restoration (cf. Isa 51:3; *Jub.* 4:25-26).[5] *T. Dan* 5:9b has already stated that God will lead the exiles εἰς τὸ ἁγίασμα αὐτοῦ; vv. 12-13 thus makes clear that this ἁγίασμα is to be identified with the eschatological temple of the last days.[6]

This reading of *T. Dan* 5:8-13 has two significant implications for understanding the manner in which Isaiah's new exodus was read around the time of the writing of the NT. First, it suggests that Isaiah's new exodus and restored Zion/Jerusalem were closely related and understood within the framework of temple-building traditions. The use of divine warrior imagery in vv. 10-11a, an integral feature of temple-building traditions, makes this an especially tenable conclusion. Second, it suggests that Isaiah's new exodus

---

3. On the use of the verb ἐλεέω in relation to Isaiah's new exodus, see p. 27.

4. The clause "he will make war against Beliar" in v. 10 in particular portrays YHWH as a victorious divine warrior.

5. The use of the root ερημο- in v. 13 to describe the end of Jerusalem's plight (καὶ οὐκέτι ὑπομένει Ἰερουσαλὴμ ἐρήμωσιν) confirms that v. 12 evokes restored Zion/Jerusalem traditions as this lexeme is frequently used to describe Zion/Jerusalem's desolate state in Isaiah (e.g., Isa 44:26; 51:3; 52:9; 54:1; 61:4; 62:4; 64:9). Furthermore, the verb εὐφραίνω is used to describe the response of joy associated with Isaiah's new exodus and restored Zion/Jerusalem in Isa 42:11; 49:13; 52:8; 62:5; 65:19.

6. The relative clause, "which shall be eternally for the glorification of God" in v. 12c makes it likely that this temple is to be understood in an eschatological sense.

was linked with an *Urzeit-Endzeit* typology.[7] In particular, the designation of the ἁγίασμα as "Eden" in v. 9 and the "New Jerusalem" in v. 12 point in this direction (cf. Rev 3:12; 21:1-2; 22:1-2).

Sib. Or. 3:767-95 also helpfully clarifies how Isaiah's new exodus was read within Second Temple Judaism.[8] This passage begins by describing God's establishment of "a kingdom for all ages among men" (*Sib. Or.* 3:767-68). An eternal temple also plays a significant role within this picture of the end (*Sib. Or.* 3:773-75).[9] *Sib. Or.* 3:772-73 also describes the nations bringing "incense and gifts" to this eschatological house of worship, a prominent motif in several Isaianic texts (e.g., Isa 2:1-3; 60:1-4; 66:18-24). Isaiah's prophecy is also evoked in *Sib. Or.* 777-79, which uses imagery often associated with cosmological renewal in Isaianic new exodus texts (cf. Isa 40:3-5; 41:18-19; 43:19-21; 49:9-11).[10] Finally, *Sib. Or.* 3:785-95 brings together the restoration of Zion/Jerusalem with language that clearly recalls the blissful conditions associated with the "new heavens and new earth" in Isa 65:19-25 (cf. Isa 11:6-12; *2 Bar.* 32:1-6; 44:5-15).[11]

---

7. A similar merging of temple-building traditions and *Urzeit-Endzeit* typology may also be found in 4Q174. Throughout 4Q174 3:1-13, there are several quotations of texts from the Old Testament (Exod 15:17-18; 2 Sam 7:10-14a; Amos 9:11) frequently associated with temple-building (cf. Beale, *Temple*, 63, 235-38). There is also mention of a מקדש אדם in line 6. This phrase has been translated in various ways (e.g., "a temple of men," "a temple among men"). See Zimmerman (*Messianische Texte*, 107-10) for a helpful discussion of the history of interpretation of this phrase. One of the more appealing suggestions is that of Wise ("4QFlorilegium," 103-32), who argues that the phrase refers to an eschatological "temple of Adam" that (like the expressions "glory of Adam" and "inheritance of Adam"; cf. CD 3:20; 1QHa 4:15; 1QS 4:23; 4Q171 3:2) is grounded in an *Urzeit-Endzeit* typology. Cf. Swarup, *Self-Understanding*, 119-26.

8. The third book in the collection known as the Sibylline Oracles is generally dated around the middle of the first century BCE. Cf. Collins, "Sibylline Oracles," 366-67.

9. Note the statement in line 773-74, "There will be no other house among men, even for future generations to know."

10. Cf. Buitenwerf, *Book III*, 290. According to *Sib. Or.* 3:777-80, "All the paths of the plain and rugged cliffs, lofty mountains, and wild waves of the sea will be easy to climb or sail in those days, for all peace will come upon the land of the good." The implication would seem to be that God has removed any possible geographic limitation for those participating in the worldwide confluence to his eschatological temple. Similar hints of cosmological restoration are found in *Sib. Or.* 3:741-55. Finally, the prominence of the notion of peace in Isa 52:7-11 and Isa 57:14-21 suggests the clause, "for all peace will come upon the land of the good" in *Sib. Or.* 3:780 may also draw upon Isaianic tradition.

11. Cf. ibid., 292. The restored Zion/Jerusalem is personified as a woman in Isa 62:11 (cf. Isa 1:8; 10:32; 16:1; 37:22; 52:2; Zech 2:10). The command to "rejoice . . . and be glad" in *Sib. Or.* 3:785 also recalls such texts as Isa 25:9; 35:2; 60:5; 65:18; 66:10, 14. Furthermore, the statement, "You will have immortal light" in *Sib. Or.* 3:787 strongly evokes the description of the restored Zion/Jerusalem in Isa 60:1, 3, 19-20.

It is difficult to avoid the conclusion that significant themes from Isaiah's prophecy have been skillfully interwoven into *Sib. Or.* 3:767–95. We may safely conclude from this passage that Isaiah's new exodus was correlated with the establishment of an eschatological temple. Furthermore, *Sib. Or.* 3:767–95 demonstrates that Isaiah's restored Zion/Jerusalem was closely aligned with the "new heavens and new earth" of Isa 65–66 and an *Urzeit-Endzeit* typology around the time of the first century CE.[12]

Pss. Sol. 11 is also pertinent to this analysis of the use of Isaiah's new exodus within the Second Temple period.[13] This passage begins with a pronounced allusion to Isaiah's new exodus. The phrase ἐν Ἱερουσαλὴμ φωνὴν εὐαγγελιζομένου in *Pss. Sol.* 11:1 is likely a conflated allusion to Isa 40:9 (τὴν φωνήν σου ὁ εὐαγγελιζόμενος Ιερουσαλημ) and Isa 52:7 (εὐαγγελιζομένου ἀκοήν).[14] It is clear from the ensuing statements that *Pss. Sol.* 11 primarily concerns the repopulation and restoration of Zion/Jerusalem. The worldwide return of the exiles in *Pss. Sol.* 11:2–3 may also evoke the scope of restoration associated with Isaiah's new exodus (cf. Isa 40:5; 49:12; 52:10).[15] New exodus imagery occurs throughout vv. 4–6 and describes the manner in which God cared for the exiles as they returned home (cf. Isa 40:11; 49:9–11).[16] *Pss. Sol.* 11:4–6 also seems to depict a theophanic manifestation of God leading the exiles home in much the same manner as Isa 40:3–5, 9–11; 49:9–10; 52:7–10. The image of a theophany is especially evoked in *Pss. Sol.* 11:6, which describes the exiles being guided "under the supervision of the glory of their God."[17] The clause ἔνδυσαι Ιερουσαλημ τὰ ἱμάτια τῆς δόξης in v. 7 is also likely an allusion to Isa 52:1 (ἔνδυσαι τὴν δόξαν σου Ιερουσαλημ) and confirms that the author is presenting Zion/Jerusalem as the goal of the new exodus that is described in vv. 4–6 (cf. Bar 5:1–4).

In summary, this brief overview of *T. Dan* 5, *Sib. Or.* 3:741–95, and *Pss. Sol.* 11 has provided a strong degree of support for the reading of Isaiah's

---

12. The brevity of *Sib. Or.* 3:767–95 makes it difficult to determine with certainty whether this passage might depict the universalistic scope of salvation one encounters in such Isaianic texts as Isa 66:18–24. The extent to which Isaiah is evoked in this text, however, opens the door to this possibility.

13. On the dating of the *Psalms of Solomon*, see Atkinson ("Redating," 95–112).

14. Ibid., 223–25.

15. The restored Zion/Jerusalem is here personified and instructed to "look at your children" who are assembled from the "east," "west," "north," and "far distant islands" (cf. Bar 4:36–37; 5:5–6).

16. The clause ὄρη ὑψηλὰ ἐταπείνωσεν εἰς ὁμαλισμὸν αὐτοῖς in v. 4 is particularly evocative of way imagery in new exodus texts such as Isa 40:3–4; 43:16, 19–20; 49:11; 57:14 (cf. Bar 5:7).

17. Bar 5:9 creates an even stronger picture of a theophany through the statement, "God will lead Israel with joy."

new exodus presented in this chapter. In my analysis of Isaiah's new exodus, I primarily argued that this important theme: 1) is closely aligned with ANE temple-building traditions; 2) has the restored Zion/Jerusalem as its goal; 3) is frequently associated with anthropological, cosmological, and ecclesiological renewal; and 4) is often linked with an *Urzeit-Endzeit* typology. The Second Temple texts highlighted in this excursus demonstrate that Isaiah's new exodus was interpreted in much the same manner by Jewish interpreters around the time of the first century CE.[18]

---

18. Additional Second Temple texts (e.g., 1 *En.* 1:3–8; Wis 19:1–22; Bar 5:1–9; 1QM 12:9–18; 4Q176; *T. Mos.* 10:1–5) could be marshalled in support of this reading of Isaiah's new exodus, especially with regard to its correlation with Isaiah's restored Zion/Jerusalem theme. Finally, there is undoubtedly a strong emphasis on cosmological renewal within the three texts investigated in the preceding analysis.

Bibliography

Adai, J. *Der Heilige Geist als Gegenwart Gottes in den einzelnen Christen, in der Kirche und in der Welt: Studien zur Pneumatologie des Epheserbriefes*. Regensburger Studien zur Theologie 31. Frankfurt: Peter Lang, 1985.

Adams, E. *Constructing the World: A Study in Paul's Cosmological Language*. Studies of the New Testament and its World. Edinburgh: T. & T. Clark, 2000.

———. "Graeco-Roman and Ancient Jewish Cosmology." In *Cosmology in the New Testament*, edited by J. Pennington and S. McDonough, 5–27, Library of New Testament Studies 355. London: T. & T. Clark, 2008.

Albl, M. *"And Scripture Cannot Be Broken": The Form and Function of the Early Christian Testimonia Collections*. Supplements to Novum Testamentum 96. Leiden: Brill, 1999.

Alexander, P. *The Qumran Songs of the Sabbath Sacrifice and the Celestial Hierarchy of Dionysius the Areopagite: A Comparative Approach*. Manchester: University of Manchester, 2006.

Allen, L. *Ezekiel 20–48*. Word Biblical Commentary 29. Nashville: Thomas Nelson, 1990.

———. *Psalms 101–150*. Word Biblical Commentary 21. Nashville: Thomas Nelson, 2002.

———. "Structure, Tradition and Redaction in Ezekiel's Death Valley Vision." In *Among the Prophets: Language, Image and Structure in the Prophetic Writings*, edited by P. Davies and D. Clines, 127–42. Journal for the Study of the Old Testament Supplement Series 144. Sheffield: JSOT, 1993.

Allen, T. "Exaltation and Solidarity with Christ: Ephesians 1:20 and 2:6." *Journal for the Study of the New Testament* 28 (1986) 103–20.

Arnold, B. *Genesis*. New Cambridge Bible Commentary. Cambridge: Cambridge University Press, 2009.

Arnold, C. *Ephesians*. Zondervan Exegetical Commentary on the New Testament 10. Grand Rapids: Zondervan, 2010.

———. *Ephesians, Power and Magic: The Concept of Power in Ephesians in the Light of its Historical Setting*. Society for New Testament Studies Monograph Series 63. Cambridge: Cambridge University Press, 1989.

———. "Returning to the Domain of the Powers: Stoicheia as Evil Spirits in Galatians 4:3, 9." *Novum Testamentum* 38 (1996) 55–76.

Atkinson, K. *An Intertextual Study of the Psalms of Solomon: Pseudepigrapha*. Studies in the Bible and Early Christianity 49. Lewiston, NY: Edwin Mellen, 2001.

———. "Towards a Redating of the Psalms of Solomon: Implications for Understanding the Sitz im Leben of an Unknown Jewish Sect." *Journal for the Study of the Pseudepigrapha* 17 (1998) 95–112.

Aune, D. "Apocalypticism." In *Dictionary of Paul and His Letters*, edited by G. Hawthorne, et al., 25–35. Downers Grove, IL: InterVarsity, 1993.

Aus, R. "Paul's Travel Plans to Spain and the 'Full Number of the Gentiles' of Rom 11:25." *Novum Testamentum* 21 (1979) 232–62.

Aymer, A. *Paul's Understanding of "KAINE KTISIS": Continuity and Discontinuity in Pauline Eschatology*. Ann Arbor, MI: UMI Dissertation Services, 1983.

Baasland, E. "Persecution: A Neglected Feature in the Letter to the Galatians." *Studia Theologica* 38 (1984) 135–50.

Baltzer, K. *Deutero-Isaiah: A Commentary on Isaiah 40–55*. Hermeneia. Translated by M. Kohl. Minneapolis, MN: Fortress, 2001.

Barclay, J. *Obeying the Truth: A Study of Paul's Ethics in Galatians*. Studies of the New Testament and Its World. Edinburgh: T. & T. Clark, 1988.

Barnett, P. *The Second Epistle to the Corinthians*. New International Commentary on the New Testament. Grand Rapids: Eerdmans, 1997.

Barr, J. *The Semantics of Biblical Language*. Oxford: Oxford University Press, 1961.

Barrett, C. K. *The Second Epistle to the Corinthians*. Harper's New Testament Commentary. New York: Harper & Row, 1973.

Barstad, H. *A Way in the Wilderness: The 'Second Exodus' in the Message of Second Isaiah*. Journal of Semitic Studies Monograph Series 12. Manchester: University of Manchester Press, 1989.

Barth, M. *Ephesians: Introduction, Translation, and Commentary on Chapters 1–3*. Anchor Bible 34a. New York: Doubleday, 1974.

Barthélemy, D. *Critique textuelle de L'Ancien Testament*. Orbis Biblicus et orientalis 50/2. Göttingen: Vandenhoeck & Ruprecht, 1986.

Batto, B. *Mythmaking in the Biblical Tradition: Slaying the Dragon*. Louisville, KY: Westminster John Knox, 1992.

Baumgarten, J. *Paulus und die Apokalyptik: Die Auslegung apokalyptischer Überlieferung in den echten Paulusbriefen*. Wissenschaftliche Monographien zum Alten und Neuen Testament 44. Neukirchen-Vluyn: Neukirchener, 1975.

Beale, G. K. "The Old Testament Background of Reconciliation in 2 Corinthians 5–7 and Its Bearing on the Literary Problem of 2 Corinthians 6:14–18." *New Testament Studies* 35 (1989) 550–81.

———. *The Temple and the Church's Mission: A Biblical Theology of the Dwelling Place of God*. New Studies in Biblical Theology 17. Downers Grove, IL: InterVarsity, 2004.

Becking, B. "Jeremiah's Book of Consolation: A Textual Comparison, Notes on the Masoretic Text and the Old Greek Version of Jeremiah XXX–XXXI." *Vetus Testamentum* 44 (1994) 145–69.

Bedale, S. "The Meaning of κεφαλή in the Pauline Epistles." *Journal of Theological Studies* 5 (1954) 211–16.

Beetham, C. *Echoes of Scripture in the Letter of Paul to the Colossians*. Biblical Interpretation Series 96. Leiden: Brill, 2008.

Beker, J. *Paul the Apostle: The Triumph of God in Life and Thought.* Philadelphia: Fortress, 1980.

Belleville, L. *Reflections of Glory: Paul's Polemical Use of the Moses-Doxa Tradition in 2 Corinthians 3:1–18.* Journal for the Study of the New Testament Supplement Series 52. Sheffield: Sheffield Academic, 1991.

Berkeley, T. *From a Broken Covenant to Circumcision of the Heart: Pauline Intertextual Exegesis in Romans 2:17–29.* Society of Biblical Literature Dissertation Series 175. Atlanta, GA: Society of Biblical Literature, 2000.

Berger, K. *Das Buch der Jubiläen.* Jüdische Schriften aus hellenistisch-römischer Zeit 2.3. Gütersloh: Gerd Mohn, 1981.

Best, E. *A Critical and Exegetical Commentary on Ephesians.* International Critical Commentary. London: T. & T. Clark, 1998.

———. "Dead in Trespasses and Sins (Eph 2:1)." *Journal for the Study of the New Testament* 13 (1981) 9–25.

———. "Ephesians 2.11–22: A Christian View of Judaism." In *Text as Pretext: Essays in Honour of Robert Davidson,* edited by R. Carroll, 47–60. Journal for the Study of the Old Testament Supplement Series 138. Sheffield: JSOT, 1992.

———. *One Body in Christ: A Study in the Relationship of the Church to Christ in the Epistles of the Apostle Paul.* New York: Macmillan, 1955.

———. "Who Used Whom? The Relationship of Ephesians and Colossians." *New Testament Studies* 43 (1997) 72–96.

Betz, H. *Der Galaterbrief: Ein Kommentar zum Brief des Apostels Paulus an die Gemeinden in Galatien.* Hermeneia. Munich: Kaiser, 1988.

Bird, M. "Incorporated Righteousness: A Response to Recent Evangelical Discussion Concerning the Imputation of Christ's Righteousness in Justification." *Journal of the Evangelical Theological Society* 47 (2004) 253–75.

Black, M. *The Book of Enoch or 1 Enoch.* Studia in Veteris Testamenti Pseudepigrapha 7. Leiden: Brill, 1985.

———. "The New Creation in 1 Enoch." In *Creation, Christ and Culture,* edited by R. McKinney, 13–21. Edinburgh: T. & T. Clark, 1976.

Blenkinsopp, J. *Ezekiel.* Interpretation. Louisville, KY: John Knox, 1990.

———. *Isaiah 40–55: A New Translation with Introduction and Commentary.* Anchor Bible 19a. New York: Doubleday, 2002.

———. *Isaiah 56–66: A New Translation with Introduction and Commentary.* Anchor Bible 19b. New York: Doubleday, 2003.

———. *Opening the Sealed Book: Interpretations of the Book of Isaiah in Late Antiquity.* Grand Rapids: Eerdmans, 2006.

———. "The Structure of P." *Catholic Biblical Quarterly* 38 (1976) 275–92.

Block, D. *The Book of Ezekiel: Chapters 25–48.* New International Commentary on the Old Testament. Grand Rapids: Eerdmans, 1998.

Breytenbach, C. *Versöhung: Eine Studie zur paulinischen Soteriologie.* Wissenschaftliche Monographien zum Alten und Neuen Testament 60. Neukirchen-Vluyn: Neukirchener, 1989.

Brooke, G. "Miqdash Adam, Eden, and the Qumran Community." *Gemeinde ohne Tempel/ Community without Temple: Zur Substituierung und Transformation des Jerusalemer Tempels und seines Kults im Alten Testament, antiken Judentum und frühen Christentum,* 285–301. Wissenschaftliche Untersuchungen zum Neuen Testament 1.118. Tübingen: Mohr Siebeck, 1999.

Brown, R. "Semitic Background of the New Testament Mysterion." *Biblica* 40 (1959) 70–87.
Broyles, C. *Psalms*. New International Biblical Commentary. Peabody, MA: Hendrickson, 1999.
Bruce, F. F. *The Epistles to the Colossians, to Philemon, and to the Ephesians*. New International Commentary on the New Testament. Grand Rapids: Eerdmans, 1988.
———. *The Epistle of Paul to the Galatians*. New International Greek Testament Commentary. Exeter: Paternoster, 1982.
Bryan, D. *Cosmos, Chaos and the Kosher Mentality*. Journal for the Study of the Pseudepigrapha Supplement Series 12. Sheffield: Sheffield Academic, 1995.
Buitenwerf, R. *Book III of the Sibylline Oracles and Its Social Setting: with an Introduction, Translation, and Commentary*. Studia in Veteris Testamenti Pseudepigrapha 17. Leiden: Brill, 2003.
Bultmann, R. *Der zweite Brief an die Korinther*. Kritisch-exegetischer Kommentar über Das Neue Testament. Göttingen: Vandenhoeck & Ruprecht, 1976.
Caird, G. *Paul's Letters from Prison*. Oxford: Oxford University Press, 1976.
Caragounis, C. *The Ephesian Mysterion: Meaning and Content*. Coniectanea Biblica: New Testament Series 8. Lund: CWK Gleerup, 1977.
Carr, W. *Angels and Principalities: The Background, Meaning, and Development of the Pauline Phrase hai archai kai hai exousiai*. Society for New Testament Studies Monograph Series 42. Cambridge: Cambridge University Press, 1981.
Carroll, R. P. *Jeremiah: A Commentary*. Old Testament Library. London: SCM, 1986.
Charles, R. *The Book of Enoch or 1 Enoch*. Oxford: Clarendon, 1912.
———. *The Book of Jubilees or The Little Genesis*. London: Adam & Charles Black, 1902.
Childs, B. *Introduction to the Old Testament as Scripture*. Philadelphia: Fortress, 1979.
———. *Isaiah*. Old Testament Library. Louisville, KY: Westminster John Knox, 2001.
Clayton, J. and E. Rothstein. "Figures in the Corpus: Theories of Influence and Intertextuality." In *Influence and Intertextuality in Literary History*, edited by J. Clayton and E. Rothstein, 3–36. Madison: University of Wisconsin Press, 1991.
Clements, R. "The Prophecies of Isaiah and the Fall of Jerusalem in 587 B.C." *Vetus Testamentum* 30 (1980) 421–36.
———. "The Unity of the Book of Isaiah." *Interpretation* 36 (1982) 117–29.
Clifford, R. "The Unity of the Book of Isaiah and its Cosmogonic Language." *Catholic Biblical Quarterly* 55 (1993) 1–17.
Clines, D. *The Theme of the Pentateuch*. Journal for the Study of the Old Testament Supplement Series 10. Sheffield: JSOT, 1978.
Cohen, S. *The Beginnings of Jewishness: Boundaries, Varieties, Uncertainties*. Hellenistic Culture and Society. Berkeley: University of California Press, 1999.
Collange, J. *Énigmes de la Deuxième Épître de Paul aux Corinthiens: Étude Exégétique de 2 Cor. 2:14–7:4*. Society for New Testament Studies Monograph Series 18. Cambridge: Cambridge University Press, 1972.
Collins, J. J. *Apocalyptic Imagination: An Introduction to Jewish Apocalyptic Literature*. 2nd ed. Grand Rapids: Eerdmans, 1998.
———. "The Sibylline Oracles." In *Jewish Writings of the Second Temple Period: Apocrypha, Pseudepigrapha, Qumran Sectarian Writings, Philo, Josephus*, edited

by M. Stone, 357–81. Compendia Rerum Iudaicarum ad Novum Testamentum 2. Assen: Van Gorcum, 1984.
Cook, J. "Greek Philosophy and the Septuagint." *Journal of Northwest Semitic Languages* 24 (1998) 177–91.
Cotterell, P., and M. Turner. *Linguistics & Biblical Interpretation*. Downers Grove, IL: InterVarsity, 1989.
Craigie, P. *Psalms 1–50*. Word Biblical Commentary 19. Waco, TX: Word, 1984.
Cross, F. *Canaanite Myth and Hebrew Epic: Essays in the History of the Religion of Israel*. Cambridge, MA: Harvard University Press, 1973.
Cullmann, O. *Christ and Time: The Primitive Conception of Time and History*. Rev. ed. Translated by F. Filson. Philadelphia: Westminster, 1964.
Dahl, N. *Studies in Ephesians: Introductory Questions, Text- and Edition-critical Issues, Interpretation of Texts and Themes*. Wissenschaftliche Untersuchungen zum Neuen Testament 1.131. Tübingen: Mohr Siebeck, 2000.
Danker, F. W., ed. *A Greek-English Lexicon of the New Testament and Other Early Christian Literature*. Chicago: Chicago University Press, 2000.
Das, A. "Paul of Tarshish: Isaiah 66.19 and the Spanish Mission of Romans 15.24, 28." *New Testament Studies* 54 (2008) 60–73.
———. *Paul, the Law, and the Covenant*. Peabody, MA: Hendrickson, 2001.
Davenport, G. *Eschatology of the Book of Jubilees*. Studia Post-Biblica. Leiden: Brill, 1971.
Dawes, G. *The Body in Question: Metaphor and Meaning in the Interpretation of Ephesians 5:21–33*. Biblical Interpretation Series 30. Leiden: Brill, 1998.
de Boer, M. *Galatians: A Commentary*. New Testament Library. Louisville, KY: Westminster John Knox, 2011.
———. "The Meaning of the Phrase τὰ στοιχεῖα τοῦ κόσμου in Galatians." *New Testament Studies* 53 (2007) 204–224.
———. "The New Preachers in Galatia: their Identity, Message, Aims, and Impact." In *Jesus, Paul, and Early Christianity: Studies in Honour of Henk Jan de Jonge*, edited by R. Buitenwerf, et al., 39–60. Supplements to Novum Testamentum 130. Leiden: Brill, 2008.
Dexinger, F. *Henochs Zehnwochenapokalypse und Offene Probleme Der Apokalyptikforschung*. Studia Post-Biblica 29. Leiden: Brill, 1977.
Dinkler, E. *Im Zeichen des Kreuzes: Aufsätze von Erich Dinkler*. Beiheft zur Zeitschrift für die neutestamentliche Wissenschaft 61. Berlin: Walter de Gruyter, 1992.
Dodd, C. *According to the Scriptures: The Sub-structure of New Testament Theology*. London: Nisbet, 1952.
Dumbrell, W. *Covenant and Creation: An Old Testament Covenantal Theology*. Exeter: Paternoster, 1984.
———. "The Purpose of the Book of Isaiah." *Tyndale Bulletin* 36 (1985) 111–28.
Dunn, J. D. G. *Christology in the Making: A New Testament Inquiry into the Origins of the Doctrine of the Incarnation*. Philadelphia: Westminster, 1980.
———. *The Epistle to the Galatians*. Black's New Testament Commentaries. London: Hendrickson, 1993.
———. *The Theology of Paul the Apostle*. Grand Rapids: Eerdmans, 1998.
———. "Works of the Law and the Curse of the Law (Galatians 3.10–14)." *New Testament Studies* 31 (1985) 523–42.

Ekblad, E. Jr., *Isaiah's Servant Poems according to the Septuagint*. Contributions to Biblical Exegesis and Theology 23. Leuven: Peeters, 1999.

Elliger, K. *Deuterojesaja*. Biblischer Kommentar Altes Testament 11. Neukirchen-Vluyn: Neukirchener, 1978.

Endres, J. *Biblical Interpretation in the Book of Jubilees*. Catholic Biblical Quarterly Monograph Series 18. Washington, DC: Catholic Biblical Association of America, 1987.

Faust, E. *Pax Christi et Pax Caesaris: Religionsgeschichtliche, traditionsgeschichtliche und sozialgeschichtliche Studien zum Epheserbrief*. Novum Testamentum et Orbis Antiquus 24. Göttingen: Vandenhoeck & Ruprecht, 1993.

Fee, G. "II Corinthians VI.14–VII.1 and Food Offered to Idols." *New Testament Studies* 23 (1977) 140–61.

———. *God's Empowering Presence: The Holy Spirit in the Letter's of Paul*. Peabody, MA: Hendrickson, 1994.

Feinberg, C. *The Prophecy of Ezekiel: The Glory of the Lord*. Chicago: Moody, 1969.

Fischer, G. *Jeremia 26–52*. Herder's Theologischer Kommentar zum Alten Testament. Freiburg: Herder, 2005.

Fishbane, M. *Biblical Interpretation in Ancient Israel*. Oxford: Clarendon, 1985.

———. *Text and Texture: Close Readings of Selected Biblical Texts*. New York: Schocken, 1979.

Fitzgerald, J. *Cracks in an Earthen Vessel: An Examination of the Catalogues of Hardship in the Corinthian Correspondence*. Society of Biblical Literature Dissertation Series 99. Atlanta, GA: Scholars, 1988.

Fitzmyer, J. "Qumran and the Interpolated Paragraph in 2 Cor. 6.14–7.1." *Catholic Biblical Quarterly* 23 (1961) 271–80.

Fletcher-Louis, C. *All the Glory of Adam: Liturgical Anthropology in the Dead Sea Scrolls*. Studies on the Texts of the Desert of Judah 42. Leiden: Brill, 2002.

Fraser, J. "Paul's Knowledge of Jesus: 2 Corinthians 5.16 Once More." *New Testament Studies* 17 (1971) 293–313.

Frey, J. "Die paulinische Antithese von 'Fleisch' und 'Geist' und die palästinish-jüdische Weisheitstradition." *Zeitschrift für die Neutestamentliche Wissenschaft und die Kunde der älteren Kirche* 90 (1999) 45–77.

Fung, R. "Body of Christ." In *Dictionary of Paul and His Letters*, edited by G. Hawthorne, et al., 76–82. Downers Grove, IL: InterVarsity, 1993.

Funk, R.W., ed. *A Greek Grammar of the New Testament and Other Early Christian Literature*. Chicago: Chicago University Press, 1961.

Furnish, V. *2 Corinthians*. Anchor Bible 32A. Garden City, NY: Doubleday, 1984.

Gärtner, B. *The Temple and the Community in Qumran and the New Testament: A Comparative Study in the Temple Symbolism*. Society for New Testament Studies Monograph Series 1. Cambridge: Cambridge University Press, 1965.

Gaston, L. *No Stone on Another: Studies in the Significance of the Fall of Jerusalem in the Synoptic Gospels*. Supplements to Novum Testamentum 23. Leiden: Brill, 1970.

Georgi, D. *The Opponents of Paul in 2 Corinthians*. Philadelphia, PA: Fortress, 1986.

Gignilliat, M. *Paul and Isaiah's Servants: Paul's Theological Reading of Isaiah 40–66 in 2 Corinthians 5:14–6:10*. Library of New Testament Studies 330. Edinburgh: T. & T. Clark, 2007.

Gladd, B. *Revealing the Mysterion: The Use of Mystery in Daniel in Second Temple Judaism with its Bearing on First Corinthians*. Beihefte zur Zeitschrift für die neutestamentliche Wissenschaft und die Kunde der älteren Kirche 160. Berlin: W. de Gruyter, 2008.

Gloer, W. *An Exegetical and Theological Study of Paul's Understanding of New Creation and Reconciliation in 2 Cor. 5:14–21*. Mellen Biblical Press Series 42. Lewiston, NY: Edwin Mellen, 1996.

Gnilka, J. *Der Epheserbrief.* Herders Theologischer Kommentar zum Neuen Testament 10. Freiburg: Herder, 1971.

———. "2 Kor 6,14–71 im Lichte der Qumranschriften und der Zwölf-Patriarchen-Testament." In *Neutestamentliche Aufsätze. Festschrift für J. Schmid*, edited by J. Blinzler et al., 35–52. Regensburg: Pustet, 1963.

Goldingay, J. *Psalms, Volume 3: Psalms 90–150*. Baker Commentary on the Old Testament Wisdom and Psalms. Grand Rapids: Baker Academic, 2008.

———. *The Message of Isaiah 40–55: A Literary-Theological Commentary*. London: T. & T. Clark, 2005.

Goldingay, J., and D. Payne. *Isaiah 40–55: Volume I*. International Critical Commentary. London: T. & T. Clark, 2006.

Gombis, T. "Ephesians 2 as a Narrative of Divine Warfare." *Journal for the Study of the New Testament* 26 (2004) 403–18.

Goppelt, L. *Typos: The Typological Interpretation of the Old Testament in the New*. Translated by D. Madvig. Grand Rapids: Eerdmans, 1982.

Gordley, M. *The Colossian Hymn in Context*. Wissenschaftliche Untersuchungen zum Neuen Testament 2.228. Tübingen: Mohr Siebeck, 2007.

Gräßer, E. *Der zweite Brief an die Korinther: Kapitel 1,1–7,16*. Ökumenischer Taschenbuchkommentar zum Neuen Testament 8.1. Gütersloher: Gütersloher Verlagshaus, 2002.

Greenberg, M. *Ezekiel 1–20*. Anchor Bible 22A. Garden City, NY: Doubleday, 1983.

———. *Ezekiel 21–37*. Anchor Bible 22B. New York: Doubleday, 1997.

———. "The Design and Themes of Ezekiel's Program of Restoration." *Interpretation* 38 (1984) 181–208.

Grudem, W. "Does κεφαλή ('Head') Mean 'Source' or 'Authority over' in Greek Literature: A Survey of 2,336 Examples." *Trinity Journal* 6 (1985) 38–59.

Gunkel, H. *Creation and Chaos in the Primeval Era and the Eschaton: A Religio-Historical Study of Genesis 1 and Revelation 12*. Translated by K. Whitney Jr. Grand Rapids: Eerdmans, 2006.

Haag, E. "Der Weg zum Baum des Lebens: Ein Paradiesmotiv im Buch Jesaja." In *Künder des Wortes: Beiträge zur Theologie der Propheten*, edited by L. Ruppert, et al., 35–52. Würzburg: Echter, 1982.

Hafemann, S. *Paul, Moses, and the History of Israel: The Letter/Spirit Contrast and the Argument from Scripture in 2 Corinthians 3*. Wissenschaftliche Untersuchungen zum Neuen Testament 1.81. Tübingen: Mohr Siebeck, 1995.

———. "The Comfort and Power of the Gospel: The Argument of 2 Corinthians 1–3." *Review & Expositor* 86 (1989) 325–44.

Halpern-Amaru, B. "Exile and Return in Jubilees." In *Exile: Old Testament, Jewish, and Christian Conceptions*, edited by B. G. Wright III, 127–44. Supplements to the Journal for the Study of Judaism 56. Leiden: Brill, 1997.

Hanson, P. *Dawn of Apocalyptic: The Historical and Sociological Roots of Jewish Apocalyptic Eschatology*. Rev. ed. Philadelphia, PA: Fortress, 1979.

Hardin, J. *Galatians and the Imperial Cult: A Critical Analysis of the First-Century Social Context of Paul's Letter*. Wissenschaftliche Untersuchungen zum Neuen Testament 2.237. Tübingen: Mohr Siebeck, 2008.

Harris, M. *The Second Epistle to the Corinthians*. New International Greek Testament Commentary. Grand Rapids: Eerdmans, 2005.

Hartin, P. "ΑΝΑΚΕΦΑΛΑΙΩΣΑΣΘΑΙ ΤΑ ΠΑΝΤΑ ΕΝ ΤΩ ΧΡΙΣΤΩ (Eph 1:10)." In *A South African Perspective on the New Testament*, edited by J. Petzer and P. Hartin, 228–37. Leiden: E. J. Brill, 1986.

Hay, D. *Glory at the Right Hand: Psalm 110 in Early Christianity*. Society of Biblical Literature Monograph Series 18. Nashville: Abingdon, 1973.

Hays, R. *Echoes of Scripture in the Letters of Paul*. New Haven: Yale University Press, 1989.

Hoehner, H. *Ephesians: An Exegetical Commentary*. Grand Rapids: Baker Academic, 2002.

Holladay, W. *Jeremiah 2: A Commentary on the Book of the Prophet Jeremiah Chapters 26–52*. Hermeneia. Minneapolis, MN: Fortress, 1989.

Hollander, J. *The Figure of Echo: A Mode of Allusion in Milton and After*. Berkeley, CA: University of California Press, 1981.

Hong, I. *The Law in Galatians*. Journal for the Study of the New Testament Supplement Series 81. Sheffield: JSOT, 1993.

Hooker, M. "Interchange in Christ." *Journal of Theological Studies* 22 (1971) 349–61.

Hoover, H. *The Concept of New Creation in the Letters of Paul*. Ann Arbor, MI: UMI Dissertation Services, 1979.

Hubbard, M. *New Creation in Paul's Letters and Thought*. Society for New Testament Studies Monograph Series 119. Cambridge: Cambridge University Press, 2002.

Jackson, T. *New Creation in Paul's Letters: A Study of the Historical and Social Setting of a Pauline Concept*. Wissenschaftliche Untersuchungen zum Neuen Testament 2.272. Tübingen: Mohr Siebeck, 2010.

Jeal, R. *Integrating Theology and Ethics in Ephesians: The Ethos of Communication*. Studies in Bible and Early Christianity 43. New York: Edwin Mellen, 2000.

Jeremias, J. "Der Eckstein." *Angelos* 1 (1925) 65–70.

Jervis, L. *Galatians*. New International Biblical Commentary 9. Peabody, MA: Hendrickson, 1999.

Jewett, R. *Romans: A Commentary*. Hermeneia. Minneapolis, MN: Fortress, 2007.

———. "Agitators and the Galatian Congregation." *New Testament Studies* 17 (1971) 198–212.

Jónsson, G. *The Image of God: Genesis 1:26–28 in a Century of Old Testament Research*. Coniectanea Biblica: Old Testament Series 26. Translated by L. Svendsen. Lund: Almqvist & Wiksell, 1988.

Joyce, P. *Ezekiel: A Commentary*. Library of Hebrew Bible/Old Testament Studies 482. Edinburgh: T. & T. Clark, 2007.

Kaminsky, J. "The Concept of Election and Second Isaiah: Recent Literature." *Biblical Theology Bulletin* 31 (2002) 135–44.

Käsemann, E. *New Testament Questions of Today*. Translated by W. Montague. London: SCM, 1969.

———. *Perspectives on Paul*. Translated by M. Kohl. Philadelphia, PA: Fortress, 1971.

Keown, G., P. Scalise, and T. Smothers. *Jeremiah 26–52*. Word Biblical Commentary 27. Dallas. TX: Word, 1995.

Kiesow, K. *Exodustexte im Jesajabuch: Literarkritische und Motivgeschichtliche Analysen*. Orbis biblicus et orientalis 24. Fribourg: Éditions Universitaires, 1979.

Kim, S. *The Origin of Paul's Gospel*. Wissenschaftliche Untersuchungen zum Neuen Testament 2.4. Tübingen: Mohr Siebeck, 1981.

Kirby, J. *Ephesians, Baptism and Pentecost*. London: SPCK, 1968.

Kirchschläger, W. "Zu Herkunft und Aussage von Gal 1, 4." In *L'Apôtre Paul: Personnalité, Style et Conception du Ministère*, edited by A. Vanhoye, 332–39. Bibliotheca Ephemeridum Theologicarum Lovaniensium 73. Leuven: Leuven University Press, 1986.

Kitchen, M. "The ἀνακεφαλαίωσις of All Things in Christ: Theology and Purpose in the Epistle to the Ephesians." PhD thesis, University of Manchester, 1988.

Kittel, G., and G. Friedrich, eds. *Theological Dictionary of the New Testament*. Translated by G. Bromiley. 10 vols. Grand Rapids: Eerdmans, 1964–1976.

Knibb, M. *The Ethiopic Book of Enoch*. Oxford: Oxford University Press, 1978.

Koch, D. A. *Die Schrift als Zeuge des Euangeliums: Untersuchungen zur Verwendung und zum Verständnis der Schrift bei Paulus*. Beiträge zur Historischen Theologie 69. Tübingen: Mohr Siebeck, 1986.

Koole, J. *Isaiah III, Volume 1/ Isaiah 40–48*. Historical Commentary on the Old Testament. Translated by A. Runia. Kampen: Kok Pharos, 1997.

Kraus, H. *Psalmen*. Biblischer Kommentar Altes Testament 15.2. Neukirchen-Vluyn: Neukirchener, 1961.

Kraus, W. *Das Volk Gottes: Zur Grundlegung der Ekklesiologie bei Paulus*. Wissenschaftliche Untersuchungen zum Neuen Testament 1.85. Tübingen: Mohr Siebeck, 1996.

Kugler, R. *The Testaments of the Twelve Patriarchs*. Sheffield: Sheffield Academic, 2001.

Kuhn, K. "The Epistle to the Ephesians in the Light of the Qumran Texts." In *Paul and Qumran: Studies in New Testament Exegesis*, edited by J. Murphy-O'Connor, 115–31. Chicago: Priory, 1968.

Kwon, Y. *Eschatology in Galatians: Rethinking Paul's Response to the Crisis in Galatia*. Wissenschaftliche Untersuchungen zum Neuen Testament 2.183. Tübingen: Mohr Siebeck, 2004.

Lalleman-de Winkel, H. *Jeremiah in Prophetic Tradition*. Contributions to Biblical Exegesis and Theology 26. Leuven: Peeters, 2000.

Lambrecht, J. "'Reconcile Yourselves . . .': A Reading of 2 Corinthians 5, 11–21." In *Studies on 2 Corinthians*, edited by R. Bieringer and J. Lambrecht, 363–412. Bibliotheca Ephemeridum Theologicarum Lovaniensium 112. Leuven: Leuven University Press, 1994.

———. "The Favorable Time: A Study of 2 Cor 6, 2a in Its Context." In *Vom Urchristentum zu Jesus: Für Joachim Gnilka*, edited by H. Frankemölle and K. Kertelge, 377–91. Freiburg: Herder, 1989.

Levenson, J. *Creation and the Persistence of Evil: The Jewish Drama of Divine Omnipotence*. Princeton: Princeton University Press, 1988.

———. *Theology of the Program of Restoration of Ezekiel 40–48*. Harvard Semitic Monographs 10. Cambridge, MA: Scholars, 1976.

Levin, C. *Die Verheißung des neuen Bundes in ihrem theologiegeschichtlichen Zusammenhang ausgelegt*. Forschungen zur Religion und Literatur des Alten und Neuen Testaments 137. Göttingen: Vandenhoeck & Ruprecht, 1985.

Liddell, H. G., et al. *A Greek-English Lexicon*. 9th ed. Oxford: Clarendon, 1996.

Lincoln, A. *Ephesians*. Word Biblical Commentary 42. Dallas, TX: Word 1990.

———. "Ephesians 2:8–10: A Summary of Paul's Gospel?" *Catholic Biblical Quarterly* 45 (1983) 617–30.

———. *Paradise Now and Not Yet: Studies in the Role of the Heavenly Dimension in Paul's Thought with Special Reference to His Eschatology*. Society for New Testament Studies Monograph Series 43. Cambridge: Cambridge University Press, 1981.

———. "The Church and Israel in Ephesians 2." *Catholic Biblical Quarterly* 49 (1987) 605–24.

———. "The Use of the OT in Ephesians." *Journal for the Study of the New Testament* 14 (1982) 16–57.

Lindars, B. "A Bull, a Lamb and a Word: 1 Enoch XC. 38." *New Testament Studies* 22 (1976) 483–86.

Lindemann, A. *Die Aufhebung der Zeit: Geschichtsverständnis und Eschatologie im Epheserbrief*. Studien zum Neuen Testament 12. Gütersloh: G. Mohn, 1975.

Loader, W. "Christ at the Right Hand: Ps. CX.1 in the New Testament." *New Testament Studies* 24 (1978) 199–217.

Lona, H. *Die Eschatologie im Kolosser und Epheserbrief*. Forschung zur Bibel 48. Würzburg: Echter, 1984.

Longenecker, B. *The Triumph of Abraham's God: The Transformation of Identity in Galatians*. Nashville: Abingdon, 1998.

Longenecker, R. *Galatians*. Word Biblical Commentary 41. Dallas, TX: Word, 1990.

Louw, J. *Semantics of New Testament Greek*. Semeia Studies. Atlanta, GA: Scholars, 1982.

Lührmann, D. *Der Brief an die Galater*. Zürcher Bibelkommentare. Zurich: Theologischer, 1978.

Lund, Ø. *Way Metaphors and Way Topics in Isaiah 40–55*. Forschungen zum Alten Testament 2.28. Tübingen: Mohr Siebeck, 2007.

Lundbom, J. *Jeremiah 21–36*. Anchor Bible 21B. New York: Doubleday, 2004.

Lundquist, J. "What is a Temple: A Preliminary Typology." In *The Quest for the Kingdom of God: Studies in Honor of George E. Mendenhall*, edited by H. Huffmon, et al., 205–19. Winona Lake, IN: Eisenbrauns, 1983.

Marcus, J. "The Evil Inclination in the Letters of Paul." *Irish Biblical Studies* 8 (1986) 8–21.

Martin, A. *La Tipologia Adamica nella Lettera agli Efesini*. Analecta Biblica 159. Rome: Pontificio Instituto Biblico, 2005.

Martin, R. *2 Corinthians*. Word Biblical Commentary 40. Waco, TX: Word, 1986.

———. *Reconciliation: A Study in Paul's Theology*. Atlanta, GA: John Knox, 1981.

Martyn, J. L. "Apocalyptic Antinomies in Paul's Letter to the Galatians," *New Testament Studies* 31 (1985) 410–24.

———. "Epistemology at the Turn of the Ages: 2 Corinthians 5:16." In *Christian History and Interpretation: Studies Presented to John Knox*, edited by W. Farmer, et al., 269–87. Cambridge: Cambridge University Press, 1967.

———. "Events in Galatia: Modified Covenantal Nomism versus God's Invasion of the Cosmos in the Singular Gospel: A Response to J. D. G. Dunn and B. R. Gaventa." In *Pauline Theology, Volume I: Thessalonians, Philippians, Galatians, Philemon*, edited by J. Bassler, 160–79. Minneapolis, MN: Fortress, 1991.

———. *Galatians: A New Translation with Introduction and Commentary*. Anchor Bible 33A. New York: Doubleday, 1997.

Matera, F. *II Corinthians: A Commentary*. New Testament Library. Louisville, KY: Westminster John Knox, 2003.

———. *Galatians*. Sacra Pagina 9. Collegeville, MN: Liturgical, 1992.

———. "The Culmination of Paul's Argument to the Galatians: Gal 5:1–6:17." *Journal for the Study of the New Testament* 32 (1988) 79–91.

Matlock, R. *Unveiling the Apocalyptic Paul: Paul's Interpreters and the Rhetoric of Criticism*. Journal for the Study of the New Testament Supplement Series 127. Sheffield: Sheffield Academic, 1996.

Mauser, U. "Isaiah 65:17–25." *Interpretation* 36 (1982) 181–86.

Mayer, A. *Sprache der Einheit im Epheserbrief und in der Ökumene*. Wissenschaftliche Untersuchungen zum Neuen Testament 2.150. Tübingen: Mohr Siebeck, 2002.

McHugh, J. "A Reconsideration of Ephesians 1.10b in the Light of Irenaeus." In *Paul and Paulinism. Essays in Honour of C. K. Barrett*, edited by M. Hooker and S. G. Wilson, 302–9. London: SPCK, 1982.

McKane, W. *A Critical and Exegetical Commentary on Jeremiah, Vol. 2*. International Critical Commentary. Edinburgh: T. & T. Clark, 1996.

McKelvey, R. *The New Temple: The Church in the New Testament*. Oxford Theological Monographs. Oxford: Oxford University Press, 1968.

Mell, U. *Neue Schöpfung: Eine traditionsgeschichtliche und exegetische Studie zu einem soteriologischen Grundsatz paulinischer Theologie*. Beiheft zur Zeitschrift für die neutestamentliche Wissenschaft und die Kunde der älteren Kirche 56. Berlin: Walter de Gruyter, 1989.

Meyer, R. *Kirche und Mission im Epheserbrief*. Stuttgarter Bibelstudien 86. Stuttgart: Katholisches Bibelwerk, 1977.

Middlemas, J. "Divine Reversal and the Role of the Temple in Trito-Isaiah." In *Temple and Worship in Biblical Israel: Proceedings of the Oxford Old Testament Seminar*, edited by J. Day, 158–84. Library of Hebrew Bible/Old Testament Studies 422. London: T. & T. Clark, 2007.

Miletic, S. *"One Flesh": Ephesians 5.22–24, 5.31: Marriage and the New Creation*. Analecta Biblica 115. Rome: Pontificio Instituto Biblico, 1988.

Milik, J. "Problèmes de la littérature hénochique à la lumière des fragments araméens de Qumrân." *Harvard Theological Review* 64 (1971) 333–78.

Moo, D. *The Epistle to the Romans*. New International Commentary on the New Testament. Grand Rapids: Eerdmans, 1996.

Morales, R. *The Spirit and the Restoration of Israel: New Exodus and New Creation Motifs in Galatians*. Wissenschaftliche Untersuchungen zum Neuen Testament 2.282. Tübingen: Mohr Siebeck, 2010.

Moses, R. *Practices of Power: Revisiting the Principalities and Powers in the Pauline Letters*. Emerging Scholars. Minneapolis, MN: Fortress, 2014.

Moritz, T. *A Profound Mystery: The Use of the Old Testament in Ephesians*. Supplements to Novum Testamentum 85. Leiden: Brill, 1996.

Muddiman, J. *The Epistle to the Ephesians*. Black's New Testament Commentaries. New York: Continuum, 2001.

Münderlein, G. "Die Erwählung durch das Pleroma: Bemerkungen zu Kol. i.19." *New Testament Studies* 8 (1962) 264–76.

Mussner, F. *Christus, das All und die Kirche. Studien zur Theologie des Epheserbriefes*. Trier: Paulinus, 1968.

———. *Der Galaterbrief*. Herders Theologischer Kommentar zum Neuen Testament 9. Freiburg: Herder, 1974.

Nanos, M. *The Irony of Galatians: Paul's Letter in First-Century Context*. Minneapolis, MN: Fortress, 2002.

Nickelsburg, G., and J. Vanderkam. *1 Enoch: A New Translation*. Minneapolis, MN: Fortress, 2004.

Nickelsburg, G. *1 Enoch 1: A Commentary on the Book of 1 Enoch, Chapters 1-36, 81-108*. Hermeneia. Minneapolis, MN: Fortress, 2001.

Niditch, S. "Ezekiel 40-48 in a Visionary Context." *Catholic Biblical Quarterly* 48 (1986) 208-24.

North, C. "The 'Former' Things and the 'New' Things in Deutero-Isaiah." In *Studies in Old Testament Prophecy*, edited by H. H. Rowley, 111-26. Edinburgh: T. & T. Clark, 1950.

O'Brien, P. "Ephesians 1: An Unusual Introduction to a New Testament Letter." *New Testament Studies* 25 (1979) 504-16.

———. "The Church as a Heavenly and Eschatological Entity." In *Church in the Bible and the World*, edited by D. A. Carson, 88-119. Exeter: Paternoster, 1987.

———. *The Letter to the Ephesians*. Pillar New Testament Commentary. Grand Rapids: Eerdmans, 1999.

Oswalt, J. *The Book of Isaiah: Chapters 40-66*. New International Commentary on the Old Testament. Grand Rapids: Eerdmans, 1998.

Overfield, P. "Pleroma: A Study in Content and Context." *New Testament Studies* 25 (1979) 384-96.

Pate, C. *Adam Christology as the Exegetical and Theological Substructure of 2 Corinthians 4:7-5:21*. Lanham, MD: University Press of America, 1991.

Patrick, D. "Epiphanic Imagery in Second Isaiah's Portrayal of a New Exodus." *Hebrew Annual Review* 8 (1984) 125-41.

Patzia, A. *Ephesians, Colossians, Philemon*. New International Biblical Commentary 10. Peabody, MA: Hendrickson, 1990.

Pokorný, P. *Der Brief des Paulus an die Epheser*. Theologischer Handkommentar zum Neuen Testament 10/II. Leipzig: Evangelische Verlagsanstalt, 1992.

———. *Die Epheserbrief und die Gnosis*. Berlin: Evangelische Verlagsanstalt, 1965.

Potter, H. "The New Covenant in Jeremiah XXXI 31-34." *Vetus Testamentum* 33 (1983) 347-55.

Propp, W. *Exodus 1-18: A New Translation with Introduction and Commentary*. Anchor Bible 2. New York: Doubleday, 1999.

Räisänen, H. *Paul and the Law*. Wissenschaftliche Untersuchungen zum Neuen Testament 1.29. Tübingen: Mohr Siebeck, 1983.

Rantzow, S. *Christus Victor Temporis: Zeitkonzeptionen im Epheserbrief*. Wissenschaftliche Monographien zum Alten und Neuen Testament 123. Neukirchen-Vluyn: Neukirchener, 2008.

Rendtorff, R. *Kanon und Theologie: Vorarbeiten zu einer Theologie des Alten Testaments*. Neukirchener: Neukirchen-Vluyn, 1991.

———. "Zur Komposition des Buches Jesaja." *Vetus Testamentum* 34 (1984) 295-320.

Renz, T. *The Rhetorical Function of the Book of Ezekiel*. Supplements to Vetus Testamentum 76. Leiden: Brill, 1999.

Roberts, A., and J. Donaldson, eds. *The Apostolic Fathers with Justin Martyr and Irenaeus*. The Ante-Nicene Fathers, vol. 1. Grand Rapids: Eerdmans, 1956.

Robinson, J. A. *St. Paul's Epistle to the Ephesians*. 2nd ed. London: Macmillan, 1909.

Roetzel, C. "Jewish Christian-Gentile Christian Relations: A Discussion of Ephesians 2:15a." *Zeitschrift für die Neutestamentliche Wissenschaft und die Kunde der älteren Kirche* 74 (1983) 81–89.

Rosel, M. *Übersetzung als Vollendung der Auslegung*. Beihefte zur Zeitschrift für die alttestamentliche Wissenschaft 223. Berlin: de Gruyter, 1994.

Sailhamer, J. *The Pentateuch as Narrative*. Grand Rapids: Zondervan, 1992.

Sanders, E. P. *Paul and Palestinian Judaism: A Comparison of Patterns of Religion*. Philadelphia, PA: Fortress, 1977.

Sandmel, S. "Parallelomania." *Journal of Biblical Literature* 81 (1962) 1–13.

Schaper, J. *Eschatology in the Greek Psalter*. Wissenschaftliche Untersuchungen zum Neuen Testament 2.76. Tübingen: Mohr Siebeck, 1995.

Schlier, H. *Der Brief an die Epheser*. Düsseldorf: Patmos, 1968.

———. *Der Brief an die Galater*. Kritisch-exegetischer Kommentar über Das Neue Testament 13. Göttingen: Vandenhoeck & Ruprecht, 1965.

Schmeller, T. *Die zweite Briefer an die Korinther*. Evangelisch-Katholischer Kommentar zum Neuen Testament 8.1. Neukirchen-Vluyn: Neukirchener, 2010.

Schnackenburg, R. *Der Brief an die Epheser*. Evangelisch-Katholischer Kommentar zum Neuen Testament 10. Zürich: Neukirchener, 1982.

———. "Die Kirche als Bau: Epheser 2.19–22 unter ökumenischem Aspekt." In *Paul and Paulinism: Essays in Honour of C. K. Barrett*, edited by M. Hooker and S. Wilson, 258–71. London: SPCK, 1982.

Schneider, G. "Die Idee der Neuschöpfung beim Apostel Paulus und ihr religionsgeschichtlicher Hintgrund." *Trierer theologische Zeitschrift* 68 (1959) 257–70.

———. "KAINH KTISIS: Die Idee der Neuschöpfung beim Apostel Paulus und ihr religionsgeschichtlicher Hintergrund." PhD diss., Universität Trier, 1959.

———. *Jesusüberlieferung und Christologie: Neutestamentliche Aufsätze 1970–1990*. Supplements to Novum Testamentum 67. Leiden: Brill, 1992.

Schnelle, U. *Neutestamentliche Anthropologie: Jesus—Paulus—Johannes*. Biblisch-theologische Studien 18. Neukirchen-Vluyn: Neukirchener, 1991.

Silva, M. "Eschatological Structures in Galatians." In *To Tell the Mystery: Essays on New Testament Eschatology in Honor of Robert H. Gundry*, edited by T. E. Schmidt and M. Silva, 140–62. Journal for the Study of the New Testament Supplement Series 100. Sheffield: Sheffield Academic, 1994.

Sommer, B. *A Prophet Reads Scripture: Allusion in Isaiah 40–66*. Contraversions: Jews and Other Differences. Stanford: Stanford University Press, 1998.

Schreiner, T. *Galatians*. Zondervan Exegetical Commentary on the New Testament 9. Grand Rapids: Zondervan, 2010.

———. "Is Perfect Obedience to the Law Possible: A Re-Examination of Galatians 3:10." *Journal of the Evangelical Theological Society* 27 (1984) 151–60.

———. *The Law and Its Fulfillment: A Pauline Theology of Law*. Grand Rapids: Baker, 1993.

———. "'Works of Law' in Paul." *Novum Testamentum* 33 (1991) 217–44.

Schweitzer, A. *The Mysticism of St. Paul*. 3rd ed. Translated by W. Montgomery. New York: Macmillan, 1960.

Schweizer, E. "Slaves of the Elements and Worshipers of Angels: Gal 4:3, 9 and Col 2:8, 18, 20." *Journal of Biblical Literature* 107 (1988) 455–68.

Schwindt, R. *Das Weltbild des Epheserbriefes: Eine religionsgeschichtlich-exegetische Studie.* Wissenschaftliche Untersuchungen zum Neuen Testament 1.148. Tübingen: Mohr Siebeck, 2002.

Scott, J. *"On Earth as in Heaven": The Restoration of Sacred Time and Sacred Space in the Book of Jubilees.* Supplements for the Journal for the Study of Judaism 91. Leiden: Brill, 2005.

———. *Paul and the Nations: The Old Testament and Jewish Background of Paul's Mission to the Nations with Special Reference to the Destination of Galatians.* Wissenschaftliche Untersuchungen zum Neuen Testament 2.84. Tübingen: Mohr Siebeck, 1995.

———. "The Use of Scripture in 2 Corinthians 6.16c-18 and Paul's Restoration Theology." *Journal for the Study of the New Testament* 56 (1994) 73-99.

Scroggs, R. *The Last Adam.* Oxford: Blackwell, 1966.

Sellin, G. *Der Brief an Epheser.* Kritisch-exegetischer Kommentar über das Neue Testament 8. Göttingen: Vandenhoeck & Ruprecht, 2008.

Simian-Yofre, H. "Exodo en Deuteroisaias." *Biblica* 61 (1980) 55-72.

Stanley, C. *Arguing with Scripture: The Rhetoric of Quotations in the Letters of Paul.* New York: T. & T. Clark, 2004.

———. *Paul and the Language of Scripture: Citation Technique in the Pauline Epistles and Contemporary Literature.* Society for New Testament Studies Monograph Series 69. Cambridge: Cambridge University Press, 1992.

Steck, O. "Der neue Himmel und die neue Erde. Beobachtungen zur Rezeption von Gen 1-3 in Jes 65, 16b-25." In *Studies in the Book of Isaiah: Festschrift Willem A .M. Beuken,* edited by J. V. Ruiten and M. Vervenne, 349-65. Bibliotheca Ephemeridum Theologicarum Lovaniensium 132. Leuven: Leuven University Press, 1997.

Stendahl, K. "The Apostle Paul and the Introspective Conscience of the West." *Harvard Theological Review* 56 (1963) 199-215.

Stockhausen, C. *Moses' Veil and the Glory of the New Covenant: The Exegetical Substructure of II Cor. 3,1-4,6.* Analecta Biblica 116. Rome: Pontifical Biblical Institute, 1989.

Stordalen, T. *Echoes of Eden: Genesis 2-3 and Symbolism of the Eden Garden in Biblical Hebrew Literature.* Contributions to Biblical Exegesis and Theology 25. Leuven: Peeters, 2000.

Strachan, R. *The Second Epistle of Paul to the Corinthians.* Moffat New Testament Commentary. London: Hodder & Stoughton, 1935.

Stuckenbruck, L. *1 Enoch 91-108.* Commentaries on Early Jewish Literature. Berlin: de Gruyter, 2007.

Stuhlmacher, P. "'Er ist unser Friede' (Eph 2,14) Zur Exegese und Bedeutung von Eph 2,14-18." In *Neues Testament und Kirche: Für Rudolph Schnackenburg,* edited by J. Gnilka, 337-58. Freiburg: Herder, 1974.

———. "Erwägungen zum ontologischen Charakter der καινή κτίσις bei Paulus." *Evangelische Theologie* 27 (1967) 1-35.

Stuhlmueller, C. *Creative Redemption in Deutero-Isaiah.* Analecta Biblica 43. Rome: Biblical Institute, 1970.

Suh, R. "The Use of Ezekiel 37 in Ephesians 2." *Journal of the Evangelical Theological Society* 50 (2007) 715-33.

Sumney, J. "Studying Paul's Opponents: Advances and Challenges." In *Paul and His Opponents*, edited by S. Porter, 7–58. Pauline Studies 2. Leiden: Brill, 2005.

———. *"Servants of Satan," "False Brothers," and other Opponents of Paul*. Journal for the Study of the New Testament Supplement Series 188. Sheffield: Sheffield Academic, 1999.

P. Swarup, *The Self-Understanding of the Dead Sea Scrolls Community: An Eternal Planting, a House of Holiness*. Library of Second Temple Studies 59. London: T. & T. Clark, 2006.

Talbert, C. *Ephesians and Colossians*. Paideia Commentaries on the New Testament. Grand Rapids: Baker, 2007.

Thielman, F. *Ephesians*. Baker Exegetical Commentary on the New Testament. Grand Rapids: Baker Academic, 2010.

Thompson, J. *The Book of Jeremiah*. New International Commentary on the Old Testament. Grand Rapids: Eerdmans, 1980.

Thrall, M. "The Problem of II Cor. VI.14–VII.1 in Some Recent Discussion." *New Testament Studies* 24 (1977) 132–48.

———. *The Second Epistle to the Corinthians I: Introduction and Commentary on II Corinthians I–VII*. International Critical Commentary. Edinburgh: T. & T. Clark, 1994.

Tuell, S. "The Rivers of Paradise: Ezekiel 47:1–12 and Genesis 2:10–14." In *God Who Creates: Essays in Honor of W. Sibley Towner*, edited by W. Brown and S. McBride Jr., 171–89. Grand Rapids: Eerdmans, 2000.

Turner, M. "Mission and Meaning in Terms of 'Unity' in Ephesians." In *Mission and Meaning: Essays Presented to Peter Cotterell*, edited by A. Billington et al., 138–66. Carlisle: Paternoster, 1995.

Usami, K. *Somatic Comprehension of Unity: The Church in Ephesus*. Analecta Biblica 101. Rome: Pontificio Instituto Biblico, 1983.

Vanderkam, J. "1 Enoch, Enochic Motifs, and Enoch in Early Christian Literature." In *The Jewish Apocalyptic Heritage in Early Christianity*, edited by J. VanderKam and W. Adler, 33–101. Compendia Rerum Iudaicarum ad Novum Testamentum 3. Assen: Van Gorcum, 1996.

———. *Enoch and the Growth of an Apocalyptic Tradition*. Catholic Biblical Quarterly Monograph Series 16. Washington, DC: Catholic Biblical Association of America, 1984.

———. *Textual and Historical Studies in the Book of Jubilees*. Harvard Semitic Monographs 14. Missoula, MT: Scholars, 1977.

———. *The Book of Jubilees*. Guides to Apocrypha and Pseudepigrapha. Sheffield: Sheffield Academic, 2001.

Vanhoozer, K. *Is There a Meaning in This Text?: The Bible, The Reader, and the Morality of Literary Knowledge*. Grand Rapids: Zondervan, 1998.

Van Kooten, G. *Cosmic Christology in Paul and the Pauline School: Colossians and Ephesians in the Context of Graeco-Roman Cosmology, with a new Synopsis of the Greeks Texts*. Wissenschaftliche Untersuchungen zum Neuen Testament 2.171. Tübingen: Mohr Siebeck, 2003.

Van Roon, A. *The Authenticity of Ephesians*. Translated by S. Prescod-Jokel. Supplements to Novum Testamentum 39. Leiden: Brill, 1974.

Van Ruiten, J. *Primaeval History Interpreted: The Rewriting of Genesis I-II in the Book of Jubilees.* Supplements for the Journal for the Study of Judaism 66. Leiden: Brill, 2000.

———. "The Intertextual Relationship between Isa 11,6-9 and Isa 65,25." In *The Scriptures and the Scrolls: Studies in Honour of A. S. Van der Woude on the Occasion of His 65th Birthday,* edited by F. Garcia Martinez, et al., 31-42. Supplements to Vetus Testamentum 49. Leiden: Brill, 1992.

———. "The Influence and Development of Is 65,17 in 1 En 91,16." In *The Book of Isaiah: Les oracles et leurs reflectures unite et complexité de l'ouvrage,* edited by J. Vermeylen, 161-66. Leuven: Leuven University Press, 1989.

Van Winkle, D. "The Relationship of the Nations to Yahweh in Isaiah xl-lv." *Vetus Testamentum* 35 (1985) 446-58.

Von Rad, G. *Theologie des Altens Testaments.* München: Kaiser, 1960.

Vouga, F. *An die Galater.* Handbuch zum Neuen Testament 10. Tübingen: Mohr Siebeck, 1998.

Wallace, D. *Greek Grammar Beyond the Basics: An Exegetical Syntax of the New Testament.* Grand Rapids: Zondervan, 1996.

Wagner, J. *Heralds of the Good News: Paul and Isaiah 'in Concert' in the Letter to the Romans.* Supplements to Novum Testamentum 101. Leiden: Brill, 2002.

Walker, W. Jr., *Interpolations in the Pauline Letters.* Journal for the Study of the New Testament Supplement Series 213. London: Sheffield Academic, 2001.

Watson, F. *Paul and the Hermeneutics of Faith.* London: T. & T. Clark, 2004.

———. *Text and Truth: Redefining Biblical Theology.* Edinburgh: T. & T. Clark, 1997.

Watts, J. *Isaiah 34-66.* Word Biblical Commentary 25. Waco, TX: Word, 1987.

Webb, W. *Returning Home: New Covenant and Second Exodus as the Context for 2 Corinthians 6:14-7:1.* Journal for the Study of the New Testament Supplement Series 85. Sheffield: JSOT, 1993.

Wedderburn, A. J. M. *Baptism and Resurrection: Studies in Pauline Theology against Its Greco-Roman Background.* Wissenschaftliche Untersuchungen zum Neuen Testament 1.44. Tübingen: Mohr Siebeck, 1987.

Weima, J. "Gal 6:11-18: A Hermeneutical Key to the Galatian Letter." *Calvin Theological Journal* 28 (1993) 90-107.

Weinfeld, M. "Jeremiah and the Spiritual Metamorphosis of Israel." *Zeitschrift für die Alttestamentliche Wissenschaft* 88 (1976) 17-56.

———. "Sabbath, Temple and the Enthronement of the Lord—The Problem of the Sitz im Leben of Genesis 1:1-2:3." In *Mélanges bibliques et orientaux en l'honneur de M. Henri Cazelles,* edited by A. Caquot and M. Delcor, 501-12. Nuekirchen-Vluyn: Neukirchener Verlag, 1981.

Weippert, H. "Das Wort vom Neuen Bund in Jeremia 31:31-34." *Vetus Testamentum* 29 (1979) 336-51.

Wenham, G. *Genesis 1-15.* Word Biblical Commentary 1. Waco, TX: Word, 1987.

———. "Sanctuary Symbolism in the Garden of Eden Story." In *Proceedings of the Ninth World Congress of Jewish Studies: Division A—The Period of the Bible,* edited by World Union of Jewish Studies, 19-25. Jerusalem: World Union of Jewish Studies, 1986.

Westerholm, S. *Perspectives Old and New on Paul: The "Lutheran" Paul and His Critics.* Grand Rapids: Eerdmans, 2004.

Westermann, C. *Das Buch Jesaja: Kapitel 40-66.* Das Alte Testament Deutlich 19. Göttingen: Vandenhoeck & Ruprecht, 1966.

Wevers, J. *Notes on the Greek Text of Exodus*. Society of Biblical Literature Septuagint and Cognate Studies 30. Atlanta, GA: Scholars, 1990.

Whybray, R. *Isaiah 40-66*. New Century Bible Commentary. London: Marshall, Morgan & Scott, 1975.

Wilk, F. *Die Bedeutung des Jesajabuches für Paulus*. Forschungen zur Religion und Literatur des Alten und Neuen Testaments 179. Göttingen: Vandenhoeck und Ruprecht, 1998.

Wilson, T. *The Curse of the Law and the Crisis in Galatia: Reassessing the Purpose of Galatians*. Wissenschaftliche Untersuchungen zum Neuen Testament 2.225. Tübingen: Mohr Siebeck, 2007.

Wintermute, O. "Jubilees: A New Translation and Introduction." In *The Old Testament Pseudeigrapha*, edited by J. Charlesworth, 35-142. Garden City, NY: Doubleday, 1985.

Wise, M. "4QFlorilegium and the Temple of Adam." *Revue de Qumran* 15 (1991) 103-32.

Witherington, B. *Paul's Narrative Thought World: The Tapestry and Tragedy of Triumph*. Louisville, KY: Westminster John Knox, 1994.

Wolff, C. *Die zweite Brief des Paulus an die Korinther*. Theologischer Handkommentar zum Neuen Testament 8. Berlin: Evangelische Verlagsanstalt, 1980.

———. "True Apostolic Knowledge of Christ: Exegetical Reflections on 2 Corinthians 5.14ff." In *Paul and Jesus: Collected Essays*, edited by A. J. M. Wedderburn, 81-98. Journal for the Study of the New Testament Supplement Series 37. Sheffield: JSOT, 1989.

Wolff, H. *Anthropologie des Alten Testaments*. München: Kaiser, 1973.

Woyke, J. "Nochmals zu den 'schwachen und unfähigen Elementen' (Gal 4.9) Paulus, Philo und die στοιχεῖα τοῦ κόσμου." *New Testament Studies* 54 (2008) 221-34.

Wright, A. *The Origin of Evil Spirits: The Reception of Genesis 6.1-4 in Early Jewish Literature*. Wissenschaftliche Untersuchungen zum Neuen Testament 2.198. Tübingen: Mohr Siebeck, 2005.

Wright, N. T. *The Climax of the Covenant: Christ and the Law in Pauline Theology*. Edinburgh: T. & T. Clark, 1991.

———. *Justification: God's Plan and Paul's Vision*. Downers Grove, IL: InterVarsity, 2009.

———. *The New Testament and the People of God*. Minneapolis, MN: Fortress, 1992.

———. *Paul and the Faithfulness of God*. Minneapolis, MN: Fortress, 2013.

———. *The Resurrection of the Son of God*. Minneapolis, MN: Fortress, 2003.

Yates, R. "Re-examination of Ephesians 1:23." *Expository Times* 83 (1972) 146-51.

Yee, T. *Jews, Gentiles and Ethnic Reconciliation: Paul's Jewish Identity and Ephesians*. Society of New Testament Studies Monograph Series 130. Cambridge: Cambridge University Press, 2005.

Zenger, E. "Der Gott des Exodus in der Botschaft der Propheten—am Beispiel des Jesajabuches." *Concilium* 23 (1987) 15-22.

Zimmerli, W. *Ezechiel*. Biblischer Kommentar Altes Testament 13.1. Neukirchen-Vluyn: Neukirchener, 1969.

Zimmerman, J. *Messianische Texte aus Qumran: Königliche, priesterliche und prophetische Messiasvorstellungen in den Schriftfunden von Qumran*. Wissenschaftliche Untersuchungen zum Neuen Testament 2.104. Tübingen: Mohr Siebeck, 1998.

Index of Authors

Adai, Jacob, 150
Adams, Edward, 1-2, 4-5, 39, 76, 79, 81-82, 84-85, 102, 104, 107, 178
Albl, Martin C., 134
Alexander, Phillip, 7
Allen, Leslie C., 47, 50, 133
Allen, Thomas G., 131-32
Arnold, Bill T., 182
Arnold, Clinton E., 78-79, 123, 125-26, 138-39, 141, 143, 145, 149, 164
Atkinson, Kenneth, 190
Aune, David E., 74
Aus, Roger David, 38
Aymer, Albert, 1

Baasland, Ernst, 70
Baltzer, Klaus, 18, 20-21, 27-28
Barclay, John, 72, 80, 83-84, 179
Barnett, Paul, 90, 93, 98-100, 106-7, 110-11, 116
Barr, James, 127
Barrett, C. K., 93, 95, 99-100, 104, 107-8
Barstad, Hans, 16, 24
Barth, Markus, 122, 124-25, 127, 129, 131, 137-39, 143, 153, 155-56, 159-61, 163, 167
Batto, Bernard F., 23, 181, 184
Baumgarten, Jörg, 103
Beale, G. K., 5-6, 34, 36, 47, 49-50, 104, 110-12, 116, 121, 140-41, 165-66, 168, 182-83, 189
Becking, Bob, 56

Bedale, Stephen, 126
Beetham, Christopher, 140, 152
Beker, J. Christian, 74-75
Belleville, Linda, 89
Berger, Klaus, 63
Berkeley, Timothy W., 11
Best, Ernest, 123, 125-26, 128, 131-32, 138, 142-43, 146, 149, 153-54, 157, 159-60, 161, 163, 165, 167, 178
Betz, Hans Dieter, 69, 71-73, 79, 84
Bird, Michael, 108
Black, Matthew, 58, 61-62
Blenkinsopp, Joseph, 17-22, 25, 27, 37-38, 49-50, 183, 187
Block, Daniel I., 49-51
de Boer, Martinus, 70-72, 78, 80
Breytenbach, Cilliers, 100, 106-7
Brooke, George, 66
Brown, Raymond, 123
Broyles, Craig, 134
Bruce, F. F., 70, 71, 73, 77, 79-80, 84, 124, 129, 145, 157, 165
Bryan, David, 61-62
Buitenwerf, Rieuwerd, 189
Bultmann, Rudolf, 74, 93, 95, 97-98, 102, 106

Caird, G. B., 145, 163
Caragounis, Chrys C., 122-124, 126, 128, 129, 161
Carr, Wesley, 143
Carroll, Robert P., 53, 55

INDEX OF AUTHORS

Charles, Robert H., 61, 65
Childs, Brevard S., 17, 19–21, 24, 27–28, 30, 33–34, 37
Clayton, Jay, 9
Clements, Ronald, 24
Clifford, Richard J., 23, 25
Clines, David J., 158
Cohen, Shaye J. D., 70
Collange, Jean-François, 89–90, 95, 99, 116
Collins, John J., 58, 63, 189
Cook, John Granger, 182
Cotterell, Peter, 126, 130
Craigie, Peter C., 134
Cross, Frank Moore, 23, 181
Cullmann, Oscar, 75

Dahl, Nils A., 153
Das, A. Andrew, 38, 72
Davenport, Gene L., 65
Dawes, Gregory W., 127, 138–39
Dexinger, Ferdinand, 62
Dinkler, Erich, 95, 102, 109
Dodd, C. H., 12
Dumbrell, William J., 16, 54
Dunn, J. D. G., 69–71, 76, 80–81, 84, 87, 91, 95, 99, 135, 146, 157

Ekblad, Eugene Robert, 113
Elliger, Karl, 15, 17
Endres, John C., 63

Faust, Eberhard, 156, 163
Fee, Gordon, 116, 132
Feinberg, Charles, 49
Fischer, Georg, 56
Fishbane, Michael, 8, 183
Fitzgerald, John, 116
Fitzmeyer, Joseph, 116
Fletcher-Louis, Crispin H. T., 90, 183, 185
Fraser, J. W., 99–100
Frey, Jörg, 80
Fung, Richard Y., 138
Furnish, Victor P., 93, 95, 97–101, 107, 111

Gärtner, Bertil, 164

Gaston, Lloyd, 167
Georgi, Dieter, 93, 99–100
Gignilliat, Mark, 6, 15, 18, 99, 104, 108, 112
Gladd, Benjamin, 123
Gloer, W. Hulitt, 2
Gnilka, Joachim, 116, 147, 149, 154, 164, 167
Goldingay, John, 17–23, 25, 27–29, 113–14, 133
Gombis, Timothy, 121, 135–36, 142, 162
Goppelt, Leonhard, 4
Gordley, Matthew, 135
Gräßer, Erich, 93–95, 98, 102, 106
Greenberg, Moshe, 44–45, 49–50
Grudem, Wayne, 126
Gunkel, Hermann, 4

Haag, Ernst, 24
Hafemann, Scott J., 89–91, 97
Halpern-Amaru, Betsy, 66
Hanson, Paul, 4, 35–36, 181
Hardin, Justin K., 70–71
Harris, Murray J., 92, 95, 98–100, 106–7, 110–111, 116
Hartin, Peter, 122, 126
Hay, David M., 132
Hays, Richard B., 8–12, 89
Hoehner, Harold W., 7, 123–25, 128–29, 131, 139, 145, 147, 152, 154–55, 157, 164–65
Holladay, William L., 56
Hollander, John, 9
Hong, In-Gyu, 72, 78, 84
Hooker, Morna D., 108
Hoover, Joel H., 1
Hubbard, Moyer, 1, 3, 5–7, 13, 15, 34–35, 44–45, 47, 52, 54, 57, 64–65, 67–68, 70, 75–76, 80–81, 83–87, 89–91, 93, 97–99, 101–5, 107, 110, 120, 144–45, 170, 173, 178

Jackson, T. Ryan, 1, 2, 5–7, 13–16, 19, 34–35, 39, 54–55, 79, 81, 83–87, 96, 99, 102–4, 107, 110, 149, 173, 177–79
Jeal, Roy R., 131
Jeremias, Joachim, 167

Jervis, L. Ann, 70, 74
Jewett, Robert, 70–71, 145–46
Jónsson, Gunnlaugur A., 134
Joyce, Paul M., 44, 46–47, 51

Kaminsky, Joel, 19
Käsemann, Ernst, 74, 80, 108, 178
Keown, Gerald, 56
Kiesow, Klaus, 22
Kim, Seyoon, 6, 90, 98
Kirby, John, 149
Kirchschläger, Walter, 76
Kitchen, Martin, 127
Koch, Dietrich-Alex, 110
Koole, Jan Leunis, 18, 22, 25
van Kooten, George, 127
Kraus, Hans Joachim, 133
Kraus, Wolfgang, 1–4, 34, 38–39, 67–68, 84, 87, 105, 107, 120, 173, 178
Kugler, Robert, 187
Kuhn, K. G., 122
Kwon, Yon-Gyong, 75–76, 84

Lalleman-de Winkel, Hetty, 54
Lambrecht, Jan, 94–95, 97, 99–101, 106–7
Levenson, Jon D., 50, 183
Levin, Christof, 54
Lincoln, Andrew T., 31, 122–24, 130–32, 135, 140, 146–47, 149–50, 152–53, 155–56, 159–67
Lindars, Barnabas, 61
Lindemann, Andreas, 125, 159, 161
Loader, William R. G., 132
Lona, Horacio E., 127
Longenecker, Bruce, 72, 78–79, 82
Longenecker, Richard, 69, 71–73, 79–80, 82, 86
Louw, Johannes P., 130
Lührmann, Dieter, 69, 71
Lund, Øystein, 15, 17–18, 22–25, 113, 115
Lundbom, Jack, 54, 56
Lundquist, John M., 8

Marcus, Joel, 80
Martin, Aldo, 122, 134–35, 151

Martin, Ralph P., 93, 95, 98, 101, 104, 106–7, 111, 155, 160
Martyn, J. Louis, 69–76, 80, 85–87, 98–101
Matera, Frank J., 69, 71, 82, 84, 90, 93, 96–98, 101–2, 106, 108, 111
Matlock, R. Barry, 75
Mauser, Ulrich, 37
Mayer, Annemarie C., 160
McHugh, John, 5, 122, 128, 130
McKane, William, 54, 56
McKelvey, R. J., 164–65, 167–68
Mell, Ulrich, 1, 3, 6–7, 15, 35, 43, 53, 64, 67–68, 77, 84–85, 97, 99, 104–5, 120, 145, 173, 178
Meyer, Regina P., 139, 141
Middlemas, Jill, 36
Miletic, Stephen F., 5, 148, 151, 158
Milik, Józef T., 61
Moo, Douglas, 96
Morales, Rodrigo, 50, 72
Moritz, Thorsten, 29, 132–35, 149, 151, 159, 161–62
Moses, Robert E., 78
Muddiman, John, 124, 138–39, 140, 143, 152–53, 155–56, 160–61, 164, 166, 167
Münderlein, Gerhard, 138–39, 141
Mussner, Franz, 70, 73, 77, 84, 125, 150–51

Nanos, Mark D., 71–72
Nickelsburg, George W.E., 58–62
Niditch, Susan, 49
North, Christopher R., 24, 190

O'Brien, Peter, 122, 126, 132, 138, 140, 142–43, 145, 147, 149, 152–53, 155–57, 159, 164
Oswalt, John, 17, 25–29, 37–38, 40, 112, 114
Overfield, P. Derrick, 140

Pate, C. Marvin, 95
Patrick, Dale A., 23
Patzia, Arthur G, 167
Payne, David, 18, 20–21, 25, 27–28
Pokorný, Petr, 149, 160, 163–64

Potter, Harry D., 54
Propp, William H. C., 23

von Rad, Gerhard, 54
Räisänen, Heikki, 146
Rantzow, Sophie, 163
Rendtorff, Rolf, 16, 54
Renz, Thomas, 45–46, 49
Robinson, Joseph Armitage, 140
Roetzel, Calvin J., 155–56
van Roon, Aart, 122
Rosel, Martin, 182
Rothstein, Eric, 9
van Ruiten, Jacques, 37, 62–63

Sailhamer, John, 183
Sanders, E. P., 146
Sandmel, Samuel, 182
Scalise, Pamela, J., 56
Schaper, Joachim, 133
Schlier, Heinrich, 76, 78, 124, 126–27, 138, 156, 163–64, 166
Schmeller, Thomas, 95, 99, 101–2, 106, 111
Schnackenburg, Rudolf, 29, 125, 127, 131, 139, 142, 149, 150–51, 153–56, 160, 163–64, 166–68
Schneider, Gerhard, 1, 2, 6, 7, 34, 52–54, 57, 64, 103
Schnelle, Udo, 2, 80
Schreiner, Thomas, 71–72, 77, 86, 146, 157
Schweitzer, Albert, 74
Schwindt, Rainer, 143
Scott, James M., 38, 65, 116–17
Scroggs, Robin, 97
Sellin, Gerhard, 126–27, 135, 137, 150, 160, 165
Silva, Moisés, 77
Simian-Yofre, Horacio, 24
Smothers, Thomas, 56
Sommer, Benjamin D., 53
Stanley, Christopher D, 11–12, 110
Steck, Odil H., 37
Stendahl, Krister, 178
Stockhausen, Carol Kern, 54, 90
Stordalen, Terje, 36–37
Strachan, Robert Harvey, 1

Stuckenbruck, Loren T., 62
Stuhlmacher, Peter, 1, 6, 34, 64, 84, 99, 101, 149, 151, 160–61
Stuhlmueller, Carroll, 17, 25, 37
Suh, Robert H., 44
Sumney, Jerry, 70
Swarup, Paul, 189

Talbert, Charles H., 155
Thielman, Frank, 122, 124, 126–27, 156–57, 159, 165, 167–68
Thompson, John, 53–54
Thrall, Margaret E., 90, 92, 95, 97–98, 100–101, 103, 107–9, 111, 116
Tuell, Steven S., 49–50
Turner, Max, 5, 122, 126, 130

Usami, Kōshi, 126–27

Vanderkam, James C., 58, 60, 61, 63
Vanhoozer, Kevin, 9
Vouga, François, 71, 73, 84

Wagner, J. Ross, 10–12
Walker, William O, 116
Wallace, Daniel, 94–95, 97, 123
Watson, Francis, 8, 152
Watts, John D., 17–19, 36–37, 39, 112
Webb, William J., 5–6, 34–35, 53, 55, 94, 102, 104, 110, 112–17, 121
Wedderburn, Alexander J. M., 144
Weima, Jeffry, A., 69, 71, 73, 82, 84, 86
Weinfeld, Moshe, 54, 182
Weippert, Helga, 54
Wenham, Gordon, 158, 182
Westerholm, Stephen, 146
Westermann, Claus, 17, 20, 27–28, 35, 37–39
Wevers, John William, 23
Whybray, Roger N., 18
Wilk, Florian, 6, 90
Wilson, Todd, 70
van Winkle, D. W., 19
Wintermute, O. S., 63
Wise, Michael O., 189
Witherington, Ben, 131
Wolff, Christian, 93, 95, 98–99, 100–101, 106–7

Wolff, Hans Walter, 54
Woyke, Johannes, 79
Wright, Archie, 58
Wright, N. T., 4, 71, 75–76, 156, 158

Yates, Roy, 140

Yee, Tet-Lim, 149, 153, 155–56, 159–60, 162–63, 167

Zenger, Erich, 24
Zimmerli, Walter, 45
Zimmerman, Johannes, 189

Scripture Index

Old Testament

Genesis

1–2	4, 37, 90–91, 142, 148, 151–52, 168–69, 172–73, 181–83, 185
1–3	4, 36–37, 40, 50, 52, 60, 67, 97, 171
1:1	37
1:1, 7, 16, 21, 25, 26, 27, 31	37
1:1–31	182
1:1—2:1	185
1:2	182, 185
1:3	90
1:3, 6, 9, 14, 20, 24, 26	182
1:20–21	50
1:26–27	90
1:26–28	134
1:27	152
1:28	158, 185
1:31	183
1:31—2:3	183
2–3	36, 60, 183
2:1	183
2:1–4	62
2:1–3	182, 183
2:2	183
2:2–4, 18	37
2:3	183
2:6	185
2:9	36
2:15	183
3	4, 119, 169
3:1, 2, 4, 13, 14–15	37
3:1–24	130
3:15	36
3:17, 22, 24	36
5:21–24	58
6:1–4	12
6:5	80
8:21	80
9:9	36
11:27	158
12–17	158
12:1–3	158
12:2	156, 176
12:2–3	59, 158
12:3	4
12:7	36
14:17–20	133
15:1–21	158
15:13	163
17:1–4	70, 158
17:1–6	156, 158, 176
17:2, 6, 8	158
17:4	4
18:18	4
22:16–18	158
23:4	158

Genesis (continued)

26:3–4, 24	158
28:3	158
35:11–12	158
47:27	158
48:3–4	158

Exodus

2:22	163n184
3:8	76
4:23	24
6:1, 6	20
6:3–7	117n239
7:4–5	23
7:16	24
8:1, 20	24
10:7	30
13:13–16	23
14:11	23
15:1–3	23
15:1–17	184
15:1–18	24
15:1–19	21, 23, 181
15:3	23
15:6	20
15:13	113n216
15:13, 16–17	24
15:13, 17, 19	23
15:17	56, 166, 183n11
15:17–18	23, 184, 189n7
15:18	184
17:6	113
18:3	163n184
18:4, 8–10	76
19:6	163n186
20:12	155
25–31	182
25–40	24, 182
25:1	182
25:7	184n11
25:8	8, 56
28:9–12	184n11
29:44–45	8
30:11, 17, 22, 34	182
31:1, 12	182
31:12–17	182
32:11	20, 113n214
34:29–35	89
36:1	48
39:32	183
39:42–43	183
39:43	183
40:33	183

Leviticus

18:6, 12, 13	164
19:33–34	50
19:36	113
20:3	48
23:34–36	183
26:11–12	117

Deuteronomy

4:34	20
5:15	20
5:16	155
6:4	79, 154n144
6:6	54n47
6:21	20
7:6	163n186
7:8, 19	20
7:16	21n67
8:15	113
9:26, 29	20
11:18	54n47
23:2–6	50
26:8	20
27–30	72n20
27:26	72
28–34	65n108
28:16, 22, 24, 38–40, 42	59n75
28:49	149
29:4	61n87
29:22	149
30:1–5, 9, 16	5975
30:5, 6, 14	54n47
32:8–9	79:56

SCRIPTURE INDEX

Judges

8:27	30n67

Ruth

2:10	163n184

1 Samuel

4:4	45
6:2	45
16:7	93n116

2 Samuel

7	184
7:1–6	183
7:10–11	184
7:10–14	184, 189n7
7:11–16	158
7:21	123n13
7:23–24	117n239

1 Kings

5:4–5	183
6:18, 29, 32	184n11
6:38	183
8:2, 31–55, 65	183
8:10–13	8n20
8:15, 56	122n5
8:39, 43, 49	166

2 Kings

22–23	53
23:4, 6, 10, 12	56n63
25:17	167
25:27–30	53

1 Chronicles

22:8–10, 18–19	183

26:27	165n195
28:2	48n24
29:1	165n195

2 Chronicles

6:30, 33, 39	166
7:9	183
28:23	30n67
30:27	166
34:3–7	53

Nehemiah

2:7–11	17n16
9:14	123n13

Job

10:3	147n118
14:15	147n118

Psalms

2:6 LXX	31n70, 36n83
8 LXX	132, 134–35, 137
8:3	134n62
8:6–8 LXX	134n63
8:7 LXX	121, 134n61, 137, 141, 147n118, 169, 175
14:1 LXX	36n84
15:3 LXX	163n186
23:1 LXX	138n84
23:3 LXX	36n84
23:3–6 LXX	136n72
25:8 LXX	8n20
28:3, 10 LXX	183n11
35:9–10 LXX	184n11
42:3 LXX	36n84
45:5 LXX	50
47:2–3 LXX	31n70, 36n83
47:8–14 LXX	136n72
49:12 LXX	138n84
63:8–9 LXX	147n120

Psalms (continued)

63:10 LXX	147n116, 147n118, 147n120
67:1–11 LXX	18
67:17 LXX	140n95
71:18 LXX	122n5
76 LXX	22n37
76:18–20 LXX	113
76:20 LXX	22
77:15–16 LXX	113
77:52 LXX	113n216
77:52–55 LXX	24n43
77:69 LXX	8n20
88:4–15 LXX	183n11
88:12 LXX	138n84
90:4	65
91:5 LXX	147–48, 175
92:1–5 LXX	183n11
97:1–3 LXX	27
97:2 LXX	123n13
98:1 LXX	45
98:1–5 LXX	183n11
98:9 LXX	36n84
101:26 LXX	147n118
102:7 LXX	123n13
104:37 LXX	23
104:41 LXX	113
105:48 LXX	122n5
109 LXX	132–135, 137
109:1 LXX	121, 141, 169
109:1, 4 LXX	134n61, 175
109:5–7 LXX	134n61
117:22 LXX	166–167
118:19 LXX	163n184
118:64 LXX	138n85
131:7–8, 13–14 LXX	183n11
131:8–9, 13–14 LXX	8n20
132:7–8, 13–14 LXX	183n8
138:8 LXX	147n118
142:5 LXX	147–148, 175

Ecclesiastes

3:11	147–48, 175n6
7:13	147–48, 175n6
8:17	147n116, 147n120
11:5	147n116, 147n120

Isaiah

1–39	24, 34
1:8	189n11
1:21–27	36n82
2:1–3	189
2:1–4	19n24, 19n27, 36n82, 41n105, 166
2:2–4	29, 39
3:6	164
4:1–6	36n82
4:2–6	41n105
4:3–5	25n52
5:26	149
6:3	138n85
6:10	31, 61n87
8:23	34
9:1	34, 90
9:6–7	154n146
9:7	31
10:31	189n11
11:1–12	128, 136, 175
11:1–27	20n31
11:1—12:6	36n82
11:6–8	35n80
11:6–9	4n8
11:6–12	189
11:10	33n74, 115
11:12	115
12:1–6	16
16:1	189n11
18:5–7	36n82
19:18–25	19n24
19:22	31
24:19–23	36n82
24:22	36n83
25:9	189n11
27:1–2, 12–13	20n31
27:6–13	36n82
27:13	31n70
28:16	167–70, 176
29:16	147–148, 175n6
30:18–19	36n82
30:26	31
30:27–33	20n31
31:1–5	36n82
31:4–9	20n31
32:12–20	26n53

32:17–18	31	40:9	20, 27n56, 64n104, 190
33:13	31	40:9–10	20n29, 36, 41
33:20	64n104	40:9–11	18n22, 19, 20, 21n35, 27, 115
33:20–22	36n82		
33:20–24	16	40:10	17n11, 21, 113n218, 188
34:5–7	20n31		
35:1–10	17, 41n105	40:10–11	21n35, 113
35:2	189n11	40:11	21, 113n218, 190
35:3–4	21n35	41:17–20	26n53
35:4–10	26n53	41:18	113n216
35:8–10	36n82	41:18–19	189
35:10	25n52	41:22	24n47, 25n49
37:22	189n11	41:25–27	36n82
37:31–32	16n10, 36n82	42:1–16	39
40–55	16, 18n18, 19n24, 25–29, 30n68, 32, 34–36, 37, 39, 41n105, 104, 112–13	42:9	6n14, 24n47, 25, 34, 37
		42:9–16	15n7
40–66	18n18, 24, 112, 114	42:10–17	25n51
40:1	27n56	42:11	188n5
40:1–2	17, 31, 115n228	42:15–16	113
40:1–2, 9	36n82	43:1–15	22n37
40:1–2, 11	27n56	43:5	115
40:1–4	20n30	43:5–6	114
40:1–5	19, 41n103, 85n83, 17n11, 172	43:8–15	22
		43:9	24n47
40:1–5, 9–11		43:9, 18–19	25n49
40:1–11	15–16, 18–19, 19n26, 20–21, 27–31, 33, 39, 113n218	43:16	22
		43:16, 19	113
		43:16, 19–20	105, 190n16
40:3	17–18, 21, 21n33, 22n36, 30, 188	43:16–17	22–23, 25
		43:16–21	15, 17n11, 23–24, 25n52, 26–27, 36, 41n103, 41n104, 136, 172, 175, 181
40:3, 10	17n11		
40:3, 10–11	33n74		
40:3–4	20n30, 23, 105, 113, 190n16		
		43:17	22–23
40:3–4, 10–11	113n216	43:18	25
40:3–5, 9–11	27n59, 39, 41n104, 136, 172, 175, 188, 190	43:18–19	6n14, 15, 22, 24, 25n51, 104n177
		43:19	17n11, 22n36, 25–26, 34, 37
40:3–5	17, 18n22, 18n23, 21, 39, 113n221, 114, 189		
		43:19–20	22n39, 23, 113–14
40:4	18, 21	43:19–21	189
40:5	18–19, 19n24, 19n25, 21, 27n59, 28–29, 32, 39–40, 114, 117, 150, 166, 190	43:20	22, 35n80, 114
		43:20–21	23, 25n52
		43:21	24n43, 115
		44:3–4	26n53
43:6	29	44:23	114

Isaiah (continued)

44:23–28	36n82
44:26	188n5
46:8–13	36n82
46:9	24n47, 25n49
48:1–11	15n7
48:3	24n47
48:3, 6	6n14, 25n49
48:7	34, 37
48:20	28
48:21	113n216
49	110, 112, 115
49:1	113
49:1, 6–8, 11–26	174
49:1–6	112
49:1–7	112, 114
49:1–12	113n218
49:1–13	112–15
49:1–21	20n30
49:4	112
49:5–6, 8	110n204
49:6	112n213, 113, 114n224
49:6–12	29
49:7	113
49:8	110, 112, 114
49:8–12	114
49:8–13	112, 113n215
49:9	112–13, 114n227, 120
49:9–10	20n29, 41, 188–90
49:9–12	113, 114n223, 114n224, 114n227, 115, 174
49:10	113, 188
49:10, 13	27n56
49:11	113–14, 190n16
49:11–13	20n30
49:12	114–15, 190
49:13	114, 115n228, 188n5
49:13–21	36n82
49:14–21	20n30
49:14–26	112, 114, 18n16
49:18	115
49:19–20	115
49:20	112
49:22	33n74, 115
49:23	185
51:1—52:10	36n82
51:3	4n8, 25n52, 27n56, 35n80, 50n34, 52, 188
51:3–5, 9–11	41n103, 41n105, 172
51:9	21n33
51:9–10	24n46
51:9–11	20n31, 24n46, 25n49, 41n104, 115, 136, 172, 175
51:9–12	24n46
51:12—52:10	28
51:22—52:6	27
52:1	38, 190
52:1–2, 7–9	64n104
52:2	189n11
52:7	6, 17n11, 26–29, 31, 44n5, 136–37, 149, 152, 161, 169, 188–90
52:7–10	27n56, 41, 136, 172, 174–75, 188, 190
52:7–11	36, 115, 117–18, 120, 174, 189n10
52:7–12	15–16, 20n31, 26–29, 117
52:8	27, 28n59, 118, 188n5
52:8, 10	113n221, 150
52:8, 12	20n29
52:8–9	27n56
52:9	188n5
52:10	27–29, 40, 114, 117, 190
52:11	28, 110, 116–17, 120
52:12	27n56
52:13—53:12	108n194
53	108n194
53:5	31
53:10	108n194
53:11	108n194
54:1	188n5
55:7	188
56–66	16, 18n18, 30n68, 34–35, 36n83, 41n105, 104, 112
56:1–7	19n24
56:1–8	29, 39, 41n105
56:7	36n84
56:9—57:13	30–31
57:3–13	30

57:13	30, 31n70, 33	64:7	147n118
57:14	17n11, 30–32, 33n74, 113	64:9	188n5
		64:10	64n104
57:14, 17–18	33, 190n16	64:10–11	41n105
57:14–19	29–30, 41n103, 172	65	60n81
57:14–21	15–16, 30, 31n70, 32–33, 39, 150, 189n10	65–66	14, 19, 19n26, 20, 25–26, 28, 33, 35, 42, 62n93, 64, 66–67, 170, 172, 190
57:16	31		
57:16–18	32		
57:17	30–31	65:7, 16–17	24n47
57:18	20n29, 27n56, 31–32	65:11	36n84
57:19	6, 26, 29, 31–32, 44n5, 137, 149, 150–52, 154, 161, 169	65:15–20	59
		65:16	37
		65:16–17	6n14, 26, 34, 42n106
58:12	114n224	65:17	34–35, 37, 104n177
59:16–21	20n31, 36n82	65:17–18	64n104
59:20	16n11	65:17–25	4n8, 15–16, 16n11, 17n11, 35–38, 40, 41n103, 42n106, 67, 119, 128, 172–73
60	185n16		
60–62	16, 16n11, 17n11, 33n74		
60:1	114n224	65:18	35n81, 37–38, 189n11
60:1, 3, 19–20	189n11	65:18–19	16n11, 35
60:1–16	39	65:19	37, 188n5
60:1–4	19n24, 19n27, 189	65:20	38
60:1—63:6	36n83	65:20–25	40n102
60:3–7, 10–16	17n11	65:21–22	59n76
60:10–22	16n11, 36n82	65:22	36, 38
60:14	38, 115, 185	65:22–23	17n11
60:16	76n44	65:25	35, 37–38
61:1	31	66	39
61:1–6	36n82	66:7–14	16n11
61:4	24n47, 34, 114n224, 188n5	66:10, 14	189n11
		66:14–24	20n31, 136, 175
61:4–7	16n11	66:15–17	39
62:1–4, 10–12	16n11	66:18	19n27, 113n221
62:1–12	36n82	66:18, 23–24	39–40
62:4	188n5	66:18–19	19
62:5	188n5, 189n11	66:18–21, 23	29, 39
62:8–9	17n11	66:18–22	19n25
62:8–12	21n35	66:18–23	19, 33n74, 41n105
62:10	17n11, 33n74, 115	66:18–24	4, 15–16, 16n11, 19, 29, 36–40, 41n103, 42n106, 87, 115, 117, 119, 150, 166, 172, 189, 190n12
62:10–11	33n74		
62:10–12	41n103, 172		
62:11	17n11, 189n11		
63:1–6	20n31		
63:11–13	21n33	66:19	38n92
63:11–14	113n216	66:19–20	38
63:18	31n70, 36n84	66:20	31n70, 38

Isaiah (continued)

65:20–23	65
66:20–24	64n104
66:22	104n177
66:23	19, 40

Jeremiah

2:1—25:14	53
2:3	56n63
4:6	54
5:20–25	54
7:22–23	117n239
9:22–25	83n74
11:3–5	117n239
14:8	163n184
17:1, 9	54
17:12	56n64
18:2	54
19:4–5, 13	56n63
23:5	55n58
23:23–24	138n85
25:11–12	44
29[36]:14	57n66
30–33[37–40]	55
30[37]:3	55, 57
30[37]:8, 10	55
30[37]:8–10, 17–22	57n67
30[37]:9	55n58
30[37]:9, 21	55
30[37]:17–22	55
30[37]:18	55, 57n66
30[37]:18–22	55–56, 172
30:20	57, 67n115
30[37]:20	56
31[38]:4–7, 12	55
31[38]:4–10, 12, 15–17, 27–28	57n67
31[38]:7–10, 15–17, 27–28	55
31[38]:12–14, 23–24	55n53
31[38]:21–22	53
31[38]:23	57n66
31[38]:31	57
31[38]:31–33	55n56, 117n239
31[38]:31–34	54–57, 67n115, 144n108, 172
31[38]:38–40	56–57
31[38]:39–40	57
32[39]:35	56n63
32[39]:36–40	144n108
32[39]:36–44	55n57
32[39]:44	57n66
33[40]:7, 11, 26	57n66
33:15–26	53
[37]:18	57, 67n115
[38]:40	57–58, 67, 172
39:1–10	53
51:31–34	53
51:45	112n214
52:1–30	53
52:31–34	53

Lamentations

5:2	163n184

Ezekiel

1	51
1:1, 4, 26–28	51
1:1, 26–28	44
1:1–3	49
1:28	44
1:29	44
2:3–4	44
3:4–5	44
4–7	45
4:1—5:4	45
5–9	44
5:6–7, 9, 11	45, 51
6:1–7	45
6:1–7, 9, 11	45, 51
6:9	46
7:4, 8–9, 20	45, 51
7:20	45
7:21–22	45
8–11	48n23
8:1–3	49
8:3–18	51
8:5–18	45n9
8:6	51
9–11	45, 51
9:3	45, 51

10:3–4, 18–19	45, 51	37:5–6, 9–10, 14, 23–24	48
11:16	45	37:9–14, 21, 25	52
11:17–20	45n10, 117n239	37:11	47
11:18–19, 21	46	37:11, 15–28	52
11:19	55n56, 90	37:12–14	47n20
11:22–23	45, 51	37:12–14, 21–22, 25–28	48
12:2	61	37:13	48n22
14:3–7	46	37:14	47, 144n108
17:17	165n195	37:15–28	47, 48
20:16	46	37:16–17	48
20:33–34	27	37:18–28	48
20:40	36n84	37:23	45n10
26:25–27	90	37:23, 27	48
28:13–18	184n11	37:24–25	55n58
29:17	44	37:26–28	49n26, 52, 67, 172
33	46n13	37:27	117
33–48	46	38–48	49n26, 67
34:24	55n58	40–42	49
34:27	76n44	40–48	45, 47, 49–52, 57, 67, 172
36–37	45n10, 51–52		
36:17, 21–22	47	40:1–2	49
36:22, 28, 32, 37	52	40:2	49, 165n195
36:22, 32, 37	48	43:1–5	50
36:22–28	47	43:2–5	45, 51
36:22—37:14	47–48	43:5	138n85
36:22—37:28	46, 48	44:4	45, 51, 138n85
36:24, 28, 33	52	44:5–9	50, 52
36:24–38	57	44:5–16	50
36:25–26, 29, 33, 38	51	44:6–9	50
36:25–28, 33, 37–38	55n57	44:7, 9	51n37
36:25–33	46	47:1–12	4n8, 49–50, 52, 67, 184n11
36:25	46		
36:25, 38	46	47:9	50n34
36:25–28	45n10, 47, 144n108	47:21–23	50, 52, 172
36:26	46–48, 52, 172	47:22	50n36
36:26–27	55n56	47:22–23	51n37
36:27	46–48	48:10	36n84
36:27–28	48	48:21	56n64
36:28	46, 48		
36:28–38	47n20		
36:29	46		

Daniel

36:29–35	47n17, 52, 172
36:30	46
36:33	46
36:35	50n34, 52, 173
37	44, 45n10, 47, 48
37:1–14	47, 76n42, 90
37:5–6, 9, 14	47

2:19, 27, 30, 47	123, 130
2:19–47	123, 125
2:23, 28, 29, 30, 45	123n13
2:28–29, 45	123
7:27	163n186
9:15	113n214

Daniel (continued)

9:16, 19–20	31n70, 36n83
10:13–14, 20–21	79n56
12:1–3	76n42
12:7	163n186

Hosea

2:23	85
6:1–2	76n42

Joel

2:1	31n70, 36n83
2:28–32	90
3:18	50
4:17	31n70, 36n83

Amos

6:10	164n190
9:11	184, 189n7

Micah

4:1–2	39n99
4:1–8	19n27
5:5	154n146

Nahum

1:2–8	18
1:15	26

Habakkuk

3:1–13	18

Zephaniah

3:8–10	29

Haggai

2:5	113n214
2:7	138n85

Zechariah

2:10	189n11
8:3	31n70
8:7–8	117n239
8:20–23	19n27
14:8	50
14:16–21	40

New Testament

Matthew

16:18	166
22:44	133n58
24:1	165n195

Mark

1:15	78n51
12:36	133n58

Luke

20:42	133n58

John

4:20–24	150n131

Acts

2:14–21	90
2:34	133n58

7:17	78n51
10:5	90
15:1	86n87
15:13–18	184
18:4	92n112
19:8, 26	92n112
21:39	163n185
28:23	92n112

Romans

1:3	99
1:17	109
1:20	146, 148, 175n6
2:6	12n36
2:13	108
2:17–25	73n24
2:23–29	83n74
2:28–29	153n141
3:1–2	153
3:9–26	72n22
3:20, 24, 28, 30	108
3:20, 28	146n114
3:20–27	73n24
3:20–31	146n114
3:21–22, 26	109
3:27	146n115
3:31	155, 157
4:1	99
4:1–3	73n24
4:1–5	146n114
4:1–8	108
4:1–25	108
4:2, 4	146n115
4:24	76
5:2–3, 11	92n115
5:8	95
5:9–10	108
5:12–19	95
5:12–21	135
5:15–17	98
5:20–21	96
6:1–2	77n49
6:1–6	77
6:1–11	82n69, 98, 144
6:2, 10–11	77n50
6:3	102n165
6:4	77, 144n109
6:6	96
6:6, 9, 12–14	144n109
6:8	102n165, 145n110
7:1–6	144, 145n110, 155
7:2–6	77n50
7:4	77n47
7:5–6	80n59, 144n109
7:6	157
7:7–25	72n22
7:13	97n138
8:1–9	82n69
8:1–13	80n59
8:4–5, 12–13	99
8:6, 12	80
8:9	102n165
8:11	76
8:12–13	80n64
8:18–25	2n4, 75, 85, 177n9
8:19–22	114
8:34, 38–39	132
8:35	95
9:3, 5	99
9:4	153
9:11–12	146n114
9:22–23	123n13
9:30–31	108
10:4–10	108
10:15	26
10:18	99
11:32	72n22
12:2	76, 143n102
12:4–5	137n76
13:8–10	157n159
13:9	126, 127
14:5–6	78n53
14:14	102n165
14:19	165n195
15:1–3	157n159
15:2	165n195
15:8–12	157
15:17	92n115
15:24, 28	38n92
16:22	69
16:26	123n13

1 Corinthians

1:20	75, 76, 81, 143n102
1:22–23	93n120
1:26	99
1:28–31	146n115
1:31	73n27, 92n115
2:6, 8	75, 143n102
3:5–7	89
3:6–7	165
3:6–17	141
3:9	165n195
3:11	168n209
3:18	75–76
3:18–19	76, 81
3:21	92n115
4:17	102n165
5:7	95n130
5:13	12n36
6:11	108
7:17–24	139n89
7:19	82–83
7:29–31	76n40
7:31	76, 82, 85, 96, 173
8–10	79n56
8:4	79n56
8:5	79n56
8:5–6	154n144
9:1–17	92n115
9:20–21	157n159
10:3–4	10
10:11	75–76
10:19	79n56
12:12, 27	137n76
12:28	166n201
14:3, 5, 12, 26	165n195
14:23	93n118
14:29–32	166n201
15:20–22, 44–49	95
15:20–24	76
15:20–24, 35–50	96
15:20–28	75
15:21–22, 24–27	132
15:22	97
15:23–28, 51–55	85
15:27	134
15:32	12n36
16:21	69

2 Corinthians

1–5	173
1:1—5:13	88
1:1—7:16	88, 115n231, 116n231
1:5	102n165
1:12, 14	92n115
1:17	99
2–6	98n147, 100n155
2–7	99n149, 111–12
2:14—5:10	53
2:14—7:4	94, 106n182, 117, 119–20
2:15–16	98
2:16	89n96
2:17	89, 92
2:17—3:1	112
3–4	90
3:1	89n95, 92n114
3:1–3	89
3:1–6	55n56, 93n116
3:1–18	119, 157, 173
3:1—4:6	88–89, 91, 174
3:3	89
3:3, 6	53
3:3, 6, 14–18	91
3:4–6	89
3:5	89n96
3:6	89
3:7–11	89
3:7–18	89
3:8	89
3:11–18	155
3:12, 18	92
3:12–18	89
3:15	89
3:16	99n149
3:16, 18	89
3:18	89n101, 90, 91n107, 119, 174
3:18—4:6	90–91, 173
4:2	92
4:3–6	91
4:4	76, 90, 97, 143n102
4:4, 6	89, 90n101, 91n107, 119, 174
4:4–6	96, 99n149
4:6	90–91

4:11	98	5:20	106–108, 111–12, 116n231
4:16	53	5:20–21	109, 111
4:18	93n116	5:21	95n130, 106–109
5	2, 6	6:1	111–12, 116n231
5:1	165n195	6:1–18	110, 119, 174
5:5	53, 99n149	6:2	76, 99, 110–112, 115, 116n231, 118–20
5:10	94		
5:11	92, 94	6:3–10	116
5:11–13	94, 112	6:11	116n231
5:11–15	100n155	6:11–13	116n231
5:11–21	8, 13, 70, 88, 91, 118–19, 173–75, 178	6:13	116n231
5:11—6:2	116	6:14	116
5:11—6:10	116n231	6:14–16	116n231, 117
5:11—6:16	115, 116n231	6:14–18	117
5:12	70, 92–94, 104	6:14—7:1	116n231
5:12–15	73n27	6:16	5, 68n1, 110, 116–18, 120, 174, 175n5, 177, 178n12
5:13	93–94, 96		
5:14	94–97, 99n149	6:16–17	118
5:14–15	95n127, 97–98, 100n155, 101–105, 119, 174	6:16–18	111n205, 116
		6:17	110, 115–20
5:14–16	100, 105, 174	10:2–3	99
5:14–17	38, 68, 88, 92, 97, 103, 105–106, 118–20, 145n110, 174	10:8	165n195
		10:8—12:12	92n115
		10:12–13	93n120
5:14–21	95n125, 97, 107n191, 110–11, 115, 177	10:17	73n27
		11:13–23	112
5:15	96–97, 118	11:17–22	93n116
5:16	93n116, 98–101, 103, 104n177, 110	11:18	99
		12:1–7	93n116
5:16–17	98, 103	12:19	165n195
5:17	1, 3, 5n11, 6–7, 12–16, 21–22, 24n47, 34, 37–40, 42, 67, 88, 91, 96, 97n137, 99, 101–105, 107, 109–10, 115, 118–21, 159n166, 171, 174	13:1	12n36
		13:10	165n195

Galatians

1–2	70
1:1, 4	73, 81
1:1–5	69
1:1	76
1:4	75–76, 79–80, 86n87, 87n92, 143n102
1:6	71
1:10	70, 73n27, 92, 164
1:10, 15	112n211
1:10–14	83n75

5:17–21	97
5:18	102n165, 106–107, 143
5:18–19	107
5:18–21	105–106, 109, 118–119, 174
5:19	106–107, 109, 118–19, 174

Galatians (continued)

Reference	Pages
1:13	83
2:1–3, 7–21	86n87
2:3–5	70
2:3–12	71
2:9	166
2:11–16, 19–21	87n92
2:15–21	73
2:15—4:11	82
2:16	72n21
2:16–17	108
2:18–21	71
2:19	77
2:19–20	77–81, 88, 144
2:19–21	79
2:20	77, 95, 96n133
3:1–2, 10–13	71
3:1–3, 13–14, 23–26	73
3:1–5	90
3:1–19	157
3:1–29	173
3:3	80n59
3:3–14, 24	108
3:5–14	108
3:6–14, 27—4:6	86n87
3:6–29	87n91, 159n164
3:8	4n8
3:10	72
3:11–12, 21	146n114
3:13	95n130
3:13–29	79
3:15—4:11	77–78
3:19–26	77
3:21–29	87n92
3:22	72n22
3:27	102n165
3:28	83–85, 109, 152n139, 173, 177n10
3:29	102n165
4	79n56
4:1–3	78
4:1–10	73, 78, 79n56, 81, 84, 157n158, 173
4:1–11	78n53
4:3	78–79
4:3, 9	81n65, 83n77, 84
4:3–10, 21—5:1	82
4:4	75, 78, 81
4:8	79n56, 154n144
4:9	78–79
4:21–31	79, 87n91, 157, 159n164
4:23, 29	99
4:26	164
4:28–29	80n59
4:29	70n11, 71
5:1	72n21
5:1–6	72n21
5:2, 4	72n21
5:2–3	70
5:2–6, 11	71
5:3	72
5:4	82n72
5:4–6	86n87, 173
5:5	82n72
5:6	82–85, 88
5:11, 16–25	73
5:13, 16	80n59
5:13, 16, 19–21	80n64
5:13–23	80
5:13–24	82n69
5:13–26	79–81
5:14	157n159
5:24	77, 79–81
6	2, 6
6:1–4	92n115
6:2	157n159
6:4	73n27
6:11	69, 70n11
6:11–13	69
6:11–16	8, 13, 38, 68, 84, 173, 177–78
6:11–18	69–70
6:12	69–71, 73
6:12–13	69, 70n11
6:12–15	153n141
6:12–18	145n110
6:13	70–73
6:13–14	146n115
6:13–15	74n35
6:14–15	73n31, 74n35, 84–85
6:14–16	69, 87–88, 120
6:14	3, 73–75, 77–79, 81–84, 85n83, 87, 88n93, 96n133, 173

6:15	1, 2n5, 3, 12, 40, 67, 69, 73, 78, 82–87, 105n179, 118, 159n166, 173, 177		135–37, 140, 142, 152, 160, 162, 165, 168–69, 172, 175
6:15–16	39, 84n89, 88, 109, 159n164, 177	1:21	131n48, 134, 143n102
		1:21–22	129
6:16	85–87, 173	1:22	126n27, 127, 134–35, 137, 167, 169, 175
		1:22–23	160–61
		1:23	124, 137–41, 160–61, 175

Ephesians

		2	6, 41, 136, 138
1–2	6, 13, 26, 121–22, 125, 129, 164, 169–70, 175, 177–79	2:1	131–32, 142–43
		2:1, 5	131n48
		2:1–3	143–44
1:1	166n201	2:1–4, 11–13, 19	178
1:3–10	122, 130–31	2:1–6	149, 169, 175
1:3–14	122n4, 130, 169	2:1–6, 10, 15	6n13
1:4	130	2:1–7	131–32, 144–45, 148, 163n182
1:5	124		
1:7, 14, 22–23	129–30	2:1–10	129, 132, 142–43, 148–49, 161, 175, 178
1:9–10	8, 122, 125–26, 130–31, 160–61, 169, 175		
		2:1–16	136
1:9	123–25, 128–29, 175	2:1–22	6, 13, 42, 44, 133, 135, 137, 140–41, 160–61, 177
1:10	5, 78, 122, 124–31, 140n91, 140n94, 143n103, 152, 160n169, 161, 165n197, 166, 168, 175–76		
		2:1–23	131
		2:2	125n22, 129, 143
		2:2, 10	144n109
1:10, 12	133	2:2, 19–22	160n173
1:10, 20–23	6n13	2:2–3	144n109
1:15–17	139	2:3	143
1:15–19	132	2:4	143, 154
1:17	141	2:4–6, 8	98
1:17–19	139	2:4–7	145n113
1:17–23	141n98	2:4–8	145
1:18–19	137	2:4–10	145n111
1:19–20	143n104	2:5	142–43, 145
1:20	131, 133–35, 144, 169	2:5–6	96n133, 131, 143
1:20–21	133, 134n61	2:5–6, 10	6n13
1:20–22	75, 121, 132–33, 135, 137, 140–41, 160, 162, 169, 172	2:6	144–45, 148, 164, 175, 176n8
		2:7	75, 131n48, 145
1:20–23	29, 131–33, 135–37, 139–42, 175	2:8	145
		2:8–9	146
1:20—2:10	160n169	2:8–10	73, 92, 142, 145, 148, 178
1:20—2:22	8, 29n65, 41–42, 121n2, 130, 132		
		2:9	145, 146n 114
		2:9–10	145n112

Ephesians (continued)

2:10	145–48, 169, 175		160n170, 162, 169, 176–77
2:11	152, 153n141, 153n142	2:15–16	158, 160n169
2:11, 13, 19	177	2:16	137–38, 158–61
2:11–12	152, 158, 163	2:17	26, 29, 136, 150, 161–62
2:11–12, 19–22	178	2:17–18	136
2:11–13	156–57, 163n182	2:18	150, 163
2:11–14	156–57	2:19	136, 163–64
2:11–15	83, 149, 152, 155, 157–59, 169	2:19–22	6n13, 29, 121, 125, 136–37, 140–41, 150n131, 160, 162–63, 168–70, 172, 175–77
2:11–17	152		
2:11–18	149, 150n131, 158n160, 162, 163n182, 168, 176	2:20	163, 165–70, 176
		2:20–22	136, 164
2:11–19	6n13	2:21	138, 164n193, 165–66
2:11–21	6, 152n139	2:21–22	141, 164, 167–68, 176
2:11–22	29, 32–33, 38, 86n89, 125–26, 129, 132, 138n78, 143n103, 149, 151, 160n169, 161, 165, 175, 177–78	2:22	164n193, 166, 168
		3:1–13	129
		3:2–13	125
		3:3–5	123n13, 125
		3:3–6	125, 175
2:12	153, 156, 163	3:4	125
2:12, 14–15	169	3:4–6	161n174
2:12–13	156, 159	3:5	166n201
2:12–13, 16–22	32	3:5–6	125n24
2:13	149–52, 154, 156, 161–62	3:6	125
		3:9	128
2:13, 15, 17	149, 152	3:9, 11	143n102
2:13, 15, 17, 20	132, 169	3:19	124, 139–40
2:13, 17	5–8, 13–16, 21, 31–32, 40, 44, 121, 137, 142, 149, 151n136, 169, 171	4:4	138
		4:4, 12, 16	137
		4:4, 15–16	138
		4:10	128
2:13–15	158	4:10, 13	140
2:13–17	32	4:11	166n201
2:13–18	149, 151, 176	4:11–16	165
2:14	154–155, 158n160, 162	4:12, 16	138
		4:12, 16, 29	165n195
2:14–15	154n147, 155, 158n161	4:13	124
		4:15	126n27, 127n32, 165
2:14–16	159	4:15–16	165n198
2:14–18	149	4:16	165n196
2:15	32, 39–40, 121–22, 149, 151–52, 153n141, 154n147, 155–59,	4:17–24	159
		4:22	96
		4:24	152n139, 159
		5:14	143
		5:23	137

Philippians

5:23, 28, 30	137
6:2	155, 157
6:12	125n22, 129

Philippians

1:1	112n211
1:23	95
1:25–26	92n115
2:9–11	97
2:16	92n115
3:1–6	70
3:2–3	93n120
3:3	80n59, 92n115, 146n115
3:3–5	153n141
3:3–6	73n24
3:3–11	73n27
3:6	72n22
3:9	109
3:20	163n185, 164
3:20–21	132

Colossians

1:6, 10	165
1:15	90
1:15–20	135n69, 179
1:15–23	149n124
1:16, 20	128
1:18	167
1:19	124, 139–40
1:20	160n169
1:20, 22	160n169
1:22	155n149
1:27	123n13
2:2	125
2:8, 20–21	78n54
2:9	139
2:9–10	140, 141n95
2:11	153n141
2:12	144n105
2:12–13	144
2:14	155
2:16–17	78n53
2:18–19	165
2:19	138
3:1	144n105
3:9	96
3:10	152n139
3:10–11	83, 86n89, 179
3:11	152n139
3:15	138
4:3	125
4:18	69

1 Thessalonians

1:10	139n89
2:12	139n89
2:19	92n115
4:15, 13	154n144
5:6–8	93n120
5:12	99
5:24	139n89

2 Thessalonians

3:17	69

1 Timothy

2:6	95n130
5:8	164
6:17	75, 143n102

2 Timothy

2:19	166

Titus

2:12	75

Philemon

19	69

Hebrews

1:2	78n51
1:34	133n58
5:6, 10	133
6:20	133
7:1–17	133
12:18–24	164

James

2:10–11	72n22

1 Peter

2:4–8	166–167
2:4–10	150n131
2:5	166

2 Peter

2:3–6	165
3:5–13	37n91

1 John

2:17	76

Revelation

3:12	189
18:4	112n214
21–22	179
21:1–2	189
21:1—22:7	4n8, 37n91
21:14	167
21:15–17	56
21:22	60n83
22:1–2	189

Ancient Document Index

Ancient Near Eastern Documents

Enuma Elish

1:37–40, 73–76	8n20
1:37–40	182n2
1:73–76	181–182
4:28	27n57
6:1–70	8n20, 182n2
6:112	8n20

Apocrypha

Baruch

1:19–20	23
2:11	23
2:14	76
4:36–37	190
5:1–9	191
5:5–6	190
5:7	190
5:9	190
5:14	190

1 Maccabees

1:21, 36	56n64
2:12	48n24
2:46	70n10
3:51	48n24
4:46	90
5:1	56n64
9:27	90
11:38	163n184
14:41	90

1 Esdras

2:26	165n195
4:51	165n195
5:60, 73	165n195
5:65	166
6:6	165n195
8:75	56n64

2 Maccabees

4:11	153n143
7:9–36	76n42
8:17	153n143

Sirach

17:17	79
24:3	185
24:3–17	183
36:12	56
49:16—50:21	90

Tob

1:4	48n24

Pseudepigrapha

Apocalypse of Moses

13:3–4	76n42
20:2	90n106, 97
21:6	90n106, 97
28:4	76n42
41:3	76n42
43:2	76n42

4 Ezra

3:20–22, 26	46n15
4:26–27	75
4:37	125
6:7	75
6:13–28	4n8, 37n91
7:12–13, 50, 113	75
7:112–13	76
8:1	75
14:5	123

2 Baruch

5:1–9	191
14:1	125
32:1–6	17
44:5–15	17, 189
44:7–15	37
32:1–6	62, 189
32:6	37
51:1, 3	90, 97
13:5, 13–15	115
14:5	125

Wisdom

1:7	138
3:9	163
7:25–26	90
9:8	8, 48
10:15, 17	163
19:1–22	191
54:15, 21	90, 97
73:1–7	4
74:1–2	59

1 Enoch

1:3–8	191n18
6–16	12
8:2	59n74
9:6	123
10:1—11:2	58, 59
10:3	59
10:3, 18–19	173
10:3, 18–19, 21	63, 67n115
10:3, 21	4n8
10:6	60
10:7	59
10:16	59n77
10:16, 21	63, 172
10:16–17	59
10:16—11:2	59
10:17	60
10:18–19	59, 63, 104, 172
10:20	59
10:21	60n81, 172
10:22	59
11:1	59, 63, 67n115, 104, 172
18:6–9	59n79
18:8	60n80
20:5	79n56

22:4, 11, 13	60n80
24:2—25:7	4n8, 59
24:6	59
25:3	59
25:3–5	60
25:3–6	63, 67, 172
25:4–5	60
25:5	60
25:5–6	60
25:6	60, 63, 173
38:3	123
72:1	37n91, 58, 62, 67, 104
83:7	123
85:3	61
89:8–9	60n82
89:32–33, 41, 54, 74	61
89:50	61n84
89:73	61n84
90:7, 26	61
90:28–29	60–61, 63, 67, 172
90:28–29, 32–33	67n115
90:28–38	60, 62, 131n46, 166
90:32	61
90:32–33	172
90:32–33, 37–38	63
90:34	61
90:35	61
90:37	61, 63
90:37–38	61, 63, 67, 104, 173
90:38	61–62
91:11–17	131n46
91:12–13	166
91:12–17	62
91:13	62–63, 67, 172
91:13, 16	67n115
91:14	62–63, 173
91:15–17	37n91
91:16	62n93, 63, 104
91:16–17	62
103:2–4	123

2 Enoch

16:7	79
66:6	75

Greek Apocalypse of Ezra

2:23–25	147, 148n121

Jubilees

1:7, 22–23, 29	64n100
1:7, 27–29	65
1:7–14	65
1:7–29	63n96, 64–65
1:13	64n102
1:15–18	64n101
1:17, 27–29	64, 66, 172
1:17–18	64n102
1:17–29	67, 172
1:22–24	72n21
1:22–29	64n101
1:26–30	64n100
1:27–28	63n96
1:28	64
1:28–29	17n11, 66–67, 131n46
1:29	62n93, 63–64, 66–67
4:25–26	184n11, 188
4:26	17n11, 63, 65–67, 104, 131n46, 172
4:29	67
4:29–30	65–67
4:30	65
5:1–11	12
5:12	64n100
5:19	72n21
8:19	184n11
11:4–5	79n56
15:31–32	79n56
21:23	72n21
23:11–31	63n96, 64n100
23:16	72n21
23:22–31	65–67, 90, 173
23:25	65
23:25–29	104
23:27	65–66
23:27–29	65–67

Liber Antiquitatum Biblicarum (Pseudo-Philo)

3:9–10	75
3:10	4n8

3 Maccabees

2:15	166

4 Maccabees

8:7	153n143
17:9	153n143

Psalms of Solomon

9:1	188
11	190
11:1	190
11:2–3	190
11:4–6	190
11:6	190
11:7	190
17:28	163n184

Sibylline Oracles

3:741–55	189n10
3:741–95	190
3:767–68	189
3:767–95	17n11, 189–90
3:772–73	189
3:773–75	189
3:777–79	18n21, 189
3:777–80	189n10
3:780	189n10
3:785	189n11
3:785–95	4n8, 189
3:787	189n11

Testament of Abraham

9:6	147, 175n6

Testament of Asher

1:8	80

Testament of Dan

2:1	187
5	190
5:4–7	187
5:8	188
5:9	188
5:9–13	188
5:10–11	188
5:12–13	188
5:18–13	17n11, 187

Testament of Job

49:2	147
49:3	147, 175

Testament of Judah

19:4—20:5	80

Testament of Moses

10:1–5	191n18

Testament of Solomon

8:1–2	79n56
18:1–2	79n56
22:7—23:4	167

Dead Sea Scrolls

Damascus Document

3:20	90n106, 189
20:8	164

1QH

4:15	90n106
5:20	122n5
7:21–22	80n59
9:36	72n21
10:14	122n5
11:21–23	164
12:29–33	80n59
12:32	122n5
14:10–14	164
15:2–3	80
18:22–23	80n60
19:29	122n5

1QHa

4:15	189n7

1QIsa[a]

	28n59

1QM

10:5	122n5
12:1–7	164
12:9–18	17n11, 136n74, 184–85, 191n18
12:10–12	184
19:1–8	184

1QpHab

7:2	125
7:2, 13	78n51

1QS

3–4	12
3:6–12	72n21
4:18–20	78n51
4:19–21	80n60
4:23	90n106, 189n7
4:25	104
5:4–5	80n60
11:7–9	164
11:9–10	80n60
11:12	108n197
11:15–20	122n5
11:20–22	134

1Q171

3:1–2	90n106

4Q554

1–2	56

4Q171

3:1–2	90
3:2	189n7

4Q174

2:12—3:13	131n46, 184
2:14	184
3:1–13	189n7
3:6	175n5
3:7–8	184

4Q176

	191n18

4Q215a

2:2–6	75

11Q

48:7–10	163n186

11QTemple

29:7–10	131n46, 166

48:7, 10	163, 166

11Q19

29:9–10	184

Josephus

Against Apion

2:282	78n53

Jewish Antiquities

2:101	163n185
3:123, 179–87	8n20
3:91	78n53
11:59	165n195
11:294	78n53

12:46	163n185
13:257–58	70
14:264	78n53

Jewish War

4:201, 323	48n24

The Life

112–13	70

Philo

On the Life of Abraham

1:139	165n195

On the Cherubim

1:121	163n185

That God is Unchangeable

162	72n21

On Giants

6, 16, 19, 58	12

Who is the Heir?

1:249–51	93n121

Allegorical Interpretation

2:31	93n121

On the Migration of Abraham

127–30	72n21

On the Creation of the World

1:143	163n185

On Planting

1:47–50   8n20

On Rewards and Punishments

1:120   166

On the Special Laws

1:274   166

Targums

Targum Isaiah

28:16	168n207
52:8	28n60
57:14	30n69

Targum Jeremiah

30:18   55

Targum Ezekiel

36:38   46n14

Early Christian Writings

Epistle of Barnabas

5:11   127n34

Against Heresies

1:10:1	127n34
3:16:6	127n34
3:18:1, 7	127n34
3:21:10	127n34
5:20:2	127n34
5:21:1	127n34

www.ingramcontent.com/pod-product-compliance
Lightning Source LLC
Chambersburg PA
CBHW050438240426
43661CB00055B/2434